The 51st Brigade

The History of the Jewish Partisan Group from the Slonim Ghetto

By Sarah Shner-Nishmit

Translation of *HaPlugah HaChamishim v'Achat*

Translated into English by Judith Levi

Originally published in Hebrew by

The Ghetto Fighters Museum   Publication - The Israel Ministry of Defence

Published by JewishGen

An Affiliate of the Museum of Jewish Heritage - A Living Memorial to the Holocaust
New York

The 51st Brigade - The History of the Jewish Partisan Group from the Slonim Ghetto

Copyright © 2015 by JewishGen, Inc.
All rights reserved.
Second Printing: September 2016, Elul 5777

Author: Sarah Shner-Nishmit
Translator: Judith Levi
Editors of the Translation: Zvi Shefet, Mike Levy
Layout: Sheldon Z. Lipsky
Map Production: Hila Shefet-Mashiach
Image Editor: Hila Shefet-Mashiach
Cover Modifications: Rachel Kolokoff Hopper
Indexing: Lynn Mercer

This book may not be reproduced, in whole or in part, including illustrations in any form (beyond that copying permitted by Sections 107 and 108 of the U.S. Copyright Law and except by reviewers for public press), without written permission from the publisher.

Published by JewishGen, Inc.
An Affiliate of the Museum of Jewish Heritage
A Living Memorial to the Holocaust
36 Battery Place, New York, NY 10280

"JewishGen, Inc. is not responsible for inaccuracies or omissions in the original work and makes no representations regarding the accuracy of this translation. Digital images of the original book's contents can be seen online at the New York Public Library Web site."

The mission of the JewishGen organization is to produce a translation of the original work and we cannot verify the accuracy of statements or alter facts cited.

Printed in the United States of America by Lightning Source, Inc.

Library of Congress Control Number (LCCN): 2015953752
ISBN: 978-1-939561-36-7 (hard cover: 400 pages, alk. paper)

Cover Credit: From the cover of the original Hebrew book
Original cover design, maps and sketches in Hebrew by Ofer Drori

JewishGen and the Yizkor-Books-in-Print Project

This book has been published by the **Yizkor-Books-in-Print Project,** as part of the **Yizkor Book Project** of **JewishGen, Inc.**

JewishGen, Inc. is a non-profit organization founded in 1987 as a resource for Jewish genealogy. Its website [www.jewishgen.org] serves as an international clearinghouse and resource center to assist individuals who are researching the history of their Jewish families and the places where they lived. JewishGen provides databases, facilitates discussion groups, and coordinates projects relating to Jewish genealogy and the history of the Jewish people. In 2003, JewishGen became an affiliate of the **Museum of Jewish Heritage - A Living Memorial to the Holocaust** in New York.

The **JewishGen Yizkor Book Project** was organized to make more widely known the existence of Yizkor (Memorial) Books written by survivors and former residents of various Jewish communities throughout the world. Later, volunteers connected to the different destroyed communities began cooperating to have these books translated from the original language—usually Hebrew or Yiddish—into English, thus enabling a wider audience to have access to the valuable information contained within them. As each chapter of these books was translated, it was posted on the JewishGen website and made available to the general public.

The **Yizkor-Books-in-Print Project** began in 2011 as an initiative to print and publish Yizkor Books that had been fully translated, so that hard copies would be available for purchase by the descendants of these communities and also by scholars, universities, synagogues, libraries, and museums.

These Yizkor books have been produced almost entirely through the volunteer effort of researchers from around the world, assisted by donations from private individuals. The books are printed and sold at near cost, so as to make them as affordable as possible. Our goal is to make this important genre of Jewish literature and history available in English in book form, so that people can have the personal histories of their ancestral towns on their bookshelves for themselves and for their children and grandchildren.

A list of all published translated Yizkor Books in the project with prices and ordering information can be found at:
http://www.jewishgen.org/Yizkor/ybip.html

Lance Ackerfeld, Yizkor Book Project Manager

Joel Alpert, Yizkor-Book-in-Print Project Coordinator

This book is presented by the
Yizkor Books in Print Project
Project Coordinator: Joel Alpert

Part of the
Yizkor Books Project of JewishGen, Inc.
Project Manager: Lance Ackerfeld

These books have been produced solely through volunteer effort of individuals from around the world. The books are printed and sold at near cost, so as to make them as affordable as possible.

Our goal is to make this history and important genre of Jewish literature available in English in book form so that people can have the near-personal histories of their ancestral towns on their bookshelves for themselves and for their children and grandchildren.

Any donations to the Yizkor Books Project are appreciated.

Please send donations to:
Yizkor Book Project
JewishGen
36 Battery Place
New York, NY 10280

JewishGen, Inc. is an affiliate of the
Museum of Jewish Heritage
A Living Memorial to the Holocaust

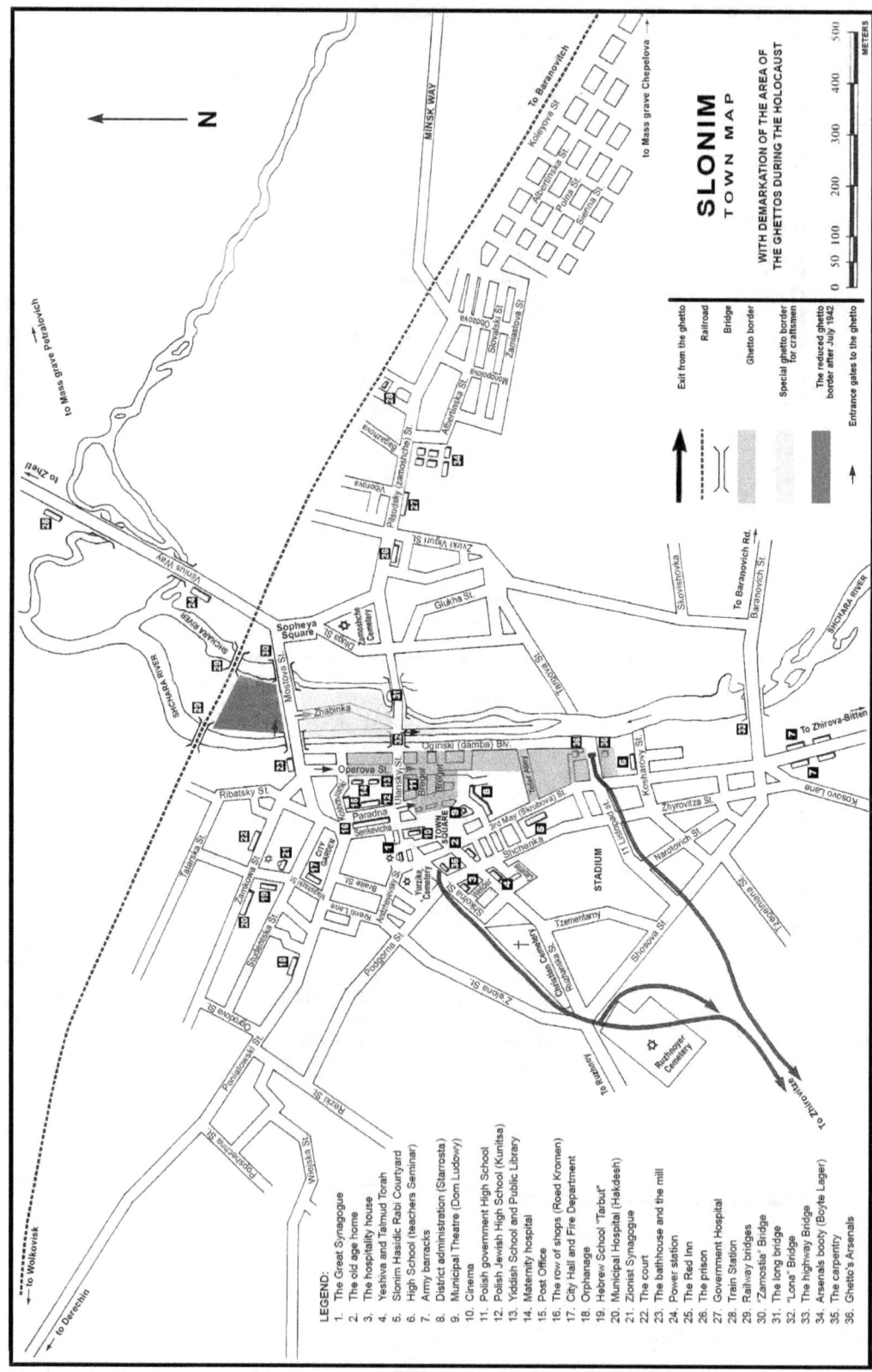

Translation of the Title Page of Original Hebrew Book

Sara Shner-Nishmit

THE 51st BRIGADE

The History of the Jewish Partisan Group from the Slonim Ghetto

Published by

The Ghetto Fighters Museum   Publication - The Israel Ministry of Defence

Background

This is the story of the fight of young Jewish people from the town of Slonim and its environs, against the German murderers of World War II and their Belorussian and Polish collaborators. The book lays blame at the feet of Soviet partisans, who abandoned their comrades in arms and incited anti-Semitic hatred towards the Jewish fighters.

The Jewish troop called *Shchors*, on the banks of the River Shchara, marched along its battle paths, fought with courage and strength and distinguished itself in battle. They buried their dead, cared for their wounded, and never abandoned their old people and children.

Throughout this cruel war in the forests and forest edges they attacked police stations and military camps and blew up trains carrying German troops and equipment.

At the end of the war, people from Slonim and the area were recruited into the Red Army and advanced with the Soviet army into German territory. The soldiers who then remained immigrated to Israel and set up their homes there.

The writer Sarah Shner-Nishmit, one of the founders of Kibbutz Lohamei HaGetaot (Fighters of the Ghetto), was born in 1913 in the town of Siena, in the Suvalki district, Poland. In 1925 her family uprooted to Lithuania. She completed her studies in Classical Languages and Philosophy at the University of Kovno, Vilna, and in 1962 she completed an advanced level course in Archival Studies at the Hebrew University.

She was imprisoned with the invasion of the Soviet Union by the German army in 1941, and fled from a German labour camp to the partisans in the forests. She was a nurse in the Soviet partisan troop until the liberation in 1944; from 1945 to 1947 she was one of the founders of the "Zionist Organisation for the Return of Jewish Children" from convents and Christian houses in Poland. From 1955 she was among the workers of "The House of the Ghetto Fighter" museum alongside her husband Tzvi Shner (director of the museum from 1950 to 1984). She published books and articles about the struggles of the Jews in the ghettoes and the forests.

Originally published by Israel Ministry of Defence, House of the Ghetto Fighters

Acknowledgement for the Translation

The preface relating the history of the Slonim Jewish community which appears in this book, was written according to the monograph by the historian Ing. Kalman Lichtenstein, the principal editor of "The Slonim Notebook" (Pinkas Slonim, 4 vol.)

This book is published thanks to the funding from the "Slonim Notebook" editorial board and from the 51st Brigade veterans in Israel.

For organising the English translation, editing and publication, thanks are due to Sheila and Mike Levy of Cambridge, England. Sheila is a cousin of Abraham Bublacki, a member of the 51st Unit.

Thanks especially are to Mr Zvi Shefet, a former member of the 51st Unit and the promoter of editing the book and its translation into English.

Abraham Boblacki

Foreword of the Translation

The English translation of this book has taken years to come to fruition. Written in 1990, the monumental account of the tragic events in Slonim, was a work of great scholarship by the late Israeli historian, Sara Shner-Nishmit. She worked with former members of the 51st Brigade, the Jewish partisan group, principally people like Zvi Shefet who assisted her in gathering the testimonies.

My interest in the story of the Jewish hero partisans of Slonim began in 1998. My wife Sheila's Aunt Betty handed over four family photographs and a couple of wartime documents. Liverpool-born Betty knew that I was interested in history and was just starting out as a Holocaust educator in England. The small black and white photographs were obviously taken in the 1930s and featured Great Aunt Eva, the sister of my wife's grandmother. She is shown with what seem to be family members: two small girls – around 8 to 11 years old - and a young man.

The documents that accompanied the photographs gave some crucial information about the people shown in the grainy little snaps. One was an enquiry sent to the International Red Cross by my wife's grandfather some time during the Second World War. Writing from Liverpool, he wanted to have some information on family members from Slonim, their home 'shtetl' in Eastern Poland. Nothing had been heard of them since the occupation of the country first by the Russians, and after June 1941, by the advancing German army.

The document helpfully lists the family members living in Slonim and by implication, I could associate their names with the people shown on the photographs. The facts seem to be that some time in the mid 1930s, Great Aunt Eva, paid a visit from Liverpool to Slonim, possibly for a family wedding. Her sister (and of course that of my wife's grandmother), had stayed in Slonim when the other siblings emigrated to Liverpool in the late 1890s.

The mysterious people in the photograph appear to be the two girls: Lebe and Blumey Boblatski. A young man in a separate photograph turned out to be Abraham Boblatski, their older brother. A search of the Yad Vashem Central Database of Shoah Victims' Names revealed a record for Abraham who it seems died in 1943. The testimony was signed by Mr E Luboshitz from Israel who described himself as a former neighbour.

My next move set in motion a series of remarkable coincidences. An Israeli friend scoured the Israeli phone book for Mr E Luboshitz, rang a series of numbers and eventually spoke to a very old man who some years before had indeed written the testimony about Abraham Boblatski. He suggested, though, that I speak to a Mr Zvi Shefet who would know much more.

Mr Shefet was, and still is, responsible for the Association of Slonim Jews and was easily traced to an apartment in Tel Aviv. I sent a copy of the photograph of the young man to Zvi who confirmed that this was indeed Abraham Boblatski (or Bublacki). He also told me something that I had no idea about until that moment: Abraham was a partisan in the 51st Brigade. No one in my wife's family had heard of Abraham and certainly not that he had been a partisan. The next piece of news was if anything even more remarkable: Zvi was organizing a study trip to Slonim the following week. This was July 2008. I dropped all plans, booked tickets and joined the Slonim tour as the only non-Israeli.

Led by Zvi, the seven-day tour took us to the three sites of Jewish martyrdom in the forests near Slonim. We had a walk around the town including the site of the former ghetto, important landmarks in Slonim's Jewish history and the story of Zvi's astonishing escape from the Nazi murderers.

I also discovered the existence of this book – written in Hebrew, telling the story of the Slonim partisans (not least the part played by Cousin Abraham).

We spent many months trying to find a translator of the book and eventually a good friend from our home town in Cambridge (England), offered to take on the mammoth task without any charge. Judith Levi told us that to translate the book would be a mitzvah but it would take her time. It took her around a year of careful work fitting in the task whenever she could. Judith, a former resident of Israel, translated the book by speaking into a Dictaphone. We then gave the recording equipment to two audio typists who offered to transcribe Judith's words to text.

The translation that you see here was the work of Judith Levi who cannot be thanked enough for offering us this wonderful mitzvah. Thanks are also due to Ruth Greene and Jane Elia for working so hard on the audio transcriptions.

We hope that the translation of Sara Shner-Nishmit's magisterial work will open a relatively forgotten part of modern Jewish history. It is of course essentially a story of deep tragedy – most of the Jewish citizens of Slonim were murdered by the Germans and their collaborators.

It is to all the victims of the savage and murderous policy of the Nazis that we would wish to dedicate the English translation of this book.

Above all we dedicate this translation to Zvi Shefet, one of the most remarkable men I have ever met. Zvi has made the memory of the Jews of Slonim a lifelong task. He has been back to Slonim many times, ensured that the roof of the now derelict Slonim synagogue was repaired has organised a Jewish memorial site in the former cemetery there and three forest memorials marking the spot where thousands of martyrs were murdered.

This is a tragic story of victims, but also an inspirational story about heroism: Jewish heroism.

Mike Levy

Cambridge England, 2014

In memory of

The martyrs of the town of Slonim and its

Surroundings

Who perished in the Holocaust,

The fighters who fell in the ghetto, in the forests

and in the liberation armies.

Map of Belarus with Slonim

Geopolitical Information:

Alternate names: Russian: Слоним. Belarusian: Слонім. Yiddish: סלאנים

Slonim is located at 53°05' North Latitude and 25°19' East Longitude
108 mi WSW of Minsk

	Town	District	Province	Country
Before WWI (c. 1900):	Slonim	Slonim	Grodno	Russian Empire
Between the wars (c. 1930):	Słonim	Słonim	Nowogródek	Poland
After WWII (c. 1950):	Slonim			
Today (c. 2000):	Slonim			

Nearby Jewish Communities:
Ozernitsa 13 miles W
Hałynka 15 miles NW
Byten 16 miles SSE
Kozlovshchina 16 miles N
Polonka 17 miles ENE
Derechin 20 miles NW
Zelva 21 miles WNW
Molchad 23 miles NE
Pavlovo 23 miles SW
Ruzhany 23 miles SW
Kosava 24 miles SSW
Dvorets 24 miles NNE
Novaya Mysh 24 miles E
Ivatsevichy 25 miles S
Dzyatlava 27 miles N
Novoyel'nya 29 miles NNE
Baranavichy 30 miles E

Short Note about the Jewish Community of Slonim

Jews were living in Slonim as early as 1388. At the beginning of the twentieth century there were about 11,500 Jews living in town, about 73% of the population. In 1940 at the time of the Soviet occupation there were about 35,000 Jews living in Slonim, half of them were refugees from the occupied Poland by the Nazi Germany. When the Nazi forces occupied Slonim in 1941 Jews were shot in the woods. Some hundreds survivors escaped into the forests or were hidden. About 200 survived the war.
Their stories are presented in Volume II of "Pinkas Slonim"

Today there are a few descendants of Slonim, especially in Israel.The once vibrant Jewish community of Slonim is no more.

Today there are no Jews living in Slonim.

Note to the Reader:

Also please note that all references within the text of the book to page numbers, refer to the page numbers of the original book.

Note on Second Printing:

The second printing differs from the first printing only in that the List of Partisans in Appendix 4 has been corrected to reflect their proper places and dates of death of the partisans and a few minor typographical and spelling errors.

Owners of the first edition can write to Mike Levy <mike@keystage.org> to obtain a file containing the corrected Appendix 4 that can be printed and inserted into the first printing of the book.

Contents

	Page
Introduction	
A) Social structure in the Soviet partisan movement in Western Belorussia	**6**
B) Some notes on the Soviet historiography of partisan warfare	**13**
C) Is the wealth of detail relevant to the history?	**14**
D) Sources	**16**

Preface - Slonim - A large Jewish town   23
    Location of the town, its history, the annihilation of the Jewish community

Chapter One - Slonim in the grip of the slaughterer   29
    At the outbreak of war, the first decrees and Actions, the German civil administration, the establishment of the ghetto

Chapter Two - Beginnings of the partisan movement in the Slonim area   39
    The Fiedrik group, Lieutenant Proniagin's group, organization in the ghetto, debate over the goals of the underground, contacts with the forest and amassing weapons, disappointment in seeking links with the partisans, Herzel Shepetinski joins the underground

Chapter Three - The period of "Actions" of mass annihilation   51
    The massacre of 14th November, the death march, after the bloodbath, liaison is made with the partisans in the forest, smuggling arms out of the German loot camp, new members in the organisation, the Pusovitz and Mogilev missions, first exodus to join the partisans, girls in the organisation, the massacre of 29th June, 1942, how A. Orlinski and Dr. Noah Kaplinski were rescued, life in the small Mostova ghetto, the story of Eliyahu Abramovski, Shusterovitch's report

Chapter Four - On the forest paths – to the partisans   91
    Zerach Kremin leads Jews to the forest, Shabtai Moshkovski leaves for the partisans, Avraham Doktortchik leaves for the partisans, the killing of Mariampol, first day in the fighting unit, the destruction of the underground shelter in the carpenters' workshop, Avraham Orlinski reaches the partisans, Dr. Cheslava Orlinski leaves for the forest, between hope and despair

Chapter Five - How the young women suffered on their way to the forest   111

The experience of Krussi Abramchuk, the story of Judith Shelubski-Graf, the story of Tanya (Tamar) Gellerstein-Imber, what happened to the Mukasay sisters

Chapter Six - Stages in the setting up of the Jewish (partisan) group   118

The establishment of the "Shchors" troop, the establishment of the Jewish group 51, Captain Fyodorovitch: the commander of the Jewish group

Chapter Seven - In the Jewish group   124

The early days, the end of the underground in the Slonim ghetto, a plan which was not put into action

Chapter Eight - The battle pathway of the 51 group   134

The Kosovo operation, in the camp on the day of the Kosovo mission, the Komsomol meeting in the brigade, first activities of the youngest member of the group, in the family camps, on the first watch, a mishap in the pasture, an acquisition mission for the family camp, the Gavinovitch operation, the destruction of the Biten Jewish community, the route of the young Yisrael Slonimski from Biten to the partisans

Chapter Nine - The "Shchors" troop on the march to the east   163

The first Selection and the rejection of the Jews, the confiscation of weapons in the village of Tchemeri, the battle of Tchemyeli, group 51 on the march eastwards

Chapter Ten - In the days of the siege and the manhunts   169

The battle of Samitchin, the battle of the Tenth Dam, the death of the commander, the transfer of wounded, the partisan field hospital, the panic flight and leaving behind the wounded, abandoned on guard duty, the heroism of Golda Gartsovski, a new commander for group 51 and the arrival of Brinski and Tchorni

Chapter Eleven - The family camps under siege   193

Deserted and abandoned, the Belorussian partisans turn the Jews out of the forest, Bobkov reorganises his troop, the renewal of the manhunts, Boris Heiman's group, the chapter of suffering of the women of Slonim and Biten unfolds in the days of the manhunt: (Masha Mukasai, Tanya Gellerstein-Imber), the personal story of Mina Volokoviski

Chapter Twelve - The "Shchors" troop in the autumn of 1942   **208**

The journey to Kriboshin, members' loss of life, the killing of Natan Sapirstein, the venom of anti-Semitism simmers, the Khatinichi mission, the German spy Ragimov and the battle of the 5th of October, blaming Jewish partisans, the first "Shalman" (rejection of Jewish partisans), integration into the "Vasiliev" troop, the tribulations of Judith Shelubski, the Tukhevichi operation and an incident on patrol, the battle on the river Laan, organising intelligence in the area, the Deniskovichi operation.

Chapter Thirteen - "Shchors" in the Pinsk division   **227**

"Shchors" stationed at Gotzk, the Berkovitch incident, the disbanding of the Jewish group 51, the unsuccessful Starobin mission, the arrival of the Kovpak and Kapusta camps, in the days of siege and manhunt of February 1943, breaking through the enemy surround, the killing of Kandelstein, the panic flight from the village of Puczini, Shimon Milikovski falls in battle, the death of Ziama Shusterovitch

Chapter Fourteen - Parting from the Pinsk division and the end of the march eastward   **240**

The battle for Svyataya Volya and the return to Lake Vigonov, the Orlovski incident, anti-semitism and parasitism in the troop, the second and third "Shalmans" and the delegation of the rejected to the "Shchors" battalion, the dispersal of the reject group and the murder of Avraham Bublatski, the fate of other people in the reject group, twists and turns in the story of Mishka Pertzov.

Chapter Fifteen - Under the command of Sergei Ivanovitch Sikorski   **260**

Setting up the Brest division, the arrival of Linkov, the reorganisation in Volchye-Nori, from the deeds of the Budioni troop (the battle of Antopol, the action in Peski, the bombing of the forest and activity on the landing strip, activity on the enemy's transport lines), the rescue of Jews by Jewish partisans

Chapter Sixteen - The war on the enemy's lines of transport   **275**

"The war of the rail tracks" and the "Concert", some of the exploits of the Jewish saboteurs: a sabotage mission in which A. Imber participated, Imber's second sabotage mission, abandoned in the field of action, among the paratroopers, commander Shomilin falls in battle; excerpts from the memoirs of Ya'akov Khatzkelevich, Zerach Kremin in the Kotovski troop: (my new sub-machine gun, alone in the rye field, how they taught me to drink, how we closed the Brest-Warsaw line, the war of flags)

Chapter Seventeen - Members of group 51 in the "Vasiliev" troop   291

Good integration, the battle of Krasnaya Sloboda, winter 1942-1943: daily life in the troop, coping, producing home-made explosive in the troop, Jewish craftsmen in the troop), during the February 1943 manhunt: (the rifle incident, the killing of the Jewish violinist, in the Gotzk region, Herzel Shepetinski dies in battle), the foundation of the "Lenin" brigade, the plan to visit Volchye-Nori, 1st. of May celebrations

Chapter Eighteen - Vasiliev's fighters of the "Lenin" brigade in the "The war of the Rail tracks"   304

Blowing up the railway lines, the revenge of Avraham Hirshler, the Germans' partners (the Italians, the Hungarians, the Belgians), the war of pamphlets and posters, stepping up discipline and party indoctrination, taking a message to Komarov, the battle of the Deniskovichi sawmill, the splitting up of the "Vasiliev" troop, an event near the village of Lushcha

Chapter Nineteen - Winter and spring of 1944   314

Entrapping through "Lashon" (Tongue), Ukrainian spies, the quandaries of liberation, Zvi Shefet in his home town of Slonim

Chapter Twenty - The Brest division on the road to liberation   321

Spring 1944, Zhenia Eichenbaum falls in battle, twists and turns of liberation, the Odyssey of Archik Bandt, some outcomes – Itche Rabinovitz, Shmuel Guterman, the epilogue of Zerach Kremin, to the Land, the Land!

Appendices
1) From enemy reports **337**
2) A report of the destruction of Jewish partisans **343**
3) An excerpt from the logbook of the "Shchors" troop **344**
4) A list of the Jewish partisans in battalion 51 **348**
5) A partisan bulletin **356**

Index **357**

Introduction

A) Social stratification of the Soviet partisan movement in Western Belorussia

To leave the valley of death, to join the partisans and avenge the blood that had been spilt was the dream of many young Jewish men and women. But who are the partisans? How do they function? What is their way of life? And how do they fight? How is it possible to keep going in the forests during the winter at the height of the cold? How do you find somewhere to hide from the cold, and bread to eat?

The young people of the ghettos did not know how to answer these questions. Even when they managed to obtain arms and learned how to use them, the forest was still a puzzle and a mystery for them. They were in need of direction from experienced partisans. However, the latter refused to accept Jews and train them.

The people who left the ghetto were often bitterly disappointed in their contacts with the partisans. More than once, they came across partisans who were far from ideologists, but rather, dubious characters and even criminals, who exploited the innocent trust of the ghetto Jews and wrung out of them everything they could get hold of, robbed them when they came, following to instructions, to the forests, and frequently also murdered them.

The partisans who populated the forests of western Belorussia did not come from a single national, social or cultural origin, and their moral standard was also varied. There is no truth in the version appearing in many of the Soviet history books, that most of the fighters in the forest who joined the partisans were motivated by honest patriotism and an enthusiastic desire to fight against the conquerors of their homeland. It is true that the people who set up the partisan movement, its organisers and chief commanders, were patriots who went out to the forests from idealistic motives. Not so with the majority of partisans, the tens of thousands who streamed to the forests in the later years of the war. Comparisons of the size of the partisan movement in 1941 and even in the first half of 1942, when German columns were marching forwards into the very heart of the Soviet Union, with the dimensions that grew and swelled after the victory of Stalingrad and the defeat of the Germans on various fronts, prove clearly that most of the forest fighters joined the partisans out of practical and opportunistic considerations.

In order to organise the partisan movement in Belorussia and to develop it during the first years of the war, they (the Soviets) had to send leaders and partisan organisers from the Soviet rear, this is described in official Soviet history:

"In the second half of 1941, 437 troops and partisan groups, totalling 7, 254 men were organised and sent into the regions of Minsk, Vitebsk, Mogilev, Pinsk, Baranovitch, Vileika and others.... In January 1943, 512 troops, numbering 57, 700 men were operating in conquered Belarus, and in June, there were already 553 troops - 80, 700 men, in November, 720 troops - 122, 600 men."[1]

Another official Soviet report says:

"The growth process of the partisan movement in Belarus is reflected in the growth of particular partisan divisions. In sixteen partisan brigades, in the northern areas of the Baranovitch district, out of the overall number of 11, 885 partisans who joined the partisan troop: in 1941 - 243 men; in the first half of 1942 - 672 men; in the second half - 1, 135; in the first half of 1943 - 2,153; in the second half - 3, 506; in 1944 - 3, 477."[2]

Jews who had been wandering through the forest and sought contact with the partisans were often received with mocking and contempt: " You've come here to save your skins behind our backs!" but the truth is that many of the commanders and the partisan fighters in the Soviet troops, were, in the period of the Soviet regime, members of the Bolshevik party and active in the socialist government, and they themselves fled to the forest in order to save their lives, since they were the first who the invader sought to eliminate. And in fact, there is nothing improper in the fact that they went to the forest to save their lives. We don't value the partisan movement for the motives which propelled its fighters to flee to the forest for partisan warfare, but according to their deeds behind the enemy lines and their contribution to its defeat.

Let us now examine the waves of volunteers to the partisan movement in its different strata.

The first to leave for the forest were people whose lives were in danger - activists in the party and the communist youth organisation, people in the management and the clerks of the Soviet regime, militiamen in the service of

---

[1] *Istoria Velikoi Otechestvennoi Voiny Sovetskovo Soyuza 1941-1945. Moskva 1960-1961, Vol II, p.126; Vol III, p.460*

[2] *L.N. Bitchkov, Partizanskoye dvizhenye gody velikoi otechestvennoi voiny 1941-1945. Moskva 1965, p.355*

the Soviet police. Among these, there were ideological communists, activists in the party from the days of independent Poland, and ex-political prisoners. There were those who had jumped on the communist bandwagon only with the setting up of the Soviet regime in the area, after the fall of Poland. The ideological communists were some of the first who set up fighting partisan groups, whereas the people of the other kind wanted to spend the difficult years in the forest or to hide in the villages until the storm had passed, until the enemy was expelled and the Soviet regime re-established. Some traitors emerged from among these people who wanted to 'atone' for the crime of their service to the Soviet regime, by means of dedicated service to the Germans, as spies or informers on their comrades and by taking an active part in the murder of Jews.

Among the first partisans were also numbered officers and soldiers of the Red Army who hadn't managed to break through the German surround, but weren't prepared to be taken prisoner. They chose the forest and partisan warfare. They united with the groups of communist activists who roamed through the forests and set up the first partisan groups. They came to terms with each other: the local people knew the conditions in the territory and the population. They knew who one could trust and of whom one had to be careful. They were also able to recruit intelligence and partisan contacts in the villages and small towns, whereas the military men excelled in leading and commanding military operations.

Refugees from German captivity belonged to the second stage of forest dwellers. They, too, were different in character and motives. There were those who wanted to pass the time quietly until the Red Army returned and all they did in the forest was take clothing and foodstuffs from the peasants. But there were also many refugees from captivity who reached the forest who were penetrated with a deep desire to take revenge on the enemy. They saw their comrades, soldiers, dying in their thousands in the prisoner of war camps, rotting of hunger and thirst, freezing from the cold, beaten and humiliated. The inhuman abuse of prisoners of war filled them with a burning hatred of the enemy. When they came across groups of partisans in the forest, they were only too happy to join them and fight. Some of them also organised independent fighting groups. These partisans carried out many heroic acts, through danger and personal self-sacrifice.

However, the period when these prisoners of war had stayed in the camps had badly affected their moral nature. They had absorbed vicious Nazi anti-Semitism, propaganda which spoke of the Jews being guilty for the difficult economic situation among the population of the Soviet Union. All Stalin's crimes, the enforced collectivisation, the mass exiles to camps, the brutal murders and imprisonments were attributed to the Jews, who were supposed to be political commissars, the evil advisers of Stalin who had taken control of

'Mother Russia'. Many prisoners, in particular the Ukrainians, accepted the German offers of recruiting to their service in the camps.

There were all kinds of people among the refugees from captivity, some completely ignorant and some intellectuals, and army and police commanders who became organisers and partisan commanders of courage and talent. However, their relationship with the Jews was often reserved and even hostile.

Partisans who were contemptuously nicknamed "the bridegrooms" belonged to the third sector. These were Soviet officers and soldiers who went to the villages and made their homes in the peasants' farms as agricultural labourers when they hadn't been able to break through the German surround and their units crumbled. Many men had been recruited to the army at the outbreak of war, and so the farmers' wives were only too happy to accept a cheap workforce for their farms. There were those who made personal connections with the farmers' wives, and others who married daughters of the farmers and thought they would pass the years of the war pleasantly and quietly instead of being killed or wounded at the front. Unfortunately for them, the Germans began to register the population and ordered the Soviet citizens to present at their command offices and then the "bridegrooms" began to flee to the forest. They joined existing partisan groups or organised new ones. These bands fought the enemy very little. Mainly they would go out to acquire food and other supplies or frequently simply robbed farmers. In order to arm themselves, they would put pressure on the peasants in the area to hand over their weapons, which had been left behind by the Red Army soldiers as they retreated. Sometimes they would kill a German or lone policeman who they would come across on the road and take his weapons. They also would ambush a lone German vehicle which was travelling along the road, stop it, kill the occupants and take their weapons. This low level of activity had not yet developed into real partisan warfare. But by the summer, and particularly in the autumn of 1942, parachutists were already appearing in the forests of western Belarus, envoys from the Soviet rear and representatives of the Bolshevik party. They began to organise the lone partisan battalions, which up until then had each functioned independently, and urged them into active warfare against the enemy.

In 1943, partisans of the fourth type appeared in the forests of western Belarus – "the recruits". When the number of German fatalities grew with their defeats at the fronts, they began to recruit men in the villages and small towns, and send them to work in Germany, to replace the large numbers who had been sent to the front. Many of the Belorussian and Polish youth were hunted - there is no other word for it - and transported against their will to forced labour in Germany. The youth began to hide. The partisans wanted to beat the Germans to it and organised recruitment operations of their own in their rural areas, though many sons of the peasants reached the partisans on their own initiative.

But they too were full of hatred of the Jews, which they had absorbed from the German propaganda. Moreover, their looting of Jewish property with the destruction of the ghettos contributed to anti-Semitism. During the murderous Actions, local residents, both urban and rural, would come to the ghetto to rob, furnished with sacks and carrying away their loot on carts. This, and the Jews who had left their property in the peasants' houses gave the peasants hope they would not remain alive to come back after the war and ask for their belongings back.

The fifth sector consisted of people released from the Soviet labour camps. During the years of the Soviet regime, many hundreds of prisoners were brought to Western Belarus, some political and some criminal, who were employed in fortifying the borders, building the airstrips, laying the roads and other activities. Most of them hated the Soviet regime. The Germans released the prisoners of these camps and they dispersed in all directions. Because of the war, the released prisoners couldn't return to their homes. They went to the villages and hired themselves out for agricultural work in return for a roof over their heads and food. When the German authorities eventually came to arrest them, they also fled to the forests. The criminal elements among them formed gangs there, which frequently robbed the peasants and passers-by and they killed Jews who they chanced upon on the road. Both types were a danger to the Jews of the forests. The ex-political prisoners blamed the Jews for the Bolshevism of Mother Russia and for the suffering which the authorities had caused them. There were among them people whose suffering in the forced labour camps had not put out the flame of love for their motherland. The cruel deeds the German conquerors inflicted on their people - the mass murders, the hanging of civilians, among them women and young people, and the burning of whole villages with their inhabitants - brought these people to the ranks of the avenging partisans. However, among them there were not a few who accepted the German offer of enrolment to their service, to army units and their police, like the support units of the Ukrainians and the Baltic peoples, who served the enemy and did the work of hangmen for the Germans in the ghettos and in the concentration and extermination camps. Many had been trained in this work in the camp of Trabeniki in Poland. They worked with the Waffen SS., and under their command, also fought against the Soviet partisans.[3]

Units of Ukrainians, Lithuanians and Latvians and also Belorussian police, took part in the destruction of the Jews of Slonim, Biten and small towns in the region.[4]

---

[3] *In the report of General Jorgen Stroop on the suppression of the Revolt in the Warsaw Ghetto, they are called "The men of Trabeniki" (Travnikleute).*

[4] *Gruppe Arlt, Taetigkeitsbericht, Minsk, 25.10.1942.*

In 1944, the last sector of the partisans appeared in the forests of Belarus. These were the people, who up until now, had served in the enemy army and police. During this period, the defeat of the Germans was already near and certain, as was the moment for reprisals on the traitors. Many collaborators wanted to atone for their sins to the motherland by means of joining the partisans. Whole police units of Belarusians and Ukrainians moved now with their weapons to the partisans. This sector, too, which up until now had been drenched in much Jewish blood, could not be counted as friends of the Jews in the forests. Those who lived in the family camps were forced to be extremely careful not to meet them.

Until the end of 1942, and even to the middle of 1943, there ruled a noticeable degree of lawlessness in western Belarus. Various partisan units would each act as they saw fit and enjoyed a great deal of independence in their operations. Not all the commanders, as has been said, fought out of ideology and frequently competition and struggle for command and rule prevailed among them. There were also acts of murder of commanders by their competitors in order to take their place. Jewish commanders particularly suffered and it happened that a Jewish partisan commander of an initiative was shot by his comrades in arms so that he wouldn't disturb their peace with his battle plans.[5]

In the wake of the broadening of the partisan movement and the joining of various criminal elements, the atmosphere in the troops into which these "partisans" were absorbed was spoilt and they made life very difficult for the Jewish partisans. With this, one must point out that there were commanders whose relationship with the Jews who were in their units was decent and they also aided the family camps, which were within their jurisdiction and supplied them with a little food.

The first period in the forests was a period of great mobility of partisan groups, and they would go from area to area as they thought fit. There were units that wandered eastwards in the hope of crossing the front line and joining the regular forces.

However, at the end of 1942, and particularly in 1943, roaming was forbidden and the partisan units were pinned down to one area of functioning. Envoys from the Supreme Partisan HQ and representatives of the Belorussian communist party came to the forests of Volchye-Nori and the forests near to

---

[5] *The lawyer Alter Davoretzki was shot in this way. He organised a partisan organisation in Zhatel (Zdzienciol), Diatlovo in Belorussian, and left for the forests. He wanted to attack the labour camp Dvoretz, to liberate hundreds of young Jews and bring them to the forest to fight as partisans. It is suspected that the organiser of the Derechin partisan group, Dr. Atlas, was shot in the back by a partisan in the course of a battle against the Germans.*

the towns of Slonim, Biten, Kosovo and others from the Soviet rear, and they imposed law and order and military discipline on the partisan movement. Separate partisan units were forced to unite into larger units and to accept the authority of the envoys from the Soviet rear, who had come from the 'Great Land'.[6] The envoys wanted full accounts of their operations from the partisan commanders and supervised the carrying out of tasks and instructions. The territory of western Belarus, which had formerly been under Polish rule, and also that of eastern Belarus, which prior to the war had been under the control of Soviet Russia, was divided into regional centres (Mezhray tzentr) in which resided representatives of the party. The partisan units were united into divisions (Soyedinenye), divisions into brigades (Brigada's) and these into battalions (Otriady), the battalions into troops (Roty), the troops into the platoons (Vzvody) and the platoons into squads (Otdelenye). In addition to the commanders, there were appointed to each battalion and troop, commissars and polytrouks (lieutenants), whose role was to serve as the deputies to the commanders and political educators to the partisans. Often the authority of the commissar was greater than the authority of the commander. An HQ worked by each troop, headed by a chief of staff or an operational officer and likewise, the special platoon (osoby otdiel), whose role was to supervise the political correctness of the partisans and the faithful execution of tasks. It was also within the authority of the head of section to judge and punish offenders.

This was a relief for the Jewish partisans, and many of them who had been banished earlier to the partisan camps were brought back to the fighting units. This was also done because of the need to enlarge the number of partisans in the units when the troops became brigades and the battalions became troops. Now partisans who had plotted against the Jews and were convicted of unlawful killing had to pay the price and were punished.

During the Red Army offensive on Koursk and Uriol in the summer of 1943, fighting along enemy transport lines was intensified. Smaller, select partisan units were trained and specialized in these operations: blowing up German military trains, sabotaging the railway tracks and burning bridges. The military equipment for these operations was supplied by the Soviet rear. Accordingly, the problem of supplies of weapons and ammunition lessened, as previously the partisans had been forced to produce these from shells and bombs that had not exploded in a primitive manner and in danger of their lives.

In the operations of the "War of the Rail-track", as it was called, the operation to paralyse the movement of enemy trains, Jewish saboteurs excelled. Airfields were now set up in almost every partisan area on which planes from the Soviet rear would drop military equipment - bricks of explosive

---

[6] *The Soviet hinterland (rear?) was called "The Great Land", and the territory under partisan control, "The Little Land".*

material TNT. ("Tol" in Russian) and medicines and first aid materials. Eventually, landing strips were set up in the forest, where instructors and army commanders would land, and on the way back, the planes would take back those who were seriously wounded.

B) Comments on the Soviet historiography of partisan warfare

We are concerned with the question of objectivity of history books. In fact, the question has often been raised: is there such a thing as an objective history book? It seems to me possible to conclude that every history book is to a greater or lesser degree, subjective, and is affected by ideology, the world view and school of thought to which the writer of the book belongs, and the spirit of the period (a completely unscientific concept - perhaps the fashion?) in which the book was written. And if this is the case with historical essays, categorised as scientific, how much more so with books of memoirs, where the subjective foundation is particularly prominent?

There is no doubt that the description of the people in whose company the writers of memoirs worked is very influenced by the relationship between the writer and those described. In Soviet books of memoirs, the part of the Bolshevik party in partisan fighting and the contribution of the party to the victory over Germany altogether usually stands out. The contribution of commanders and commissars, who were party members, and their initiative in leading battles and obtaining victories over the enemy are particularly emphasised and their part in failures is glossed over. The commanders and the rank and file who were party members are usually described as people without blemish. Indeed, many of the Soviet partisans, commanders and ordinary fighters, carried out life-threatening deeds of extreme heroism out of unreserved love and devotion for their homeland. However, not all of them were shining examples. Comparisons and evaluations of the descriptions of non-Jewish Soviet authors and the memoirs of Jewish partisans, who fought under their command or by their side, frequently present a different picture. The literature of Soviet memoirs does not in essence reveal the true personalities of their protagonists; it frequently hides mistakes of judgement and failings in battle which cost precious lives.

Of course, human errors are an understandable and well known phenomenon, and even the most able make mistakes sometimes, but this literature frequently conceals the facts about moral corruption, such as the pursuit of power, vindictiveness, drunkenness, cruelty, the humiliating treatment of female partisans, and in particular the Jewish women among them. This literature ignores manifestations of cowardice which certain commanders revealed by not telling the truth and by laying blame for failure on others. Moreover, it ignores incidents that happened not infrequently when a commander falsely blamed another partisan in order to get rid of him and execute him.

The official historiography, and likewise the books of memoirs, tends to minimize the part played by the Jews in the partisan fighting, and indeed, when the name of an outstanding Jewish partisan is recalled, his origin is never mentioned. In contrast, from time to time, it refers to the national identity of other peoples and even tribes from Asia or Western European peoples, who were drawn for various reasons into a Soviet partisan unit.[7] The exception among these books is the book: *Andreyev, Sovershennoye Imi Bezsmertno, izd. "Visshaya Shkola", 1986,* which mentions the identity of Jewish heroes.

However, memoirs of Jewish partisans are also subjective. Here, one is aware of a desire to bring back from oblivion the names of Jewish partisans, in particular those who fell, and even those of people who did not excel in the bravery of their spirit or in their attainments of battle at all. The memoirs of Jewish partisans are in fact a response to the forgetting and concealment of the Soviets.

Another characteristic of the memoirs of Jewish partisans is the abundance of reports about the problems which the Jews from the ghetto were forced to overcome when they left to join the partisans and also the many descriptions of difficulties and injustices which their anti-Semitic comrades in arms caused them. And accordingly, the witness accounts – the memories – are coloured with strong emotion. Descriptions of the activities in which they took part and the conditions in which they are involved are much more detailed. Probably the reason for this is that the memoirs of the non-Jews are almost all those of commanders and even senior commanders. They saw the general picture; they described the political situation, the contacts with commanders of nearby units and the residents of the area and also the mood of the civilian population where they were active. However, they did not always take part themselves in the operations which they describe, whereas the Jewish memoirs were rank and file fighters or junior commanders, and they described the partisan fighting in which they took part personally and which they experienced in the flesh.

C) Is the wealth of detail relevant to history?

The question can be asked, "Is the wealth of detail that appears in the memoirs of Jewish writers relevant? Do they have historical value? Are they history?" - a question posed by the historian E.H. Carr in his book, *What is History?*

---

[7] *For example: in the official book of the partisan War in the Republic of Belarus it says: "In the partisan troops of Belarus there were over 1.500 Poles, and some hundreds of Czechs, Slovaks, Yugoslavs, Germans, Rumanians, Austrians and Italians." Note: There is no mention of the fighting of thousands of Jewish partisans. The gains of the Jewish partisans are credited to the non-Jewish people of the republic.*

One must accept that many details (obviously not all of them) which appear in the memoirs of Jewish partisans have a decisive historical value in writing about the history of the Jews in the period of the Second World War, and evidently in the history of this period in general. These details throw light on the problems and difficulties which a young Jew who wanted to fight encountered. They answer many questions which have been asked by people who didn't experience this period and wonder at the behaviour of the Jews in those years. These details describe the relationships between the officers and their Jewish men, the relationships between the non-Jewish partisans and their Jewish comrades. They answer to a great extent the question of how the Jews behaved in the ghetto; the piercing and troubling question as to why large numbers of young Jews didn't leave for the forests and why did they wait so long to rebel? There is no mention, no response to these questions in non-Jewish historical writing.

I will present several examples from the book before us:

The response of Bobkov, commander of the Sovietskaya Belorussia brigade to the reports of the Jews from the family camp in the forests of Volchye-Nori, and the many inhuman losses which they suffered in the murder of their relatives, was in these words: "Now it'll be easier for you, because you've got rid of so many barakhlo" (rags in Russian).

These wicked and cynical words were said by a commander within whose jurisdiction the family camp lay and whose people needed his care and should have been able to accept his help. Bobkov said this twice.[8] Bobkov's deeds are not recalled in the memoirs of his senior commander, the commander of the Shchors troop, Proniagin, who was the one who handed over the command to him and who praises his brave spirit. Yet this man, who murdered people with his own hands, and whose men frequently murdered the Jews of the forests, was nominated to receive the decoration "Hero of the Soviet Union".[9]

The Jewish partisan, Berkovich an active reconnaissance soldier, who was constantly on the roads, directly carried out the order of his commander and shot a peasant who had been found guilty of collaboration of the enemy. Berkovich was sentenced to death for that by the commander and commissar of the Komarov division, since the commander of the Korzh division claimed that the man who had been shot was trusted by him and a relative. Berkovich was shot on the order of Korzh, also a "Hero of the Soviet Union", without being able to justify himself, without investigation, without witness evidence and without a trial, whereas Fedya, who gave the command, came clean out of

---

[8] Moshe Pitkovski, "Azoi iz un untergegangen die Yiddishe Kehilah in Biten", in: the Biten folder, p.295, 303. He heard these cited words from the partisan Boria Yudkovski, who served as liaison between the H.Q. of Bobkov and the family camp. After he immigrated to Israel, Yudkovski was a member of Kibbutz Lochamei haGetaot and active in the Kibbutz Hameuchad organisation.

[9] Bobkov was not awarded the highest decoration after Jews who had survived Volchye Nori gave evidence of his anti-semitic abuses.

the whole matter. This detail, too, does not appear in the memoirs of the commanders of the divisions. Acts of execution of Jewish partisans on the brutal orders of Soviet commanders were not uncommon.

In the memoirs of Proniagin, the commander of the Shchors troop, whose exploits are considered in this book, the name of Dr. Avraham Blumovitch (Atzmon), the chief medical officer of the troop, and subsequently, of the division, is not recalled even once. Dr. Blumovitch was an outstanding surgeon who operated in the forest in difficult partisan conditions, without an operating theatre and without vital surgical equipment. He saved the lives of many wounded partisans. Is his name not mentioned in the book because he was a proud Jew and immigrated to Israel? By contrast, Dr. Lakomtsev, the Russian, is highly praised, whilst he worked in another troop, and would be less likely to be mentioned than Blumovitch, whose rank was higher than that of the Russian.

There is no reference, either in official partisan literature or in memoirs, to the fact that during the initial period of organisation in the partisan movement, Jewish doctors and nurses supplied the forest almost entirely with medical support. Polish and Belorussian doctors didn't feel they needed to go to the forest to treat wounded partisans, whereas Jewish doctors went willingly when a contact was found for them. They did this not only to save their own lives, but because they were also looking for a channel to fight and take revenge on the enemy. That is how Dr Blumovitch behaved and also Dr Yehezkel Atlas, from Kozlovshchina (a region of Novogrudek), and many other doctors and nurses. In Poland, in occupied Soviet territory and also in free Yugoslavia, most of the medical teams in the forests were Jewish nurses and doctors.

D) The sources

This book has been written on the basis of;

1) Witness accounts of the Jewish 51 battalion, which were published in the memorial (Yizkor) books of the Slonim and communities;

2) The memoirs of Jewish partisans from the 51 battalion, which were written by them and delivered as monographs;

3) Witness accounts of fighters of the 51 group, which were written or recorded by their comrades;

4) Clarification discussions which partisans carried out by means of questionnaires which I sent them;

5) Memoirs of Soviet partisan commanders;

6) Soviet official history books;

7) Memoirs of Jewish partisans;

8) A report of a German operational division which murdered the Jews of the region.

The memoirs are those of:

Avraham Orlinski, A. Imber, Avraham Doktorchik, Ya'akov Khatzkelevich, Shabtai Moshkovski, Zerach Kremin, Ya'akov (Yasha) Shepetinski, Zvi Shepetinski – Shefet.

Witness accounts:

Abramovich Luba, Abramovski Eliyahu, Dr. Orlinski Cheslava, Abramchik Bandt Lubaoba, Avramchik Krusi, Alpert-Rozenberg Hannah, Alpert Pesach, Dr. Avraham Blumovitch, Bandt Avraham, Bandt Aharon, (Archik), Gellerstein-Imber Tanya (Tamar), Gertsovski-Doktorchik Golda, Davidovitch-Stein Miriam (Sima), Volkoviski Mina, Zhagel Luba, Mukasay –Moshkovski Masha, Moshkovski Hillel, Dr. Kaplinski Noah, Krasnostavski Zhenia, Finkel Ze'ev, Finkel Natan, Rabinovitch Yitzhak (Itche), Shelubski-Graf Yehudit.

Books and articles

Abramovitch David (Dodel), **A partisan un aroitarmeier,** Tel-Aviv, 1981.

Blum, Dr. Leon Miron Leshem, **A Geshonken leben**, Ferlag Yiddishland, Buenos Aires.

Holtz, Y ,**The Jews of Slonim under the Nazi occupation**, an anthology of the heritage, Pub. Moreshet booklet 30, November 1980.

Major-General P. Varshigora, **The route-marches of Kovpak**, the history of a partisan brigade, pub." Ma'arachot", 1953.

K. Lichtenstein (Ed.) **The Slonim Folder,** vol. 1, Lichtenstein Klein and Yekhezkel Raban, (Eds.), vol. 2.

The Biten Folder, Oifkum un Untergang fun a Yidishe Kehile, redagirt Dodel Abramovitch un Mordechai V. Bernstein, Buenos Aires, 1954.

M. Pertsov, **The Lad from Osovo (Ways of Life),** in duplication.

Sh. Straus-Marka **Poylisher Yidden in die Velder**, Tel-Aviv, 1979.

Letters

Partisan letters of the "Shchors" group, held in the Soviet Union, mainly from the year 1960.

The letters of P.A. Proniagin, ex- Shchors troop commander, to Yasha Shepetinski, of 13th. March 1960, 7th. October 1960; Proniagin to Nyonia Tsirinski, of 11th. June, 1960 – most of it about the plan for the book which he was to write.

The letters of Nyonia Tsirinski from the city of Omsk to Yasha Shepetinski, of 25th. April, 1960, 3rd. September 1960 – mostly about meetings fellow partisans and his visits to Slonim, Brest and other places; 15th. November 1960, and 15th. August 1965.

G.A. Dudko, ex- Shchors troop Commissar, to Yasha Shepetinski, of 16th. March 1960, and 5th. September 1960

Dr. W.A. Lakomtsev, 13th. March 1959.

Sources

1. Ainstein Reuben, **Jewish Resistance in Nazi Occupied Eastern Europe** Paul Elek, London, 1974.
2. Bitchkov L.N. **Partizanskoye Dvizhenye v Gody Velikoi Otechestvennoi Voiny**, 1941—1945, Kratki Ocherk, Moskva, 1965.
3. Braiko Petr, **Kalinenko Oksana, Vnimanie Kovpak.** Moskva, 1971.
4. Brinski A. **Po Tu Storonu Fronta**, Vospominania Partizana. Moskva, 1971.
5. **Bug v Ognie**, Minsk, 1977.
6. **Druga Vojna Sviatowa**, Ksiazka I Wiedza, Warszawa, 1987.
7. **Istoria B.S.S.R**, Akademia Nauk Belorusskoi SSR, v Dvuch Tomach, Minsk, 1961.
8. **Istoria Velikoi Otechestvennoi Voiny** Sovetskovo Soyuza, v 6 Tomach, 1941 — 1945, Institut Marksizma — Leninizma Pri .C.K. Moskva, 1961.
9. **Iz Istorii Partizanskovo Dvizhenia v Belorussii**, Sbornik Vospominanii 1941 — 1944. Minsk, 1961.
10. Kovpak A.S., **Od Putiwla do Karpat**, Prasa Wojskowa, Warszawa, 1949.
11. Kovpak A.S., **Iz Dvevnika Partizanskich Pochodov**, Moskva, 1964.
12. Linkov G.L., **Voina v Tylu Vraga**, Moskva, 1951.
13. Liventsev V. **Partizanskii Krai**, Minsk, 1969.
14. **Partizanskoye Jormirovanie Belorussii** v Gody Velikoi Otechestvennoi Voiny (June 1941 — July 1944), Minsk, 1983.
15. Proniagin P.V., **U Samoi Granitzi**, Minsk, "Belarus", 1979.
16. **Ruch Podziemny v Ghetach i Obozach**, Materialy i Dokumenty, Ajzensztajn, Opracowala Betti Ajzensztajn, Warszawa, Lodz — Krakow, 1946.
17. **Soviet Partizans in World War II**, edited by John A. Amstrong, the University of Wiskonsin Press, Madison, 1964.
18. Starozhilov N.B., **Partizanskie Soyedinenya Ukrainy** v Velikoi Otechestvennoi Voine, izd. "Vishcha Shkola", 1983.
19. **Vsenarodnaya Borba v Belorussii** Protiv Nemetsko — Fashistskikh Zakhvatchikov, 3 Toma, Minsk, 1984, 1985.

2. БЫЧКОВ Л. Н. ПАРТИЗАНСКОЕ ДВИЖЕНИЕ В ГОДЫ ВЕЛИКОЙ ОТЕЧЕСТВЕННОЙ ВОЙНЫ, 1941 - 1945, КРАТКИЙ ОЧЕРК, МОСКВА, 1965.

3. БРАЙКО ПЕТР, КАЛИНЕНКО ОКСАНА, ВНИМАНИЕ КОВПАК. МОСКВА, 1971.

4. БРИНСКИЙ А. ПО ТУ СТОРОНУ ФРОНТА, ВОСПОМИНАНИЯ ПАРТИЗАНА. МОСКВА, 1971.

5. БУГ В ОГНЕ, МИНСК, 1977.

7. ИСТОРИЯ Б. С. С. Р., АКАДЕМИЯ НАУК БЕЛОРУССКОЙ ССР, В ДВУХ ТОМАХ, МИНСК, 1961.

8. ИСТОРИЯ ВЕЛИКОЙ ОТЕЧЕСТВЕННОЙ ВОЙНЫ СОВЕТСКОГО СОЮЗА, В 6 ТОМАХ, 1941 - 1945, ИНСТИТУТ МАРКСИЗМА - ЛЕНИНИЗМА, ПРИ Ц. К. МОСКВА, 1961.

9. ИЗ ИСТОРИИ ПАРТИЗАНСКОГО ДВИЖЕНИЯ В БЕЛОРУССИИ, СБОРНИК ВОСПОМИНАНИЙ 1941 - 1944. МИНСК, 1961.

11. КОВПАК С. А. ИЗ ДНЕВНИКА ПАРТИЗАНСКИХ ПОХОДОВ, МОСКВА, 1964.

12. ЛИНЬКОВ Г. Л., ВОЙНА В ТЫЛУ ВРАГА, МОСКВА, 1951.

13. ЛИВЕНЦОВ В. И. ПАРТИЗАНСКИЙ КРАЙ, МИНСК, 1969.

14. ПАРТИЗАНСКОЕ ФОРМИРОВАНИЕ БЕЛОРУССИИ В ГОДЫ ВЕЛИКОЙ ОТЕЧЕСТВЕННОЙ ВОЙНЫ (ИЮНЬ 1941 - ИЮЛЬ 1944), МИНСК, 1983.

15. ПРОНЯГИН П. В., У САМОЙ ГРАНИЦЫ, МИНСК, ((БЕЛАРУСЬ)), 1979.

18. СТАРОЖИЛОВ Н. В., ПАРТИЗАНСКИЕ СОЕДИНЕНИЯ УКРАИНЫ В ВЕЛИКОЙ ОТЕЧЕСТВЕННОЙ ВОЙНЕ, ИЗДАТ. ((ВИЩА ШКОЛА)), 1983.

19. ВСЕНАРОДНАЯ БОРЬБА В БЕЛОРУССИИ ПРОТИВ НЕМЕЦКО-ФАШИСТСКИХ ЗАХВАТЧИКОВ, 3 ТОМА, МИНСК, 1984, 1985.

Newspaper sources:

Two descriptions in the Latvian newspaper, *"Rigas Balss"*, of the trial of German and Latvian Nazi war criminals, which took place in March 1961, in the Latvian supreme court in Riga, against policemen of the 18th police battalion, who destroyed villages in Belarus and Latvia in the years 1941-1943 in areas of partisan activity in the Brest region.

In fact, the days of the existence of the Jewish 51 battalion as a Jewish partisan unit, were short (from 30th. June 1942 to the beginning of January 1943), but they were preceded by a time of stormy underground activity in the Slonim ghetto. Its members continued to fight after the independent breakup of the Jewish battalion and its dispersal among the troops of the Brest division, until they left the partisan forest. Many of those who survived fought in the ranks of the Red Army until the end of the war and the defeat of the Nazi Reich. Some ex-members of the Jewish battalion completed their war with the Nazi enemy on the soil of the collapsed Reich.

In this work of mine, I owe an acknowledgement of thanks to the members of the publishing committee: to the partisans Avraham Orlinski, Zerach Kremin, Ya'akov Shepetinski, and in particular, Zvi Shepetinski-Shefet, the chairman and vital spirit of the committee. They spared no effort and laboured in collecting the material, in gathering witness accounts and recording them, in searching for documents and maps and sketching diagrams. They were constantly at my disposal when I was working on the book, responding willingly to my every approach and request, and in this way, they made the work much easier. I owe thanks to Dr Noah Kaplinski, who read the first part of the book and made his comments. I am sure that without their help, it is doubtful whether I would have written the book.

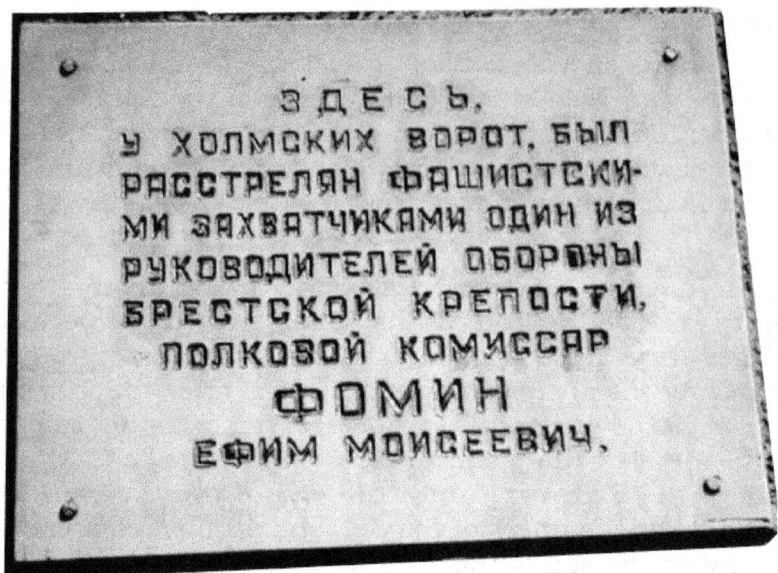

A memorial plate to Yefim Ben Moshe Fomin, brigade commissar, one of the commanders who defended the Brest fortress. He was shot at the gate of the fortress by the German fascists.

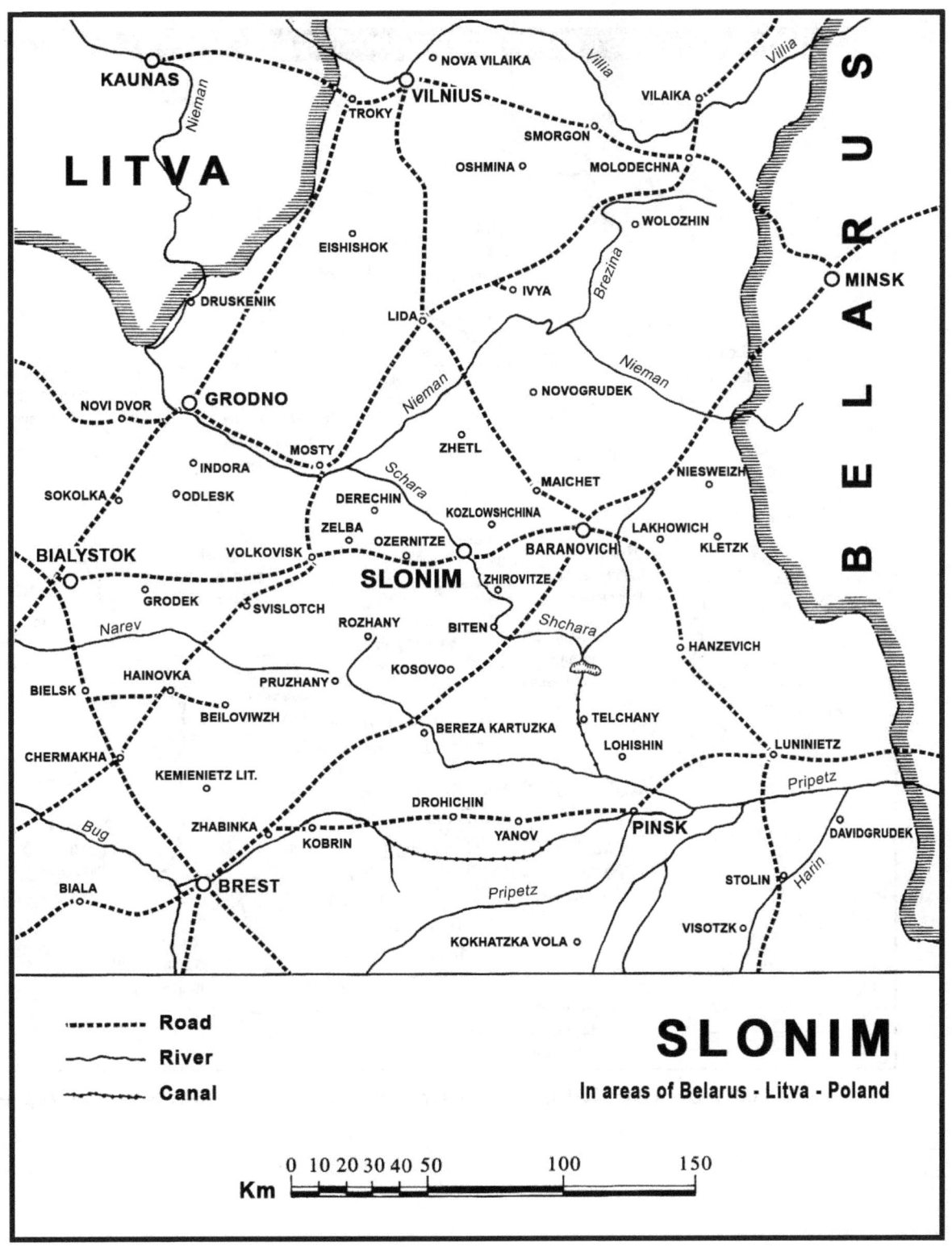

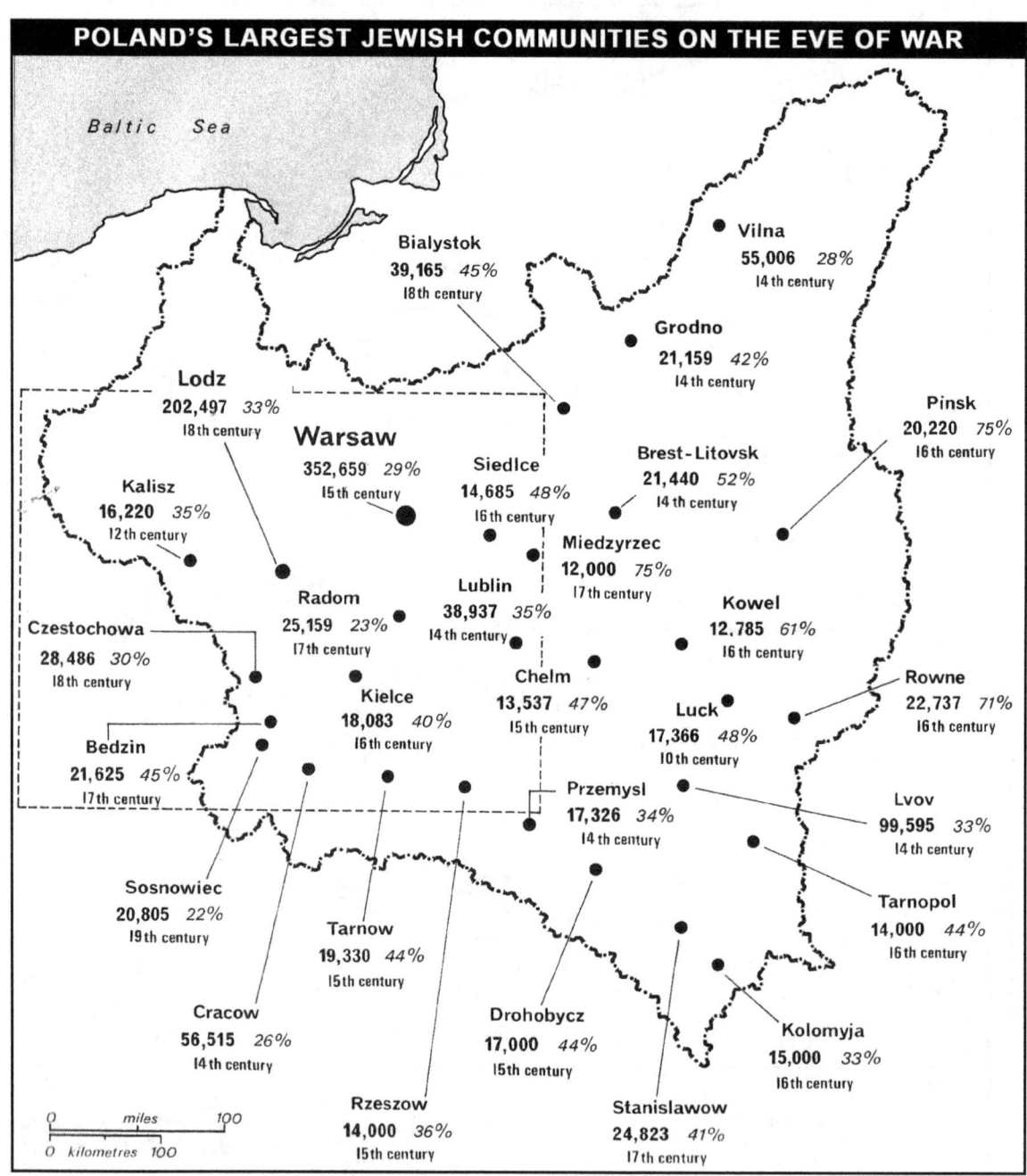

From the **ATLAS OF THE HOLOCAUST** by Martin Gilbert - Courtesy of Yad Vashem

Preface

Slonim: a major Jewish town

Location of the town

The town of Slonim dwells on the banks of the River Shchara. Its waters flow into the Niemaen, which falls away to the Baltic Sea. Until the Second World War, the town belonged to Poland, and is now part of Soviet Belarus. This strip of land has abundant forests, many parts of which have been cut down over the years and in their place, urban and rural settlements have been set up. Agricultural workers on this strip of land have not been blessed with lush crops, since much of the farmland is sandy soil, which does not produce enough bread to support a peasant family.

In the summer months, passers-by would particularly notice broad expanses of the white blossom of spelt, the 'corn' of sandy soil, between the villages. Here and there a blue carpet of flax blossom would spread out before their eyes, but in the years just before World War Two, there were fewer stretches of flax, because the preparation of fabric from it was labour intensive, and cotton, which the peasants would buy in Jewish shops when they came to the town on market day, had taken its place. Here and there, one could see a field of potatoes, and smaller areas in which ears of corn and barley would move in the wind, dotted about with blue cornflowers and the red of wild poppies.

The population was poor, only the owners of larger plots of land being blessed with abundant crops, and therefore, the peasants would supplement the income of their families with cutting wood in the local forests and transporting it to the town, and with fishing and other industries which nature offered them.

The Jewish population of Slonim and other small towns in the area was not a wealthy one, and the poor people of the town were many. Around Slonim and its subsidiary towns, the land which was once covered with dense forest was receding. Now bare patches were breaking out in the forest, and they were criss-crossed with pathways and roads which connected the settlements of the area with the central towns in the interior of the state.

At one time the forests were populated with an abundance of wildlife. At times the foxes and the wolves would reach the fences of the settlements on a winter's night. Their wailing and barking could be easily heard around the houses and their eyes would gleam in the darkness like burning coals. Now they too were fewer and only very occasionally might you still meet them.

From ancient times, the forests closest to Slonim had been called by the name of Volchye Nori, which means the caves of the wolves. This was a forest whose trees, both pine and deciduous, intertwined with branching treetops which hid the sky until a ray of light could barely penetrate through them. At the bottom, around the trunks, at the entrances to the forests and the bare patches, various bushes grew, tangled shrubs and wild blackberry, and bushes of forest nuts. During the years of the holocaust these forests were the last refuge of the remnant of the Slonim ghetto and of the small towns of the region, and a place of suffering and sorrow which the anti-Semitic partisans inflicted on the Jews.

In the spring, as the snows melted, the River Shchara became a broad channel and would sometimes flood the fields on its banks. In other places, it was very narrow but quite deep, so that it was impossible to cross on foot. The Shchara had an abundance of fish, which provided an income for many people, Jews and Christians. Eventually, the forests which were on the banks of the Shchara and its tributaries, became the places where partisan troops encamped, sometimes setting up their camps on the right bank and sometimes on the left. Because of their activities, the partisans were often forced to cross the river, sometimes when it was frozen, and they would get wet up to the neck. Sometimes, they would go a long way to neighbouring forests, or even distant ones, right up to the Niemen, where on more than one occasion they encountered white Poles – these were partisan units who were hostile to the Soviet regime and to the Soviet partisan movement, and more than they fought against the German invaders, they would attack the Soviet partisans and at every opportunity, murdered the Jews of the forest who they happened upon.

A little history

The Jewish community in Slonim has a long history of about five hundred years, though it now belongs to the Belorussian Soviet Republic. In the period of the initial Jewish settlement in the region, Slonim, like several other western Belorussian towns, belonged to the Lithuanian orthodoxy and the people of Slonim were considered to be 'Litvakim'. After the union of Lublin (1569), when Lithuania became part of the kingdom of Poland, many Jews settled in Slonim, and at the end of the 16th century, the Jewish community numbered eleven to twelve thousand souls. The community suffered a great deal from the injustices of the urban Christians and its growth was slow. The community suffered many vicissitudes and also times of economic growth, in particular in the period of Mikhal Kazimiezh Oginski (1771-1792), the enlightened prince, under whose jurisdiction Slonim came. The prince was famous for digging the Oginski canal, which links the River Pripiet and the tributaries of the Dnieper with the Shchara, creating a waterway from the Black Sea right up to the Baltic Sea. Merchandise, wood and crops were sailed along this waterway, and many people, among them Jews, found their living in this occupation, and the economic situation of many in that strip of land improved.

However, the community in Slonim also knew low points. During the years of the many wars which shook the region, the community was sorely tried with exile, blood-libels and burnings, when many of the residents of the city remained without homes.

Internal life, too, knew change: the cultural and spiritual life of the community, the ways in which their lives were organised, new reversals, conflicts and tensions, between the Chasidim and the Mitnagdim, between the educated and the conservative Charedim orthodoxies. With the penetration of the enlightenment to the region in 19th century, a struggle was conducted over the nature and education of the younger generation, and modern education cleaved a path for itself with difficulty.

Various organisations were active in the community, some of them philanthropic societies to ease financial hardship and some social and cultural organisations. One should note in particular the communal organisation in the years of the German conquest in the First World War (1915-1918). Even then, the exploitative character of German conquest stood out and made the yoke of the Jewish settlement much heavier. Many men were taken into hard forced labour; some of them were transported to great distances. The Jews of Slonim frequently lost their livelihood, and numerous families reached starvation point. Following this difficult economic situation, disease spread and many youths and children fell prey to tuberculosis. In this difficult time, the Zionist movement, the 'Hertzliyah Association', which was active even before the war, proved itself. The association called for communal help for the needy. The Blue Star of David was organised and recognised by the occupying authorities. This organisation offered medical and even practical help for the needy.

In the period of Polish independence, political activity branched out in the communities, according to various political parties. On the Jewish streets, youth organisations were active from either end of the political spectrum, from communist youth to Betar. The pioneering youth movements sent their members to preparatory kibbutzim, where they trained themselves for a life of manual labour in the land of Israel.

After the outbreak of World War Two, on 17th. and 18th. September 1939, Slonim was drawn into the area of Soviet control. The tension which broke out in the Polish community in the town was not directed against the new rulers, but turned against the Jews. The process of Sovietisation returned and hit the Jewish community hard destroying the tapestry of community life and its independent economic, cultural and philanthropic organisation. The town was filled with refugees who flowed from the Polish towns conquered by the Germans, and the number of Jews in Slonim grew in 1940 to more than 27,000 people, whereas, at the start of the invasion, they numbered 13,000 - 14,000,[10] though hope still beat in the hearts of the Jews that the times would change for the better.

However, in June 1941, an end was put to these hopes.

The destruction of the Jewish community

A week before the outbreak of war between the Soviet Union and Germany, people listening to radio programmes heard of the concentration of German troops near the border. The Red Army held manoeuvres and any rumour of tension between the Soviet Union and the Third Reich was denied. Even when the war broke out on 22nd. June, many people deceived themselves that the front was a long way from Slonim, and that Soviet tanks would not allow the enemy to penetrate into Belorussian territory.

A call-up was declared in Slonim. On 23rd. June, German planes dropped a number of bombs on the town which fell near the enrolment office. That day, at 11pm., the authorities left the town, without warning either the residents or the clerks who worked in their offices. At 6 am. the next day, German tanks entered Slonim, and then the first Jewish sacrifices fell at the hands of the Wehrmacht

---

[10] *Out of the total population which numbered over 35,000 in 1940. The Slonim folders, vol. 1, p.264*

(the German regular army). The saga of persecution and decrees also began. The German noose was tightened, and death reaped its harvest daily.

On 17th. July 1941, the first mass extermination action was held – twelve hundred men were murdered, most of them young people, and among them professionals and academics, leaders of the community, and the rabbi of the town. They were shot outside the town Shpakovo. The first Judenraat[11] was chosen, consisting of fifteen men, and a contribution (a fine) tax was imposed on the Jews of the town to the sum of two million roubles, and not in notes, but in gold. After that, the order was given to hand over all the money which Jews had and everything of value. After this order had been carried out, the men of the Judenraat were murdered together with their families. A new Judenraat was chosen and the Jews were imprisoned in a special quarter – the ghetto.

On 14th. November, the second massacre took place. The victims were murdered in the fields of Tchepelova more than ten thousand victims. The wounded, who managed to get out of the pits, were taken out of there and murdered.

In April 1942, the Jewish quarter in the ghetto was closed, and surrounded by a barbed wire fence. Many Jews prepared bunkers, that is, hiding places for themselves.

On 29th. June 1942, the third mass slaughter took place, and it was carried out by Germans and their support forces, Ukrainians, Latvians, Lithuanians and Belorussians. Many Jews hid. The slaughter went on for two weeks. On the first day, victims were brought to graves which had been prepared in the fields of Petralovitch, and on the next day and henceforth, in the fields of Tchepelovo. Poles and local Belorussians took part in the 'celebration' and hunted Jews who tried to flee from the slaughter. The Germans set fire to the ghetto and it became a killing field shrouded in flames. Jews were forced to come out of their hiding places and shot. Babies were thrown into the fire still alive. Among those who were caught, a 'Selektsia' took place and of those who were taken away for slaughter, a few people with professions who were necessary to the Germans were pulled out. However, many of the men were disgusted with life and joined their wives and their children and walked with their dear ones to the killing fields.

On 15th.July, the slaughter ended and in the ghetto there remained eight hundred 'legal' people and several hundred more who had left their hiding places and had survived. The number of Jews left in the ghetto decreased because of the fleeing of people out of the jurisdiction of the Gebiet

---

[11] *Dr. Noah Kaplinski, The Story of our Community's Holocaust, in: The Slonim Folders, Book 2, p. 42.*

commissariat (district) of Slonim into the area controlled by the Third Reich, to the towns of Rozhani, Prozhani, Volkovisk and Bialystok, where the mass extermination Actions had not yet been held, and there were a few who reached Warsaw.

During the early months of the invasion, an underground was active in the ghetto, which hoarded arms and smuggled people to the forest. And then there was nothing left for the survivors but to flee from the ghetto and reach the forests, the partisans, and the war of revenge. From now forth, the story of this book is the story of their struggle and the war of the survivors of the ghetto of Slonim and its surrounding area.

CHAPTER ONE: Slonim in the grip of the destroyer

On the day that Germany attacked the Soviet Union, many Soviet soldiers and civilians from Slonim were still enjoying the Sunday holiday and going on trips out of town. By the next day, 23rd. June, German military units appeared at the junction of the Baranovitch-Bialystok-Slonim-Rozhany roads. The Soviet army was still positioned some two hundred kilometres from the town, to the west of Bialystok, but when they reached Slonim, the Germans cut off the Red Army retreat lines along the Bialystok-Baranovitch-Minsk railway, and blocked the main road.

The speed of the German advance combined with the behaviour of the Soviet troops in not allowing citizens fleeing to the east to cross the Soviet-Polish border, meant that many escapees returned where they had come from. Only a few residents of Slonim succeeded in reaching territory which was under Soviet control. The Germans now found in Slonim a population of over twenty seven thousand, much greater than that which had existed before the war. On the very first night that the Germans entered Slonim, they immediately managed to inflict casualties.

The engineer Avraham Orlinski had chosen, on this last day off before the war, to go out fishing in the dam at the foot of the waterfall, where shoals of fish would congregate. Silence reigned all around, with only the hum of the turbine disturbing the silence, when the guard informed him that he must report immediately to the regional party secretary. When he arrived, his colleague, the engineer Mirski, manager of the municipal electricity network, was already waiting for him. The two of them were ushered into the secretary. This man asked if they had heard Molotov's[12] speech, and appointed them responsible for the black-out and maintaining a regular supply of electricity to the party offices and to strategic points in the town. The conversation concluded, but the problems had only just started.

The next morning Slonim was bombed, causing serious damage to the electricity network. The electrical engineers, many of them Polish and enemies of the Soviet regime, were in no hurry to repair the damage. A. Orlinski, as technical manager, was forced to supervise the group of workers himself. When he returned home at nightfall, his wife, Dr. Cheslava, was waiting for him at the entrance to their house, and anxiously told him that the Soviet government had disappeared from the town.

Dr. Cheslava was a member of the town council and chairwoman of the municipal health committee. The chairman of the town council who lived opposite them suggested to the Orlinskis that they should flee with him in a truck he had at his disposal. Cheslava wanted first to say goodbye to her family, to her brothers and sisters and their families, who had arrived in

---

[12] *On the first day of the war, the 22nd. June, Molotov made a speech on the radio, announcing the German attack on the Soviet Union and calling on all populations of the state to fight the German invader and show their confidence in the victory of the Soviet Union.*

Slonim from Chenstochova after its occupation by the Germans back in 1939. When she returned, she was already too late; the mayor had got out quickly, when German tanks had burst into the town and started firing. Avraham Orlinski and his wife remained under the trampling jackboot of the German conqueror.

Yasha (Ya'acov) Shepetinski had been sent to work in a co-operative in Bialystok after completing his studies in accountancy. He became friendly with a female colleague and the two of them started to embroider plans for a future together. Ya'acov was still awaiting his call-up to the army. Polish refugees had arrived in Bialystok and were telling horrific stories about what was happening under the German occupation. "But to us" recalled Yasha, "it seemed so far away; everyone felt protected by the forces of the Red Army. On the last Shabbat (Sabbath) before the German attack on the Soviet Union" Yasha told us "when I was walking with my girlfriend Esther in the municipal park in Bialystok, I felt a deep heaviness. I escorted her home and wandered round outside till two in the morning. I didn't manage to sleep much and when I woke up, I awoke to the sound of explosions. Everyone was running round scared outside. This was the first German aerial attack, but the word 'war' had not yet been uttered. Nobody knew and nobody even imagined that war had broken out."

When the situation became clear, a deathly fear reigned in the town. Yasha went to the office to enlist, but found no one there. The duty officer told him to move eastwards. Ya'acov rushed off to his girlfriend and she too told him to hurry off and she would immediately follow in his footsteps. Yasha Shepetinski's family lived in Slonim; his father worked in forestry, his mother was a housewife. His brother Herzel had just finished high school and his sister R'ayah was a pupil in Class 7, his brother Reuven in Class 8, Yechiel was in Class 3 and the youngest of the children, Uri, was only four.

Yasha hastened to reach his family in Slonim and this is how he describes the journey there. "The city had already been bombed five times; the station and the petrol tanks were burning. There were already fatalities. It was very hard to find any kind of transport." After many attempts Yasha managed to get on a lorry. On the way enemy planes were circling over the road and strafing. At times they were forced to jump from the vehicle and hide in the bushes. The next morning he reached his parents' house.

"The Germans had entered Slonim on 24th. June, and had struck fear into every heart.... everybody was terrified. On the 25th. June, Stars of David had been painted on Jewish houses, but on Christian houses there were crosses, the work of so-called "good" neighbours."

Long lines of Soviet prisoners were already marching through the streets. At home they were discussing what the boys should do. Yasha wasn't registered as a citizen so it was decided that he had to live in the underground and not go outside. His brother Herzel, who was an active member of the Komsomol, the Communist Soviet Youth Movement, would have to leave town, because everybody realised that the most immediate danger threatened those who were identified with the Soviet regime.

"A group of German soldiers and officers is going through the houses and looting underwear and socks and so forth. The night of the 26th / 27th June the family sleep in their garden. In the morning in the streets you could see lines of Soviet soldiers armed with grenades and bayoneted rifles advancing in the direction of the town centre. Shots resounded all around. The Jews were glad, they thought that the Red Army had come back and would get rid of the invaders, but just before noon the firing stopped. It turned out that a Soviet Army unit with three tanks had tried to force a way through to the East. They didn't succeed, all of them were killed.

"That evening the Germans stuck their first posters up. They went from house to house and rounded up all the male Jews into the synagogues, the cinema and the people's hall. They concentrated the non-Jews in the church and in the morning released them. Now the German Wehrmacht showed its strength against defenceless Jews. They stopped groups of Jews and forced them to sing, to jump, to dance and to perform physical exercises. They forced bearded Jews to cut off each other's beards. I, my father and my little brother were in a group that were forced to march on the spot and roll on the ground. The abuse went on until the next Monday, 30th. June. That morning we escorted Herzel out towards Lida."

Zvi Shepetinski-Shefet, Yasha's cousin, had gone out to the river before the war burst upon them, because nobody in his family had any idea what was about to happen.

"It was a day off for me", recalls Zvi who was then sixteen. "I was sitting by the bank of the river and fishing, which was my favourite pastime. From the iron bridge of the railway I heard an engine whistle. It was pulling dozens of platforms loaded with tanks, canon and all sorts of weapons. The train was moving slowly in the direction of Volkovisk. On his morning stroll my father came up to me, sat by my side on the bank of the river and said that the Germans had attacked the state and bombed the airports in the main cities.

"We hurried to leave and go back home, but what could we do now? No one knew. Again, we heard a Red Army radio call to the population, asking us to keep calm and orderly because the Red Army would vanquish the invader from the Soviet state. In our house the mood was very dejected. We knew what the Germans were capable of doing to the Jews, we'd heard what they had done to the Jews of Poland.

"Before many hours had passed a German spy was caught. In his pockets they found documents which evidenced what he was. The tension in the town rose. The Germans were bombing from the air. People who lived near to strategic areas or army establishments began to look for temporary shelter. Many of them packed their cases, but fairly soon the news spread that there was nowhere to run to because German paratroopers were peppering the roads with fire. In the evening we heard canon fire. We got out to our Uncle Yitzkhak Shepetinski's house. We thought that it would be quieter there, but we were wrong. We lay in the park behind the house all night, as the shooting built up and bullets were penetrating the house.

"The German planes were dropping incendiary bombs and many houses went up in flames. Because of the hail of bullets which the Germans were raining down on the town, it was impossible to put out the fires.

"First, a German tank entered the town. In its turret stood an officer dressed in a black uniform holding a submachine gun at the ready. The streets were completely empty, save for one Christian woman who came outside to the Germans with a bouquet of flowers.

"In the morning after a night exchanging fire with a Soviet unit which was trying to break through to the East, German soldiers looking for Russians entered our house and claimed that someone had fired on them from our windows. They picked on one of the refugees living in our house *(saying that)* that he was the man who'd fired because he had smoke marks on his fingers. Only with great difficulty were they persuaded that the man was innocent. The soldiers woke me from my sleep by shaking me roughly. I saw my whole family standing with their hands up and I raised my hands too. Then they commanded me to take off my hat and asked if I was a Russian soldier. They carried out a search in the house and looted everything they fancied. When they asked our nationality, we answered that we were Poles and then they made off.

"The break-ins to Jewish houses followed rapidly. The young German soldiers were well acquainted with the task of abusing the Jews, but the older soldiers sometimes played a part in our fate. They knew very well what was awaiting the Jews under the German regime. Josef Holtz, a refugee from the town of Kalish, set up a soda factory under German command. Several of the German soldiers told him clearly that after the regular army had left, the SS would wipe out all the Jews. The store manager of the military hospital used to visit him in his flat. He asked after Holtz's family and would bring him foodstuffs and sweets for the children. Once while they were chatting, Holtz said to him: "I hope that after the war, we'll meet in the village where you were born near Vrotzlav". To this the German answered him: "You're completely crazy if you believe that you'll survive Hitler."

Early Decrees and "Actions"[13]

In the early days of the occupation, two Jews - the lawyer Hertz Itzkovitch and the merchant Moshe Yakimovski – had been appointed liaison officers with the urban authorities (still Polish). They were ordered to bring the Germans a list of Jewish lawyers and teachers in Slonim. The two representatives had not the slightest idea of the aim of this list. They delivered a full list as requested. The next day small cars appeared in front of the houses of the men on the list. Those found in their houses were ordered to get into the

---

[13] *The term used by the Germans for the concentrating of Jews in one place prior to deportation or being taken to mass graves. (J.L.)*

cars. And from then on all trace of them disappeared and their place of execution is unknown to this very day[14].

These murders, as we know, were the first link in a chain of murders which the Germans carried out in the course of exterminating the Jewish people. The intention was first of all to "behead" the Jewish community, by destroying the stratum of the intelligentsia and the leaders of the community, who the Germans considered capable of organising Jewish opposition in the community. The Germans adopted this method in many of the largest and most developed Jewish communities.

On the 17th. July the first SS entered Slonim. They searched out men and whoever they caught, they beat cruelly and dragged off to the people's hall. They stole from them everything they had – watches and rings, and emptied their pockets, all the while with lashes from their whips. After that, they loaded them on lorries and drove them in an unknown direction. After a while, the drivers and the lorries returned empty. The Jews were told that these people – one thousand two hundred in all - had been transported for work, but doubt began to gnaw at people's hearts. The Action finished at noon. Several hundred arrested men were still left in the people's hall and they were released home, with the excuse that they (the Germans) didn't need any more labourers. When they were released to their homes, they were again beaten cruelly as they went out.

The relatives of the missing men started to try and find out where they had been taken. The Germans "calmed" the enquirers and said that it was alright, the men were well. Their families even received letters to this effect. Peasants pointed out the way the lorries had gone. Women went out to look for their husbands and sons, following the path of the lorries, as the farmers had told them. They reached the village of Derevnoye and found there a huge flat area covered with a layer of sand. A little digging with their hands was enough to reach limbs and clothes. This is how this cruel deed was discovered and the place where the crime was carried out. A religious Christian woman, the sister of a forester, arrived in Slonim and weeping, told them about the slaughter in the forest to which she had been a witness.

A shower of decrees was now rained down upon the Jews of Slonim, as the Germans had done all over Poland and in occupied Soviet territory. After the slaughter of 17th. July, the Germans ordered the establishment of a Judenraat[15]. Fifteen men were chosen, all of whom were murdered within a short time - they and their families.

---

[14]*According to the eyewitness account of Dr. Noach Kaplinski, now in Israel, a Slonim man who at the time of the German occupation was director of the maternity unit of the city hospital (in Magistratska Street). But see para. 3 on the following page.*

[15] *A committee of Jews, often prominent in the community, who were manipulated by the Germans to carry out their plans while pacifying the people. (J.L.)*

By means of decrees and abuses, the Germans ordered a second Judenraat of five men to be set up. Even though they understood what awaited them, they accepted the appointment out of concern for their fellow Jews.

Indeed, in Slonim the Germans adopted the same methods of fraudulence and deceit (Tarnung) in order to disguise their plans and finish the Jews off more easily. This was a method of falsehood, a tangle of deceit. It was designed to weaken the awareness of Jews to the lethal danger which threatened them, to prevent them organising to defend themselves, to tempt them to come out of their hiding places and to squeeze out their very marrow in hard labour before destroying them. After each bloody Action, after each mass murder, the Germans distributed to the remaining people various "Life Tickets" or "Work Tickets", each time in a different colour or accompanied by a different stamp. (*This was*) in order to confuse people and to instigate splits between them over the division of Jews into "useful" ones, who would stay alive, as it were, and superfluous Jews who would be deported, to the ghetto or another camp.

In this way the Germans conducted a war against the Jews, not only with weapons of destruction but with psychological warfare: they split the Jews from within and also created around them an atmosphere of hatred and contempt on the part of their Christian neighbours. Anyone who sympathised with the trouble and suffering of the Jews and tried to help in any way was punished.

In Slonim, a Wehrmacht (regular army) officer "explained" why they were confiscating from the Jews the stocks of food which they had laid up: the Jews store foodstuffs in unhygienic conditions. The Germans would store them in suitably hygienic conditions and this was all for the good of the Jews.

The behaviour of men of the regular army, soldiers and officers, proved them to be no better than the SS. The commanding officer of the town with the occupation was a Wehrmacht officer. As the Jews of Slonim knew, he was not a member of the Nazi Party, but it was under his regime and organisation that the first massacre of twelve hundred men was carried out.

In many instances, the Jews' neighbours and colleagues, Poles and Belorussians, took part in the activities of annihilation and plundering.

German Civil Administration - The Gebietskommissariat

On 1st. September, 1941, the regional civil administration (Gebietskommissariat) arrived in Slonim. The first Governor was Gert Erren[16], but matters were mostly directed by the Head of General Department, Hick, who was a cruel hangman. In time he was replaced by Gunter Stehle, whose title was official spokesman and negotiator (Persoenlicher Referent und Staendiker Vertreter). The Jews who were not familiar with the titles and official positions of management officials called everyone, even the driver Klein, by the name of Shtabsleiter (Head of Staff). One of these officials, Ritmeyer,

---
[16] *According to the report of Gebietskommissar Erren, of 25.1.1942, document no. CXLVa-0*

when walking round the town and later in the ghetto, would cast dread on the Jews and they always tried to get out of his way. There were other murderers, often at lower ranks, but they all took part in the slaughter and would get drunk and celebrate whenever Jews had been murdered. The officer in charge of the extermination battalion in Slonim was H.J.Neuendorf. Alfred Metzner was the official translator and in 1942 he was appointed director of the factories. All these men abused the Jews and all of them took care that Jews wouldn't be able to smuggle a morsel of bread into the ghetto.

With the confiscation of Jewish stocks of food, distress grew. Only in factories outside the ghetto where Jews were employed to work was it possible to have any contact with the local residents in order to exchange clothing or foodstuffs.

Some Poles, acquaintances from earlier days, would help Jews to obtain food and sometimes rewarded them for the support that they (the Jews) had given them in the Soviet era, but such people were few. In most cases the Polish residents of Slonim were happy that the Germans were killing the Jews and anticipated their humiliation and the acquisition of Jewish property.

The Setting up of the Ghetto

After the Germans murdered the twelve hundred Jewish men, they gained confidence that they would not encounter any demonstration of Jewish opposition in Slonim. At the beginning of August the decree was made public to establish the Ghetto and the Jews were ordered to move in to it within twenty four hours. The territory that was allocated for the Ghetto was in the shape of a rectangle: it bordered on the Shchara on the east side and with the Third of May Street on the west, with Mikhailovski Lane in the south and Mostova Street in the north. It included the streets Ulanska and Operova, and the alleys through which the Oginski Canal flowed; the meagre Zhabinka Street, which was on the other side of the Canal, was incorporated in the Ghetto. In this way it was easy for the Germans to wipe out the Ghetto, divided by the river, when their forces congregated on the bridges and shot every Jew who tried to escape the slaughter by jumping in the river.

They had imposed on the Jews a financial contribution to the sum of two million golden roubles. All the desperate efforts of the men of the Judenraat to raise this huge sum came to nothing. On 7th. November the gendarmes arrested the members of the Second Judenraat (having got rid of the first one) and their whole families - two hundred souls. Only three of them were released for a ransom in five days and the rest were killed.

After the murder of the second Judenraat, and the establishment of the smaller Ghetto, Yelishevitz was placed at the head of the Jewish community, having volunteered for the "job". He was single man and claimed that with his death he would not leave a bereaved family and therefore he was ready to be sacrificed for the community.

The German occupation descended in force on Slonim quickly. It was caught in the grasp of the German predator and oscillated between hope and despair without its leaders grasping what was awaiting them. The wise people of the community and its loyal financial supporters were shocked at the cruel treatment by the Wehrmacht, who had murdered Jews and plundered their property right from the first days of occupation, and by the hail of decrees and laws that poured down upon them with the establishment of the civil regime.

Following the first Action, the Jews of Slonim still deluded themselves, as did Jews right across the German occupation, that the wave of killings would stop, and they found all sorts of arguments to support this. The financial supporters of the community sought to pacify the murderers with the help of bribes - with silver, with money, with gold and valuable objects, whereas many of the ordinary people began to build "bunkers" - hiding places. Anyone who had acquaintances in the villages sought refuge with them.

But the youth, who had social and political awareness, caught on more quickly that the Germans were deceiving the Jews, since their plan and their goal was to wipe out all the Jews. With this recognition they began to organise for the struggle, for self-defence and for revenge.

There were those who agonised over it at first in the units, each with his doubts and anxieties, with his fears for the fate of the family. Others had heartfelt debates on the situation with two or three of their close friends, friends from the youth movement or from a particular political stream. Some embarked on the path of opposition later, with the help of friends who had already become organised. In this way, out of difficult internal struggles and bitter experience, from one bloody Action to another, the organisation arose, the way became clear, the weapons were gathered and the path was paved to the forest, to partisan fighting.

In fact, in the partisan forest, among the non-Jewish fellow fighters, the path of the Jewish partisan was not paved at all. Here, too, a number of obstacles piled up for the Jewish fighters. In the forests too anti-Semitism ruled; local residents who had reached the forests had been influenced by vicious Nazi propaganda. Even in the forests Jewish partisans were shot for various reasons and Jews, remnants of the ghettos seeking a refuge in the forests, were also murdered and looted. Even in the company of partisans, the Jew was first of all a Jew. And so, out of an unremitting struggle for the right of the young Jew, survivor of the ghetto, to bear arms, to fight and take revenge on the murderers of his loved ones and his community, there arose in the forests of Rafalovka, near Slonim, and Volchye Nori, the fighting Slonim Jewish battalion, the 51st. group of the troop called "Shchors".

From the **ATLAS OF THE HOLOCAUST** by Martin Gilbert - Courtesy of Yad Vashem

CHAPTER TWO: Beginnings of Partisan Movement in the Slonim Region

News of partisan action in the area began to filter through into the ghetto. The Germans and the police were often called away (to incidents) outside the town. Incidents like this inspired hope and encouraged the young people of the ghetto: here were people fighting the Germans fearlessly. Hearts went out to the partisans and there was some faint hope of reaching them, but how to go about this was not yet clear. Then there was another difficulty. How could they leave parents and younger siblings behind in the ghetto?

The Fiedrik Group

In the Soviet era a co-operative had been founded in the village of Zavershe. The chairman was a peasant with a rich Communist revolutionary past who had participated in the Bolshevik revolutionary wars. His name was Alexander Vlasowitz Fiedrik. With the German invasion he was compelled to hide and went into the forest, where he managed to unite around him a partisan group of fifteen people, and in time, his four sons also became partisans. Yasha Shepetinski's family, whose mother came from the area round this village, were friendly with the Fiedrik family, so when Herzel Shepetinski reached Fiedrik, members of the (Slonim) underground hung a lot of hope on him, that together they would be able to set up a fighting partisan unit.

Gregory Andreyevitch Dudko was the Poltruk (political leader) in Fiedrik's group. He was a junior officer in the Red Army and had been surrounded with his unit near Bialystok. Some of the men of the unit had been captured, and some had scattered in the villages. In the course of his wanderings Dudko arrived near Slonim, and in the village of Tchemeri he made contact with an underground cell whose secretary was Yasha Iskrik. Dudko, with several men from this village, had joined up with Fiedrik's group and was now appointed politruk. The group encamped in the forest of Rosakovo.

In November 1941 Alexander Fiedrik fell in battle near the village of Rosakovo, apparently following a tip-off from a traitor. The Germans took the partisans by surprise - some were killed and some dispersed. The Germans took cruel revenge on Fiedrik's family: his mother, his wife and his daughter were burnt alive, but his sons, who were then partisans in the forest, survived. The most active among them was his son Viktor, and he carried on his father's war until he too fell in battle. Through Herzel Shepetinski, Viktor set up links with the underground in the ghetto.

Lieutenant Proniagin's Group

There was another partisan group active in this area, still taking its first steps, but which eventually became the nucleus of the Shchors troop. Lieutenant Piotr Vasilievitz Proniagin's unit was hit in the Baranovitch district.

Proniagin was in command of a section in a battle in which both his battalion and another were hit hard. They were forced to retreat, leaving behind them dead and wounded.

On 27th. June 1941 columns of German forces were still flowing eastwards with heavy artillery. The remnants of Proniagin's stricken battalion were joined by the remnants of several other units and thus they numbered as many as five to six hundred men. They tried to break through the ring around them by force of arms, but they fell back and were beaten. After they had lost about two hundred men they retreated and scattered in various directions. Only fifteen men remained with Proniagin. He relates in his memoirs[17] that he suggested moving to guerrilla style fighting and that they accepted his suggestion, setting up a group which, according to him, had already started to fight by the end of 1941. They set up ambushes on the roads and wiped out enemy vehicles, with their passengers.

The truth is that matters developed much more slowly than Proniagin relates in his book, since in fact, in the winter months of 1941-42, Proniagin was living in the village of Zapolyeh. Over time, his group had armed themselves to some extent, since at the time of their defeat, most of them had lost their weapons, or had thrown them away in order to hide their military role, should they fall into enemy hands.

Proniagin's group moved close to Slonim and made contact with the Fiedrik/Dudko group. (Proniagin managed to meet up only with Dudko as Alexander Fiedrik had fallen in battle.) The two groups merged; Proniagin was elected commander and Dudko politruk. With the help of Fiedrik's son Viktor, they made links with the underground movements in the surrounding villages, who helped arm the group. A small quantity of arms and ammunition was lifted off the river-bed of the Shchara, where soldiers of the defeated Red Army had thrown it. At that time the partisans were living in shelters made out of plaited branches, since they were always on the move. The partisans lacked warm clothes and shoes for the winter and when they made contact with the ghetto underground, members of the ghetto organisation supplied them with clothes and boots, and met their other needs.

Getting organised in the Ghetto

Persecution and abuse of the Jews in the ghetto sparked the spirit of rebellion among the young people of Slonim and the wish to defend themselves and fight. This complete change of mood was slow. The idea of fighting gradually spread during the bloody Actions which inflamed more and more people each time, and not only the youth but older people of various political views - pioneers and Communists, and members of Beitar and the Bund - but it had not yet become clear how to start the struggle or how to direct it.

---

[17] P.V., *Proniagin, U Samoi Granitzi, Minsk, "Belarus", 1976, where this source is noted: Proniagin & the page number.*

Anshel Delatitski had been a communist from the days of independent Poland and like many others, he had tried to escape to the Soviet Union without success. He had come back to Slonim on 17th. July and hid at home for a whole fortnight for fear of being seen in the street. After that he decided that the time had come to act. However, in order to do that, he would have to leave his hiding place and take on work.

They had to hide his communist past. The Judenraat obtained a certificate for him showing there were no claims against him on the part of the authorities and Delatitski was accepted for work in the water board. The committee of the Jewish community allocated him four hundred grams of bread a day with a helping of soup like all the other workers; he was given a "Life Certificate" and he started to work. According to Avraham Doktortchik, one of the first to join the underground:

"In the month of July 1941 Fanya Feignbaum, who was a first aid nurse by profession and a refugee from Lodz, approached me and asked me to come to a meeting with a few friends. The meeting took place on the embankment of the Shchara. It was attended by Noah Servianski, Zelig Milikovski, Rina Doktortchik and Anshel Delatitski.

"Delatitski introduced himself as a communist and one-time political prisoner and also introduced people who were not from Slonim, but who had arrived at the town as a result of the war and now were joining the underground organisation. Anshel told us that in Slonim there were veteran communists, members of the Communist Youth and members of the left wing Zionist Youth who wanted to do something. As an active communist underground member, he suggested we organise ourselves along the lines of the communist underground in independent Poland. In the meeting Anshel took the role of representative of the committee and responsibility for the organisation of the general underground. The people who took part in the meeting would be considered as the cell of the first underground members."

This underground cell, says Doktortchik, met three or four times in the period between July 1941 and July 1942, but apart from talking nothing happened.

In the ghetto other independent and separate underground cells started to organise. Doktortchik testifies that he also organised a cell in which the members were: Abba Yudelevitch, Zlata Yochvidovitz, Henya Yochvidovitz, David Blumenfeld and his wife Lili. But only after the slaughter of 14th. November did they start to hoard weapons.

According to Pesach Alpert, who was one of the first in the underground, the idea of resistance became real only after the Action of 14th. November 1941. Pesach returned to Slonim in August 1941 after a failed attempt to escape to the East and after the slaughter of the twelve hundred, and then conceived the idea that they needed to defend themselves. The matter was debated between the comrades Moshe Ogushevitz, Anshel Delatitski, Zhama Shusterovich, Jacob Pripshtein.

The first consideration was to **organise self defence in the ghetto**. After the massacre of 14th. November, about which more later, the separate cells organised into one central underground. However, the manner of the struggle and its methods were still not clear to these inexperienced young people. They invited David Epstein to a meeting. He was a baker in the ghetto and he had experience in the running of a communist underground from the days of independent Poland. Pesach Alpert remembers that meetings of members of the underground took place sometimes in the apartment of Dr. Avraham Blumovitch who was from Lomzha and had reached Slonim as a refugee, and sometimes at the home of Haim Azef. In time the underground acquired many more meeting places, most of them in workshops or various factories where the members worked - for instance, the bakery, the saw mill, the carpenter's workshop and the forge.

The main concerns of the organisation were directed in two ways: (a) storing arms; (b) seeking links with a general underground outside the ghetto and particularly with the partisans in the forest. David Epstein arranged a meeting between the members of the organisation and an underground member in the town, the young Polish anti-Nazi Vatzek Vilchinski who became in time the runner between the ghetto and the forest.

Pesach Alpert recalls that once an envoy from the forest arrived at the saw mill where he was working, seeking to make contact with people of the underground in the ghetto. Pesach was sent to a meeting with him. When he came back, he said "The envoy is Russian. I asked him what to do in order to get Jews out to the forest. He avoided answering and just asked for warm clothes and weapons. He also asked about the watches on the bridges over the Shchara". Clearly this meeting had no practical outcome for the ghetto underground, whose members continued to seek links with the forest.

Discussion of the Underground's Goals

Discussions and arguments about the aim and the functioning of the united organisation started with its establishment. The members of the Communist Party who were in the (underground) organisation decided to get together Party members for consultation. David Epstein was elected chairman. It was decided that the underground in the ghetto would not be a communist organisation and the reasoning was that in the Soviet Union they always waited for a command from above, for authorisation, but here in the ghetto nobody could give authorisation to set up a communist underground.... maybe one already existed somewhere, and then you might have people crossing boundaries - taking upon themselves matters which were not within their remit. In consultation, the chairman suggested that the underground organisation would function according to the model of left wing Jewish self defence units in the days of the pogroms in Tsarist Russia, and its aim would be to protect the ghetto.

Delatitski suggested setting up a partisan training camp which would function not in the ghetto, but in the forests. He thought that they should include all the movements in Slonim. To protect the ghetto would be an act of heroism, an act of Kiddush Ha'shem[18] only, but it would have no real results, that is, in hitting the Germans. The members who took part in the consultation went their separate ways without having reached a well thought out decision.

Prevarications and internal struggles about authorisation from above were not features of the Zionists among the members of the underground, but they also weighed up the two possibilities - defence of the ghetto or an exodus to the forest for the purpose of partisan fighting. The idea of an uprising in the ghetto was rejected as impossible to put into action. In fact, the Jews of Slonim were crammed into tiny alleyways between the river bridges and the ghetto was surrounded by water like a peninsula (that part was even called The Island). After the bloody Action of 14th, November, when ten thousand souls were taken to their deaths, it was already very clear to everyone that there was no possibility of staging an uprising in the ghetto, and all hopes and efforts were focused on partisan warfare. The members of the underground now concentrated on three operational areas: (1) to seek contact with the partisans; (2) to hoard weapons and ammunition; (3) to broaden the human base of the organisation.

Links with the Forest and Amassing Arms

It was difficult to create links with the forest and on more than one occasion when it seemed that contact had been made, the members were rewarded with bitter disappointment when they came up against extortion and exploitation of the ghetto Jews in order to make personal gain from them. The first contacts with the underground in the ghetto were made, as described above, with Alexander Fiedrik from Zavershe and with Jacob Iskrig from Tchemeri, who was the secretary of an underground communist cell in the village. After Fiedrik was killed in action in November 1941, those links were cut off and the members of the underground continued to seek contact.

Contact was in fact created. Fanya Feigenbaum, a nurse by profession, had made contact with Vatzek Vilchinski. This young Pole arrived at a meeting bringing with him an envoy from the forest who wanted the ghetto underground to supply a representative to the forest. It was decided to send Fanya Feigenbaum. To get out to the forest she needed papers. Delatitski approached the then head of the Judenraat, Yelishavitz, who listened to him attentively and issued a permit for Fanya. However, her mission did not bear fruit.

It should be noted that the Judenraat knew about the underground activities in the ghetto and did not oppose them, and even always responded positively when they were approached for help. For example, it happened that when David Epstein was taken to a work camp, he was released on the intervention of Kvint, who was in charge of the Jewish Department of Employment. When the Germans required the Jews to give up their warm clothes, the Judenraat decided to give warm clothes to the underground. (Kvint

---

[18] Heb: "Sanctification of the Name". The act of martyrdom

and his assistant in the Work Department, Max Rabinowitz, were not members of the Judenraat.)

The main ammunition resource for the organisation in the ghetto was the "Beutelager" - the big armoury where the Germans amassed and stored the large amount of looted weaponry left behind by the Red Army as they retreated. In the loot stores were amassed tons of ammunition and heavy military equipment, tanks and canon. Some of the weaponry was in a good condition and usable, but some of it was damaged and spoiled. The Germans brought it all to the stores, which occupied an extensive area. Young people from the ghetto worked there. Those with skills matched the missing pieces, polished up and repaired the damaged firearms and put canon, machineguns and rifles back together. Jewish girls polished the parts of the weapons and the bullets and everything was hoarded in the huts in the camp.

The person responsible for work in the loot store was the German sergeant Mutz. An arms cache was set up in the cellar of the carpenters' workshop in Podgorna Street, which was outside the ghetto and which before the war used to belong to a Jewish carpenter called Shelubski. The whole thing was possible[19] because the workers in the carpenters' workshop were Jews, mainly members of the underground, and consultations with the underground took place in the workshop. There were also caches for arms and explosives within the ghetto. One such store was set up in the Shepetinski house in Mikhailovski Lane and another in the backyard of the house of Shabtai Moshkovski and David Perel. The Germans allowed the workers in the loot camp to take back home bags of sawdust for whatever they needed. In these bags were hidden parts of rifles and ammunition which had been taken out of the camp. Delatitski recalls that in a very short time the underground already had twelve rifles and fifteen pistols, two chests of grenades and a large quantity of ammunition. In time further weapon stores were set up both in the ghetto and outside it.

A.Imber, a native of the town of Ostrov Mazovietski, was twenty at the time of the invasion of Poland. He fled with his family to Bialystok. When the Soviets entered, they drove out the refugees, and so they were forced to wander eastwards to distance themselves from the border areas. The Imber family reached Slonim. His mother and his sister died in the Actions and he was left alone with his father, with whom he later reached the partisans. He knew that there was an underground in the ghetto, but for a long time was unable to make contact with them. He made sure that he got work in the armoury as a light mechanics worker because he understood that in a place which was such a large weapons dump, he would be able to get something out to defend the ghetto. Imber guessed that in the camp there were people from the underground, and started to investigate and ask questions, but people refused to speak to him, just as they refused to speak to anyone who wasn't known to them and trusted. His questions aroused their suspicions and the members of the underground started to fear him.

---

[19] *The instigator of the shelter and one of its builders was the carpenter Shelubski, who died in the Action of 29th. June: evidence of Itche Rabinovitz.*

Once, two young men from his town – Ya'acov Timan and Israel Sokolik, who were members of the underground - asked him if he knew the engineer Orlinski. They hinted that Orlinski had sent them to him to help them to get weapons out. They even asked him to prepare a submachine gun (P.P.D) for Orlinski. Imber soon managed to meet their request. Now he had a connection with the underground and he was happy that he could help. He looked for a temporary hiding place for weapons within the loot camp, a hiding place from which the liaison men would be able to pass weapons to the ghetto when the time came.

At that time the workers spent the night on the campsite. Aviezer set up his weapons store in a niche in a big oven in the corridor of the house where they slept. The underground liaison used to take the weapons out to the ghetto and from there to the forest. Those who were most active in doing this at that time were: Liuba Abramovitch, Nionia Tsirinski, Halinka Rudinstein, Zelig Milikovski and Zerach Kremin. The transfer of weapons was fraught with difficulties and mortal danger. On one occasion Nionia Tsirinski took an assembled rifle, with the butt, and hung it on his body underneath his clothes. The rifle rubbed his leg and Nionia started to limp. Unfortunately, when the workers on their way to the ghetto reached the bridge, the Germans stopped them and commanded Nionia to help them load a vehicle. They were afraid that the rifle would be discovered on him because it was hard for him to bend over. In the end, his comrades managed to get the rifle out to an open field and everything passed safely. The workers didn't only "nick" weapons from the loot camp, they also engaged in sabotage. They poured water and salt acid over the weapons and ammunition.

Shabtai Moshkovski came from an agricultural Jewish family which went back for generations. Once they had owned a large farm. When the war broke out Shabtai was studying Law in Lvov. He returned to Slonim with great difficulty after the murder of the twelve hundred. After the massacre of 14th. November his family uprooted and moved into the ghetto. A fellow student of Shabtai's, a Belorussian boy, organised work for him in the forge and he learned the profession with a skilled blacksmith. Aharon Bandt, one of the active underground members, introduced him to the members and Shabtai started to be active in arms acquisition. In a hiding place near his house in Mikhailovski Lane, together with Aharon (who was known to his friends as Archik), he hid rifles and explosives. Another well camouflaged hiding place for arms was in the shelter of the carpentry workshop in Podgorna Street.

Disappointments in Making Contact with the Partisans

The underground in the ghetto had already managed to build up a sizeable stock of weapons, but had not yet made contact with the forest. On one occasion, the members managed in their searches to meet up with two Soviet army officers, prisoner-of-war escapees, who were living in villages close to Slonim. The ghetto representatives suggested giving them arms on condition that they would set up a partisan unit. The officers agreed, as it were, but their reply amazed the underground members. "We have more weapons than we need, a whole division. We need boots, felts, soap, cigarettes, suits and so on". These were goods that were hard to obtain at that time. The young people of the ghetto needed the co-operation of partisans who were military men to train them in guerrilla style fighting and in organising life in the forests and therefore they agreed to supply the officers with their request but their requests aroused suspicion.

Supplying the required goods was beset with dangers. It was hard to obtain these goods from the ghetto Jews whose property had all been looted. The only source that remained was the German loot camp, where, in addition to weapons, property which the Germans had looted from the Jews was hoarded. The young men would have to get the particular items required from the camp, to smuggle them to the ghetto and from there to the forest. Despite the danger they embarked on the job.

The loot camp was near a suburb at Zamoshtcha some distance from the ghetto. The task of smuggling anything out from it required engaging in various ruses. The arrangements in the camp were supervised by the German sergeant Mutz; he was concerned with the workers and in the days during the actions he used to take them out of the town so that they too wouldn't be taken for mass destruction. However, in the task of smuggling, they obviously had to be extremely careful of him.

The loot camp had pastures where a fifteen year old Jewish boy shepherded the sheep belonging to the German commander of stores. The shepherd whose name was also Shabtai was a young member of the underground. Every day he used to bring hay for the sheep and hide in the bundles of hay boots and soap which the underground members brought him. These items were stored in the same yard as the piles of hay. The members would smuggle the soap and the boots from the camp and deliver them to the officers.

However disappointment from these contacts was not short in coming. The underground members found out that the officers were selling the items in the villages for alcohol and were getting drunk. They had no intention of engaging in partisan fighting. And so it was decided to break off contact with them and to look for other connections. In the meantime, they continued to bring weapons and ammunition out of the loot camp and to store them in the underground's secret caches.

Yasha (Ya'acov) Shepetinski Joins the Underground

Yasha was the elder brother of Herzel Shepetinski, one of the original activists in the underground, one of the first to make contact with the forest, and this is what he recounts about how he joined the underground and his activity in the loot camp. At the end of August 1941 Yasha saw that his younger brother Herzel, who had just completed high school and was a member of the Komsomol, was not at home. To his mother he had said that he would spend the night at a friend's. Herzel returned home after three days, during which his family had been very worried about him. Yasha noticed that Herzel's mood was good and this puzzled him. He didn't know that Herzel had visited the village of Zavershe and spoken to the partisans Fiedrik and Dudko.

After about a month, Yasha bumped into Herzel by chance on the roof of their house. In Herzel's hand was a Nagan (a Russian pistol). Yasha was very excited. Herzel felt his brother's excitement and wouldn't leave him alone all evening so that he could watch what Yasha said. In the evening they left the house and Yasha insisted on an explanation from Herzel. "How can you possibly conduct a war single-handed? Suppose you kill one German but in revenge they'll hang the whole of our family". Herzel listened and said to him, "We're all going to be lost, all of us, and we have to pay the highest price with our lives and for that reason we have to prepare for an active struggle". He hinted that he was not alone in that view and made his brother swear to keep the secret even from their parents. Herzel suggested to his brother that he join the underground and in a few days he would receive classified instructions.

Several days later Herzel instructed him to go to the employment office of the Judenraat, to say there that he was a fitter and suggest that they send him to work in the loot store (Beutenlager). Ya'acov was very agitated and at that time he was amazed at Herzel's calmness. When he arrived in the morning at the employment office, he remembered that he wasn't registered at all on the register of ghetto residents and he was afraid of what would happen to him. However, he decided to go the window where a refugee who he didn't know was sitting. To his amazement, when he said his name the clerk got out his card where it said that he was a fitter, put it on one side and instructed him to appear at ten o'clock when Sergeant Mutz would arrive. Yasha understood that "the machine" was working.

At the appointed time he reached the place where the Jewish workers were concentrated. Mutz appeared holding in his hand a whip. It was very obvious that the German was quite tipsy. Those present got into a line. Mutz went along the line and examined all of them from top to bottom with vicious laughter. If you were touched on the stomach with the whip or whipped around the legs, this was a sign that you had been accepted. At the end of the inspection he took them to the workplace.

The looted arms camp was next to the railway. Opposite the open part there stood a crane, and a lorry was bringing in weapons and ammunition. Mutz handed them over to a cross-eyed sergeant and he called to the head of the group of workers, a refugee from Germany whose name was Erich Stein, and gave him instructions. The group of Jewish workers was sent to unload the weapons that had arrived on the lorry and to sort them.

When Yasha got home after his first day of work, he felt that he was a man of the underground; it was a good feeling. He expected instructions about clashes with the enemy but the first instruction he had was to work well and prove his dedication and not to have unnecessary conversations. He was also expected to learn how to use a machinegun. Yasha says, "I got into a whole pile of weapons, took apart and assembled machineguns and rifles. When Mutz looked at me, I tried to work energetically and when he called me I stood in front of him in a military style. My efforts weren't in vain - Mutz appointed me the weapons chief of the first hut and together with me, my friend Vova Abramson from Leningrad. Twenty young women also worked in the store and they polished up the parts of the weapons. Our role was to take the weapons apart and reassemble them. We were forbidden to absent ourselves from our workplace. The finished weapons were delivered to the storehouse in the place where the greasers worked. Behind the storehouse there was an open space where they tried out the machineguns. That's what the soldiers on duty and Mutz used to do. Sometimes our work managers - Stein and Sibosh - used to shoot there as well.

One day a group of workers saw how the "unter" (sergeant) Mutz, who was obviously drunk was shooting a target with a machinegun. He was a good marksman and he was proud of that. Then my companion, Vova Abramson, dared to ask for permission to try shooting. To my amazement Mutz agreed, but on condition that if Vova missed, he would be beaten on his backside. I agreed to this condition too. Obviously we were beaten because we had never tried to hit the target before. The main object was to get some practice in shooting. Mutz mocked us, but was pleased and from then on I practised firing every day. It helped us a lot. After about a year almost all our armourers were machine gunners with the partisans. At that time the Germans were sure that the Jews were incapable of carrying out any sabotage or organising any kind of opposition.

I spent the whole month of September 1941 becoming acquainted with the weapons and getting to know the German soldiers who were on guard. We worked from eight o'clock in the morning to six in the evening. To get to work and back home, they would take us organised in lines. Only a few people who worked in the domestic camp were allowed to go without a guard. At the beginning of December I received an instruction to get weapons out of the Beutenlager to the ghetto. At first I was careful what I did, a few bullets in my pockets or explosives for grenades, but later I started to take whole grenades. It was a test of nerves, for I was aware of the consequences of failure. Another difficulty in our activities was being careful of other workers. Out of the underground people I knew only Herzel and Archik Bandt".

Meanwhile, the terror in the ghetto was just as strong. Every day there was a public execution. There would be someone caught with a potato in his pocket or attempting to throw a piece of bread over the fence. Once a drunken SS guard decided at whim to amuse himself murdering Jews. However life in the ghetto went on and people still hoped. The remnants of the Jews were turned out from the small towns of the area into the ghetto and there were dark days when the Jews were hunted like wild animals and deported to "a new settlement".

At the beginning of October 1941 Sergeant Mutz obtained permission for his workers to reside in the loot camp. He knew that (the Germans) were preparing a large scale Action in the ghetto and he wanted to keep workers whom he needed, and so forty men lived in a hut close to the loot camp. This was a hard blow to the underground because it was no longer possible to bring out of the camp the whole collection of weapons that they'd prepared - grenades and hundreds of bullets - and they could do nothing but wait to see how events unfolded.

In the Shepetinski house the nutrition problem was extremely bad. There was no food at all and neither were there any articles that they could exchange for food. The hardest thing was seeing the children suffer hunger. Ya'acov decided to do something in order to obtain foodstuffs for the hungry people in his home. He thought and he came up with an idea. It was soap that could save them.

From time to time Mutz would "borrow" his workers for other jobs outside of his camp. While he was working in the camp, Yasha noticed hidden crates of soap. This was the merchandise that Mutz was preparing for himself. He would take the crates of soap and transport them in his vehicle. So on one occasion at the end of work, Yasha secretly went right into the store. It was his plan to stay there until dark and to fill his sack with sixty pieces of soap, which would weigh twenty four kilograms, and then make off with them at night. It was possible to carry this out because the storehouses of the camp were not locked. Ya'acov learned thoroughly the movements of the guards in the camp. The deed was extremely dangerous but he only saw before his eyes the starving faces of his little brothers and his sister and the tormented face of his mother, so he decided to take the risk.

Ya'acov managed to get out of the camp and to make off through the barbed wire fence and turn towards the ghetto. On the way he had to cross the Shchara. He did this part walking, part swimming, and then again through another barbed wire fence surrounding the ghetto, and then he was almost home, trembling with cold and tension, but happy that he'd managed for the time being to save his family from hunger. In exchange for the soap, it was possible to get foodstuffs from the Christians. Nobody noticed his absence from the loot camp.

In time Mutz housed some of the women who worked for him in the camp. He stood guard next to the workers' barracks. His role was to prevent people coming from outside to the workers and also access of the SS. In his conversation with the management of the region and the gendarmerie, Mutz would refer to "my Jews". He held on to the loot camp by the skin of his teeth, because he knew that if it were wiped out, he would be sent to the front.

Fear and dread was growing among the Jews of the ghetto. Many workers who didn't actually reside in the camp used to hide at night in the barracks instead of going home to sleep.

In the ghetto two classes, effectively, had been created: "essential" Jews who worked for the Germans and mainly had a professional skill; and "just Jews" who the Judenraat would enrol according to the commands of the Germans for all sorts of occasional jobs like mending roads, knocking down houses that were damaged through the activities of the war and cleaning jobs in the town. All these people worked without reward.

CHAPTER THREE: The Period of "Actions" and Mass Elimination

The Massacre of 14th. November 1941

While efforts were being made to make contact with the partisans in order to build up a store of weapons and organise for whatever may come, the ghetto in its misery was stunned on the 14th. November by a bloodbath which swept away about ten thousand people. Again, this Action descended on the Jews of Slonim very suddenly. After the first massacre of the twelve hundred men, people realised that those who had been well hidden had stayed alive, and so many of them started to prepare hiding places in the ghetto.

Engineer Avraham Orlinski says: Staff Sergeant (Shtaabsfeldfebel) Eichinger, deputy of the town commandant was billeted in the Orlinski house. His house was managed by a one-time Jewish prostitute who now pretended to be a Tartar. Before the massacre, the "Tartar" revealed to Dr Cheslava's (Orlinski's wife) sisters, with great distress, that an Action was about to take place.

From the end of October to early November, the director of the region had already been distributing yellow certificates to skilled men and workers who worked for the Germans. The authorities "explained" that the certificates entitled their owners to additional portions of food, but no one yet realised the true meaning of this distribution. Orlinski hadn't worked since the city had been occupied. As there was talk of an Action against the non-workers who, according to rumour, would be expelled from the town, a friend advised him to register for work in the office of the employment manager, Kwint. Orlinski registered as a mechanic and was appointed work manager for a small group of ten Jews, who prepared building materials from bricks which had been taken from wrecked houses. After that he worked as a mechanic in a textile factory. On the second day he was working the Germans took groups of workers for a certain job outside the town. (Later it emerged that they had been taken to dig pits).

Now Orlinski's main concern was to get hold of a yellow certificate, a life certificate as it were. Everyone tried to register as many family members as possible on this certificate, supposing that this would protect them from being deported. Orlinski put down his wife and the son of his sister-in-law, a child of five, as his own son.

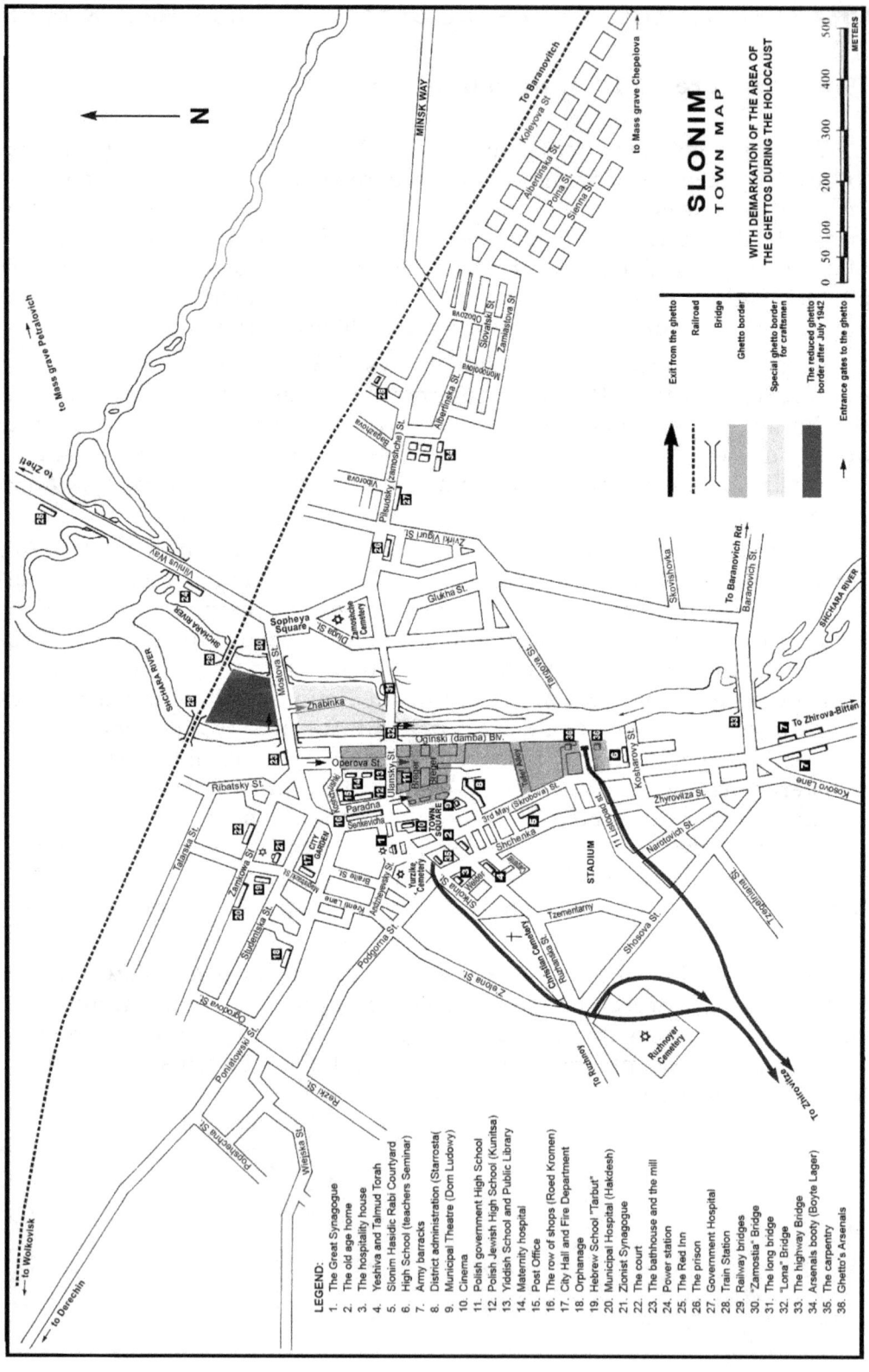

In the evening the "Tartar" let them know that the Action would start the next day, the 14th of the month, and that the town commandant and Werhmacht soldiers would be taking part. In the Orlinski house they had set up a hiding place in the cellar, which was locked because the municipality kept potatoes there. They could get down to the cellar through a tiny window which looked out on the yard. Orlinski moved his mother and other members of his family into his house. All through the night nobody slept. At four in the morning he peeped outside and this is what he saw:

"I saw that the whole command area was brightly lit. This was confirmation that the Germans were planning to act. I woke the family and put them in the cellar. I left my mother, who was seventy-six, in the house, thinking that I would have time to hide her at the last minute if necessary. I was afraid she would be too cold in the cellar. My mother, Cheslava and the little boy all stayed in the house.

"In our house there was a tiny room by the kitchen from which a ladder led up to the loft. From this empty little room I watched what was happening in the street. In a short while large numbers of lorries full of soldiers drove through the street. Their uniform was brown with brown velvet collars. The soldiers quickly jumped down from the lorries and spread out in the houses. The surprise was enormous because I hadn't imagined to myself that this operation would start from the centre of town, close to the German command. Past experience was that the vehicles passed the centre of the town quietly. They were already pulling Jews out of this street, which belonged currently to the Aryan side. We had remained in our own place on account of Cheslava, as they hadn't yet imprisoned doctors in the ghetto. My wife had carried on working in the municipal hospital. I grabbed my mother and passed her through to the loft and then I heard the voice of Cheslava shouting out below and calling my name. I went down quietly, opened the door of the tiny room under the kitchen as if I'd been there all the time, and I saw five burly soldiers trying to get my wife out. When I opened the door they stopped. Cheslava called out to me that they're asking for the yellow certificate. I gave it to them. The first one indicated us and said: 'Orlinski, his wife and son'. The child stood pale in the corner and watched what was happening. The soldiers gave me back the certificate and cleared off. Only now did the significance of the yellow certificate become clear to us."

This is Zvi Shepetinski's (Shefet) experience of the Action when he was a boy of sixteen:

"On the morning of 14th. November, workers were no longer allowed to go out to their jobs. From one end of the ghetto to another the voices of the murderers reverberated, "Get out, you accursed ones, out, quick". My father and I hid in a stable between the logs for heating. My mother locked us in from outside and so did my uncle. Everybody supposed that this time too they would take only men, and so the women and the children remained in their houses.

"But this time it wasn't like that. From every one of the neighbours' houses we could hear the weeping of women and children. It's hard to describe the impression that those voices made on a man hiding, who couldn't grasp what was happening. This time they're taking his mother, his wife, his sister and his children - where were they taking them? Should he stay in the hiding place, or go out and join his loved ones?

"These thoughts are tormenting. Twenty plans go through my head, and they trap you like a tangled net from which you can't escape. The fear is hard to bear - not just the crying of the women and the screaming of the children, but the voices of our Christian acquaintances with whom we'd been friendly for decades. The things that they were saying froze your blood and the things they did paralysed all initiative. And then I hear them dragging my aunt, Chaya Ribatski out of the house with her little son Vovik. She is pleading with them to let her take something out of her belongings for her little child, provisions for the journey. Despite this, the brutal soldiers mock her that it would be hard for her to carry and where she is going she will get everything she needs."

The family of Zvi Shefet was saved by his mother. The Germans entered the house and asked where the men were. The rest of the family was hiding behind the door into another room. The door was fixed with nails and hung with a blanket, and on the nails which stuck out there were hung various clothes. The Germans went round the house searching. She said that the men had gone out to work. The Germans interrogated her as to where her husband was working and if he had a yellow certificate. She answered that her husband had taken the yellow certificate to his workplace and they went and left the mother in the house. One of the Germans ordered her to lock the house and not to answer any knocking. After everything around them had died down, she brought them food.

Particularly dreadful experiences fell to Yasha Shepetinski, Zvi's cousin, and this is his story:

"On 13th. November a soldier gave me a present, a tin of preserves. I also took a spring for the disc of a 63-bullet machinegun and I brought it all home safely. I left the house in order to go back to the loot store. At the gate of the ghetto I met Rivka, a refugee from Poland, and the pair of us managed to get safely over the bridge and enter the suburb of Zhabinka. But all our efforts to get out of the ghetto and to get to the barracks in the loot camp were in vain; they weren't letting anyone go out and all our explanations were useless. The response of the guards was "Go tomorrow". With no alternative we went to sleep in Rivka's house. She lived in an attic and the crowding was worse than in our house.

"Rivka read a lot that evening; she loved poetry and recited passages from classical Polish literature beautifully. I found myself a place where I could stretch out and I fell asleep without getting undressed."

"We woke up to the sound of bitter crying. Down below they were shouting and crying. Had something terrible happened? Were we really finished? And then we saw and heard SS. men armed from top to toe, and Belarussian and Lithuanian police were turning everyone out into the street. We heard their shrieks: "Get out, get out, fast, out!" The whole ghetto was echoing with shouting and moaning, and above it all we could hear the children crying. A family with a baby lay in the loft. Rivka and I hid ourselves. I could see through a crack in the roof how they were sitting all the people in the street on the ground in a tight group, with guards all around. I saw an officer explaining something; apparently he allowed one of a family to go into his house to take some belongings. And one of them jumped up and called out to us in the loft that they were going to shoot us because this would be an Aryan sector.

"People just didn't know what to do. Lots of them went out, others, like us, remained indoors. All the people who went down to the street were organised in lines and taken away. And now the Germans went from house to house poking around everywhere. We crawled into one of the corners. They were shooting at sick people and anyone who refused to come out. The shots were continuous. In our loft children burst out crying. The police heard the crying and they burst into the loft and shot the children one after the other. This time we went out. They pushed us out into the street where about three hundred people had already been collected. The police and the Lithuanians were drunk and they pilfered from the houses bundles of belongings and suitcases, and piled them up. An officer riding on a bicycle went up to our group and declared, "In accordance with the orders of the town commandant, we're carrying out 'Uebersiedlung' (resettlement). Anyone who shouts or makes a noise will be killed on the spot. In the new place everyone will get work and clothes and food." One old man got up and went towards the officer, wanting to ask something. The officer beckoned him with his finger to come closer, and shot him. After this murder, the mothers started to put their hands over their children's mouths."

The Death March

Yasha's story continues:

"By now I knew that the end was near for us, and the one thought running through my brain was: "Flee!" People were marching slowly, trying to prolong their lives. The Lithuanian guard and the local police were hurrying them up. Passing through Ulanska Street, over the bridges, in front of the prison they turned right along the Baranovitch road. There's no chance of escaping. I'm marching at the end of a line, useless plans going through my head: maybe I could attack the guard and strangle him? Better to wait, maybe I could still manage to escape. And so it goes on, kilometre after kilometre. The line moves, the children are wailing. They don't understand orders and go on crying. They sense what's about to happen and with their stiff arms, they cling to the necks of their mothers. Their fathers stare at the ground as if guilty. Others pray under their breath. I'm looking around for acquaintances, maybe some of my relatives are here and I could say goodbye to them.

"Before the junction we hear machinegun fire. They stop us in order to tidy up the lines, and somewhere they're shooting and shooting. I notice several acquaintances. We say farewell with our looks. Behind us there are some carts, and on them there sit old people whose strength has failed them. How very thoughtful!

"The shooting has stopped and we've been sitting on the wet ground for about twenty minutes already. And then the order to get up comes again. We walk. Behind me there marches an old grandmother and a young mother carrying a baby in her arms. The grandmother is humming a lullaby to get her grandchild to sleep. I see it's hard for them to carry the child and suggest that I help them. They refuse. There's nowhere to flee, the land is just open. I wouldn't manage to go even five steps. I walk on and curse the German who gave me the tin of preserves. I can't forgive myself for falling into their hands over a tin of preserves. Instead of that, I should have brought a machinegun home and then let them see if they can catch me.

"I have already lost count of how many kilometres we've done. There's a lump stuck in my throat. Some people are marching and crying quietly, whilst others tell them off: "Stop frightening the children". They stop us and push us to the right side of the road. I notice that the whole area is covered with footsteps. It's obvious that they have already brought a lot of people here.

"And suddenly I hear "Yasha!" It's Rivka. I had lost her on the road. She was walking at the head of the lines. I push up beside her with difficulty. We hug each other and say goodbye like people who are close. She says, "They'll pay for this one day".

"We're surrounded with (hangmen) murderers. They force us to get all our things together in another place. We see a big pile has been made there. It's obvious we've reached the place of slaughter. Now they start to sort people with the butts of their rifles, forcing us to take our outer clothes off. It's hard to describe what's happening, hearing the curses, words of farewell and the most dreadful of all - the children's crying.

"I was in the first group that they took to the trench. I was wearing an overall dirty with grease, so they didn't force me to take it off. The trench was about half full with shot bodies, many of them still groaning. My brain seemed to go silent, I just wanted to fall somewhere. When I got near the edge of the trench, I lost my balance. It seems that I heard shots and apparently I fell. I didn't take in what happened after that, because I lay unconscious in the trench and I didn't even notice that it filled up with bodies.

"When I regained consciousness, I felt that I was suffocating, it was hard for me to breathe. At first I couldn't grasp where I was and what was happening to me, but when it became clear, I felt sick with horror. It seemed to me that something was moving in my brain, but half of it was going over the other half. With all the strength I could muster, I started to crawl out. I grabbed bodies, hands and legs, all of them, I think, immersed in boiling hot blood. I'm choking but I'm crawling out to the air. I listen. All around me silence. From up above the sounds of distant gunfire reach my ears.

"Finally the stars flash before me. Another effort and I'm already up on top of the bodies. In the distance, on the sides of the roads, bonfires were burning and around them were sitting the murderers. My first thought is to flee, to get far away from them. I climb up over the bodies, which are still warm. I crawl in the sand, getting away from the atrocity. I stop. Maybe this is just an illusion? No I'm alive and whole, and I must save myself.

"I tell myself to be careful, not to act in panic. I crawl silently through the bushes, getting further from the road, and then I stand up and run. I feel as if my legs are flying and don't even touch the ground. Nobody's chasing me, and nobody noticed that I escaped.

"Now I'm calmer. I go up to the river - what should I do now? Where can I go? To the forest? But where? I remembered my parents, my brother and my sister, and decided to go home and see if they're alive. I go right along the bank of the river. Before the bridge I turned right and crawled across the road. The night was dark and a strong wind was blowing by the saw mill. I crossed the Shchara swimming and it seemed to me that it had become deeper and its waters were as cold as ice. I reached the opposite bank with the last ounce of my strength. I slipped through the barbed wire fence surrounding the ghetto and then I'm walking along Michailovski Lane. In the darkness the walls of our house rise up. I go running up to it and sick horror grabs me: the doors are burst wide open, that means that nobody's at home, they're all lying in the trench. Why have I been left alive?

"I went inside, I leaned on the wall and I burst out crying. I had never wept like that. Suddenly I heard my mother - "Yankele!" Even when she hugged me I couldn't calm down."

After the Blood Bath

The situation in the ghetto is terrible, people are afraid to leave their houses. The workers go to work and those who are left hide in the hiding places which have been set up in all sorts of places. And again the Germans adopt strategies of misleading and deception that are typical of them, and they promise those who are left that their lives are safe and that there will no more Actions. The Germans allocated new rations of food, but many people refused to accept them for fear that this would reveal the families in hiding. The regime took further steps to reassure them and forbade the officials of their various authorities and the SS to enter the ghetto. The Jews were in fact a little reassured and began to come into the streets.

The blood bath had opened the eyes of many people. The Germans were not to be trusted. People of the underground intensified their efforts, their activity was strengthened and many more members joined, more firearms were hoarded, and they continued to look for links with the partisans.

The ghetto population was dreadfully crowded. In the homes of the Shepetinski brothers, for example, in an area of sixty square metres, seventeen people were living. Within the ghetto it was forbidden to grow flowers or plants, and fruit trees and bushes were torn up. The death sentence was imposed for the birth of a baby. All around the ghetto leaflets were dropped which said that the Jews were guilty of all the troubles of the war which were affecting various peoples.

Winter arrived, and with it new fears for survival - for food and wood for heating. It was hard to heat the houses. Every day when the workers came home from work, they would stand by the entrance gate holding bundles of small twigs to heat the house and anyone who managed to get his bundle through into the ghetto was happy.

The families were starving. It was hard to look at the faces of the hungry children who were becoming shrivelled from lack of food. At first they would ask for food and cry, but after that they evidently understood the situation and fell quiet. The mother of Yasha and Herzel Shepetinski took off her yellow patch sometimes and went out to the town. In the fields she also used to gather ears of corn which had been left after the harvest and brought them home. She made a soup from the kernels. Only the father of the family, who worked in the saw mill, had the right to receive a small ration of food.

After they fenced off the smaller (reduced) ghetto in April 1942, the families of the medical team, who until now lived outside the ghetto, were ordered to move into it. The engineer Volfstein, a refugee from Poland, was appointed to build the fence around the ghetto.

Contacts are made with the Partisans in the Forest

Herzel Shepetinski was one of the first who sought to liaise with the forest. However, after the father of the Fiedrik family fell in battle, and his sons went into the forest, contact was cut off.

Yasha Shepetinski remembers that from time to time all sorts of people would come to his younger brother, Herzel, with whom he would go and confer secretly. Among them was a short man with a hump. This was Anshel Delatitski, one of the communist activists.

Anshel made contact with Vatzek Vilchinski, a young Polish man active in the Communist Youth in the town, and from him he heard about the beginnings of partisan organisation in the area and about the Proniagin group. He decided to make contact with the partisans. He gave Vatzek's address to Herzel and Zerach Kremin, who were in fact the first to make contact with the Proniagin-Dudko group.

Zerach Kremin came from the small town of Belitza in the Novogrodek district. He was a teacher by profession. With the outbreak of war, he had also tried to escape to the east and reached the River Berezina, but there the Germans overtook him and he went back to Belitza. First of all, the Germans would start by exterminating the Jewish intelligentsia, and so Zerach fled to Slonim and lived there with his uncle Dr. Moshe Kremin. There he met his friend Nionia Tsirinski and the two of them began to plan their move to join the partisans.

Zerach met the officers Proniagin and Dudko. At the time, the Germans were allowing the Jews to go out to the villages in order to collect debts that the farmers owed them - in exchange for giving over half the sum to the Germans. Zerach got himself authorisation and went out in March 1942 to the village of Zavershe, where he met with the two officers, who were the commanders of the group. They both told him that in the spring they were planning to move into the forest, but that they needed warm clothes and ammunition. When they asked him, Zerach told them everything that had happened to him to date, and bought saccharine and tobacco for them. In the evening he came back to the ghetto in a cart laden with potatoes as camouflage.

A further meeting with the partisan commanders took place the next week. The pair attended this meeting accompanied by a third person, Misha Pover (that is, Mishka the cook) and Zerach was accompanied this time by Aharon Bandt. These envoys of the ghetto underground organisation spent the whole of the next day with the officers, who fed them and gave them butter to take home. On the way home about twenty partisans accompanied them and they went in carts. In the village of Skolditch they acquired army clothes from the peasants, according to Aharon's instructions. The army property was in that house because its owner was one of the chief looters of Soviet equipment when the Red Army retreated. The partisans surrounded the house and knocked on the door. The peasant tried to run away through the window, but he fell straight into the arms of the partisans who were waiting for him. They found a lot of military equipment in his house. The village was next to the route via which the Red Army had retreated, and so the peasants had an opportunity to collect firearms and pilfer army equipment. There had also been incidents where peasants had stripped the clothes off wounded soldiers who were lying on the ground. The partisans accompanied the Jewish lads up to the outskirts of Slonim.

Commander Proniagin describes in his book these first contacts with the ghetto underground:

"When we encamped in the forests of Rafalovka and also Volchye-Nori, we had to ensure that we supplied ourselves with reliable contacts - first of all with Slonim, the centre of German administration for the district and where a large German force was stationed - then also with the smaller towns of Kosovo and Biten and with people at the railway junctions in Gantzevitch, Domanovo and Lesnaya. We established the contacts with Slonim through Viktor Fiedrick, Nikolai Filentchik, Vassili Michailtchik and Yosef Sushko. Our immediate contacts in Slonim were with Zerach Kremin and Grisha Shepetinski." [20]

Proniagin goes on to tell how once when he went to meet the members of the Slonim ghetto organisation, he almost fell into the hands of the enemy:

"At ten o'clock in the evening we reached a khotor[21] a distance of a few kilometres from Slonim. Michail Faschenko went with me to the meeting. He was very fit and had extremely good endurance. One of the Slonim men met us there - Grisha (Herzel) Shepetinski - and we went on with him. We got near Slonim and listened out; all around there was silence. Shepetinski told us that at nine in the evening he'd left the peasant's house where we were meant to

---

[20] *Proniagin. P. 23, the Jewish boys mentioned are Zerach Kremin and Herzel Shepetinski*

[21] *Khotor – in the local language this is an isolated farm, with a relatively small plot of land. Many khotors were created in the process of agrarian reform in Poland after the First World War, when peasant land was demarcated and the large holdings of the Polish landlords were shared out to landless peasants. Many families moved their houses from their villages to be near their holdings.*

arrive, and everything was quiet there. The owner of the house, Yosef Michalovitch Filko, was a very reliable man. He had sent away his wife and his daughter to relatives so that they wouldn't disturb us. Filko was waiting for us alone. Vilchinski and Misko were to arrive at midnight.

"We approached with confidence as if everything was all right. The owner met us in the entrance; there was a dog in the yard but while the owner was around he didn't bark. We went into the house; inside it was warm and light and the windows were well blocked. We began to talk and then suddenly we heard a sharp bark from the dog in the yard. The owner went out to check, a moment passed and another moment, silence and suddenly loud knocks on the window. And after a moment, a volley of machinegun shots in the glass. Now it was all clear, we had fallen into a trap. Michail and I had an automatic rifle SBT. and each one of us had two grenades in our belts. I told him to let everybody throw a grenade in the window and then we'd jump out immediately. Faschenko understood me with one word, "We'll do it" he replied.

"So we switch off the light, we tear the blackout from the window; we jump on the benches and with one blow break the window frame and throw out grenades. At the same time, we jump out, jump over the fence and run about twenty metres and throw ourselves on the ground. The enemy is firing random volleys from automatic rifles. The two of us lob another grenade and again throw ourselves into the darkness of the night.

"After about half an hour we returned to the khutor. Vasia Michalchik, who had been able to hear the shots and grenade explosions clearly, was anxiously waiting for us. As we found out later, the enemy had been keeping tabs on Filko's house for a long time. Only our grenades and the barking of the dog saved our lives.

"Shepetinski and Filko also managed to disappear with the sound of the automatic rifles and explosions of the grenades and warned their friends as soon as they could. Despite this we held the meeting but in a different place and at a different time."

Further on in his story Proniagin lists the names of members of the underground in the Slonim ghetto with whom he was in contact. He makes no suggestion that these were Jews from the ghetto, although he acknowledges that the men of the ghetto supplied his group with a lot of firearms and these are his words:

"Our group received a variety of weapons and a great quantity of explosives from the looted weapons store in Slonim where some people who were devoted to us worked: N.Tsirinski, A. Bublatski, Z. Shusterovitch, A. Doktortchik, S. Milikovski, G. Malach, G. Greenghauz.

"In the weapons store the store master Erich Stein directed the daily work. He was a German Jew. The fascists put their trust in him and he lived with them. He didn't have to wear a yellow patch on his back or his chest. The people of the underground decided to draw Stein over to their side.

"But how to approach him? Would he agree to work with the underground? If he should refuse, what then? What lies in store for the man who negotiates with him? Torture and an agonising death might await him.

"The people of the underground appointed Tsirinski to speak with Stein.

"N. Tsirinski was a young man of twenty, a man of initiative. When the war began he was in Bialystok. He tried to get out to the east, but only reached Minsk, as the battle-front arrived there first. He came back to his relatives in Slonim and began to work in the loot store. Tsirinski waited for the right moment and embarked on a conversation with Stein. We were very happy when we received the news that the storeman had agreed to work with the underground. Stein fully justified our hopes. He worked with the smuggling of machineguns and rifles from the weapons store and in sabotaging the arms which remained in German hands in the store. In June 1942 Stein had to leave Slonim and join the partisans. With us he served as a saboteur. In December of that year he fell while fulfilling his role in battle. "

Continuing his story, Proniagin describes the contribution of Natan Liker as miraculous.

"Natan Liker was a young, well-developed man with a quiet and measured character in whom one could recognise strong willpower. At the beginning he worked for the Germans as an electrician and in January 1942 he managed to get a job with the workshop to repair radio receivers. He used his role to help the partisans.

"We are indebted to Natan Yosifovitch Liker for obtaining radio receivers from Slonim. He joined the troop in August 1942. At first he served as a private and after that commanded a small group. He took part in blowing up twenty-eight enemy trains and in many battles. His luck was that he worked with Soviet hero Kiril Peokofievitch Orlovski and with the saboteurs and reconnaissance men whom Orlovski commanded. "[22]

---

[22] *Proniagin, p.25-26*

Smuggling Arms from the German Loot Camp

The weapons which the members of the underground smuggled out of the German loot camp and secreted in hiding places in the ghetto and town needed to be transferred into the forest. Just smuggling weapons out of the Beutenlager was a complex and dangerous operation in itself. They generally had to dismantle a weapon into its parts and pass the parts through, hidden on the body or the clothes of the smuggler. The way to the gate of the ghetto was paved with dangers since every policeman and every gendarme[23] was authorised to stop a Jew and search him, and they also had to be checked at the entrance gate to the ghetto. Outside, by the gate, Belarussian policemen were on guard and did not treat the Jews with kid gloves; the Jew, if he was caught with arms, was without doubt going to die, and not only would the guilty person pay with his life, but also his colleagues, his neighbours and the members of his family. The members of the underground would invent all sorts of tricks in order to get weapons out of the loot camp and smuggle them into the ghetto. Sometimes they bought washing soap, obviously at a much exaggerated price, and the condition of this negotiation was that the Germans would bring the soap to the ghetto at night. However, in the parcels were wrapped up parts of weapons and explosives instead of soap and the Germans themselves brought them to the ghetto.

After they'd hidden the weapons in the underground hiding places in the town or the ghetto, they had to get them through to the forest and neither was that easy. Proniagin, the commander of the Shchors brigade, describes the smuggling of firearms to the partisans in the forest, in his memoirs. According to him most of the weapons were brought out by "the people of Slonim coming to the partisans"[24] but some were passed to the forest by the contact liaisons of the troop and among these people Nikolai Filipovitch Filenchik stands out in particular. He would travel back and forth between Slonim and Zelesye in the winter on a sleigh and in the summer in a cart, bringing all sorts of merchandise. He would hide the weapons and the explosives among the merchandise under the hay. He also encountered difficulties, since from time to time there were policemen or Germans stopping his cart on the way and demanding to search it. This man would get rid of the inspectors with the help of bottles of spirit which he thrust into their hands.

Approaching New Year 1942 Yasha received instructions to smuggle a dismantled machinegun into the ghetto. The main point of the exercise was to prepare the machinegun parts, to hang them under a coat and to put the coat on without anyone seeing. Then, he had to pass the guard at the gates and get the treasure into the ghetto. In order to avoid the search, Yasha Shepetinski tells us:

---

[23] *Policeman – a local person. Gendarme – a German policeman.*

[24] *Proniagin, p.26. Proniagin does not reveal in his book that the people of Slonim who brought the arms when they joined the partisans were mainly Jews, members of the ghetto underground.*

"I used to stand at the head of the queue. The guards used to make me leave to one side the bundles of firewood which we would carry and they made do with this and didn't search our tools. I would pass my load to Herzel without them seeing, and he would take it to a secret place. In the month of March firearms were already hidden in our home. In March to April I got out of the loot camp three machineguns, eight disks, over a thousand bullets and about ten hand grenades.

"Mutz didn't treat his workers badly, although he always had a whip in his hand. He wanted to keep his workplace and so there were times when he ordered us to take apart rifles and machineguns whose assembly had already been completed, and polish them anew in order for the work to go on as long as possible. And the Jews worked as slowly as possible and sabotaged as much as they could. The engineer Erich Stein from Frankfurt directed the sabotage; he was a graduate of the Naval Officers' School and a very intelligent and brave man. Stein had fled from Germany to Poland after Kristallnacht. In the loot camp he worked as chief armourer, but in 1943 he was killed as a partisan when he was returning from sabotaging the railway track close to the village of Budcha.

"We would generally sabotage weapons that the Germans had already checked. We would shorten the firing pin and the weapon wouldn't fire. When we worked on the disks, we would tighten the springs so that they had no contact with the bullets and thus more thanonce the police returned the weapons which they didn't manage to operate. I remember once in the spring of 1942 the police brought in a machinegun which didn't fire. In their presence Mutz ordered Stein to check it. Stein released the spring with a screw without them understanding what he was doing and the machinegun worked beautifully. Mutz made fun of the police and cursed them, saying in front of the complainers that they needed to learn how to work the instrument. The police commander apologised and didn't come back and complain anymore."

"In the spring of 1942 Herzel disappeared twice from home for several whole days. At that time the arrogance and self-confidence of the Germans were decreasing. They no longer marched out to collect loot with the same confidence. At the beginning of April they loaded ten of our people onto a lorry; we drove to the village of Tovtaki to fetch anti-aircraft canon. The accompanying guard was armed with helmets and full battle-dress and an armoured car went in front of the lorry. As soon as we turned into the forest, the Germans transferred us to the cabins of the lorries and hid behind. This behaviour showed us that they were afraid of the partisans.

"However, we didn't manage to keep our secret at home. At the end of April we decided, Herzel and I, to set up the machinegun in the cowshed, oil it and hide it in the earth. When everybody had fallen asleep in our house, we stole out secretly to the cowshed and began to assemble it. I managed to oil the machinegun and Herzel dug the hole and suddenly the door of the cowshed squeaked and there in the doorway was standing Mum and behind her Dad. It turned out that our mother had guessed that we were doing something dangerous. "My sons", she whispered and started to cry. She held and kissed us and Dad stood thunderstruck and just whispered, "What good boys, may G-d look after you". So now the three of us hid the machinegun and heaped firewood upon it. We trusted our parents that they wouldn't tell anyone our secret. For our mother, the revelation was difficult. Every time a German or a policeman passed by our house, she used to think that they were coming to get the machinegun out.

"Archik Bandt used to take most of the weapons that I managed to get out, over to the forest. Herzel oversaw the work and I struggled all the time with the question, why don't we ourselves go to the forest? We're likely to miss the chance. First Herzel was silent and after a while he said that he'd received instructions from the forest to stay put in order to supply them with more weapons.

"At the beginning of May I had an accident. They took all the men to load damaged 14mm. canon. While we were working, the barrel of the canon slipped from the platform and crushed my left foot; I couldn't stand up any more. Fortunately for me the gendarme didn't notice it - for the wounded and the sick were exterminated immediately. My comrades lifted me up secretly onto the platform and I tried to stand up leaning on to the railing and pretending that I was working. During the lunch break the head of the group told Mutz about the accident and asked for his help. Mutz brought a lorry up, my comrades lifted me onto the cabin and two of our boys sat behind on a box and that's how we travelled. They brought me to the fence of the ghetto, to Krasnoarmeiskaya Street, to the ghetto hospital. When they sat me in the lorry, one of the boys held out to me the bag of a gas mask which was absolutely full of something and asked me to deliver it to the doctor. Only while we were driving did I catch on that the bag contained grenades. All during the journey I didn't let the bag out of my hands. When I came to the hospital I delivered it to Dr. Blumovitch, who was then our doctor in the ghetto hospital.

"During this whole operation I was amazed at Mutz's behaviour. When I was already on the other side of the barbed wire fence, I said to him: "Thank you very much, Sergeant". He answered me, "Alles Jacob", meaning, "It's all that I could do". I can say without exaggerating that at that time Mutz saved my life.

"In the hospital they laid me down in the Department for Infectious Diseases where the Germans wouldn't go. There was a crack in the sole of my foot. They plastered me up and after a few days I was allowed to go home. The days passed and I was thinking all the time about going out to the forest. However, they were still asking for more and more weapons."

New Members in the Organisation

New members were joining the ranks of the organisation all the time, but people quickly made contact with the underground. Ze'ev Finkel remembers how he was enrolled to the underground service. He was a refugee from Suvalki:

"One day a lean young man approached me with burning eyes, and asked me if I work in the loot camp. I replied in the affirmative. And then he asked me if I was interested in joining the underground and going out to meet the partisans. This was Zerach Kremin. I agreed to all the conditions that he set before me. Presently Zerach taught me how to use a pistol and a hand grenade."

Ze'ev was integrated into smuggling weapons into the ghetto.

Hillel Moshkovski joined the underground by means of a pistol which he was repairing for Zerach Kremin. After a while Mitos Snovski got in touch with him and needed him to get a radio transmitter out of the office of the town commandant (Ortskommandant). The two of them went into the German's office in the middle of the day and Mitos showed Hillel what to take. Hillel asked no questions, took the instrument and brought it to Mitos' house, where he still lived outside the ghetto.

In July 1942 envoys from the forest reached Hillel with an order to obtain a printing press for the partisans. The only press then in Slonim was in the management of a Jew, but he refused to give the machine up with the letters. The partisans decided to take the letters without permission. Hillel followed the owner of the press and one morning, when the latter left his house, broke in through a window with a hand grenade in his pocket, removed the letters, took them out to the dairy in Podgorna Street and hid them there. In the meantime, the maid went into the dairy and Hillel had to get out quickly. The next day he transferred the press to the underground shelter and from there it reached the forest and was used by the partisans to print leaflets. [25]

After some time, the liaison of the group, Volodya Fiedrik, came to Zerach and asked him, on behalf of the partisans, to get a doctor. Since Zerach knew from his cousin, Yasha Kremin, that Dr. Blumovitch very much wanted to join the partisans, he approached him in the Jewish hospital. He arrived safely, introduced himself and asked if the doctor was ready to join the partisans. Dr. Blumovitch declared that he was prepared to go as soon as possible.

Avraham Blumovitch completed his medical studies in the University of Vilna. With the German invasion of Poland, he had tried to escape from Lomzha where he was working but was wounded on the way. The Germans picked him up and hospitalised him in a field hospital in the small town of Azernitsa and from there he reached the hospital in Slonim. His colleague from student days in Vilna, Dr. Noah Kaplinski, was working in the hospital. Back then a friendly relationship had grown up and this continued in occupied Slonim. In the organisation of health services in the ghetto, Dr. Blumovitch fulfilled the role of director of the clinic, which was in the high school on Operova Street. Working in the ghetto hospital in Mikhailovski Lane, there were Dr. Berger, a refugee from Poland and Dr. Gvorin, while the professional doctors Paretzki, Smolinski, Kaplinski, Wiesenfeld and Cheslava Orlinski worked in the city hospital. During the afternoon, Dr. Blumovitch, Dr. Kaplinski and others would come to the hospital in the ghetto. The Orlinski couple and Dr. Kaplinski were close friends, as Cheslava had worked with Kaplinski from 1939. In the early months of 1942 they lived in an apartment together.

---

[25] *Witness evidence of Hillel Moshkovski*

During the many conversations they had about how to survive, joining the partisans was often mentioned. However, for Dr. Kaplinski, that was an impossible path to take because he had to look after his three-year old daughter, whilst his wife and his five-year old son had stayed in the Soviet Union.

Dr. Blumovitch had thought about joining the partisans back in the days when he was hospitalised in Slonim and there were two wounded Soviet officers with him, with whom he had planned to get out to the forest. However, a few days before they were due to leave the hospital, the Germans came and took all the Soviet wounded to a prisoner-of-war camp. Fortunately for Blumovitch there were two nurses in the hospital who hid him and thus he was saved. During that period there was as yet no connection between the Jews and the partisans.

Avraham Orlinski was looking for contact too. One of the prisoners who was taken out of the hospital mentioned the name of Zhama Shusterovitch to him. Shusterovitch was active in the Communist Party and with the German occupation had been forced to live in a double underground.

In the meantime, the ghetto was set up and the situation in Slonim deteriorated. A Jewish hospital was organised and the Jewish patients were transferred from the city hospital to the Jewish hospital in the ghetto. Zhama Shusterovitch wanted to store the underground's weapons in the shelter which had been built in the Jewish hospital, but it wasn't possible to do that. The organisation made efforts to attract doctors and nurses to the underground in order to get them to the forest when the time came. In the end Dr. Blumovitch met Shusterovitch and passed him a list of doctors and nurses.

The partisans wanted Blumovitch to supply the forest with medication and medical equipment. Their requests were met and the doctor waited for his instructions to leave for the forest.[26]

Kaplinski heard about Blumovitch's defection to the forest only from Dr. Orlinski. Because of the necessity for extreme secrecy, Blumovitch hadn't told Kaplinski his plan to go over to the forest, nor did Dr. Kaplinski know about the conversations that Blumovitch had had with other doctors.[27]

One evening in May 1942, Dr. Blumovitch was given the news that the time had come for him to go to the forest. A group of people was gathered in the backyard of Archik Bandt's house on Mikhailovski Lane, and he was supposed to transport them to the forest, but it turned out that no one could find him in the ghetto, so the exodus was postponed. In the meantime two new blows fell upon the ghetto: the outcome of Operation Puzovitch which drained the last strength of the people who were caught; and Operation Mogilev which shed the blood of hundreds of people. Dr. Blumovitch went over to the partisans only on the 3rd. June with the first group led by Zerach Kremin and Aaron Bandt. Blumovitch

---

[26] *Witness evidence of Zerach Kremin.*

[27] *Witness evidence of Dr. Noah Kaplinski*

was in contact with Dr. Berger and he, for his part, had links with Cheslava, the doctor who was in contact with Kaplinski. He helped her to collect medicine and medical equipment which he would "nick" from the city hospital.[28]

After Dr. Berger was killed in the Action of 29th. June, Cheslava lost contact with the underground. It was later renewed through Vatsek Vilchinski.

The Puzovitch and Mogilev Operations (22nd. May 1942)

In the ghetto an atmosphere of dread prevailed. Incidents of Jews being murdered for the smallest of reasons were increasing. In the middle of the street a young carpenter was shot by the gendarmes because they found half a bottle of milk on him. It was now impossible to buy food because of the danger of death for anyone who bought or sold alike. In the ghetto rumours were going around that all the ghettos in the area were to be wiped out and everyone realised that the Slonim ghetto was facing its final days.

Ukrainians reached the ghetto and fear fell upon its residents. Young Zvi Shepetinski, his father Shlomo and uncle Yitzhak Shepetinski worked in building construction. One day an order was received that all the Jewish men would have to appear in the open place near the bridge; they should bring food parcels for two days with them. People felt that a disaster was about to happen in the ghetto.

The forge which worked for the regional manager was required to prepare quantities of hammers to make gravel. The atmosphere was electriv.

The Jews had gathered by the bridge and then they (the Germans) made one of them sit on it and at the German command, the Jewish police were forced to beat the Jew. If one of the policemen noticed that the blows of the Jewish policemen were too weak, he beat the Jewish policeman. After that two Germans from the regional management passed along the line and pulled Jews out of it for work in the Puzovitch camp, where they were to make a road. Shabtai Moshkovski was also pulled out of the row, and he remembered that in his sack he had the slip ordering the smithy to make hammers for the Germans, so he went up to the German engineer and held the order out to him. The German read what was written and sent him back to the forge.[29]

In the house of Zvi Shepetinski they were debating what to do - to appear or to hide. It was decided to wait till morning and see which way the wind blew. After a night watch, frequently peeping outside, they saw that movement in the street had lessened and become more cautious. Men with knapsacks moved like shadows to the place where they were collected, but the movement on the Aryan side looked normal. Zvi and his father decided to report. Jews responsible for building work ordered their workers to wait on the spot.

---

[28] *Evidence of Dr. Noah Kaplinski; witness evidence of Dr. Orlinski*

[29] *Witness evidence of Shabtai Moshkovski*

After a little while, lorries full of Ukrainians passed by them, travelling in the direction of the ghetto. Hearts sank, everyone was sure that the Ukrainians were about to carry out an Action. They heard the command to move and the Jewish workers were taken in the direction of the small town of Kozlovshchina. They went through fields and forest. Outside it was a pleasant spring day, the trees were in blossom and everything looked fresh and peaceful, as if Nature herself was mocking the suffering of the Jews. Zvi Shefet says:

"We walked for a whole day on country paths. From the men who were accompanying us we learned that they would hunt out men and take them off somewhere. In the evening we reached a peasant's hut on one of the lone farms and they left us there to sleep the night in the hayloft. They told us that an SS unit would pass Slonim on its way to the front and they would hunt out men for work. The regional management and the Wehrmacht command from Slonim were not able to oppose the SS, and therefore they decided to take those workers they most needed a long way from the town, to ensure that they would have them for themselves. We were ordered to lie down quietly. We lay in complete silence, a group of Jews whose hearts were torn apart from sorrow and worry for their dear ones who had remained in the ghetto. We thought about our fate. The Germans were hiding us from the SS in order to exploit us for their own needs, and for the pleasure of finishing us off themselves when they no longer needed us.

"At noon we arrived near the village of Pusovitch. First of all, they 'welcomed' us with some road labouring under the management of Christians from Slonim. The road was intended for military use. Jews brought the stones in wheelbarrows and the peasants brought them in their carts. Here and there a German was walking around and from time to time, purely for pleasure, he would land a blow on a Jew who wasn't being "careful" enough in his work. At noon a car arrived with the regional governor; they called for the craftsmen they needed and the rest, which was most of us, remained on the road. My father and my uncle were called too and I was left behind. My father held me in his arms when they called his name and wouldn't let go of me. I told him to go and I would come on soon, the work here wouldn't be particularly heavy for me. I tried to calm him down so that he would be able to go home.

"The ones who were chosen were counted a few times and taken back to Slonim. We stayed with the Jews of the camp who had long hair and were filthy. They had already been there a number of months and in a few words they described to us the appalling conditions that ruled in the camp. When we went inside, we saw the terrible reality. There were a few large huts in the camp with straw roofs and we slept on the floor which was covered with rags swarming with fleas. There were no windows here. In a small stream which flowed behind the camp, hundreds of people had to wash, naked or half naked. The water was murky and polluted, but despite this, had to be used to wash your face and to clean your teeth, as well as for drinking and cooking."

Zvi was attacked by severe stomach pains. He was told that there was a doctor in the camp. He reached the doctor who lived in a peasant's hut outside the camp. The doctor told him to lie down quietly - maybe the pains would have passed by the next day. Zvi went back to the camp and met a few people he knew from Slonim, and they lit a bonfire outside and lay by it. Zvi joined them but couldn't get to sleep.

The next day, when everyone went out to work, the doctor examined him again and told him just to lie down and rest because he didn't have any medication. The doctor told him that he had got in touch with the regional management and informed them that he had a sick person here who must be transferred to hospital. They told him that if he (Zvi) didn't work the next day, they would send their doctors, adding that not only sick Jews were superfluous but also the healthy ones.

On the evening of the third day of his stay in the camp Zvi noticed a cart approaching the gate of the camp. This was a carter who brought the Slonim workers parcels from their families. Zvi received a letter from his parents, and in a parcel he found a work ticket which had been hidden in the pocket of a garment. This was intended to enable him to get into the Slonim ghetto. The carter told him that he was due to return to Slonim at dawn and agreed to take Zvi with him. Zvi divided the contents of the parcel his parents had sent him among his friends, and told them that he was about to get out of there. He managed to get out of the camp in the cart laden with barrels as if for drawing water - and didn't return. He went to the house next to which the carter had tied up his horse and cart for the night, stealthily went into the threshing floor and burrowed into the hay.

In the morning he got on the cart and burrowed himself well into the straw. Several Christians joined this journey to town too. On the way out a policeman stopped them, exchanged a few jests with the Christians who were sitting on the cart and they left Puzovitch safely. After they'd gone a few kilometres he crawled out of the straw and sat in the cart by the side of the farmers. He listened to their conversations, which were actually full of commiseration for the sufferings of their Jewish acquaintances. When they got near to Slonim, he went back and hid under the straw. The cart passed through Bridge Street and turned into Operova Street. Nobody stopped them. The farmers got off by the entrance to the ghetto, the carter and Zvi showed their papers and went in without questions or demands. Tsvi's family was waiting for him on the other side of the fence.[30]

On the 22nd. May the news spread that Ukrainians were on their way in order to take the Jews out to slave labour in Mogilev, to build fortifications. That evening a group of underground members met: Dr. Blumovitch, Anshel Delatitski, the Shepetinski brothers, Zerach Kremin, Avraham Bandt and others - in the Shepetinski's backyard in Mikhailovski Lane. The plan was to go to the forest, but it appeared that Archik Bandt, who was to have led the group, wasn't in the ghetto. Anshel Delatitski was particularly tense since, as a communist, he had to hide all the time. When he saw Dr. Blumovitch, who was a well-known Zionist, he went up to him and asked "Do you know that we're standing on a Socialist platform?" "That's true" replied the Doctor, "but when are we going to get off this platform and move into the forest?" Delatitski had no answer to that.[31]

---

[30] *The Pozovich camp was liberated by a partisan attack by the "Bolack" troop on 2th. June, 1942, Biten Notebooks, 427-429*

[31] *Witness account of Zerach Kremin*

"We tried" Zerach tells us, "to convince Avraham Bandt to take us. After all, as a past resident of the village of Skolditch, he would know the way. But Avraham refused."

The main problem was how to get past the small town of Zhirovitza where a large German police presence and a Belarussian police force were stationed. So, not having a guide, they decided to disperse at midnight, to hide during the manhunt, and to go into the forest at the first opportunity.

On the next day, Tuesday, 23rd. May, the manhunt was carried out. A group of Ukrainians burst into the ghetto like a flock of black crows. They spread out in the alley-ways and lanes of the ghetto group by group, beating and cursing people, looting and robbing. They had Lithuanians with them and Belarussian police. The Jews hastened to hide.

Before the Action, the engineer Orlinski had gone to stay the night in the textile factory where he worked. There was no one there, but the Belarussian mechanic hid him in the steam engine hall. In the morning the Ukrainians broke into the building to look for Jews. The mechanic's assistant said that there were no Jews there and they made off again. In the afternoon, his (Orlinski's) wife, the doctor, sent a Belarussian nurse from the hospital with a green/blue certificate which could protect him from being snatched. She herself remained in the hospital.

Yosef Holtz, a refugee from Kalish, who managed a soda factory under German control in Slonim says that the Ukrainians and the Lithuanians were taking people who had the yellow certificates, but by noon they had managed to catch only three hundred men. And so they began to take men out of the factories. Out of eighteen workers who worked in the soda factory, there remained only three.

Most of the men who were transported to Mogilev died of hunger and disease. Every Sunday a parade was held here and the weak ones were taken out for execution. After seven months there was not a single one of the non-skilled workers who had been taken from Slonim. After eighteen months of unbearable life in Mogilev, the rest of the skilled workers were taken to the camp in Minsk. In about thirteen days the front drew nearer to Minsk and the Germans dragged the Jewish workers from camp to camp until, finally, they reached Mauthausen in Austria, and from there to Evenze, where most of them perished from hunger. When the Americans liberated the camp, out of four hundred and three Jews from Slonim there remained only three men. [32]

First Departures to the Partisans

After the Puzovitch and Mogilev operations, the underground became better equipped. When they made contact with the Proniagin groups, the goal seemed already in sight. At the same time, an urgent need sprang up to get three members out to the forest, as in the ghetto immediate danger awaited them. In the Mogilev days, three of the active members had fallen into enemy hands -

---
[32] *Witness account of Yisrael Yudelevitch, one of the three who survived, related to Yosef Holtz, in: Anthology of Heritage, Book 30, November, 1980.*

Avraham Bublatzki, Zhama Shusterovitch and Mitos Snovski. The latter was freed by the clerks of the district administration who needed him for work, and the other two were taken by train with the rest of the men who had been caught. On the way, they managed to jump from the carriage and went back to the ghetto. They said that they had opened a little window and jumped. Before that, they had suggested that the rest of the passengers jump but they refused and even tried to stop them for fear of German reprisals.

These two were joined by Yitzhak Gratchuk. He worked in the German loot camp and used to get out hand grenades and other weapons for the organisation. In about the middle of May he slipped four hand grenades into his knapsack and hung it on the wall so that when he returned, he could take it to the ghetto. But a Polish woman who worked as a cleaner apparently noticed what he was doing and reported it to one of the German commanders. At that time Gratchuk was outside the loot camp. Somebody told the Germans that it probably was another man who put the hand grenades in Gratchuk's knapsack and it would be a good idea to set a soldier there who would catch the man when he came to take them. And in fact that's what the Germans did. In the meantime, somebody warned Gratchuk not to go back to the camp.

When they didn't catch the "other" man, the camp commander, senior lieutenant Wertzel and his deputy Mutz announced that if Gratchuk didn't come back, they would hand over the whole matter to the district commander. The men of the underground, among them Pesach Alpert, informed the Judenraat of the incident. They bribed Mutz and his boss Wertzel with the sum of twenty or twenty-five golden roubles in order to hush the whole thing up. With a good heart produced by wine, Wertzel declared that if he caught Gratchuk, he would kill him not for stealing the grenades for the farmers - he supposed that they were intended for fishing - but because he had made such a stupid error as to hang up the rucksack on the wall instead of hiding it.

It had become clear that they could no longer postpone leaving for the forest and so on the next Saturday evening, after the Mogilev operation, on 3rd. June, 1942, the first group of partisans left the ghetto, comprising five people: Dr. Avraham Blumovitch, Anshel Delatitski, the nurse Fanya Feigenbaum and Kuba Zilberhaft. The guides were Zerach Kremin and Aharon Bandt. They set out for the forest of Rafalofka where Proniagin's group was stationed. They reached the forest safely and handed over the newcomers to the care of the commanders[33]. At daybreak on Monday the two guides went back to the ghetto. The partisans were very pleased that they had come, particularly Dr. Blumovitch who brought with him a heavy crate of medical instruments, materials for bandaging and medicines and immediately started to tend the wounded. Zerach recalls what a terrible feeling it was when he had to go back and penetrate through the barbed wire fence into the stifling atmosphere of the ghetto. From then on the guides repeated this operation a number of times, and got people out to the forest. However, not all the members of the underground had managed to get out yet. The Soviet partisans continued to

---

[33] *Witness account of Zerach Kremin*

ask the Jews to stay in the ghetto and to supply them with more and more arms, ammunition and various other commodities.

On 10th. June a second group went into the forest comprising the members: Yitzhak (Itche) Gratchuk, Avraham Yakimovski (who was nicknamed Anton), David Blumenfeld and Adek Schnur.

More members joined the organisation and the arms smuggling grew in strength. Shabtai and Hillel Moshkovski built an extra bunker which had a hidden entrance through the woodshed. The first shelter was shared between them and their neighbours and suited the needs of the underground. The new hiding place was covered with planks and behind them Shabtai and Archik Bandt hid rifles and ammunition. Some of the weapons were transferred to the backyard of the Shepetinski family and were handed over to those people who were leaving for the forest.

It was not easy for new members to find the underground. They had to be extremely careful even of Jews, who were afraid of any activity which was likely to endanger their situation. Avraham Orlinski got in touch with the underground only after the Mogilev operation; his wife Dr. Cheslava worked with Dr. Blumovitch and when he joined the partisans, she lost that contact. In the textile factory where Orlinski worked there was also a forge, where he met Shabtai Moshkovski. While they were chatting, Orlinski showed him a pistol he had with a broken spring. Shabtai took the spring from him hoping he would be able to mend it, or fix a new spring, but he didn't manage it since in the meantime the slaughter of 29th. June had started in the ghetto and the smithy craftsman with whom Shabtai worked was killed.

In exchange for a pistol, Shabtai introduced Orlinski to Yasha Kremin, who was at the time the messenger for the underground organisation. Through him Orlinski was introduced to Doktortchik and from then on he served as contact since Yasha had gone to the forest.

Orlinski was also in contact with the fitter, Ya'akov Timan, a refugee from the town of Ostrov Mazovietski, who was working in the mechanics workshop. At that time Orlinski had conceived the idea of establishing within the ghetto a partisan fighting group and he was on the lookout for weapons and ammunition. He brought orders for weapon repairs to Timan, who had similar views. When Orlinski told him about the option of joining the partisans in the forest, Timan disclosed to him that he had a friend who worked in the German loot camp and that there it was possible to get various guns. Timan suggested to Orlinski that he should transfer to work in the loot camp. He told his friend Imber about Orlinski and in this way a link was created between him and the members of the underground who worked in the loot camp.

The Girls in the Organisation

Girls also worked in the underground organisation and they did their job with great courage and dedication. Rita (Rivfka) Mukasei Moshkovski recounts:

"In the autumn of 1941 I met Anshel Delatitski. He asked if I would agree to collect clothes and money for certain needs, but he didn't explain what they were. When I agreed, he suggested that I get four other people to join me in the job. I chose Yisrael Rabinovitch, Yosef Shelubski, Cheikel Kokoshitski and Yekutiel Goldin. And so we were a 'quintet' in the underground organisation, and whatever we collected I passed over to Anshel. Later Delatitski disclosed to me that the goods were intended for the partisans in the forests. On the day of the slaughter of 14th. November we all hid in bunkers. From my hiding place I saw how they were leading away Jews in Operova Street - men, women and children. After the Action, our house was included within the boundary of the ghetto and we weren't supposed to pass through. We stayed there until the massacre of 27th. June 1942. All that time we were in touch with Delatitski and I collected money, clothes and tobacco for the partisans. In time they included me in the fighting brigade which was on the point of going into the forest."

Young women were active in the organisation and took part in hiding weapons and ammunition, smuggling it from the loot camp to the ghetto. Among the arms smugglers was Halinka Rodinstein, a brave and agile young woman. Some of them were caught and paid for this with their lives. Nevertheless, it was hard for the girls to get into the fighting group in the forest. The partisan command accepted very few young women to its unit and chose to absorb Russian rather than Jewish women.

Young women worked in service jobs - cooking, laundry and standing guard. Some of them worked as first-aiders and nurses and some used to accompany the partisans when they went out on missions. Their role was to take the wounded away from the battlefield and to care for them. Others treated the wounded and the sick in the clinics in the camp, which were organised in special underground dugouts. Most of the young women suffered a humiliating attitude on the part of partisans who were coarse and disrespectful. And those who refused to be mistresses of the commanders were sometimes expelled from the troop to a family camp. Only a few Jewish girls won the right to be counted among the fighters, to carry weapons and to take part in battles. The fate of the girls who had a husband or a brother among the fighters in the troop who could protect them was better. The situation for those who belonged to the medical team was also better.

After the bloody Action of 29th. June, Rita's 'five' no longer existed. Yekutiel Goldin and Yosef Shelubski were killed in the Action; Kheikel Kokoshitski died in Mogilev and only Yisrael Rabinovitch reached the partisans, though he fell in the forest. Rivka (Rita) Mukasei Moshkovski came to the forest together with her two sisters - Masha and sixteen year old Yocheved, the youngest of the sisters. In the forest Rita was accepted into the Jewish 51 Battalion; her two sisters were sent to the Biten family camp and Yokheved, the younger one, was killed in the manhunt which the enemy carried out in the forest in the autumn of 1942.

The other girls, too, brave and active young women in the underground organisation in the ghetto, suffered terribly in the forest both before they reached the partisans and afterwards, but more of that later.

The Action of 29th. June 1942

Tension reigned in the ghetto; everybody sensed that something dreadful was about to happen. The only hope for the time being was in the news of trains carrying large numbers of German wounded from the front, trains which rushed through mainly at night. However, the Germans were still at the height of their strength and the day of deliverance was far off. There were still barges sailing on the Shchara, bringing wood to the saw-mills which before the war had been Jewish property. Now they were working for the Germans, operated by Jews decorated with yellow patches - some of them members of the underground organisation, who were making their plans for revenge and storing up weapons.

On 28th. June the Germans began to arrest Poles, particularly from the stratum of the intelligentsia. And so there were instances of lone Poles and even families seeking refuge in the ghetto. Even though it was already well known that the Germans were apt to divert attention from their defeats at the fronts by carrying out bloody Actions in the ghettos, despite this many Jews still supposed that this time the German intentions were directed at the Poles.

On the eve of the Action the members of the underground met to confer. Doktortchik suggested distributing weapons to the people and calling on the ghetto to defend itself. Zhama Shusterovitch didn't see any point in that and the meeting broke up without a decision. The Jews of the ghetto, and among them the members of the underground, went down into the shelters. On the morning of 29th. June, horror flooded through Jewish dwellings; the Germans and their Lithuanian helpers raced around the backyards of the ghetto, pulling out the people who were hiding in their shelters and when they couldn't find them, they set the houses on fire. Partisan Itche (Yitzhak) Rabinovitch has given an account of this extermination Action.

He worked in the carpenters' workshop on Podgorna Street with the underground members Zelig Milikovski and Eliahu Abramovski, and they were also responsible for the underground shelter, which had been started by Mendel Shelubski. After the Action of 14th. November, Itche lost his whole family; now he remained alone and lived with his friends in Mostova Street by the river, in a house which was outside the ghetto. From there they used to go to work without needing to cross through the ghetto gate.

One day Mendel Shelubski asked Itche to accompany him to the ghetto in order to visit his sister. They took tools with them and were walking in the direction of the gate, but near the ghetto gate they noticed a German car and by it there were Germans from the district administration. Next to them stood Gershon Kvint, who was in charge of the employment office, talking to them. At a certain moment, Ritmayer took out his pistol and shot Kvint, who immediately collapsed on the ground. Itche understood that the murder of Kvint was an omen of the terrible bloodshed which was about to be carried out in the ghetto. He refused to go on and turned back to the carpenter's on Podgorna Street, whereas Mendel went on to the ghetto and was killed.

We can read what happened to the Jews of Slonim in those days of terror in the witness accounts of the few survivors. Zvi Shepetinski says:

"In the Sunday evening you could hear drunken singing in the ghetto from the seminar building of Skrobova Street where the Lithuanian murderers were staying. Their voices stopped us sleeping. All night one of us was keeping watch outside. At three or four before dawn, Herzel, who was on guard outside told us that large groups of Germans, Lithuanians and Belarussian police were surrounding the ghetto; they were taking up positions and their machineguns were trained towards us.

"It was obvious that they were preparing a massacre. We woke the whole family. Everybody got dressed and went down to the shelters. Our hiding place was in an underground trench that had been dug underneath the shed, and the entrance to it was camouflaged by a sideboard, on which a padlock was hung. In order to get into the hiding place you had to lift up the bottom shelf which covered a floorboard. The hiding place ran the length of our house, a metre and a half in width and depth. The floorboards of the entrance could be closed from inside with a bolt and it was hard to find it from outside.

"Having the experience of the previous Actions, we left all the doors in the house open and we scattered the clothes and bed linen through all the rooms, so as to give the impression that the Action had already taken place here.

"The shooting and screaming went on till the afternoon and then it was a little quieter around us. The air in the hiding place was unbearably thick and so with our hands we dug a number of holes in order to reach the air. The holes reached the potato plot and so it was not possible to notice them from outside.

"At four in the afternoon the murderers renewed their searches; this time in larger groups overseen by someone from the civil administration. They checked every corner and shot people who they dragged out of their hiding places. They poked around in our yard too, picking at the firewood in the shed. One policeman wanted to set light to the shed but the Germans forbade him, it was a pity to burn such good material.

"Twilight fell upon the ghetto and now a car approached and sprinkled stuff on our houses, and within a few minutes we felt from the air holes that the house was going up in flames. It started to collapse and burning embers fell into our hiding place. The smoke gnawed at our eyes and choked our throats. We decided to crawl out while holding on to planks and pillars which were burning. We were forced to go forward crawling on our bellies between the stalks of the potatoes and we reached the shed covered with burns."

Aharon Bandt was with the Shepetinski family as he had stayed to spend the night with his friends. Now he decided to go to the forest. They had to go through Mikhailovski Lane in the direction of Archik Bandt's house. They ran one after the other. The guard who was standing at the end of the alley by the river didn't notice them. While they were running, they passed dozens of bodies lying in the alley. Archik had already gathered around him a band of young men and women ready to leave, some of them armed. People threaded themselves through a little window which looked out onto a yard and they reached Skrobova Street where the German watch was marching. They took advantage of the moment when the guards were further off, passed along the road running and under cover of darkness left the town weltering in the blood of its Jews. With them went the whole of the Shepetinski family - the parents and the little children; the only person missing was their young son Reuven.

While they were running through Mikhailovski Lane in the direction of the house of Archik Bandt, Reuven had jumped into the drainage canal near the house. Bodies of the murdered people were lying in it. Because he was in shock, the lad became confused and turned in the direction of the Shchara which flowed past about fifty metres away. Reuven, who was a good swimmer, jumped into the river and managed to cross it despite the shots of the murderers who had noticed him. He escaped into the saw mill on the opposite bank and hid there among the planks. The next night, after he had recovered, he went out on the road that led to the village of Zavershe to the Fiedrik family. They fed him and brought him to the forest of Volchye Nori, to the 51 group, and there he was reunited with his brothers Yasha and Herzel.

Yasha Shepetinski has this to say about how the large group, which had left the ghetto on the night of slaughter, came to the forest:

"We unearthed a second machinegun[34] and some more armed lads joined us. Archik Bandt took the command; he had been a sergeant in the Polish army. The families organised themselves. Not everybody went out into the forest even though about two hundred people gathered, among them all of our family, save for Reuven of whom we had no news. We set two machineguns at the crossroads; at the head went Archik and at the rear Avraham Bandt and Yasha Shepetinski. It was Sunday night. Among those walking were: the two Bandt brothers and their father Yechezkel, their mother Nechamah, their sister Matla Luninski and her two children, five year old Chaim and three year old Tzilla, Liuba Abramchik, her sister Leah, David Perl, his sister with her husband and their two year old daughter, our parents Yitzhak and Hanna, my brother Herzel, our sister Raya, our little brothers Yechiel and Uri, Hershel Shepetinski (now Zvi Shefet), his father, who was our uncle Shlomo Shepetinski, and his mother Hannah, his sister Sonia, two thirteen year old boys and so on.

"We crossed the road and by the brick factory we turned towards the forest. We marched quickly and quietly. It was a short summer night and so we had to be quick in order to arrive in time. We took turns at carrying the small children in our arms. I have to say that the children were really grown up and understood the threat of danger."

That night another large group left the ghetto under the leadership of Zerach Kremin. It included Avraham Bublatski, Heniek Malach, Irka Weisselfisch and also many of the families of the members of the (underground) organisation.

---

[34] *In addition to the machine-gun which was hidden in the backyard of the Shepetinski house.*

"Everyone was full of hope that considering all the partisans' demands which they had met, they would be received with open arms, but the reality was completely different. The Jews who streamed towards the forest, among them elderly people and children, were a burden in the view of the non-Jewish partisans - extra mouths to feed, an unwanted and superfluous element in the forest which they thought belonged only to them. The anti-Semitic face of many of the partisans was revealed in its full ugliness.

In this Action, which lasted for two weeks, many of the members of the organisation who hadn't managed to find a hiding place were murdered. Some of the survivors have told us what happened to them, and these are the experiences of the future partisan, the young Imber:

"Suddenly the Germans picked up everyone working in the loot camp, and sent us to the ghetto. This was foreboding, though many people found it encouraging: if they're taking us back to the ghetto, it means there won't be an Action.

"The whole ghetto had gone down into the hiding places. The Germans caught a few Jews who they forced to accompany them and to call to the Jews in Yiddish to come out, that nothing bad would happen to them. Many Jews, when they heard Yiddish, were tempted to come out and were led off to the pits.

"At noon on the first day of the Action a lorry from the loot camp drove through the streets of the ghetto, and from it Mutz was declaring through a loudspeaker that the camp workers could come out and approach the lorry without fear for their lives. People cautiously popped out of their hiding places and ran to the lorry and I did the same. In fact, people who weren't counted among the workers of the loot camp ran towards it. The lorry, loaded with people, went quickly off to the camp, but here it was evident that this too was a trick. An officer of the civil administration, Hick, appeared and sorted the people. Anyone he didn't like the look of was placed at the side. Among those who were turned out to the side was an experienced carpenter from Slonim, one of the camp workers. He said that he had a "life certificate" from the ones which had been distributed to the camp workers. Mutz went up to him, took out his pistol and killed him on the spot.

"Now no illusions remained, we knew what was waiting for us. After a few hours we heard Hick's voice: 'We still need some more men to fill the quota and the loot camp must find men to make up the missing places'. Mutz applied himself immediately to carrying out the command and ordered some men to get up on the lorry, among them our friend Ya'akov Waxman. He understood very well where they were taking them, so when the lorry was on the way to the prison where people who were intended for extermination were being concentrated, he jumped off the vehicle and fled. When the lorry reached the prison, Mutz noticed someone was missing. He went back to the loot camp and threatened that if somebody didn't present himself immediately in place of the one who'd escaped, he himself would choose ten men in his place. Mutz left us five minutes to meet his demands, and then among the people standing around we heard the voice of Liovek Katz, a refugee from Poland and the faithful servant of Mutz. He was so devoted to his role that we were afraid of him, we saw him as a spy. Liovek volunteered to go in place of the one who'd escaped. Mutz didn't take Katz' loyal service into account at all, and ordered him to get on the lorry and took him off to his death."

The Germans burned house after house in the ghetto. People, who became live torches and tried to save themselves by jumping out of a burning house, were immediately shot by the rounds of bullets that were waiting for them all around the house. Others tried to jump in the Shchara but there too the bullets of the murderers reached them. In this Action there was no longer any difference between Jews who were defined as 'useful' and just Jews. The brothers Ze'ev and Natan Finkel managed to hide in the loft of their house; they had weapons and they had decided to fight. But the murderers didn't go up to their loft.

In the house of the brothers Avraham and Aharon Bandt, they'd built two hiding places, in one of which were hidden weapons belonging to the underground. They went down to the hiding place. In the bunker where Avraham was sitting a policeman thrust a bayonet through a crack and it was a miracle that he wasn't stabbed.

The underground member David Perl hid weapons in a shed in Mikhailovski Lane. When the Germans set fire to the house, the fire reached the shed and the explosives hidden in it blew up.

Shabtai Moshkovski who was caught in the Action says this about his difficult experiences and about his rescue:

"I, my brother Tsvi and my brother-in-law Yisrael, together with most of the tenants of our house, went down to the hiding place and we shut the lid on top of us. The yard was full of Germans and their aides and they were looking for hiding places. We heard blows and screams. After a while, the lid was lifted from our hiding place and Germans and their aides in various uniforms, armed from top to toe, stood above us holding grenades in their hands and called out, "Come out, or we'll throw the grenades". We climbed out while they chivvied us with blows. There were about forty of us. In the yard they arranged us in rows and put with us some more Jews who had been taken from their hiding places. My brother Tsvi jumped out of the row into the house and I and my brother-in-law remained standing.

"The Jews generally did not cry and plead, even though they knew what was awaiting them. All around there were all sorts of Germans: SS., Wehrmacht, Todet organisation[35], clerks from the district management, railway guards and Belarussian policemen. They surrounded us like predators, keeping watch on the rows so no one could escape. In addition to their yelling, they spoke the language of clubs and rifle butts.

"We had just passed Mikhailovski Lane and gone on to the bank of the Shchara when a terrifying sight was revealed to us: columns of smoke and flames rose up from the houses of the ghetto. Jews, who couldn't survive the fire, came out and joined the lines of those who were being led away. We went

---
[35] *Todet: a German engineering firm which employed Jewish slave labour. (J.L.)*

forward with slow steps and stopped from time to time because it was impossible to move. We went a little way along the left bank and then they turned us to Mostova Street, whose houses were burning.

"When we passed the first bridge, we went down to the neighbourhood that's called 'Zhabinka' or 'the island'. Until then it was the 'safest' place because most of the 'essential' Jews lived there. This time these Jews had no rights and they too had no chance of survival. You couldn't build hiding places in the earth here because as soon as you reached a depth of one metre, the water would come up into the hole, and so most of the Jews built hiding places inside the houses between double walls or in the loft, but the houses in Zhabinka were all made of wood and now they burned.

"We continued to move forward slowly and I had enough time to look around me. On the right the houses of Zhabinka were going up in flames. Pairs of Germans passed from house to house, breaking the windows with their rifle butts, collecting clothes and piling them on the tables. After that they poured on petrol and set fire to it. I saw this through the windows of the houses which were lower than the bank where we were marching. And the house of Abba Yudelevitch, a member of the Ha'shomer Hatsa'ir movement and of the underground, was already going up in flames. This was an unusual house in the neighbourhood because it was built of bricks. Their hiding place was in the loft. I saw Abba and his brother Motke later that day, but their family were all burned alive.

"I saw people burning like candles in front of the Jews who were standing in a line, and before the eyes of the German murderers. And now smoke was coming up off a child's back; another twenty metres and he would reach us. The smoke grew thicker and the child was standing in flames, a living candle running towards us. A German dressed in civilian clothes with the sign of the Swastika on his lapel drew out a pistol and with two shots put an end to the child's life.

"A baby is crying in its mother's arms. The woman tries to run to the river to get some water for the thirsty child. The German trains his rifle on her and threatens to kill her. The woman falls back and the baby continues crying. A young carpenter jumps into the water. From time to time he raises his head to draw air, and swims along with the current. A German trains his weapon on him. Round after round splits the air and the bullets fall into the water, searching for the young swimmer, 'this cheeky one, who dares to save his life'. Another round of bullets and the water turns red. The head goes down, comes up again and finally sinks."

It was about one in the afternoon when Shabtai reached the second bridge, a wooden bridge slanted over the Shchara where the people being led away to their death were crossing. It was extremely crowded so that the Germans couldn't control the situation. The rows got all mixed up, there were no lines. There was a crowd of women standing on it and there was barely room to move. Shabtai was standing at the bottom and above, in Mostova Street which ran about four metres above them, order was again established. 'Battalions' of

Jews, each about one hundred people, were moving on the slope of the street towards the Zamoshcha neighbourhood on their last journey to the killing pits.

And Shabtai too was now on the other side of the bridge. Every few moments a group of Germans would burst out with cruel blows into the midst of the crowd, and cut a part of it out as if with a knife. And these people would rearrange themselves as they went up onto the pavement according to the 'commands' of clubs.

Shabtai fell back and distanced himself from the attackers; there was no reason to hurry. Not far from him stood Abba Yudelevitch with his brother Motke. He approached them, "Abba, perhaps we can do something. Maybe we could find some way to get out of here". Abba smiled sadly, "There is no way out. I'm going with everyone". Had despair taken hold of strong, athletic Abba? Abba, who was an outstanding scout in the Pioneer youth movement, who served two years in the army, who was on pioneering leadership and but for the war would have emigrated to Israel. After all he was also a member of the underground..... Abba grasped Shabtai's hand until it hurt, and then left him. He went up to an acquaintance of his, the wife of a Jewish teacher who had already been killed. She was standing with her children; Abba took the little one in his arms and went on with the line. Shabtai accompanied them with his eyes.

Again the kidnappers burst into the crowd, but Shabtai didn't give in and stepped backwards. And now there were people in white coats going up the steps. At the head of them walked the Dr. Yosef Gvurin who came from Slonim, and behind him the nurses. The day was nearing its end. It was becoming difficult to escape the grasp of the kidnappers. Shabtai was trying to co-ordinate something, but still, he was forced to go up the steps.

A scream accompanied by blows: they're moving forwards. Everybody's marching quietly; there's no weeping heard. Several hundred metres past the second bridge on Mostova Street, opposite the church, there is a big yard. Two Germans from the district administration stood at the gate of the yard. They pulled out of the rows isolated Jews whose work they needed, so that they would work for them before they were murdered. For a moment the line stopped walking; one of the Germans went up to the first row and pulled the engineer Volfstein out of it, and the line moved forward. At the same time, a German Feldfebel came out of the yard dressed in Wehrmacht uniform and started to call out to the Jews, "Which of you is from a furniture factory?" In a fraction of a second Shabtai jumped out of the row; in fact he got a blow on the head but he stood by the Feldpavel and in one breath said, "I'm an expert smithy". He pushed him into the yard and said: "Ja, das is gut. Vir brauchen eine schmide maister" (It's good. We need an expert smithy).

About one hundred and fifty Jews. Shabtai is already in the yard among all the rest facing the wall. Here, while leaning their heads on the wall, they gave vent to their tears.

One Jew bewails the bitterness of his fate that didn't allow him to die together with his family. Another on his right is weeping silently, that he didn't have the courage to oppose the German who pulled him out of the row and cut him off from his family. He speaks with admiration of his colleague, Yosef

Payevski, who marched in the same group with his son and wife. The Germans, when they saw Payevski who was known to them as an excellent accountant, hastened to take him out of the row, but he pushed the German back with force and said that he preferred to die with his son and his wife, and they went on their way arm in arm. The man related this with regret and envy.

It's starting to get dark. The Germans order Volfstein the engineer and another Jew to record those remaining alive according to their names and their profession and their place of work. The list is prepared and another inspection, just in case somebody 'unnecessary' has crept in. And then comes a kind of committee - the commander of the action and Germans from the civil directorate. The murderers went along the whole row, the Jew would say his name and his job and the German from the civil directorate who was interested in a particular job would confirm the necessity of this Jew.

Evening fell and the people left the yard accompanied by armed Germans. They were marched in Dluga Street devoid of people, only here and there Gentiles peeped out through the windows, some in fear, some in commiseration and some with a mocking smile. They were taken into the yard of the furniture factory which bordered on the saw-mill and there they were left to their own devices.

The next day, the morning of 30th. June, they transferred them to Bernadiska Street. The houses in this street hadn't been burned. They were employed taking out Jewish property from the houses under the watchful eye of the Belarussian local police who were busy at that time searching for Jews who were hiding. Jews who had come out of their hiding places joined them and worked with them. Germans came from the district administration and began to mark them: on the chest and back - next to the Star of David they marked a white cross. After the Germans had gone, dozens of Jews joined them who had come out of hiding places, and they marked each other with this extra sign. In the evening they were all transferred to the loot camp in Zamoshcha Street.

On 1st. July people came from the administration and ordered the Jews to organise themselves according to their professions. Shabtai Moshkovski joined a group of leather workers. In the end they transferred them to the reduced ghetto on Mostova Street. During the day its population grew by several hundred, with professional people who had been released from prison and transferred to the small ghetto.

Shabtai met Yasha Kremin who he already knew, and also the other members of the underground - Noah Servianski and Adolf Waxman. Afterwards Liuba Zhagel and Doktortchik and others joined the band.

However, the slaughter in the ghetto continued; many Jews supposing that the action had finished, came out of their hiding places and were hunted down, brought to the prison and transported in lorries to the pits.

In one of the groups which were taken off to be murdered in Tchepelova was a member of the underground, Shmuel Gutterman, a refugee from Poland. Those being taken to die were forced to sit on the floor of the lorry with their heads on their knees and they were forbidden to utter a word. When the lorry reached Albertin, a suburb of Slonim, Gutterman grabbed the rifle of one of the policemen and threw him off the lorry with a blow from the butt of the rifle. He himself jumped and disappeared with the rifle in the alley. He reached the partisan battalion 51.

How A. Orlinski and Dr. N. Kaplinski were saved

On the day of the Action of 29th. June, Orlinski woke early in the morning from fear and dread. When he peeped outside, he saw a German soldier opposite their house and he was armed from top to toe. Orlinski understood that they were surrounding the ghetto and that an Action would take place, and immediately called everyone in the family. Dr. Kaplinski, who lived next door, told them all to go into hiding.

The next morning the people sitting in hiding heard voices of people walking around in their house and in the yard, and they were removing belongings from the apartments. They realised that the Action was continuing. At night Orlinski went down into the house. Everything was broken open; the doors of the cupboards were open and various things were missing. On the third day of the action the conditions in the hiding place were difficult: there were sick people and other people whose nerve had been weakened, behaving as if they had gone crazy.

In the afternoon they heard a knocking at the entrance to the hiding place and after that the voice of Dr. Honigstein, the brother-in-law of Dr. Kaplinski, and to their amazement he called them to come outside. People started to leave the hiding place. Outside the gendarmes were waiting for them and Shtehlle, the head of the section for Jews in the district administration, was training a submachine gun at the entrance.

Everyone was taken out of their shelter and taken off to the prison. On the way a gendarme went up to Dr. Orlinski and told her to be calm. She and her husband and Dr. Honigstein and his wife would be released. Avraham Orlinski didn't believe the German's promise; he was certain that they were being taken on their last journey. He was tired and despairing. By the one-time national Polish gymnasium (high school) they happened to come across several acquaintances, Christian Poles who were passing in the street, and furtively gave him looks of embarrassment and fear. A deep pain hit him that they should see him in this state.

When they reached the yard of the prison, they immediately separated Dr. Cheslava and her husband from their group and after that Dr. Honigstein and his wife. The German gendarme brought them to the loot camp and there they met some more people who the Germans had kept to work for them, and Dr. Kaplinski with his daughter and her nanny. There were about six hundred Jews. They received 'life certificates' in the form of a slip of card with a number, and they were ordered to fix them on their clothes. After a few days had passed, they were taken to the now reduced ghetto. Skilled workers had to work at their craft and the others collected all the property of the murdered people for the Germans.

In the coming days Orlinski continued with the work of collecting the property of the dead and continued to meet hidden Jews. Any men he happened to meet, Orlinski would attach, with the help of his comrades, to the group of workers and in this way they would go into the ghetto, and stay there for a certain length of time without a life certificate until one was obtained for them. In a few cases those people who didn't have certificates managed to leave the Slonim ghetto and go to the small town of Ruzhani and from there onwards to places where there were still Jews living. Those who left would leave behind their certificates if they had them, for the sake of those in the ghetto who didn't have certificates.

Orlinski was saved thanks to the fact that the Germans needed the work of Dr. Cheslava who treated their wives and their mistresses, whilst the survival of doctors Kaplinski and Honigstein is linked to a young German soldier by the name of Hans Zeifel, who was a medical student before the war.

This is Dr. Kaplinski's story:

"A few weeks before the massacre, a young German soldier appeared in front of me, and with a politeness that was unusual at the time on the part of Germans speaking to Jews, he asked to speak to me.

"He introduced himself and told me that he was a medical student who had been enrolled to the Medical Corps and had been sent to the garrison which was stationed in Slonim. The soldier admitted that as a student he would be likely to encounter medical problems with which he didn't know how to deal and therefore he was asking for the help of our medical experience. I promised him our help; I brought my brother-in-law Honigstein, who was a young doctor and they became friendly. The soldier used to sometimes bring cigarettes and also other goods, and developed a real attachment to us. And now when I was standing there despairing of life, the soldier Zeifel came running along, upset and agitated. When he had discovered what was happening, he started to look for "his" doctors. When he saw me, he immediately approached Ritmayer. I saw that he was conferring and arguing with the chief of the murderers. Ritmayer went up to our group and pulled me and my daughter with me out of it."

Dr. Kaplinski was one of the first from their house who was taken to the collection point of the victims. He had refused because of his little daughter to go in the hiding place in their house and so he was taken off to the riverside together with his daughter, her nanny and his sister-in-law who had remained in the house and not gone into hiding. That was where dozens of Jews who were under the supervision of Ritmayer were concentrated. After Zeifel's intervention Ritmayer handed over Dr. Kaplinski with his daughter and his sister-in-law Sonya (who he had described as his wife) and the nanny (as his sister) to a soldier, with instructions not to put them into the group which was being taken to their deaths.

Then Zeifel asked him what had happened to Honigstein. When he heard that he was in the hospital, he ran there immediately. After about two to three hours, the soldier moved them to one of the houses in Operova Street and they had to wait there. Towards evening a messenger arrived who led them to the collection place in the yard of the Catholic church.

Meanwhile Zeifel had moved heaven and earth in order to free those trapped in hiding places. Dr. Honigstein brought Shtehlle and Zeifel to the hiding place where the Orlinski couple and their family were staying and called to those in hiding to come out. When they came out, they were taken to the loot camp and from there to the smaller ghetto. The improvised hospital of the ghetto had gone up in flames together with its patients. The team of workers had found their deaths in the pits of Petralovitch. Drs. Cheslava and Kaplinski continued in the meanwhile working in the municipal hospital and passing medical material to the partisans. The Orlinski couple went out to the partisans while Kaplinski with his daughter and the survivors of his family moved to the town of Volkovisk.

In the appalling bunkers of that town where the remainder of the Jews of Volkovisk were trapped, Dr. Kaplinski passed some dreadful days together with the other Jews of the town. He lost his little daughter who couldn't cope with the inhuman conditions of the place. He was fortunate in surviving till the day of liberation, and emigrated to Israel in 1945,[36] where he was reunited with his wife and their son, who had already managed to emigrate from Russia during the war.

Life in the little ghetto of Mostova

Now there was no point at all in obeying the repeated orders of the non-Jewish partisans to remain in the ghetto in order to supply them with weapons and to fulfil their every request for various goods. The members decided to realise their ideal of going into the forest in order to fight and take revenge, and so those members and their families who had survived continued to infiltrate out of the ghetto into the forest.

Guides from the organisation would come back from time to time to the ghetto to take more people out, and they carried on bringing out of Slonim weapons and ammunition which they had managed to hide in the town before the massacre. And so they went back and forth from forest to ghetto on most days in July and August, until the underground organisation ended with the final annihilation of the ghetto.

Halfway through the month of July 1942, the air is still suffused with the smell of burning and the smell of burnt human flesh. The slaughter has stopped. Nothing but a pile of hot ash is left of most Jewish houses; the Jews who have survived are crowded into a few houses in a small section of Mostova Street, between the suspension bridge and the fence of the sawmill that once used to belong to the Jew Yezerski and now is worked for the Germans.

---

[36] *Prior to immigrating to Israel, Dr. Kaplinski told the police about Zeifel's actions and his humane behaviour in the ghetto, so that they could collect evidence from him of German crimes in Slonim. Zeifel was found and gave his evidence. He gave up his medical studies and worked in the post office. Several German criminals, among them the district governor, Erren, stood trial and were punished. Zeifel died in old age.*

Most members of the (underground) organisation have died; a few have managed to escape to the ghetto of Baranovitch or to ghettos in an area which is annexed to the Reich, but where extermination Actions have not yet been carried out. Of the municipal committee of the underground there remain Pesach Alpert and Avraham Doktortchik, the rest have died. However, the underground activity in the ghetto and outside it continues and has even been extended as more members have joined. The supply of weapons from the loot store has been reorganised and the people working in it were as follows: Erich Stein, A. Imber, Helinka Rodenstein, Sibosh, Manya Ackerman, Itzel Anuchnik, Genya Khanchinski, Nionia Tsirinski, Vova Abramson[37], Ya'akov Timan, Eliyahu Abramovski.

There was a change in the mood of the people of the ghetto. Now they were convinced that their situation was at its worst and they could not expect any improvement. Everyone was convinced that there was no escape from extermination. The link with the forest was renewed. The organisation took on an almost popular character and large, armed groups of members and their families started to move to the forest. However, this activity was now seventy times harder, as Jews were now made to walk to work arranged in lines according to their workplace. They were accompanied by guards and they had to return in the same order to the ghetto.

The story of Eliyahu Abramovski

Before the war Eliyahu, a carpenter by trade, owned a carpentry workshop. In the ghetto he had made contact with members of the underground, and he was one of the most active suppliers of weapons. During his time in Slonim, in the ghetto period and until they left for the forest, he worked in several carpenters' workshops. In one workshop he worked with Itche Rabinowitz, who was also an underground member. When he made contact with the underground, he took orders from Bublatski. Eliyahu tells us about his activities and his experiences in the ghetto of Slonim in his witness account:

"In the other workshop, where I'd worked with Itche Rabinowitz, we had to make coffins for Germans who'd been killed. At half past eleven we would go out in a group to the ghetto for lunch. Once, before we went out, we noticed that the bloodthirsty Hick, who often murdered Jews, was standing some way off in the window and looking in the direction of our workshop. We saw that as mortal danger and so we waited, hoping that he'd go off, but when Hick hadn't moved from his vantage point and it was already twelve o'clock, we started to go. When we passed close by where he was standing, he signalled us to stop and ordered me to go up to him. When Hick moved and started to come forward to me, I broke away from the group and ran away to the ghetto. Hick started to shout, "Where is he?" They told him I'd run off. He was boiling with anger and shouted hysterically, "Shmutzigeh Yuden, loos" (Get out, dirty Jews).

---

[37] *Vova Abramson didn't manage to get out of the loot camp and was killed.*

"I hid in the shelter for nine days until Hick left Slonim and went to Minsk. I had to hide because the engineer Volfstein, who was responsible for construction work, told me to report to Hick, and promised me that nothing would happen, he would just talk to me. But I didn't believe him.

"All during this time I was looking to make contact with the partisans. On orders from Bublatski, I approached Volfstein and asked him to send me to work in the carpentry workshop which was formerly under the ownership of the Jew Shelubski, and now was worked for the German district director. Zelig Milikovski and Shefchuk also worked in this workshop. After Shefchuk joined the partisans, I worked with Zelig. Our role was to pass onto the partisans arms and other goods which we would receive from the German loot camp. The order of work was like this: lunch break in the loot camp was from 11.30 am until 12.00 am. In that window of time we used to go into the camp. In the toilet which was on the right side of the entrance, not far from the main gate, our comrades who worked in the camp would already be waiting for us, and they would have the weapon parts which were destined to be smuggled out. Our meeting would be short.

"We used to take the "trefa"[38] and turn back towards the carpenters' workshop. However, smuggling weapons and ammunition out was not easy and it was not at all simple to walk the whole way with weapon parts hidden on your body.

"In the month of Tammuz I was allocated to transfer a Russian rifle with a length of 98cm. I wore a long coat and stuck the rifle into the trousers which I was wearing. I had to pass through Paradna Street, past the German employment office and after all, at any moment, I could have bumped into a German who would have stopped me. Another time I 'lifted' seven hundred bullets for the PPD. (Soviet submachine gun) on my way to the carpenters' workshop. By the yard of the synagogue a Belarussian policeman ordered me to stop. I ran off through the yards. I made a few detours and arrived safely at the workshop. It also happened once when I was taking parts of a PPD. submachine gun that we encountered German army soldiers who took us to the market square where Jews were hauling rocks back and forth. The Germans found this funny and were laughing and taking photographs. We worked there until sunset; I was forced to work with the hidden parts rubbing my body. I didn't get back to the workshop till evening.

"In the last days before I went out to the forest, I remained working only with Zelig. The rest of the workers were with their families in the ghetto. I used to stay the night in the carpenters' workshop. Almost the whole week partisans would arrive from the forest and take back with them people and weapons.

"One day we were told to go to Burski, which was in Zamoshcha Street, and bring some skins which were intended for the partisans to the workshop. We spoke to the Jews who collected the refuse from the town and we put on their clothes like sanitary workers, and hid the skins in the rubbish. We managed to

---

[38] *Non-Kosher - in this case, forbidden objects.*

bring them to the workshop where our comrades were already waiting for us and helped us hide all the skins up in the loft.

"The next morning, Ravitz came to the carpenter's workshop. He was a tailor by trade. He cut the skins into the leg shape of boots, and then there was nothing left to do but pass the cut skins to Ravitz's workshop, which was under the supervision of the civil directorate, and for him to sew the front and backs so that they could make the boots from them in the forest.

[39] Shusterovitch's Report

In the first half of the month of July 1942, Zhama Shusterovitch and Avraham Bublatski came to the ghetto from the forest. Their goal was to get out of the ghetto trunk-loads of ammunition which had been hidden before the day of the massacre. They went into the underground's shelter which was on the Aryan side of Podgorna Street. Zelig Milikovski and Karpel Shefchuk were responsible for this, but in order to be able to go into the ghetto you had to join one of the groups of Jewish workers who left in the morning for the burnt-out areas of the ghetto. A refugee from Warsaw, Mariampol, was responsible for the groups. The envoys from the forest met with Pesach Alpert and other comrades in order to synchronise the operation. Pesach and Avraham Doktortchik arranged to meet in the cellar of the underground movement and everyone went about his business. Avraham went to meet Nionia Tsirinski, and Pesach Alpert went to meet engineer Volfstein who was appointed to the work of clearing the ruins, and arranged with him that the next morning the envoys from the forest would be able to carry out their mission. As he was leaving the garden of his house, Doktortchik noticed Nyunya walking towards the house; the lad looked unusually fat. Avraham ran across the few metres separating him and Nionia and went after him into his narrow, dark little room. Here Nionia started to divest himself of the weapons and ammunition which he had tied round his body in the loot camp, and suddenly they became aware of sounds of panic which had seized the neighbours in the nearby rooms. Someone whispered to them across the partition, "Ritmayer is at the gate of the ghetto". Ritmayer was one of the murderers appointed by the civil district directorate. The boys shot out as quickly as they could, both they and their dangerous load with them, to the large vegetable patch which was behind the house and they hid among the stalks of peas and beans which grew all along the high wooden fence of the sawmill and were interlaced around high supports. After a little while they recovered and tied the tools which were so costly and dangerous around their bodies with a rope. For a long time yet they remained in that place.

When the sun sank, Nionia and Avraham crawled out of their hiding place, took the Star of David patch off their clothes, and via the nearby gardens and yards they reached the promenade of the Oginski canal. They crossed the canal on pine logs from unloaded cargoes and got out onto the bank by the Street of the Potters. Here they looked each other in the face and with hesitant steps, their

---

[39] *According to the memoirs of A. Doktortchik*

faces running sweat, they started to walk in the Aryan streets. When they encountered the curious glances of the first Gentiles who happened on their way, their self-confidence returned. They gave their walk the kind of suppleness and lightness peculiar to young people for whom there are no cares but the moment.

From a considerable distance they could see the carpentry workshop with the underground's shelter. The young men hastened their steps. The people who were responsible for the shelter could see them through the window. They waited by the door of the entrance, then the two weapon smugglers were swallowed up in the opening. Karpel Shefchuk told them that Pesach was already inside. They went down to the cellar and dismantled the load. By the flickering light of a kerosene lamp the two semi-automatic rifles were assembled and handed over to Waxman who was called Adolf by his comrades. Afterwards they embarked on a discussion about getting out the explosives and about the group that was to pass the load to the forest and join the partisans. Nionia went back with Avraham Bublatski and Adolf Waxman to the ghetto to be able to join Mariampol's group the next day, whereas Pesach and Avraham Doktortchik stayed in the shelter to hear from Zhama Shusterovitch about what was happening in the forest.

And this is what Zhama Shusterovitch, the ideologue of the underground, told them:

"Matters in the forest are not encouraging; in fact they are extremely worrying. Relationships between the Jewish and non-Jewish partisans are very undermined. Trust and vision have faded away. All the nice talk of brotherhood of the peoples has no basis in reality. In the forest the brute strength of the fist prevails. Fears and doubts have finished off the last spark of hope for a man of the ghetto for a life of uprising and fighting a common enemy. In fact doubts had started to gnaw at us back in the autumn of 1941 after our first contacts with the non-Jewish officers of the Red Army, the members of the Bolshevik Party who were hiding in the villages near the forests of Volchye Nori and Rafalovka. They were afraid of falling into German captivity but they also hesitated to go over to the centres of popular control like Proniagin, Dudko and others. They tried to hide their identity in different ways and to stay in the villages. Only after the threats of the German conquest did they register in the winter of 1941-42 with the occupying regime, and were obliged to present once a month to the German authorities. In this way they formed a bond with each other and then the idea of going into the forest and organising in partisan groups ripened, but the decision was carried out only when the Germans ordered them to report. Our organisation tried to get the partisans' support with weapons and ammunition. When we were asked to send them experts, we sent Dr. Blumovitch, the nurse Fanya Feigenbaum and the radio operator Ya'akov (Kobi) Zilberhaft, and Anshel Delatitski also went out to them. Then they praised our underground work and crowned us with superlatives - heroism, courage, Soviet patriotism and dedication to the Communist Party. However when we raised our claim for them to absorb our youth groups from the ghetto as fighters among their ranks, they put off our repeated request with all sorts of excuses. 'You must work within the boundaries of the town, to sabotage the civil and military institutions, to direct propaganda against the Germans, to act for us as intelligence and liaison, and to supply all our needs. That's your role' they claimed, 'and in this way your activity will be extremely useful.' All our counterclaims neither influenced nor convinced them. They barely agreed in the month of May, after the failure to get ammunition and hand grenades out of the loot camp, to take Itche Garchok, his sister and myself, Avraham Bublatski and David Blumenfeld into their group."

Crisis point was reached on 30th. June, when thirty men came to the forest following the slaughter of 29th. June. This the Soviet partisans could no longer digest and the abscess burst. They were startled by the Jewish 'invasion' of the forest. When the groups of Archik Bandt and Zerach Kremin arrived, they wouldn't accept them. A heated argument raged between them. The chief speaker was Mishka Povar ('the cook' in Russian), a primitive type, who decorated his chest with the military commendation "super cook", and to show off his standing, he had hung it on a shiny background made from the back of a rustic comb decorated with sparkling pieces. 'Why do we need them?' he claimed. 'When people know in the ghetto that we have absorbed so many of them, they'll all start to flow in their hundreds and there won't be any space for them in the Russian forests.'

"The more extreme threw at us: 'The Jews aren't fighters; they're cowards and they only want to save their despicable souls. We don't need parasites. Why do we need them, for heaven's sake? Let them go to hell. Little Jews like this will only give us a rotten smell in the view of the farmers around us. The local patriots won't see us as freedom fighters and insurrectionists any more, dedicated avengers of the German invader, but as hated friends of the 'Jewish community' which aspires to a regime of tyranny, which will come back and deprive them of their lands and imprison them in Kolkhozes or the camps of Siberia in order to 'put them straight'. We'll make the Mujiks resent us."

Mishka Povar had bent towards Dudko and whispered, "Please, let the little Jews come. They've got gold and lots of good things. We'll take everything from them and we'll bury them under the trees, there are enough trees for that. Little Mother Russia has broad hands and also deep, we'll find room for all the Jews in her depths."

That's how they contrived and schemed their plots. The few more aware among them didn't dare to condemn them, whether out of fear or out of disinterest in the whole thing.

"Well, but we're all Soviet people". Artiom, an Armenian railway engineer, tried to soften the hostile atmosphere with a gentle voice, but Mishka Povar turned with a movement of his hand to his comrades and said: "Well, come on then, comrades, let's go."

"How can you abandon a badly wounded friend with no pangs of conscience? Can you not see that he needs the devoted care of Dr. Blumovitch?" Artiom tried again to arouse their pity and pointed to his Georgian friend Seriozha, whose right hand had been crushed whilst sabotaging a telephone box on the Ruzhani Road.

"Oh, go to hell all of you", Mishka let out with a spit of contempt.

"On 30th. June in the evening Mishka and his gang left the forests of Raflovka. We remained nineteen people who had left the ghetto of Slonim and several non-Jews, and among them Pavel Vasilievitch Proniagin, a Russian mathematics teacher, Vasili Andreyevitch Volkov, Grigori Sergievitch Dudko, Kazak Kobani, the Armenian Artiom, the wounded Georgian Seriozha and his friend Morat Gadzheyev Haustin.

"We remained where we were, stunned with shock. In the darkness we took our few bits and pieces and moved into the nearby forests of Volchye Nori. Downcast from the experiences of the day, we stretched out to sleep on an open hill surrounded by pine trees.

"When 1st. July dawned, Andrei Leontiev appeared, a disguised Jew, commander of the 54 group, and with him a few comrades from the group. They brought some buckwheat cereal to break our fast and a little comfort for our grieving souls. Andrei approached us with, 'There are experienced fighters in our group. It wouldn't be a good thing to bring people from the ghetto into the group who are not yet trained in battle. You're Jews and here's a Jewish commander who escaped from captivity' and he pointed to Elioshka, the graduate of the infantry school in Kiev. 'Your group will be the 51st group and he will be your commander.'"

Zhama concluded his story about the setting up of the Jewish 51st group and these words were like daggers in the hearts of Pesach and Avraham Doktortchik. The two of them didn't linger anymore and left the shelter silently, as if Zhama's words had buried their last hope and trust in the future. In complete silence they made their way back to the ghetto and parted by the gate. Doktortchik went back to his tiny room where he was living with his father-in-law, the father of his wife Rina. He tried to fall asleep in order to release the tension, but difficult thoughts wouldn't leave him alone. The words that he had heard from Zhama, next morning's anticipated operation, the fate of the Jews who were drowning in a sea of blood and hate, gave him no peace.

"What's the purpose of our struggle?" he pondered. How can you explain the hate, that all the peoples hate us when they too are groaning under the yoke of the German jackboot? And now even those who could be our comrades-in-arms in the struggle have joined them. Will we be utterly destroyed and not even the slightest remnant of us? And even if lone Jews survive out of the avengers, they will find no peace and no comfort ......

Avraham Doktortchik wanted at least one moment before his death when he wouldn't feel humiliated, and to see even just once the fear of death in the eyes of the oppressor. In the morning he woke up tired, as if he hadn't slept at all. He said goodbye to his father-in-law and went out to his work in Borski, making leather goods for the Germans from the civil directorate. The work went very slowly and he had plenty of time to think without drawing the attention of the rest of the workers.[40]

---

[40] *From the memoirs of Avraham Doktortchik. On the day of the massacre of 29th. June, Rinah tried to move to another hiding place, but she was caught and killed. She still managed to shout:"Avraham, take revenge for me!" From then on Avraham lived with his father-in-law.*

CHAPTER FOUR: On the forest paths - to the partisans.

Zerach Kremin leads Jews to the forest

The move to the forest continued, despite the betrayal of the Slonim ghetto survivors by those who should have been their comrades-in-arms, and despite the disparity between the behaviour and the official declared ideology of the Bolshevik Party. It was a fact of life and the members of the Slonim ghetto underground had no other option, but every move to the forest was a national drama, and for every one of the Jews who sought to be accepted by a partisan troop it was personal drama.[41]

Zerach Kremin, who led out Henik Malach, Avraham Bublatski and Irka Weiselfisch on the evening of the massacre of 29th. June, tells how news of the Soviet partisans' behaviour shocked him:

"On the morning of 30th. June we reached the village of Zavershe. When we went into see our contact, he was scared and told me the place was crawling with Germans and police. He asked us to go into the forest and hide. When evening came he would tell the partisans, who would look for us.

"We were broken and exhausted after the day of massacre and a night of walking, but we had no alternative but to walk to the forest. There we saw a German lorry which was apparently collecting the last of its men, and we fled. It was hot and we were thirsty, but luckily, we found a spring. We took up a position by a tree which the partisans had felled in the middle of the road. From there we could see everyone who was going into the forest, whilst we were invisible. Towards evening we observed from our lookout point an armed group approaching us. From a distance it was hard to identify the people. I left my comrades on the spot and went to the edge of the forest towards the people who were coming, and then I recognised Archik Bandt with his group and David Perl and Herzel Shepetinski. Such joy in that meeting!

"Aaron told us that a large group of Jews, including the Shepetinski family, was now in the forest of Pruszkovo near Slonim, and they needed bringing here. We decided in the meanwhile to look for the brigade to which we were now attached, so we would know where to bring the people who came from the ghetto.

"We walked to the forest, to a crossroads, and the 51 group passed by us. We joined it and walked to where it was stationed. As evening approached we saw that bit by bit all the partisans of the 51 group were disappearing and we had no choice but to go to Volchye Nori, to the rest of the groups who had come from the ghetto."

---

[41] *There was much soul-searching over these issues: 1.Would other Jews (left behind) pay for the "crime" of their escape to the forest? 2. A personal drama – how could they leave family behind in the ghetto, parents or little brothers and sisters, who they couldn't take to the partisans?*

Zerach Kremin, who had not been broken by the tribulations and sufferings of the ghetto but rather whose strength to face the future had been toughened, describes what he and his friends felt when they learned about the shabby treatment by their Soviet comrades-in-arms:

"Our pain was sharp and the insult burned. How could these people, who called themselves Soviets, Communists, exploit the Jews of the ghetto who knew the true meaning of suffering, in this disgraceful way? People in whom we had trusted, who had daily endangered our lives so we could supply their needs in the forest, and equip them with weapons and ammunition…. And now, they'd taken the weapons and made off….!.

The survivors of the ghetto didn't feel humiliated, only insulted and angry at the betrayal. After all, they had made superhuman efforts in order to reach the forest as fighters and avengers. It hurt them that they had trusted people without conscience, whose level of morality was no higher than that of the Belarussian police who served the Germans.

But the members of the Slonim organisation recovered from this blow too. "We managed" says Zerach, "and by walking fast all night we reached Volchye Nori. We met several groups of partisans there who had come back from domestic acquisition missions. When they saw us, they charged us with, "Why are you going like lambs to the slaughter?" I answered, "Well, look, we're haven't been slaughtered, we're coming to the forest to fight", but they replied, 'Yes, yes, we know you'".

In the meantime, Proniagin and Dudko had left the group of Jews and gone to their partisan camp. In the afternoon they came back and brought the Jews food. As it emerged afterwards, Proniagin and Dudko had called a meeting of the group commanders and the politroks of the Shchors battalion. A stormy argument had broken out, and two resolutions crystallised: one was that of Zhenia Kazantsov, to spread the Jews out through all the groups, and the other suggestion was Andrei's - to allow the Jews to carry on in group 51. His reasoning was: if they're no good as partisans, we don't need them, and if they are, then they can organise themselves.

Proniagin and Dudko came back with the second decision. They allocated the Jews a deserted partisan camp and appointed the Jew Elioshka as commander, saying: "He's one of yours so he'll be your commander". Proniagin stayed with the Jews and later Dudko stayed too. The members of the minorities, Artiom and Morat, stayed because of Seriozha, their wounded friend, who needed the care of Dr Blumovitch. They set themselves up in the place allotted them next to the troop headquarters.

"The next day in the evening" Zerach Kremin relates: "Proniagin and Dudko accompanied us to the village of Zavershe. We went back to Slonim in order to bring arms to our brigade. I, Archik Bandt, David Perl and Herzel Shepetinski decided to go first of all to the forest of Prushkovo and bring back with us the people from the ghetto who were waiting to be accepted by the partisans. On the way we prepared food for them and looked for arms. Zvi found a rifle under the moss in the forest. In Pruschkovo we met survivors and brought them to the forest of Volchye Nori. Some of them chose to stay with peasants they knew."

On 6th. July a group set out, including Shabtai Moshkovski, Yasha Kremin, Adolf Waxman, Me'ir (Mayorek) Malach, Ze'ev Finkel, Noah Servianski, Baruch Burshstein, Mendel Galinski, Liuba Zhagel and Ya'akov Greenghauz, altogether ten men. On 13th. July, after midnight, another group went out and in it was Shepsel Greenghauz (the father), Grisha Greenghauz the son, Natan Finkel, Yakov Khatskelevitch and Yitzhak Boretski. Ze'ev Finkel, the brother of Natan, came first of all to the ghetto and explained to them the route they had to take.

In the second half of July, another group went out. Among those who went were: Avraham Doktortchik, Adolf Waxman who had returned to the ghetto, Avraham Bublatski, Zhenia Eichenbaum, Gutta Meirson, the first-aid nurse Fiera Kovarski, Itche Rabinowitch who brought out a typewriter that he'd taken from a German office, Zhama Shusterovitch, Karpel Shefchuk and others. They reached Volchye Nori on 19th. or 20th. July. However, when they reached the forest, there were bitter and testing disappointments awaiting them.

Shabtai Moshkovski joins the partisans

After the massacre of 29th. June Shabtai worked in a group of leather workers. On 4th. July he left his work, and this was his last day of work in the ghetto. Lili Blumenfeld now joined the group - Lili had previously come to the leather workers and worked as a cleaner in the workshop. Her husband David had already been in the 51 group for some time.

The members of the underground met after work and collected all the weapons that were there to take out to the forest. At the meeting it was decided to organise themselves as a separate group and to leave armed about ten minutes after the work groups went out. They had to go up the steps on the bridge to pass the town and carry on to the underground bunker in Podgorna Street. Everyone was carrying work tools to disguise this.

Sunday 5th. July 1942 before 6am. The little company was waiting in the ghetto behind the house for the craftsmen to leave for their jobs outside the ghetto. All the members of the group were armed, carrying parts of rifles, hand grenades and ammunition. After about ten minutes the group of those going to the forest moved towards, and through, the gate and turned towards the steps which led to the bridge. At the last moment they noticed that a member of the regional directorate, the "Shtahbsleiter", Shtelle, was standing on the bridge. At that moment they changed direction and went along the embankment to the end of the Shchara, to the second bridge, in order to get out to Ulanska Street and from there to the underground hiding place. They had only gone a few dozen metres when they heard behind them shouts of "Halt!" They had no alternative but to go back to the first bridge. They started to go up the steps. Shabtai was very troubled by the barrel of the rifle which was hung under his coat and reached up to his armpit. Just when they got to the bridge, and were already standing in two rows opposite the German, he asked, "Who are you, and to which professional group do you belong?" They replied that they were a group of workers going to collect electrical goods from abandoned houses in the ghetto. Shtelle yelled again, "Why are you late going out to work?" Just then engineer Volfstein, who was responsible for the Jewish workforce in the ghetto, appeared on the bridge. Of course, he didn't know where they were going either. Volfstein turned towards the German and said, "Allow me, Herr Shtabsleiter, to punish these people myself". Shtelle answered, "This time I'll let it go, but if it happens again I shall kill all of them" and he ended with a shout of "Loos" (Get out!).

It was as if a stone had rolled off our hearts, says Shabtai. We were saved, and with us our weapons. We went on our way, this time according to the plan we had laid down. We reached Podgorna Street and the carpentry workshop and we went down into the bunker through the secret opening in the sideboard, and put our weapons in it. In the workshop we found Burshtein who up till now had been a policeman in the ghetto. When he saw what was happening and the weapons we had brought, he asked to be included in our group. After a consultation, we decided to respond positively.

Burshtein and Shabtai remained in the bunker and the rest of us made another trip into the ghetto to the loot camp and back, and brought some more parts of weapons and ammunition. That night, the night of 5th. July, four people slept in the bunker - Moshkovski, Burshtein, Liuba Zhagel and another man.

On 6th. July there was much hustle and bustle in the workshop above the bunker. The members of the underground, Zelig Milikovski, Eliyahu Abramovski and Yitzhak Rabinowitch worked in it, sawing wood, banging with hammers and deliberately making a lot more noise than usual. And underneath in the bunker during the day more members of the group collected who were preparing to leave for the forest. They put together rifles and distributed ammunition. When the carpentry workers were about to return to the ghetto, everybody was all ready to set out for the forest.

The carpenters went and closed the main door behind them. Now they had to be really quiet so that the neighbours wouldn't notice that there were still people in the carpentry workshop.

"Life certificates" of the people who were going were collected and given to one of the members, who was responsible for staying and handing them over to the underground to distribute in the ghetto amongst those Jews without certificates. At midnight the camouflage lid was lifted on the bunker and everyone went out through the back door of the workshop. Silence reigned outside. Shabtai remembered with pain how he often used to go along that route when he was a scout in the Shomer Hatsa'ir movement.

They turned eastwards to the hills of Podgorna, keeping the Christian graveyard on the left side, and on through the sown fields, jumped over a broken fence, crossed the Ruzhani road and then they were on the right of the Jewish cemetery. Now they had crossed the Slonim boundary. Behind were the pits of Cheplovo and Petralovitch where the bodies of their dear ones rested. In the little ghetto of Mostova there were still members of the underground who were impatiently and hopefully waiting for news from them.

After describing a semicircle round the town, they went through the fields on a wide dirt track which leads to the small town of Kosovo and is also the route to the forest. Mendel Galinski was now leading the group as he knew the area. They didn't know exactly where the other groups were stationed who had gone out before them; they only knew that they would make contact in the village of Zavershe via the radio operator Volodya Fiedrik.

When they got very close to the village they stayed, waiting in the woods and Yasha Kremin and Galinski went into the village with pistols and hand grenades in their hands. In the house of the radio operator they met two Russian partisans from the group of Mishka Povar. These people asked where the weapons were; they replied that they were a big group and that they had left their rifles with their friends. From the Russians they learned about the setting up of the Jewish 51 group which was stationed at Volchye Nori and Volodya showed them the way to the forest. They carried on in the morning light and reached the forest of Rafalovka; on the way they saw the forester's house, but they didn't know who the people in the house were. To be on the safe side, they made a big detour in the forest and came out on the same road a distance of a kilometre and a half from the house, and then they decided to stay there for the rest of the day. It was 7th. July by then.

With sunset they continued on their way. Between Rafalovka and Volchye Nori, the group came across some armed people who approached them. These were Jewish partisans and Aaron Bandt and Zerach Kremin were with them. They fell upon each other, weeping for their murdered families and friends. The group led by Bandt and Zerach Kremin was on its way to the town in order to find out what had happened after 29th. June, as they had left for the forest on the night of the Action. Now they had some feedback and returned with the people who had come to Volchye Nori. On 8th.July Shabtai's group joined the Jewish 51 group.

The members of the underground had transferred Dr. Kremin and his wife from the Snovski metal workshop to the carpenters' workshop. Zerach went back to the ghetto to bring his uncle, Dr Moishe Kremin, and his aunt Anya[42] to the forest. They had been accepted in the Tchapayev troop which was commanded by Captain Fedotov.[43]

After three days, Bublatski went back to the ghetto, bringing a list of needs from the partisans in the forest. The city was full of Ukrainians and Latvians and they were on guard outside the town. Bublatski was not able to enter into the town and spent a whole day in the field, hungry and tired. Only at ten o'clock at night, when it was dark, could he enter and reach the carpentry workshop.

---

[42] *They did not survive to the liberation, and died in the forest.*

[43] *Fedotov was called "The bearded captain" by the partisans, because he liked to grow a beard.*

Avraham Doktortchik joins the partisans

The morning after the messengers from the forest had come to the ghetto, Zelig Milikovski told Doktortchik that he must come to a meeting. At the lunch-break Avraham got away from the place where he was working and went to the underground shelter. In the shelter he found Pesach Alpert, the messengers from the forest and with them Mariampol, a very scared Mariampol. Pesach said that the whole operation had failed; non-Jewish lads who had looted the houses of the murdered Jews in the ghetto had noticed how the members had piled suspect baggage on a cart and hidden it under fragments of linen. They informed that the Jews had hidden away gold under rags. Police stopped the cart by the gate of the ghetto and ordered them to take apart what was in it. Avraham Bublatski and Adolf Waxman made off immediately and fled to the underground shelter. They took Mariampol with them too so that he wouldn't be able to reveal the whole thing if he were arrested. The whole Jewish work group which was working to clear the ruins in the burnt ghetto scattered.

Among those who'd escaped was engineer Volfstein, who was at that time in charge of the construction of a club for the Germans. He would come and go from the offices of the Gestapo and the regional directorate. On one of his visits, a Gestapo worker asked him to show him his identity card. Volfstein offered his ID card; however the Gestapo worker said, "Not this one, the other one". Volfstein replied that he had no other certificate, but apparently the Gestapo had heard about forged certificates with Polish and Belarussian names that the Jews of the ghetto had been producing for themselves. Volfstein understood that he was suspect in the eyes of the Germans and got out of town. The Germans arrested his wife and imprisoned her in the cells of the local police station. However, she managed to escape on the same day. The traces of this couple disappeared and their fate is unknown to this day.[44]

The Germans wanted the whole group of workers who were working that day in the ruins of the ghetto (and trying to smuggle out weapons) to be handed over, just as they had wanted the Volfstein couple. They threatened to execute five hundred Jews. Those who'd escaped were not caught and the Germans returned to their normal routine without carrying out their threats.

Pesach informed Doktortchik that the organisation had decided he must immediately join the group that was leaving the ghetto that evening, because he was known in the ghetto in his blue work overall. "Had it not been for my wife's illness and my daughters", Pesach continued "I too would have gone straight away." Doktortchik accepted the decision without hesitation. He wrote a few words of goodbye to his father-in-law on a slip of paper and handed it to Pesach to deliver to the destination after he had gone.

During the afternoon, all the people in the group which was leaving went into the shelter, then slipped away with darkness. They organised into a single

---
[44] *Evidence of Dr. Noah Kaplinski*

file about a hundred metres from the shelter, in this order: Adolf Waxman and Avraham Bublatski with the "Mauser" and shoulder bags full of hand grenades marched at the head, behind them Mariampol with a shoulder bag full of rifle bullets, Doktortchik with a semi-automatic "Diegtyerov" rifle and a shoulder bag full of grenades and magazines; behind them Zhenia Eichenbaum and Gutta Meirson with shoulder bags full of rifle bullets, the nurse Fera Koverski with two bottles of pure spirit, various medicines and dressings in a rucksack, Itche Rabinovitz carrying a typewriter in a special rope harness on his shoulder, Zhama Shusterovitch with a "Mauser" rifle and a shoulder bag full of bullets, and Karpel Shefchuk with a semi-automatic "Diegtyerov" rifle and a shoulder bag full of hand grenades and magazines for his rifle.

They marched with fearful hearts. In fact, the clear night, sprinkled with stars and moonlight filled them with fear, these people who only yesterday had been prisoners. Every rustle, every chirrup of a bird, made their flesh creep. And now, there was the threat of five hundred Jews being killed. They moved cautiously along the path, which wound between grassy knolls, seven men and three women, laden to exhaustion for the trek, which to them was now the most precious in the world.

Every time they bumped into an obstacle it would echo in their ears like thunder, but the desire to wrestle with the enemy and to take revenge overcame everything. They marched all night and when dawn broke, they realised that their guides, Bublatski and Waxman had lost their way, and they were only a little distance from Slonim. When they stopped by a large field of rye, they inspected the area and determined that they were near the village of Skolditch, which was only about three or four kilometres from their town. For fear of the danger of discovery, they decided to go into the rye field and spend the night in the tall ears of rye. Only one person was left to keep watch, lying stretched out on the ground, and the rest of them lay among the tall ears and slept.

At noon they awoke, thirsty and hungry, dripping with sweat. In order to distract themselves a little from their situation, they began to crush ears of rye between their fingers and chew the ripe kernels. When it grew dark, they left the rye field and continued their march. They quickly came to a crossroads, and again, the guides didn't know which way to turn. They decided that Avraham should be in command, since he was a committee member of the (underground) organisation, and so should take the responsibility.

Avraham had served in the Polish army and taken part in battles at the outbreak of war. He had managed to escape from German captivity. Now he took the command and ordered everyone to lie flat in the dykes at the side of the road. He set up a guard, and, with Waxman, approached a nearby hut and knocked on the door. A woman's voice answered: "Who's there?" Avraham replied: "Partisans". A bolt was drawn, a man opened the door a crack, peeped out and welcomed Avraham with a greeting. Avraham asked him for a bucket of drinking water, a mug and a loaf of bread, and Waxman passed it all to the group. They then asked him to harness his horse and cart. The women got up on the cart and laid their burdens in it, the men marched on foot, and the farmer brought them to the village of Zavershe, where they arrived close to midnight. Here, they let the farmer go with his vehicle and went to the house of Fiedrik, their contact. The contact was not at home, but his wife described the route to the village of Okuninovo to them, and advised them as to where to get a horse and cart to continue their journey.

Unfortunately, there was neither house nor living soul to be seen anywhere. They could only make out the tree-tops on the horizon. Avraham Doktortchik decided to let the horse and cart go back to their master on their own, and the group deviated from the high road into the forest. At noon they reached a village, and found that it was in fact Okuninovo. Now Waxman and Zhama became leaders again. The group was divided into three bands and each one went separately into various houses to eat. After they had quelled their hunger, they got in two lines and went to a ramshackle shed which the partisans called "Woyenkomat" (the military office), or "Komandatura". The place served the partisans as a transit station or filter for people who wanted to be accepted to a troop. Usually the advance guard of the troop's camp stayed here. The three guides, Bublatski, Waxman and Shusterovitch, ordered the rest to wait there and they themselves disappeared among the forest trees.

The refugee group from the ghetto reached its destination, the camp of the 51 brigade, which was now stationed in the forest of Volchye Nori. This was on the 19th. or 20th. July, 1942.

The killing of Mariampol

The "Woyenkomat", was a broken down shed belonging to the past forestry authority, and stood on the edge of Volchye Nori, about half a kilometre from the forest. Doktortchik's group was ordered to wait here, even though the people belonged to the ghetto underground.

One of the principles according to which candidates who wanted to join the partisans were assessed was their social background. Of course, they weren't as bothered about non-Jews as about those who had fled the ghetto. Since the initiative and control in the partisan units was in the hands of the communists, they preferred first and foremost the people who belonged to the party or to the communist youth.[45]

The escorts Bublatski, Waxman and Shusterovitch took a narrow path which wound between tall grasses and bushes, and disappeared into them. They reported to headquarters on the failure in the task of getting arms and ammunition out of the ghetto, and on the seven people they had brought with them. Headquarters called in the central members of the 51, to hear their

---

[45] *This was also how people from other ghettos were judged – in the forests where the communists had set up partisan units. The situation was different where the instigators of the underground movements and partisan units were Jews. For instance: in Dr. Itlis' brigade, where most people were from the ghetto of Deretchin, in Misha Gildman's brigade from Koritz, in the P.P.O. Vilna brigade, in the Kruk troop in Vohelin, etc. The path of young people from the ghettos was often blocked due to these party considerations.*

opinion of the newcomers. They showed a positive attitude to those waiting in the Wienkomat, except for Doktortchik and Mariampol. Regarding Doktortchik, who had latterly been responsible for underground activity in the Slonim ghetto, they expressed resentment that the post in the ghetto had been abandoned. But those questioned also said that he had been active in the ghetto underground organisation, but that his social origin was dubious –he was from the class of the property owners. When Dr. Blumovitch heard this, he tried to persuade the commander that there was no foundation to the suspicions about Avraham, he knew him well and there was no reason to lay any fault at his door because of his social background. In Mariampol's case there were other considerations. A suspicion was voiced that it was he who had caused the operation to fail. The command asked what support those with reservations had for their suspicions. The prosecutors replied that Mariampol had collaborated with the invader. Dr. Blumovitch again tried to refute the claims: after all, Mariampol had fled with the others. If he had been a collaborator he would have stayed put, in order to identify the envoys from the forest and arrest them. The command decided to attach everyone to the 51 group, save for Doktortchik and Mariampol, and to leave them meanwhile in the forest close to the camp, so that they could hear more, detailed, evidence concerning them, and decide the men's fate at their discretion.

Shortly after, the silence of the forest was split by a sharp whistle. Aharon Bandt, Ya'akov (Koba) Zilberhaft and other comrades had come out of the forest to greet the newcomers. They welcomed the newcomers to the group gladly and took them to the camp.

The forest was dense and dark, and silence reigned, broken from time to time by the sounds of night birds. After an exhausting walk, hopping over uprooted trees, jumping over puddles and a shallow rivulet, they reached a bare hill, surrounded by tall trees. On the top there projected a look-out made of criss-crossed logs, and a shelter covered over with birch branches, stuck out on its northern edge. They stopped here. The whole group except for Doktortchik and Mariampol went on their way, but the two of them were ordered to stay where they were. They were puzzled as to what this meant, and with trepidation watched the others moving into the distance. Then they sat by the shelter and fell silent. Suddenly they heard a rustling of twigs, and Archik Bandt appeared in front of them with half a loaf of bread, honey and a bucket of cool water.

When Mariampol went into the shelter for a moment, Archik whispered to Avraham that he must spend the night there with Mariampol and keep an eye on him, as tonight they would discuss his history in the ghetto and his fate would be decided. Archik left them and the pair remained alone.

In the darkness of the forest night fireflies flashed over rotten tree trunks, lighting up and fading by turns. Avraham couldn't sleep. The thought was troubling him: Why was he in particular prevented from entering the camp? What was his crime? Mariampol was also turning from side to side, trying to go over what he had done in the ghetto.

Dawn broke. Anshel Delatitski and David Blumenfeld stood in the entrance to the shelter. Doktortchik and Mariampol got to their feet immediately and went towards the camp. They marched in twos, David Blumenfeld and Mariampol first, and Avraham and Anshel behind them. After a few moments, Blumenfeld quickly drew his pistol and shot Mariampol in the back. The latter managed only to shout "Oi!" and collapsed in a heap. Doktortchik froze, numb with shock and amazement, burning with anger. Drops of cold sweat covered his body. Delatitski gave a glance of vicious scorn, raised his right shoulder and from under his army tunic, he drew three small spades and offered one to Avraham. However, Doktortchik was unable to hold the spade. The other two quickly dug a hole, laid Mariampol's body in it and covered it with earth. After that they trod on the mound of the grave, firmed the sandy soil with their feet and carefully covered it with fallen pine needles.

Doktortchik was deeply disturbed by the manner of Mariampol's killing and trailed behind the pair back to the camp. All the way he tried to keep level with them, or behind them – maybe they would put a shot in his back? Who knew? Maybe someone had falsely accused him, and he too had been sentenced to death? Pale and sunk in thought, Doktortchik went into the camp. He was immediately brought before the commander, Fyodorovitch, who was sitting by his tent with Zhenia Eichenbaum, who from their first meeting the day before had captured his heart with her youthful charm.

Just then Dr. Blumovitch approached the commander's tent. He welcomed Doktortchik with a silent smile. The commander instructed them both to be seated, turned to Doktortchik and asked him about the events of the final days in the ghetto. Avraham recounted their inability to get the arms out of the ruins and about the members' decision that he should leave the ghetto. The commander was deep in thought and one could see that he was wrestling with a problem over Doktortchik. A moment later he turned to him and said: "Who is responsible now for the activities of the organisation?"

"A senior member, Pesach Alpert, a fighter of the Red Army, an experienced underground man from the days of the Polish Republic and a member of the municipal committee of the underground from its inception" answered Avraham.

The commander weighed this up for a moment and declared: "You're staying here, you can go".

Then Doktortchik went up to Fira Kovarski and she told him that the day before the Headquarters of the troop had sat in judgement with the brigade commanders. David Blumenfeld, Anshel Delatitski and Irka Weiselfisch had prosecuted Mariampol – they said that Mariampol, whilst a manager for the work of clearing the ghetto ruins, had once, for some reason, beaten a Jewish boy. Opinions were divided: there were those who suggested the death sentence, while others suggested sending him back to the ghetto or transferring him to another ghetto. The radical group was the decisive one.

Day one in the combat group

Archik Bandt invited Doktortchik to his tent and made room for him. The tent was constructed like all the rest, a triangle covered with birch branches. Five young men and one young woman were living there: Liuba Abramchik-Bandt, Archik's brother Avraham, Shabtai Moshkovski, David Perl and Aharon. Archik brought Avraham a Russian rifle and magazine, and told him that he was to go out that very evening with the group on "food acquisition", and he would learn about partisan activity from experienced comrades. Meanwhile, he must prepare his weapon.

They were already beginning to prepare lunch in the kitchen when the group went out to a clearing in the forest and trained in laying road blocks with felled trees, in making an assault, in digging foxholes for the single fighter and shooting practice. During the exercise, the unit commander, Lieutenant Borisovitch Podolski From Stalino, who had escaped the Stattin prisoner of war camp, approached Doktortchik, saying: "Look, I'm a Jew, but I know nothing about my people, neither its distant nor its recent past, nor about its culture. I have no idea why we are being persecuted. Why are we hated - and not only by the "Fritzs"? In the P.O.W. camp, I was afraid of fellow fighters. I know of many instances of informing and arrest of Jewish comrades by Russian, Ukrainian and even "Naatzmeni" P.O.W.s. (the ethnic minorities of the Soviet Union). You, Doktortchik, have grown up among Jews, have received a Jewish education, and you must know a lot about our people. Can you explain it all to me?"

Doktortchik and his commander agreed to try to go on missions together in future, so then they would be able to talk about it freely and at length.

The exercises were finished to the satisfaction of the troop's operations officer, Merzliakov. They went back to the camp and sat down to eat a lunch of soup with grits, potatoes and slices of pork. In his unit, Podolski organised a section for a new acquisition mission, and included Doktortchik in it.

The destruction of the Underground shelter in the carpenters' workshop

Eliyahu Abramovski has this to say about the last days in the carpenters' workshop

"Tension reigned in the town, as the partisans had burned a house six kilometres away from the town. When Bublatski arrived at the workshop we lay down to sleep. And then at midnight, we were woken by shots close to the workshop. At first we grabbed the automatic rifles and wanted to open fire, because we could hear voices behind the door into the workshop. But we remembered that Bublatski was asleep in the basement. We woke him, explaining that we had to abandon the workshop fast. We took the most important things, and left by the back door."

The men succeeded in getting away, laden with medicines and arms. They marched at a distance of ten metres from each other. A guard, who the enemy had left near the workshop, became aware of their presence and fired after them, but they managed to get into a cornfield and wait there till the whole trio gathered. On the way they went into the village of Skolditch, took a horse and cart from a farmer and Bublatski brought them to the camp lookout of the 51 brigade. They got Zelig Milikovski into the camp immediately, but sent Eliyahu Abramovski to the family camp, since his social background as a past carpentry owner would not have been acceptable to the communist members. After Zelig Milikovski intervened, they brought him to the camp and he was accepted into the group.

The sudden appearance of Abramovski and Milikovski in the forest amazed everyone. Following orders of the (underground) organisation, they were to have remained in the ghetto until the last underground members had left. Why had they abandoned their position so early? They explained what had happened in the carpentry workshop.

Later, it emerged that Belorussian police had surrounded the house. It wasn't clear to the organisation's members how the police had found out that there was an Underground hiding place there – who had informed? After the three of them had fled, the police penetrated inside, removed the weapons and ammunition which had been left behind and set fire to the house. A report was published in the local Byelorussian newspaper of "The great police victory, which had wiped out the partisan headquarters". There was a list with fabricated details of the many partisans whom the police had killed there, and of the prisoners who had fallen into their hands.

Avraham Orlinski reaches the partisans

At one point, Dr. Cheslava Orlinski received a letter from Dr. Blumovitch in the forest, asking her to organise a group of doctors and nurses to serve with the partisans. They were to bring medical equipment and medicines. Cheslava contacted several doctors, who conveyed their willingness to enrol. But there were also doctors who refused, since they couldn't leave their families – elderly parents, wives and young children. They stayed with their families, even though they knew that they couldn't save them.

Avraham Orlinski, who was among those still working in the abandoned ghetto, was forced to escape after the failure of the operation to get the arms out to the forest. He managed to get to the small ghetto and tell his wife what had happened. Cheslava begged her husband to leave the ghetto immediately. Orlinski succeeding in getting out, but he had nowhere to go. So he went to the market square, as if he were hurrying to his work place in the factory. He reached the factory, once owned by a Jew, and saw that they were about to close and the workers were preparing to leave.

Orlinski was afraid to say that he wanted to stay and pass the night there, so he went out with them and approached another factory, in Podgorna Street. Maybe he could stay there? But from speaking to people on the spot, he realised that he couldn't tell them why he had come. Down-hearted at the situation, he turned back and sat on a bench by the house. And then, at the end of the road he saw a half-open gate with a door into a yard. A person stood at the entrance. As he approached, Orlinski recognised him – it was Vatzek Vilchinski, the underground liaison with the partisans. Orlinski had not known that Vatzek lived here, and ran towards him to tell him what had happened. Vatzek said that he (Orlinski) would be able to leave that same night, with Zerach Kremin, who was leading a group from Mitos Snovski's factory.

They went into Vatzek's house, and Orlinski showed his papers. In the evening they went over to Mitos, where Vatzek left Orlinski in the company of Zerach.

At eleven o' clock at night they both left Mitos' factory for the carpenters' workshop. It was completely silent, all the houses were asleep. Zerach knocked lightly on the workshop door. Several people should have been waiting for him the basement, but there was no answer to his knocking, and so he concluded that the group wasn't coming and decided that the two of them would go on their way. Silently, they crossed the alley and came to the Christian cemetery. They crossed the Rozhani road, went into the Jewish cemetery, and continued on their way to the field. They reached the Slonim-Kosovo path and carried on close to the small town of Zhirovitza. The place was swarming with Belorussian police, and they had to take care that the dogs wouldn't sense their presence and alert the police with their barking. With dawn they had arrived close to Zavershe.

Now Orlinski could breathe fully. The fine weather, suffused with the forest smells, inspired a good mood. He felt that he was breathing freedom. They marched quietly, each of them sunk in thought, until they reached a forest thicket. Here Zerach stopped, and said that Orlinski should wait there for him to return. He himself went into the thicket and disappeared.

Orlinski waited, feeling cut off from all the anxieties of this period. He wasn't thinking about what had happened, or about what might happen, almost as if he were absorbed in the sheer experience of nature. It seemed that not long passed before Zerach appeared with a man dressed in army trousers and boots, with the upper half of his body bared. This was a partisan commander, called Vassili Volkov. He inspected Orlinski without asking him anything, and approved his entry into the camp. The three of them passed between the trees and came to a forest clearing, and here Orlinski saw young men and women, brothers and sisters united by their fate.

From the day the Germans had entered Slonim, Orlinski hadn't known inner peace like this. He had no illusions about the difficult situation of the Jews under the Germans, albeit he had never imagined that this regime would lead the Jews to complete annihilation. Neither had he believed the news of the destruction of the Jews of nearby Zhirovitzi, which had reached him shortly before the slaughter in Slonim on 14th. November. When he had checked it out, he had found that it was true.

Initially he was preoccupied with concerns for survival and how to endure, but then he became sold on one idea: how to take revenge on the Nazi beast? How to defend themselves? And his tension had grown and grown. Now the tension receded. For the first time in his life he understood the true meaning of freedom, and it was a thrilling feeling. Exhausted from this new experience he lay on the ground and fell asleep.

Dr. Cheslava Orlinski reaches the forest

Cheslava saw her husband getting out of the ghetto, by the bridge, crossing it and going on to the city centre. Days passed without news from him. Her searches for some contact with him brought her to Vatzek Vilchinski. He told her that her husband had arrived in the right place, and that in future, contact with him would be via Mitos Snovski.

Meanwhile, many of the ghetto survivors made great efforts to save themselves from the net of death. Many people started to disappear, and the anxiety for those left behind intensified. In an atmosphere of hopelessness Cheslava remained alone. Even doctors with whom she had worked and was close to, were disappearing one after the other, some to the forest, and some seeking refuge in other towns, which had not yet been subject to the murderous Actions.

Cheslava was delighted at the news that her husband was in a partisan camp, and rushed to tell her brother-in-law, Pesach, Orlinski's brother. Pesach was only fifty-six, but considered himself too old for partisan warfare. He decided to leave Slonim and make for Pruzhani, where his relatives were still living.

Once, Mitos Snovski approached Cheslava and handed her the address of the carpentry workshop on Podgorna Street, where she could meet her husband. When she got there they took her inside. She stood in the middle of the room, looking for her husband. With the help of the comrades, she saw an opening on the floor of a cupboard standing against the wall, and just above the floor she saw her husband's face.

You could remove the floor on the left side of the lower section of the cupboard, revealing the entrance to the basement, where the arms and ammunition were hidden.

That night, Zerach, Kremin, Avraham Orlinski and Ze'ev Finkel had arrived from the forest to get spare parts of weapons and ammunition to the forest. They had entered Slonim before the night was over, and planned to return the next day at midnight. During the day, they rested in the basement.

When Cheslava saw her husband, they were both happy but worried. Orlinski had to go back without his wife, as she still had not been told when she was to leave for the forest. At the same time, her brother-in-law Pesach and Dr. Kaplinski were on the point of leaving the ghetto. Cheslava was friendly with the Kaplinski family, and they had encouraged and supported her when she was left alone. Dr. Kaplinski suggesting joining him on his way to

Pruzhani, but she longed to get to the forest, to her husband. Meanwhile, she went on working in the municipal hospital, collecting up medical instruments and medicines for the partisans. After her friends left she suffered unbearable loneliness. The Germans had noticed the disappearance of many Jews, and treated those remaining more cruelly. They shot any Jew they suspected of being about to escape.

Since the Germans were seized with anger at the disappearance of Dr. Kaplinski from the ghetto, Cheslava decided to spend the nights in the hospital, explaining that she was doing this for the patients. The head doctor of the hospital, a Polish nun, Dr. Neushevski, was fond of Cheslava and agreed to this. But the matron began to complain about the disappearance of clinical instruments, and the danger to Dr. Cheslava grew.

After her husband had left, Cheslava saw through a window in the hospital that Mitos Snovski was approaching the building. He had come to inform her that at four in the afternoon she was to report to his factory, with medicines and the medical instruments she had collected, and that night she would leave for the partisans.

Cheslava visited the patients as usual, gave her instructions for continuation of treatment, and went to the head doctor, Dr. Neushevski, with a request to be allowed out, to deal with several personal matters. The nun fixed her with a penetrating but friendly look, as if she understood her actions, and even approved of them. After that, she kissed her and said:" Go, my dear, may G-d be with you". And so they parted.

This nun's approach to the Jews was supportive, as it was to all those persecuted by the Germans. Before they withdrew from the town, the Germans murdered this doctor nun.

Now Cheslava had to take two suitcases with medical equipment, and carry them to Mitos' factory. It was beyond her strength. She imagined that the messenger, Snovski, would help her to carry the load, but he had gone off. Thus she turned for help to two Christian nurses who worked with her in the hospital and who were fond of her, both as their superior and as a good person. They decided that one of them would go with Cheslava. The nurse grasped the cases without asking what they contained or who they were for, and went out behind Dr. Orlinski, keeping a reasonable distance so that it wouldn't look as if there were any connection between them. Like that they walked to their destination until Cheslava saw Mitos coming towards her. Then she stopped the nun, asked her to put down the cases and go back, and the two of them parted as friends.

Mitos came up after the nun had gone some distance and carried the cases to the factory, where she met the partisan Piletski, a local Byelorussian, a one-time Soviet policeman, and led by him she left in the night for the partisan camp. Piletski's Jewish wife, Dora Derechinski, went with them, and Dr. Paretski and Erich Shnur.

Dr, Cheslava was walking along a path through the fields. Tall ears of corn grew up on both sides, but she didn't see which crop they were in the dark night. Piletski, who was walking in front of her, was a tall man, wearing army boots and holding a pistol in his hand. He kept a fast pace, and Cheslava felt unable to keep up with this speed. Should she tell Piletski that she couldn't go on? She debated this, and then she heard: "The Germans are about three hundred metres from us, maybe even nearer. We must quicken our pace."

A new strength now took shape within her, as it were, and she was surprised that she felt no fear, only a strange determination. She was sure they would get away from the enemy. She marched faster, so as to walk by Piletski's side, and no longer felt tired. She was just anxious for Dr. Paretski, who was carrying a heavy suitcase and breathing with difficulty. There were surgical instruments and dressings in his case. She recalled a nurse from the surgical unit, who had complained to her that someone was stealing instruments and that soon there would be no means of carrying out operations left in the hospital. "You'll have to tell the unit manager about it, so they won't suspect you. At times like this, it's best that you don't take responsibility on yourself" - Cheslava had answered her, and that day she had herself taken instruments and brought them to Dr. Paretski.

In a moment, she remembered the Jews wasting away behind the barbed wire fence, and guilt swept over her: Maybe she shouldn't have left them there? Maybe she should have remained to die with them? At that moment she heard Piletski whisper, to be alert and take note of what was happening around them: "The Germans are very close to us. If the dogs bark, we're lost." All her musings came to a stop. After a few minutes had passed he calmed her, now they were on a good road and the Germans were already behind them. They wouldn't come into the forest.

Cheslava looked around her – she hadn't even noticed that they had entered the forest. She had supposed that they were still walking between the ears of corn. Now they were able to rest a little. Cheslava peeped at Dr. Paretski, thinking how pitiful he was. He had lost his whole family and all the life had gone out of him. He was weighed down with deep emotions and only the desire for revenge burned in him. She herself felt very happy: only twenty kilometres separated her from her husband. How was Dr. Blumovitch, she wondered? In her mind's eye she could see his well-built, masculine image, his large, bald head, his wise eyes, his lovely smile. An interesting man, she thought. She remembered her conversations with him, before he left for the forest, when she told him of her wish to join the partisans. Now they would meet again within a few hours.

The next day Cheslava met up with her husband in the Shchors battalion camp. In the camp she went on caring for the sick and the wounded, and her husband was in active combat.

Between hope and despair

The pathway of other members of the organisation to the partisan troop was not easy. Many of them, particularly the women and the young, experienced empty promises, expectations and rejections - they were tossed between hope and disappointment until they were accepted. Even after that they weren't sure of their status, and many were actually thrown out after they were accepted, and sent to the family camp.

The two Shepetinski families, who had left the burning ghetto on 29th. June, had reached the outskirts of the forest at the place called the "Kommandatura" by the partisans. They were ordered to wait here. Partisans who passed by left them a little food. There were men, too, waiting there. They gathered wood for a bonfire and cooked their meagre food in a bucket hung on a tripod of sticks over the fire. In the Shepetinski families' group there were also young children of five and seven, the brothers of Yasha and Hertzel. The house where they had been staying was a long way from the nearest village and close to the forest of Volchye-Nori, where the partisans were encamped. There was a cornfield close by, and the children played among the tall ears of corn. Sometimes mounted partisans would meet the children and agree to give them a ride on their horses.

The days passed slowly amid expectations, and people still didn't know what would happen to them. Recently there had been a certain tension. They had seen a large group of armed partisans go past, and had been told that the fighters were on their way to a combat mission, but as usual, they weren't told what it was.

Zvi Shepetinski has this to say about his experiences until he reached the partisan unit: "We reached the forest on 30th. June. We lay among the trees broken and exhausted, but no one could get to sleep. We weighed up what we should do. We knew very well that all our little band, with its women, and its young and old, wouldn't get into a partisan unit. As the day dawned we noticed that the forest which we had reached was very sparse – impossible to hide there. The day was interminable, we felt neither hunger nor thirst, only one thought occupied us: how to contact the partisans.

"We looked for weapons. We poked every little mound of soil sticking out of the ground with sticks and iron bars. We discovered many signs that arms had been there, but found nothing. Apparently local peasants had collected them. And then I came across something hard beneath a tall tree, in a soft spot covered with moss. I started to dig with my hands and came up with a whole Russian rifle with bullets and with a bayonet stuck in it. This find encouraged us and we continued to search. However, we found nothing more. I went back to our families with the rifle. Bublatski, who was older and better trained than me, got the rifle, and he gave me his old rifle, which wasn't in working order.

"In the morning the young people who were armed decided to go off to the partisans and promised to return in a few days and take the rest of us. We remained under the protection of a few lads who had two rifles and a little ammunition."

The days and nights dragged on for an eternity. Two weeks passed and no one came to them. The families were hungry and despair began to gnaw at people. Zvi and two little cousins would go to the village to beg slices of bread and potatoes, though not every peasant who was approached gave anything. It was easier for the family of (Zvi's) Uncle Yitzhak. His wife Hannah came from that area, and peasants she knew would prepare parcels of food for her, and they had some hope that sooner or later, someone would come for them, as three of their sons – Yasha, Herzel and Reuven – were in the partisans, whereas Zvi was very fearful for his future and that of his family.

And then his uncle Yitzhak received a message to report to a certain place, so that the troop commander could investigate him and decide the fate of his family. On a very dark night the uncle's family left for the appointed place. Now Zvi's family was left alone, without contact and without hope.

It was risky to stay in the same place, as too many local peasants knew of their existence, and so they moved to another forest. However, in the new place they found no peace or rest either, and no food – Belorussians, pretending to be friendly, came and told them that the police visited their village regularly.

Zvi went on:

"The cold morning wind brought us to our feet and we went on our way. We reached the Slonim-Kosovo road. Farmers we came across on the way told us about the destruction of the Slonim ghetto. They said we should go to the partisans, as that was the only place where they weren't murdering Jews. One of them suggested going towards Biten and looking there for a contact with the partisans.

"In the morning we came to a big forest. A good peasant let us in to his house to wash, and even gave us his breakfast and some bread for the journey. He gave us directions to get to the village of Volchye-Nori, where we would find a partisan contact.

"We arrived in the village that same day, and on the way we met two partisans, who stopped their cart and came up to us. They interrogated us for a long time, and lectured us on why we hadn't left the ghetto earlier, said we had been working for the Germans, that we had handed over our gold and not armed ourselves. In answer to our question, how to join the partisans, they instructed us to go about ten kilometres to a certain place, and there they would wait for us at eleven o'clock with their commander. When my father got out his watch, in order to set the time, one of the partisans asked for the watch and promised to return it at the meeting. We went on our way. When we drew near to the place the two partisans had described, rapid volleys split the morning silence. We heard shouting and orders, which were hard to make out because of the distance. The whole thing seemed suspicious to us. We were suspicious of the two partisans, that they had deceived us and led us to this place in order to get rid of us. It was where, as we discovered later, the Jews of Biten had been murdered a little while previously.

"Despondent we retraced our footsteps towards Volchye-Nori. We went into a farmer's house and rested a little. There we were told of the slaughter of the Jews of Biten. The farmer gave us directions to the "Kommandatura". We also met a Jew from Slonim, who was already a partisan, but lacking weapons, had been put to work in the kitchens. He too was afraid to speak to us. He showed us the way and begged us not to let drop a word about our conversation.

"From a distance we spotted a lone shack near the forest. We crept up to it cautiously, and to our surprise, my Uncle Yitzhak and his wife and children were in it. They had arrived there several days ago. For the first time since we left the ghetto we ate till we were satisfied – bread, potatoes and boiled meat, which the partisans had brought from the town.

"The next day the command of the Shchors battalion arrived plus two people from the 51 brigade, together with Dr. Blumovitch. After I told them everything we'd been through they promised to return and take me to the troop. My Uncle Yitzhak and his family had been accepted into the 51 brigade by virtue of their three sons who were in the troop. A day later they accepted me too."

In the evening of that very day the partisans went out on the Kosovo mission. Meanwhile the parents and children stayed in the Kommandatura. A week later two family camps were set up in the area, close to the partisan camp. These were the Biten and Kosovo camps, and were called the 59 and 60 troops. Zvi Shepetinski's family was moved to the Biten camp. However, Zvi still had no weapons and so was not included in partisan activities.

THE CARPENTRY

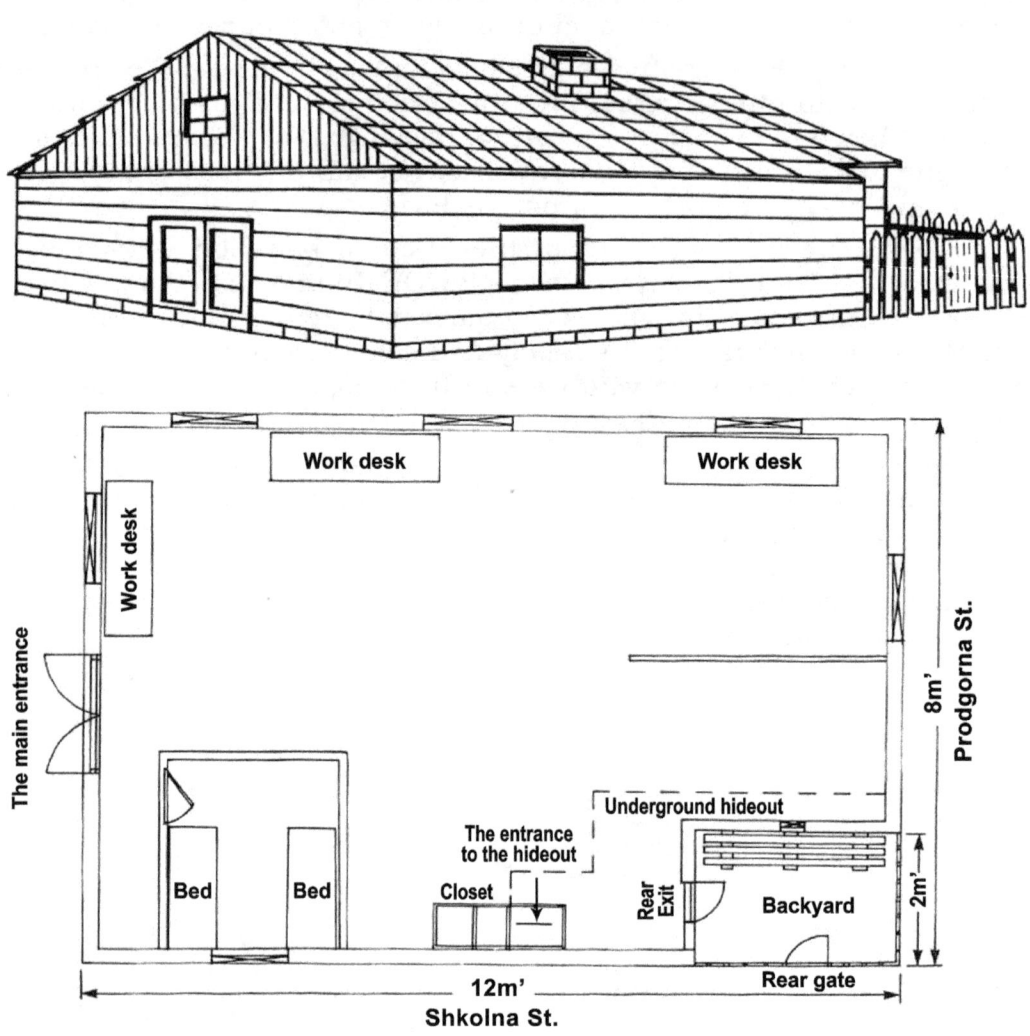

THE HIDING PLACE AND WEAPONS CACHE AT THE CARPENTRY

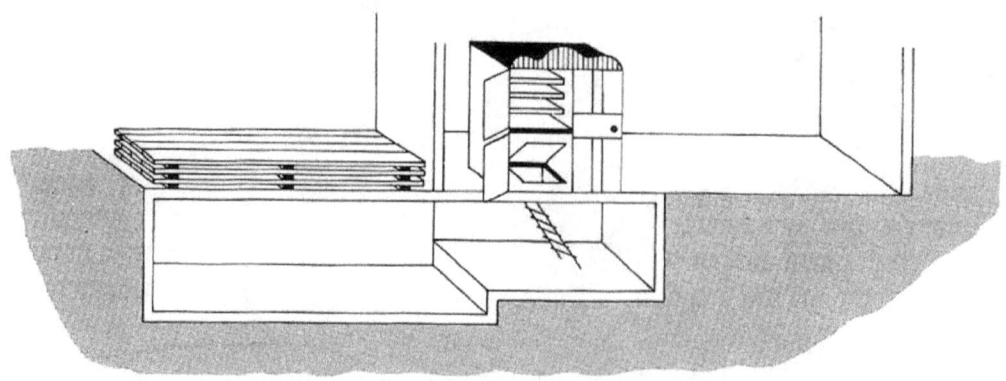

CHAPTER FIVE: The Torments endured by the Young Women on their way to the Forest

The path of the Jewish men and members of the fighting underground to the partisans was hard, but that of the women was so much harder. More than once they were forced to slip out of the ghetto on their own initiative and to wander in the fields, the villages and the forests looking for a link with the partisans. And even when they found that link, they were forced more than once to go back to the ghetto in misery and then to try a second and a third time. The partisans refused to accept young Jewish women.

Families also left Slonim for the forest, most of them brothers, sisters and parents of the partisans who had already been integrated into fighting troops with their small children. A woman whose brother was in a fighting battalion and the wife of a fighter had more chance of being accepted. Envoys would often arrive from the forest in order to get their families out but generally a young woman had to make her way under her own steam. In many cases the young girl would have lost contact with her brothers or with her husband in the troop when they changed their camp, and her way was paved with tribulations and suffering.

The Journey of Krusi Abramchick

Krusi came from Ostrov Mazovietzk and had reached Slonim as a refugee. She had survived the massacre of 29th. June by hiding in a shelter. Her sisters - Liuba and Liza - were already attached to the underground. At night, friends arrived and called her younger sisters who went out accompanied by Aaron Bandt, but Krusi was left behind because she couldn't leave their parents. During that night the people from the shelter stayed outside and saw the ghetto burning and heard the whistle of bullets. With dawn they went back to their hiding-place. In the same house there were two hiding-places, but in the confusion which broke out Krusi was separated from her family and went down into the other hiding-place. She saw crowds of peasants going into Jewish houses and looting them.

On 2nd. July they heard the voice of a Jew declaring that the slaughter was over and Jews in hiding could come out. The people hiding noticed a smell of petrol and realised that they were about to burn the house down on them. Despite that, they didn't go outside. After a little while the Germans came back and with them another Jew, and they started to dig in the house. They found the first hiding place; they caught everybody and it is not known where they took them. Krusi sat in the other hiding-place another two days. The massacre went on and she decided to go to the forest. Yonah Milikovski, who was also in that hiding-place, and knew where Archik Bandt had gone, suggested leading the people to the village of Skolditch where he thought they could meet up with the underground.

Six days from the beginning of the slaughter, eleven people left the shelter and reached Skolditch. The farmers refused to give them food so the Jews wandered round the area, hungry, for a whole week. They met peasants who told them that the slaughter in Slonim had stopped and advised them to go back to the ghetto, so they decided to go back. When they reached the brick factory Krusi and another Jew went to the house of a Polish citizen to ask what was happening in the ghetto. The Pole told them that the slaughter was continuing and Krusi went back to where the group had been, but not a soul was there because in the meantime the Germans had caught everybody. With no alternative, and in despair, Krusi went back to the ghetto. There she joined a group of workers and tried to get a "life certificate". Seeing that the Germans were still catching Jews and taking them to the pits, Krusi sold the "life certificate" which she'd received for a pair of shoes and went back to the forest. A friendly peasant took her out to the village of Skolditch and there she met Archik Bandt's father and Shimon Milikovski. Then she Kremin and Archik, and they brought her to Troop 51.

The Story of Yehudit Shelubski-Graf

Strange and difficult twists and turns of fate were the lot of Yehudit. At the time of the German occupation she was a young girl of sixteen, and when the war broke out, she'd managed to complete ten years' study at the high school in Slonim. In the ghetto she worked with fifteen Jewish girls in the vegetable garden which belonged to a German company. When the Action of 29th. June 1942 erupted, her mother went out to see what was happening in the ghetto and as she reached the ghetto gate she saw how the German officer shot Gershon Kvint, head of the employment bureau of the Judenraat, who had been standing by the gate to accompany Jewish workers going out to work. This murder was the signal for the slaughter to begin. Yehudit's family hid in a cellar during the Action. The Germans searched with the help of dogs and they threw grenades into the houses. From all sides you could hear the sound of explosions, shots, brutal soldiers screaming and the voices of the victims. The family stayed in the hiding-place until 3rd. July when suddenly they heard the voice of a Jew calling out: "Men, come out. They'll take you to work and the women can stay in the ghetto". The men who'd been sitting in the hiding-place believed it and went out. In a few moments they took the women out too. A German pulled Yehudit out of the hiding-place by pulling her hair. Everybody was taken to the prison, where they were commanded to stand all along the walls and give over everything that they had. Afterwards their belongings were searched and they were locked up in cells, men and women separately.

Yehudit was locked up with her mother. They were given no food; once a day they would be taken out to drink water but they weren't allowed to go to the toilet. The horror of the cell imprinted itself deeply in her soul. Before they were imprisoned in the cell, her mother asked a policeman: "When are you going to kill us?" and he answered her, "I don't know if it will be tomorrow, but in two days' time there'll no longer be even a memory of you here".

Yehudit knew a man in the ghetto called Avek Buzin, a refugee from the town of Zagiezh and a member of the underground who worked in the loot camp. A friend of Avek, who worked clearing up bodies from the streets of the town, saw how they dragged Yehudit and her mother to the prison and told Avek this. He decided to do something to save her. He enquired about her previous workplace, reached the German officer who had been in charge of her, and asked him to get her out of the prison. Yehudit only heard later from that officer how things had turned out. He had said:

"My first reaction was an impulse to whip out my pistol and shoot him on the spot. How dare this man come to me and ask such a thing for a Jewish woman? But I was impressed by his courage and the strength of his spirit and I asked him - who is it you want to save? I don't know her, who is she? What does she look like?"

"Several Germans got Jews out of the prison who were necessary to them", said Yehudit, "but I was only a girl of seventeen, without skills and not needed by anyone". Avek ran to the burning ghetto looking and by chance found a picture of Yehudit in their house and brought it to the officer.

"On the second day of our incarceration" Yehudit went on, "in the afternoon, the German came to the prison. I was standing at the window all the time and watching them loading Jews on lorries, to take them to the pits. Suddenly I heard a shout – "Shelubska!" The door opened and a policeman called out my name. I ran to the door, but I immediately remembered my mother who'd remained behind in the cell and I recoiled. The policeman grabbed my hand and my mother managed to shout: "A last word to my daughter!" and that is how we parted forever. The policeman brought me to the yard and there an astonishing scene met my eyes. A private car was parked there and a German driver with a swastika on his sleeve was standing by it. At door of the car stood a German who I knew from my work, who was holding my picture in his hand. He looked at me and said: "Yes, that's her". The German asked me to get into the car. I was confused. I didn't know where they were taking me. On the way he kept saying to me, your fiancé, your fiancé. I thought to myself, what fiancé? Where have I got a fiancé? Whatever is he talking about? I didn't understand any of it. I was starving and confused and on the brink of collapse. He brought me to the loot shed, called to Avek Bozin and said you owe your life to him. I asked him afterwards to save my parents who'd remained behind in the prison. He promised me to come the next day, but he was too late because the next day, at 12 o'clock, they killed everyone."

Avek hid her under the bed until she could get a work certificate which would protect her. After two days the German brought her a certificate, stating that she worked in the German transport office. This office supplied the lorries which transported the Jews to the pits. In the office Yehudit was treated humanely; she worked there for a month as a cleaner and also helped the Polish clerk. However, the only thought in her head was of getting out to the forest, to the partisans.

One day Avek told her not to go back to work, but to go to a Russian peasant who had lived once in her father's house and felt he owed something to her mother, who had helped him. The peasant had found out that Yehudit had survived and he visited her sometimes. Yehudit did as Avek told her and went to the Russian's house. Some time passed and Avek came to say goodbye to her; he was going to join the partisans. As he went, he told her that there remained very few people in the ghetto underground and he promised that when they took them out to the forest, they would take her too. Yehudit had reached the Russian but staying in his house was hard for her. His wife was very irritable and afraid. Avek didn't come to take her. After a while she found out that he had reached the town with friends in order to carry out an operation and they had come across a German who had killed them.

In the vicinity there lived a young peasant girl. It emerged that her family had contact with the partisans, and this young woman brought Yehudit to the forest. This time too she encountered much hardship, since the partisans who she met in the forest just laughed at her: she was small and thin, and looked about thirteen years old. Yehudit reached a partisan commander, who advised her to go to the house of a partisan contact by the name of Augustin Bell. She reached the village but found out that in the village there were several peasants with that name. She went from house to house, looking for this man, saying everywhere that she had come to exchange goods for bread. In the end, after much searching and great risk, she reached the house of the old man Augustin, and found temporary shelter with him. From her hiding place she saw how partisans came to him, but the old man forbade her to show herself - evidently they were anti-Semites who might well have killed her. In the end he took her to the forest. Since he was old and weak, he wasn't strong enough to bring her to Volchye-Nori, and therefore he handed her over to a young Belarussian man so that he would carry on leading her and another Jewess who had hidden in his farm. The young man relieved her of the last of her money and left them among the farmhouses of Litva. Nobody agreed to put them up. In the end she was allowed in to a Polish house. This was a village which the partisans and the Germans visited in turn; and indeed one morning she heard voices and the whinnying of horses. These were partisans from the Shchors battalion. Yehudit didn't know who they were from a distance, but she decided to take a risk and went out to greet them. Among them she knew Zerach Kremin and Doktortchik who were returning from a mission and they brought her to the Troop 51 camp. However, even then Yehudit's hardships were not over, as will be seen later.

The Story of Tanya (Tamar) Gellerstein Imber

Tanya came from Biten. She was fifteen when Poland was invaded. She and some of her family survived the German massacre in Biten on 25th. July 1942. In the ghetto she worked on the railway tracks by the bridge on the Shchara. Then the Jews in the group came into contact with a Pole who promised to supply them with arms and to lead them to the partisans. The Pole accepted payment but claimed that he couldn't find any weapons, though he allowed the Jews to stay the night in his hayloft.

Following this the German overseers informed them that they were no longer needed, as they were bringing in Ukrainian workers. Tanya decided to flee to the partisans, but first of all she went to the ghetto to say goodbye to her family. On the way she met a Belarussian girl friend who gave her some money and a letter from her eldest sister who worked in the pharmacy in Biten. When she came back, German police were approaching the hayloft and they opened fire on the Jews who were in there. Tanya fled to the nearby forest, but the Germans shot after her, and a bullet hit her, leaving a deep wound in her chest. Only Tanya, her cousin and another woman remained alive and reached the forest, out of the whole group. Tanya had lost a lot of blood, but she carried on walking with her friends to look for the partisans.

"On the way I met a Jew from Poland whose name was Lipak Vikhandler. He too was wandering through the forest looking for a place of shelter. I felt my strength fading away and that I wouldn't be able to go on with my friends. I asked them to leave me and go on without me. When they found a shelter, they could come and collect me. But they wouldn't agree to that and helped me to carry on. They really carried me on their backs until we got into the forest. There we came across some cowherds, children from the nearby villages. When they noticed us, they shouted excitedly – "Little Jews, little Jews, let's go and tell the Germans". We didn't know where we were and we had no alternative but to go deeper into the forest. The main thing was to get away from the non-Jews and the anti-Semites".[46]

Eventually the girls reached the forester's hut. Here they decided to take the risk of going inside to ask for food. To their luck, a young man opened the door to them who had been at school with Tanya. He treated them nicely and fed them, and even offered Tanya to stay in his house until the rest of them met the partisans and could come to fetch her. But her friends wouldn't agree to his suggestion and they went on together. In the end they found two partisans who brought them to the "Woyenkomat" of Volchye-Nori, where they met partisan commanders and told them their story. Tanya was already near to fainting. When she revived, she met her sister Mina, who had managed to get out of Biten.

Tanya was taken to Troop 51 and the care of Dr Blumovitch. Her pain was severe and the doctor said she needed an operation. They had no surgical equipment or anaesthetics and therefore a special messenger was sent to the small town of Biten, to Tanya's sister, who was still working in the pharmacy. The messenger brought the required equipment and Dr Blumovitch operated on her.

Tanya recovered quickly. She was hospitalised in the tent for the wounded, but so that she wouldn't have to put up with the behaviour and crude language of the Russian partisans, Yitzhak and Hanna Shepetinski transferred her to their family tent. Here they cared for her devotedly - Hannah and her daughter Rayah, who was also a young girl of fifteen. About two weeks after the operation, the Shchors troop left Volchye-Nori on its way eastwards. The

---

[46] *From the evidence of Tanya Gellerstein*

Shepetinski family, together with Tanya, were transferred to Group 59, which was the family camp of Kosova, and Tanya was cared for by Dr Tsuker, who worked there. Her sister Mina was living in the neighbouring group 60 family camp of Biten, and the two sisters would meet very often, but this idyll didn't go on for long. It ended in the days of the siege on the forest which the Germans carried out in September 1942.

The story of the Mukasay Sisters

There were three sisters; the oldest Masha, Rita, and Yocheved the youngest, who was sixteen. Masha relates: "We were saved from the massacre of 29th June in a hiding place that our family had prepared in advance. We sat for fourteen days in the hiding place, living off one rusk a day. The Germans cut off the water supply to the besieged ghetto, but luckily, there was a big tub of water in the yard where we used to do the laundry before the Action. At dead of night, Rita would go out to the yard and bring water from the tub into our hiding place. I was convinced that this time we wouldn't survive any more. I wanted to live, but I no longer believed in miracles. My prayer was that I wouldn't suffer the torture which was the lot of many of the Jewish victims who were cast in the pits while they were still alive or wounded and suffocated under the bodies which were heaped over them."

Rita was active in the underground organisation in the ghetto. When the Action ended, the members called to her to come out of the hiding place. The family came out and went to live in the smaller ghetto which was on Mostova Street. After a while they were transferred to the loot camp and the sisters received work permits. Every morning they would go out to work, like the other Jews, and come back to the camp in the evening.

The sisters were preparing to go to the forest but their father and their older brother and his ten-year old son were still in the ghetto. Masha refused to leave her father, who was weak and very exhausted from his sufferings in the Puzovich camp from which he'd been returned. But Rita persuaded her sisters that it was only after they were in the forest with the partisans that would they be able to save the remnants of their family. The Slonim cell of the underground wouldn't agree to the three sisters going out together and Rita informed them that without her sisters, she wouldn't go either. Zelig Shelubski intervened on behalf of the sisters and the three of them left for the forest on 14th August.

They managed to leave the ghetto in a group of workers, as if they were going to work as they did every morning. They turned towards the underground shelter in Podgorna Street, to the carpentry workshop, which had belonged to Zelig's father before the occupation, and went into the hiding place in the roof. They found twenty-five people already gathered there and among them Pesach Alpert, his wife and their two daughters.

That night Dr Yasha Kremin and Moshe Yankelevitch reached the ghetto so as to bring people out to the forest. In the darkness of night they left the hiding place and turned through the cemetery towards the forest. The next day

Zerach Kremin was in Slonim. He came back with the news that there had been another Action in the ghetto and the sisters' father had been killed - he and their brother with his little son. In Volchye-Nori Rita was accepted into the Jewish battalion, while Masha and Yocheved joined the family camp of people from Biten.

CHAPTER SIX: Stages in the establishment of the Jewish Group

Setting up the Shchors Troop

The partisan troop 'Shchors' underwent several metamorphoses and there are a number of versions as to how it was set up. Zerach Kremin confirms that on 1st. May 1942 several partisan groups met in the forest of Rafalovka and officially celebrated the founding of the 'Shchors battalion'. The official soviet document pays no attention to the original establishment of the troop, and as usual does not refer to the Jewish Troop 51, which was an important force in the battalion. In Volume Three of the History of the Belarussian Partisan Movement, it is noted:

"The battalion called Shchors (Commander Proniagin, Commissar Dudko, Chief-of-Staff Merzliakov) organised itself in the Brest Oblast (region) [47] in the winter of 1941-1942. In the summer of 1942 it grew to four hundred well-armed partisans. The battalion carried out combat operations. On 2nd. August the Shchors troop along with several other troops hit the large German garrison in the town of Kosovo. The Shchors led the battle. Proniagin commanded the operation.

"In the autumn of 1942 the troop moved to the Pinsk region and there it prepared for the winter. With the move to Pinsk region, the Shchors came under command of the Pinsk division (the commander was V. Z. Korzh who was authorised by the Secretary of the Communist Party, Kleshchev). In the spring of 1943 the Shchors troop was given over to the command of H. Sikorski, commander of the Brest division)."[48]

Until the spring of 1942 the group led by Proniagin and Dudko had no official name. It was called simply by the name of its commander, as was usual for partisan groups. In that period there were many groups wandering round the forests which spontaneously rallied round people who displayed initiative and daring, and who they chose to be their commanders.[49]

When the separate partisan groups declared the founding of the "Shchors" in the forest of Rafalovka, they also chose their commanders. Pavel Vassilievitch Proniagin was chosen as commander, Gregory Andreyevitch Dudko as commissar. After that Merzliakov joined them as chief of staff. The troop was divided into groups in order to hide the number of men and to mislead the enemy as to their size, and they were given the numbers 51, 52, 53 and 54. Later, groups 56, 57 and 58 were founded, most of whose fighters came from the surrounding villages.

---

[47] *Since administrative divisions in the Soviet Union do not match Israeli ones, the larger administrative unit will be called Oblast (the term for a region), and the smaller one, a district.*

[48] *Istoriya Partizanskovo Dvizhenya v Belorussii 642*

[49] *Partizanskoye Formirovaniye Belorussii, Cap. 2, P. 112*

In the Kosovan group, No. 59, there were two hundred and ten men and about fifty to sixty weapons. They set up workshops - a clothes factory, cobblers and a metal workshop. They had good skilled workers.

The Biten group, No. 60, was smaller and poorly armed. At first Mishka Fovar was appointed to the command of group 51 (this was what he was called, due to his military role as cook), but later Feodorovitch was appointed in his place. Fedor Kazanchev was given command of the 52, Bobkov the 53 and Andrei Leontiev the 54. Every group had its appointed Politruk. The 51 group camped in the forest of Raflovka near the headquarters of the troop.

In the official research into the partisan group movement in Belorussia it has been said of the building up of the Shchors troop:

"Several troops functioned continuously in connection with the organisations and underground groups. Thanks to that the partisan troops grew quickly in the spring and summer of 1942. The largest combat unit in the Brest region was a troop by the name of "Shchors". In the summer of 1942 it numbered 543 men; they were equipped with automatic rifles, two canon and forty submachine guns."[50]

It doesn't say in this document that the underground organisation which supplied most of the weaponry to the troop was that of the Slonim ghetto, and that one of the troop's canon belonged to the Jewish 51 group.

Every group enjoyed broad autonomy in its activities and in its internal life. The 51 group retained its position as the H.Q. battalion. Next to it was located the medical service with a hospital and Dr Blumovitch was the chief medical officer. Dr Blumovitch in the past had been a reserve officer in the Polish army and also an officer in the Red Army. Under his command he now had a team of doctors, nurses and sanitary workers. Every group also had its own medical service.

The troop also had an intelligence service to which were elected members from all the groups. In the summer of 1942, the troops engaged in dynamic military activity and sabotaged the main arteries of transport and traffic of the enemy, and there were many acts of sabotage on the railway lines and the roads. Ambushes set up on the roads destroyed long lines of the enemy's military vehicles with their occupants and their cargo; in addition, telephone lines were sabotaged and farms and enterprises which were active for the enemy were destroyed.

The Setting Up of the Jewish 51 Group on 2nd. July 1942

The establishment of the Jewish 51 partisan group of people from Slonim and the remnants of the Biten ghetto was in fact an outcome of anti-Semitism on the part of the Soviet partisans in the Shchors group, who refused to accept Jews to the troop. Paradoxically, the Jewish group arose in opposition to the

---

[50] *Part III (About the Brest district), p. 199*

declared Soviet policy which didn't recognise the existence of the Jewish people and was of the opinion that the partisan groups should be set up according to territorial principles. According to this policy, the Jewish partisan groups which had originated in the ghetto underground, plus those which had arisen independently in the forest from the remnants of the ghettos which had been wiped out - these were taken apart and their members dispersed among the Lithuanian, Belarussian and Ukrainian battalions. In fact, on 1st. July 1942 the non-Jewish partisans made off from Troop 51 and took with them weapons that they had received from people in the Slonim ghetto. Now they had the new struggle of risking penetrating the town as they returned to acquire armour for the Jewish fighters and to the people who flowed into the forest from the ghetto, which was in the process of being wiped out. And these are the nineteen Jews who remained in the forest of Rafalovka and constituted the nucleus of the Jewish group: Yitzak (Itche) Gratchuk, his sister Masha, Avraham Yakimovski, David Blumenfeld (a refugee from Kalish), Fanya Feigenbaum (a nurse, refugee from Lodz), Ya'akov (Kobah) Zilberhaft (from Warsaw), Dr Avraham Blumovitch (from Lumzha), Aharon Bandt and his brother Avraham, Zerach Kremin (from Belitzia), Irka Weisselfisch (from Warsaw), Avraham Bublatski, Zhama Shusterovitch, David Perl, Anshel Delatitski, Henik Malach (from Ostrov Keletski), Herzel Shepetinski, Leah (Lisa) Abramchik, Liuba Abramchik (from Ostrov Mazovietski).[51]

From among these nineteen partisans, eleven were refugees. The first to leave for the partisan struggle were the refugees, who were mainly young people, had no ties to any place or the burden of elderly parents or children and bore no responsibility for the community. It's probable that the abandonment of the Jewish partisans by the non-Jewish partisans was in fact for the best, since the Jews of the Slonim ghetto had been tried in many dangers while they were still incarcerated. They were utterly determined to set up a well equipped fighting Jewish unit, so as to take revenge on the murderers of their people and to prove to the anti-Semitic partisans that the Jews knew how to fight too. They found within themselves enough strength, bravery and initiative to attain their goals.

Envoys from the forest went back and forth to the Slonim ghetto and Volchye Nori; they brought a lot of people and weapons out of the ghetto and equipped their battalion. Not many days passed and the group of nineteen abandoned Jews, deceived and broken in spirit from the betrayal of their so-called comrades, grew to one hundred and fifty men, and went from strength to strength. It was the best equipped battalion in the Shchors troop having machine-guns, automatic rifles, grenades and a great deal of ammunition. In time they also acquired a canon. A. Imber tells how it was put together:

"Group 52 had a 45 mm. anti-tank canon. Dr Blumovitch asked me once if I knew how to put together a canon like the one in Leontiev's battalion. I approached Erich Stein and suggested that he put the canon together from the pieces that were left in the Rafalovka forest. The Jews went out to the forest of

---

[51]*Those whose place of origin is not mentioned came from Slonim.*

Rafalovka and collected various pieces, but they didn't find a bolt. On the spot there was an empty well. Dr Blumovitch went into the well, felt around with his hands and pulled out various other pieces including a bolt. Everybody was thrilled. Now they only needed two wheels and a recoil spring, but they found those too and that is how the canon of the Jewish group was put together, under the instruction of Erich Stein. They also found shells for the canon, roundabout the area."

In the group there was a gunner from the Soviet Army, Grisha Yarmolenko[52], who came from Kazakhstan. He'd reached the Shchors together with the group of Zhuravliov.[53] The canon still needed an optical instrument, but Grisha knew that you could aim it without using optical instruments, by looking along the butt. The canon was tried out successfully and served the battalion in future battles which it conducted.

Not long after, the canon was tried in a battle by the village of Chemeri, when a German train was attacked. Up till now the Jewish battalion hadn't had any experience in attacking trains. They hadn't yet carried out operations of this kind in the area. The Germans weren't yet afraid, so the train was travelling with all its lights on and well lit up from a distance. When the train passed by, Yarmolenko fired a shell at the engine. The train suddenly stopped; the carriages all went on top of each other. The Germans jumped out, took up defensive positions, started shooting and the partisans withdrew. For many Jews from Troop 51, this was the first baptism of fire.

All the summer months more people continued flowing into the battalion. At the end of July they already had a hundred and twenty fighters, in addition to the domestic group, and in August the number had grown to a hundred and fifty fighters. When the group commenced combat operations, Troop 51 was the striking force in the troop and its members were distinguished by their strength of spirit; it was not without reason that the H.Q. of the troop was next to the Jewish battalion.

Lieutenant Feodorovitch - the Commander of the Jewish Group

Lieutenant Yefim Feodorovitch, the new commander, contributed a great deal to the strengthening of the Jewish battalion. He was a Jew from Gomel, an officer in the Red Army, and had been decorated with the award of the Red Flag back in the war against Finland. He had escaped from the prisoner of war camp near Bialystok with two other prisoners; one of them was the Russian officer Merzliakov who was appointed chief of staff of the Shchors battalion and the other officer went to the East.

---

[52] *Eventually Yarmolenko commanded a unit in the 56 brigade, and subsequently in the Bodyani troop.*

[53] *He was appointed commander of a unit in a troop, and shown to be a corrupt anti-semite and a drunkard.*

The Jewish subordinates of Feodorovitch remember him as a good tempered and very dynamic man. In the headquarters of the troop, he would initiate combat activities. Contrary to other Jews who'd been born in the Soviet Union and sometimes hid their Jewishness, Feodorovitch with his warm Jewish heart, was a proud Jew. During communal meetings around the bonfire, he would ask people to tell him about the lives of the Jews of Poland and was interested in life in the land of Israel. He looked about thirty; his face was slightly dark-skinned and his black eyes expressed real human warmth. He had dark hair in which you could already see strands of silver. He was of average height, spoke slowly and his voice was deep and masculine. His whole appearance was that of a professional soldier.

He didn't pay too much attention, like the other commanders, to army etiquette. His men admired him for his simple and friendly approach to them and point out his nobility of spirit. As a commander he was clever enough to educate his people and to train them for strike attacks. Feodorovitch was aware of the anti-Semitism which was rife among many partisans, and once when he was sitting round the bonfire, he said, "If we manage to survive, the only home we'll have will be in the land of Israel".

The 51 group transferred to the more dense forests of Volchye Nori and there Feodorovitch began to train his men with intensive army exercises. He brought his group up to scratch devotedly and was knowledgeable. In the months of July and August, the men continued to train, since during this period many people came to the battalion from Slonim and the local area. In only a month this group was divided into four units: one unit was commanded by Vassily Volkov, a sergeant major in the Red Army who came from the Ukraine. Over the second was Yefim Borisovitch Podolsky, second lieutenant in the Red Army, a Jew who came from Stalino in the Ukraine, had fled the prisoner of war camp in Statin and reached the forests by crossing Poland. Aaron Bandt commanded the third unit - a reservist in the Polish Army who came from the village of Skolditch near Slonim, through which many of those fleeing from the ghetto had passed on their way to the forest. Zerach Kremin was the commander of the smaller sabotage unit.

In the 51 group there were now only five Belarussians; most of the Jewish fighters were from Slonim or refugees who had become citizens of Slonim after the fall of Poland in 1939. The 51 group retained the status of staff battalion with the medical centre next to it supervised by Dr Blumovitch, the chief medical officer, with his team of doctors, nurses and sanitary workers. Every group had its own medical service. There was a troop intelligence service, for which people were chosen from all the groups.

The Jewish Troop 51 played a part in the main battles of the troop. Its commander Feodorovitch maintained the level of morale of his group and raised it above the other groups. The moral standard of this commander and his personality helped him to toughen his group against the hostile environment. The commander of group 54, Andrei Leontiev, also a professional Soviet soldier, who was regarded with some suspicion because he was a Jew who hid his Jewishness, concentrated in his group superior Soviet army people, carefully chosen, and thus this battalion was an outstanding combat battalion. However, Fiodorovitch didn't choose his men, he received them just as they were - many whom had no military knowledge, and among them women. He trained and prepared them for combat missions. The battalion had a strong national Jewish awareness; in fact, the official language and orders were in Russian, but day-to-day the fighters spoke among themselves in Yiddish. Feodorovitch inculcated in his people a consciousness that they must not be afraid of battle and of death. There was no one who was permitted to choose between an easy role and a difficult one. They had to fulfill the tasks that were required of them, even if they were beyond their strength or abilities. In this way Feodorovitch turned his people into fighters and his group into the strongest unit in the troop.

The outward appearance of the group's camp gave an impression of tidiness and cleanliness. People lived in shelters made of plaited branches and in tents covered with tarpaulins in the military style. In the middle of the camp a large shelter was set up which served as the hospital, of which Dr Cheslava Orlinski was in charge. The sides of the shelter gleamed from the whiteness of the fabric that was stretched over them. On one side of the camp there was a kitchen under the direction of Imber Snr., who was a watchmaker by trade. At the other side end of the camp there was a workshop for repairing weapons. Here, the two 45mm. canons were tended and put together from various parts which had been collected from the roads or taken out of Slonim. Erich Stein, A. Imber and Hillel Moshkovski worked there.

The residents of the camp, in particular those who'd survived the ghetto, sought to overcome the despair in their hearts, the pain from the loss of their families, and if somebody was overcome by sorrow, they would cry privately. But the camp had a happy atmosphere. Somebody brought some record players to the camp and they played Russian and Jewish songs, and a radio was set up which worked off a battery. The news from the Front that they received was distributed to the other troops.

There was no lack of food then. Small groups were constantly sent to the villages to acquire food stuffs and sometimes the supply forces had to fight police and Germans who ambushed them on the roads.

The saboteur groups frequented the roads and paths. Absent most of all from the camp were the reconnaissance groups; they had to frequently go through the villages in order to check out the security situation in the region and to receive news of the movement of enemy forces. The Shchors battalion also, like the other partisan groups, had loyal people in the villages and in the small towns nearby and they served as intelligence. Reconnaissance were in continuous contact with underground cells in local settlements.[54]

---

[54] *Evidence of Avraham Orlinski in Lochamei HaGetaot.*

CHAPTER SEVEN: In the Jewish Group

Early Days

Most of the people in the group to which Yasha Shepetinski was affiliated were from among those who'd left the Slonim ghetto, with a few Belarussians from the village of Chemeri. The commander of the group was the Jewish second lieutenant from the Red Army, Bema Podolski.

During the month of July, the people from the ghetto trained a great deal under the supervision of the group commander, Feodorovitch. They studied partisan tactics and methods of fighting: to shoot, to camouflage themselves, go from position to position at a run, cover a comrade, throw hand grenades, advance quietly and hide all noise. After two to three weeks, Feodorovitch reported to the commander of the troop, Proniagin, that Brigade 51 was ready to carry out any combat task. Everybody was impatient to go out to battle to take revenge on the Germans and their collaborators, especially Herzel Shepetinski whose passion for revenge eventually brought about his death. In addition to training, the new partisans would go out to collect weapons and ammunition as they were still short of these. They looked for parts to complete the construction of the damaged canon that the group owned. From (spent) shells they obtained explosives. Small groups would go out to Slonim and bring back weapons which had been hidden by members of the underground in various places around the town.

At the end of July, all members of Troop 51 were already well armed. The troop had three platoons, and in each platoon, four squads. Each squad had one or two machine guns and plenty of discs. Every fighter was also equipped with hand grenades. The refugees from the ghetto had become strong in both body and spirit, and were well absorbed into the partisan environment. Friendships existed in the units and everyone was waiting to fight the enemy.

Avraham Doktortchik has described a day when a new group came to the camp from the ghetto:

"In the morning the camp was buzzing with partisans. The new people were occupied putting up tents, while others were polishing their weapons. They were busy with all the arrangements involved in joining the platoons and squads, and in taking on their roles.

"Around the kitchen, too, there was lively movement. It was located behind the tents, and in front of the tents, which were spread out in a circle between the trees, there was an open space. Several men were sitting there, stripped to the waist and taking apart weapons - rifles, semi-automatic rifles, Diegtierov machineguns, and a tank gun. They laid the parts on blankets spread out in front of them and explained to the young people and women who had just approached, the routine of cleaning, taking apart and putting back together.

Translation of an excerpt from the Russian newsletter:

The Red Star No. (L21) 12 to 18

Beasts on two legs in Slonim.

The German conquerors have brought inhuman suffering and death to the inhabitants of Slonim. We are printing below an article which has been passed to us by a resident of the town of Slonim who was a living witness to the events that occurred there from the beginning of the German occupation until now.

'Comrades, cry revenge on the Germans for the blood and tears of our people!

.......Cruel pogroms against the Jews.

The first big pogrom[55] on the Jews of Slonim was carried out by the Germans in November 1941. German police and drunken Slonim police searched Jewish houses from the morning to the evening. Children were thrown from windows and there were instances where they were torn apart alive. All the Jews were concentrated in the square, in the big synagogue. They (the Germans) carried out classification there; they released anyone who worked for the Germans and the rest they beat and loaded on lorries and took them to a field in the direction of the village of Chepelova, in the Shilovitsi district, to a place where killing pits had already been dug. At the command of the Germans, all the Jews had to undress.

The shooting started. The people stood in a line for death. They were forced to sing the song Katyushka. Several of the murderers chose girls for themselves from among the community, and promising to release them, took them between the bushes, raped them, and then killed them.

At the site of the slaughter, more than fifty people lost their minds. About nine thousand[56] people were shot that day. This bloody massacre was carried out by the sadistic Germans: Shultz Reinerg, Rener and Schtehlle. Slonim local police who stood out in their cruelty and their violence were: Sudovsky Vladimir, Boyosak Stefan, Mironchik Yosif.

After this massacre, there began the looting of the victims' property. In the summer of 1942, a further mass slaughter was carried out on the Jewish population. In order to get the population out of their hiding places, the Germans sent people to set fire to the Jewish quarter (the ghetto).'

---

[55] *The massacre of the 1.200 men was in July, 1941*

[56] *According to German reports about 10.000 victims were shot on the 'Black Friday', 14.11. 1941*

**Beasts on two legs - The partisan bulletin "The Red Star"
Which was distributed to the local population - 1942**

"Itche Mishlevitch had chopped pieces of wood which he was sawing to prepare lasts for his work as a cobbler. Erich Stein and Imber were absorbed in putting together a small anti- tank canon, which the Red Army had abandoned in the forest of Rafalovka in their panicked retreat. Hillel Moshkovski had engraved the missing part back in the ghetto, right under the nose of the factory manager, who was working for the Germans, and had sent it to the forest with the group that had just arrived. Archik Bandt had formed a group to go out and look for food. He allocated Erich Stein to this group, and amidst all the to and fro, and the preparations, the company still found the opportunity to laugh and exchange jokes.

"The sun was setting, twilight came down upon the clearing. Minkovitch, a carter from the town of Biten who worked in supplies, had set up a bonfire in the clearing. The old hands sat round it and chatted with the new people who had just arrived. They asked about the relatives who they'd left behind in the ghetto and listened in horror to the news.

"The branches of the trees which were moving with the night wind cast shadows on the faces of the people sitting round the bonfire, and the sparks and flames which coloured a forehead or a cheek or chin with a red or a bluish light, gave peoples' faces a fairy tale look - as if they were creatures from a legendary world. The discussions ended; the people stopped looking at each other and the eyes of most of them were now fixed on the flames in the bonfire where there peeped out, as it were, the faces of their dear ones whom they would no longer see. From time to time, one of those listening would get up from the circle and go to one side to give free rein to their tears. They wanted to be alone to mourn their parents, their relatives and the friends they had left in the ghetto and who were no longer alive. Others actually drew closer to the bonfire in order, by sitting around together, to distract themselves from distressing thoughts and the burning pain of the loss of their families. They sat or stood around, their eyes fixed on the flames.

"From time to time the quiet humming of a song of longing and yearning in Yiddish or Russian or Polish was borne up into the night air. At times a Hassidic nigun was threaded through in an effort to dull a little the pain of the Jewish life which had been destroyed.

"In one of the intervals between songs, Feodorovitch started to talk like a visionary about the organisation of Jewish partisan units, which would unite into a powerful army camp, liberate those imprisoned in the ghettos of Europe and take them to the land of Israel. These were words of political heresy and not everybody sitting round the bonfire heard them. Somebody tried to ask what the commander had said, but Doktortchik burst out into a patriotic Russian song - "Hey Vintovka" - and distracted him from the matter, and then everybody joined in the song again.

"It was growing late and the singing was weakening and slowly fading. A few single people and couples broke away from the circle and disappeared into their tents, while those who were left behind went on whispering for a long time and fell asleep just as they were, dressed in their clothes and hugging their weapons with their legs.

"Silence fell upon the camp; the bonfire went out and only Doktortchik who was that day "dnyevalni" (the guard on duty in the camp area) remained, sitting sleepily by the whispering coals, listening to the rustle of the dry leaves and to the voices coming from the tents. He had to struggle with slumber which made his eyes heavy, and to force his gaze and follow every little sound or movement in the area. It wasn't easy to distinguish in the dark between a tree and a tent. After that, he tried to clarify for himself the list of people who were assigned to go out on various tasks and who he was responsible for waking.

"The time to change the guard was drawing near. He made his way towards the tents in order to wake the next man on duty, and luckily he reached the right tent. If he'd made a mistake and woken the wrong man, he might well have got an earful and been "sent to hell".

"At the end of the third watch, the guard changed. A light breeze had begun to blow. The trees were swaying and dropping pinecones and the carpet of needles at the foot of the trees was silencing their fall to earth. For a moment there was a sudden sharp summer shower, but it quickly passed. The fighters who had been deeply asleep until now turned over in their beds and started to come out of the tents. The rain which had come through into the tents and wetted them had woken them up and put them on their feet, forcing them to go out from the "houses" whose floors had turned to puddles.

"Outside the boys who had got up early had lit a bonfire and sat drying their clothes by it. The people were joking and laughing out loud until everybody woke up, and the women who were cooking went off to prepare breakfast. Since daybreak the procurement group had come back from its task. Without waiting for a command from the Starshina - that is the store man, Pilsky - many of them volunteered to unpack the supplies from the carts. The tired horses needed no encouragement to gallop back to their stables. Merriment prevailed in the camp; even those who'd come back from a journey, from the tribulations of the night were infected by the general atmosphere and recounted their journeys and funny little incidents that had happened to them. The highlights of the storytellers were those of Avraham Yakimovski and Anshel Delatitski.

"Avraham Yakimovski, who was called Anton in the forest, didn't speak Russian very well and the comrades imitated his commands: "Open, strengthen, I go grenade". In the end the grenade didn't go off and these two characters and a peasant woman were slightly hurt. They were bandaged on the way by the comrades, and looked as if they were returning from battle. The way they looked only increased the joking and the teasing, and everyone was laughing at the unfortunate pair.

"The Starshina carried out a drill with the people who'd come back, checking the stock and requiring everyone to hand over all goods to the brigade's kitchen, only then allowing them to go and rest. Then the storekeeper, an ex-NKVD man, noticed Anshel's bursting rucksack and called out: "Come here, Andrei (that was his nickname among the partisans), the load you're carrying on your back is too heavy for you, come back". Anshel returned, his head bent in shame, and Pilsky took the rucksack off his back, undid it and found inside a large slice of ham. In anger and amazement, he said, "What's this?" "A piece that I kept for myself for breakfast" stuttered

Anshel, confused. "You, a past store man of the group, a communist, and you're not ashamed?" Pilsky roared at him. And he requisitioned the contents of the rucksack and let the offender go off whilst giving him a lecture."

According to partisan ethics, everyone had to eat out of the same general pot and it was forbidden that partisans coming back from an operation should bring food stuffs to have a feast for themselves. In fact, not all units kept to this principle. In many troops, there were separate kitchens for the commanders, with cooks who prepared food especially for them, and another general kitchen for the rank and file. In a number of troops, the partisans were accustomed to bring goodies with them from their trips out for the commanders and for their friends - butter, cheese, milk and onion, which was considered a very desirable commodity as many partisans suffered from vitamin deficiency. The most precious find was soap. There were units where these breaches of partisan ethics occurred without any reaction, and particularly if they were committed by non-Jews. But if the offenders were Jews, they were punished.

"'Breakfast is ready!' The chief cook announced the good news and her voice resounded in the camp like a sweet song. Life in the fresh air of the forest and also marching along the paths kept the appetite going very well. Everyone queued up for the kitchen, received their portion and started to devour it greedily, as if it was not just one night that had passed since their last meal. Doktortchik took two buckets from the kitchen, drew water from the well and retired to the bushes in order to wash. Most of the partisans who went out on operations in the villages were accustomed to wash in the houses of peasants they knew or peasants with whom they had friendly ties. The peasant women used to give them clean underwear and wash the dirty ones. In time the partisans in the more established units built wash-houses in their camps in the forest. These washing huts were particularly good in the winter days, when the partisans left the camps less so that their footprints in the snow wouldn't lead anyone to the places where they were encamped. Fleas were the partisans' worst affliction. They pervaded their clothes, which they didn't take off at night when they lay down to sleep. The men used to take off their shirts and shake them over the bonfire in order to roast the parasites that ate into their flesh, but it was of little help. They would very often boil the shirts in a bucket of water with ash.

In the days of the big chases, when the enemy made the partisans flee their huts and the fighters were forced to run from place to place for weeks on end, the fleas would make merry. There were many cases where partisans became sick with a form of typhus when they passed through one of the villages which was affected by this plague and were infected by the disease through the fleas.

The situation of those living in the family camps was extremely hard. They couldn't visit the villages, wash or change their underwear. In many family camps there were no wash-houses. In the days of the siege, when the inhabitants of the family camps were forced to flee their huts and wander in the forest for many weeks, hungry and thirsty and freezing from cold, the fleas really ate into them and many became sick and died. Most of the people who stayed in the camp had jobs: the girls washed the clothes and hung them on clothes lines stretched between the trees, and some of them mended clothes; others were involved in various jobs running the camp or improving the tents.

The End of the Underground in the Slonim Ghetto

In the second half of July 1942, weak signs of Jewish life still flickered in the Slonim ghetto, and the underground organisation still functioned. In the ghetto, which was increasingly being destroyed, and in hiding places, in lofts and in dark cellars, Jewish life - either of individuals or of families - still fluttered. Souls were tossed between hope and despair; between small sparks of hope and the continuation of a humiliating life of slavery. The Germans continued to deceive the Jews with empty promises that nothing would happen to those who remained, and that their work was essential to the Germans.

The link between the ghetto underground and the forest continued and was even strengthened. In fact in the very last period operations branched out considerably, and in the small ghetto there was no longer any factory or workshop where an underground cell didn't function. People continued to supply the forest with weapons and ammunition, medication and surgical equipment, clothes and footwear. They also brought information about the movements of enemy forces. Envoys from the forest would filter into the ghetto, whilst both weapons and people continued to flow to the forest, strengthening the armaments and increasing the number of Jews in Troop 51.

At the end of July (or the beginning of August) Zerach Kremin went out with several partisans from Volchye Nori to Slonim. They were to reach the carpentry workshop in Podgorna Street. Zelig Milikovski, Eliahu Abramovski and Itche Rabinovitch were still working there. This time, too, the objective was to get weapons and people out to the forest.

Of the people who arrived at the underground shelter during the day, some were hidden in the bunker and some in the hiding place in the loft. Four people, who worked in the barracks and had been appointed to bring rifles and ammunition, were to join the leavers. They had been given a password and a meeting place.

At dusk, the messengers left the bunker, distributed arms and instruction to the thirty people who had gathered, and were on the point of moving out to the forest. They had a machine-gun and about ten thousand bullets, several submachine-guns, and pistols. They marched the length of the Christian cemetery, crossed the Rozhani road in military file, and continued on the nearby road to Skolditch. Here Zerach Kremin stopped his group, and left with several comrades for the meeting-place with another group which had been led by Moshe Yankelevitch and Yitzhak Rosa.

As they approached they saw several figures and asked for the password. Shots were fired in response, and the figures started to withdraw. Only after some time did they start to shout the password. Zerach and his men drew close, when a bullet flew from the gun of one of the lads, and skimmed Zerach's ear. Zerach grabbed the lad, knocked him down and took his gun from his hand. It was a youngster from Ostrolenka. (Later on, he fell in the battle of the Tenth Dam.) All the other four were drunk. It turned out that they had been drinking with the German guards until the latter fell asleep, whereupon they had taken two chests of bullets and four rifles from the guardroom, and got out through a gap in the fence to go to the meeting-place with Zerach. The shots had been fired from a semi-automatic which the young boy didn't know how to use.

They went on hastily, commandeered some carts in the village, and travelled to the forests of Rafalovka, and from there to Volchye Nori. When they arrived it emerged that their whole group was on the way to a mission in Kosovo. The newcomers handed over the weapons they had brought to those going into battle.

The operations involved in getting out weapons and the flight of many Jews from the ghetto brought about many losses among the members of the underground. The Germans realised that there was ongoing partisan activity in the ghetto, and greatly increased their guard. Dozens of Germans now guarded the access roads to the town, yet parts of guns, hand grenades, machine-gun parts and a lot of ammunition were brought out of the store daily. The young women played a significant part in this.

On one occasion, a member of the underground, Leah Steindam, was caught smuggling three hundred bullets on her person. Her hands were bound with chains and she was taken to the prison, where she was severely tortured during interrogation. At first they tried to coax information out of her, to seduce her with promises, and when they didn't succeed they changed their tactics. The German hangmen knew their work well. They had excellent knowledge of the anatomy and physiology of the human body. They knew where and how to hit so as to cause the worst pain, so as to break the tortured person, and send them out of their mind.

Questions were repeated again and again with torturous blows: Who sent you? Who are the leaders in the ghetto? Who are the partisan contacts? Where do the Jews flee, and by what route? Who are the citizens helping them? Where is the partisan camp?

After the bunker was burnt, the Germans began to imprison many of the workers from workshops of the loot camp. They were interrogated and tortured terribly. Among those who were cruelly tortured was Me'ir Khoroshchanski, though they got no information out of him. He was shot in the Jewish cemetery, while crying out: "Brothers, revenge!" Sheindl Volfin and ten other underground members were also killed in the same place and the same way.

These incarcerations and executions brought to an end the chapter of daring and heroism of the underground organisation in the Slonim ghetto.

A plan which was never put into action

Erich Stein, who worked as chief armourer in the loot camp in Slonim, reached the forest at the end of July or early August 1941.[57] He knew

---
[57] *Ya'akov Khetzkeleivitch. Zichronot fon a Slonimer Partisan, Slonim Notebooks, Vol. B*

everything that was stored in the loot camp. Stein suggested blowing up the store one night. In his view, the operation should be easy, since the storehouse was guarded by only two watchmen, who would change shifts every two hours. It would be a simple matter to get rid of them. According to the plan, Stein would get a Bickford cable (a delaying fuse) out of the store, while the rest of them would carry off weapons and ammunition. They would wake the rest of the Jews, about eight hundred people, who were living in the camp after the great massacre in the ghetto, and advise them to go with the partisans. Obviously, they would first have to bring a lot of carts to the river bank, to transfer the large arms loot. After that they would blow up the storehouse.

Stein's plan fired the imagination of the Jewish partisans. They immediately contacted Nionia Tzirinski, who was still the brigade's contact with the ghetto, and told him about the plan. Similarly, they told the troop commander, Proniagin, but he wasn't at all keen on the plan. He claimed that the difficulties would be enormous, and didn't believe the operation would succeed. Nionia also put off carrying it out from day to day. It was clear that without his help the plan wouldn't be put into action. The comrades suspected that Nionia was hesitating because his mother was still among the eight hundred remnants (of the ghetto), and was afraid to take on himself responsibility lest they be hit. The brigade left Volchye Nori for the east, and the plan was never realised.

Zerach recalls that a few months later, while the troop was encamped between the villages of Razdzhalovichi and Svyetitza, a group of ten people, including Nionia, was organised under his command, and went out towards Slonim to carry out the plan. En route, at crossing points on the rail track and at one over the Shchara, they encountered concentrations of Germans, and returned to camp. Shortly after, the brigade left for Gotzek, the manhunt began, the partisans were forced to flee – and the plan was never carried out.

Zerach Kremin remembers another attempt to penetrate the town of Slonim at the end of August or early September, 1942[58]. He set out with several comrades, among them A. Doktortchik, M. Mudelevitch and Nionia Tzirinski. They left one partisan in the Jewish cemetery with a machine-gun for cover, and split up into two bands: one, led by Doktortchik, was to snatch skins and soap from the factories in Podgorna Street, and the other, which contained Zerach and Nionia Tzirinski – they were to penetrate to the centre of town up to the headquarters of the town's chief officer, and replace the Wehrmacht poster with a manifesto of the Red Army. When they got back, they were to burn the huge heaps of straw the Germans had gathered around the old cemetery and set fire to the 'Butchers' Synagogue', where the Germans were repairing two tanks, intended for anti-partisan warfare.

The men started to advance towards Podgorna Street. At Derechinski Lane, there suddenly appeared in front of them a man dressed in white. The men

---

Memoirs of Zerach Kremin

[58] *From the memoirs of Zerach Kremin*

flattened themselves against the wall, but the figure shouted "Halt!" Zerach took up his machine-gun and fired at the man, but the gun had gone silent. He tried again and fired a round. The voice of the German was weaker, but his cry of "Halt!" could still be clearly heard. Then Nionia fired another round and the man fell. The two men turned back as fast as they could, and made off towards the cemetery, where they met the rest of the party and returned to Volchye Nori without carrying out their mission. Later, it appeared that it had been a drunken German officer, who had wanted to arrest Jews. That night, and on future nights, the Germans hid for fear of partisans penetrating the town.

This was the last time the people from the ghetto actually did get into Slonim. Despite further attempts, neither Zerach nor anyone else managed to penetrate the town.[59]

On Yom Kippur, 1942, the remnants of the Slonim ghetto were murdered. In the forests of Volchye Nori, the ghetto people carried the torch of revenge in their hearts, and during the months of their activities as partisans, they hit the Germans and their helpers, the Belorussian police, hard. In the course of battle, where the people from Slonim distinguished themselves, many of them gave their lives, and together with them, partisans from the ghettos of Biten and Kosovo.

---

[59] *Zerach Kremin, Partisan inroads into Slonim, The Slonim Notebooks, vol. 2, P.132*

CHAPTER EIGHT: The battle route of the 51 group

Operation Kosovo (2nd. August 1942)

At the end of July, 1942, Sergei Yegorovitch Yegorov arrived at the Shchors troop. He had been a member of the regional communist committee for the struggle against the occupation. Before the war, this man was a secretary of the local party committee in the Moscow region. In the army, he had served at the rank of commissar of Battalion 15 in the 49th division.

Yegorov faced the commanders of the Shchors with a new task – to defeat an enemy garrison. He stressed that the troop could not allow itself any longer to be content with small missions.

At that time, the Shchors battalion was already very well armed. They had five hundred fighters in possession of forty submachine guns, a similar number of automatic rifles and many grenades. They also had a 45mm cannon in the Leontiev group and a cannon in the Jewish 51 group.[60]

Yegorov's suggestion was accepted, and the command of the troop decided on a mission to destroy the German garrison, numbering three hundred men, stationed in the town of Kosovo. The command set its patrols to check out the target area, the plan of the town, and the location of the German gendarmerie and of the Belorussian police and their armament stores. The command called for consultation with the commanders of the two adjacent troops: the troop which went by the name of Dimitrov, which was stationed in the forest of Huta-Michalin, and the troop called Voroshilov, which was stationed in the dense forest of Ruzhani. In consultation, they worked out a plan for the operation.

On the night of 2nd. August, the partisans set out for the mission. Three hundred and sixty men went from the Shchors battalion while from the two other troops, there were only one hundred and twenty. Up until now, the Shchors had carried out numerous missions limited in their range – the destruction of a small police station, the routing of police to the central towns, sabotage operations on communications and the destruction of enemy vehicles with passengers. This time, they were setting out on a battle mission with a range several times larger. For the Jewish 51 group, this was their first battle mission, which could have an impact on their status as a partisan group and on the members' sense of being Jewish fighters. The partisans were prone to feelings of despair and regret that they had remained alive, while the members of their families had been cut off. But now they had hope of revenge on the murderers of their dear ones, which instilled them with a taste for life.

On 1st. August, in the afternoon, the command was given to the group to prepare for battle. The fighters were organised to set out with the best of their arms, and just then, a large group arrived at the camp from the Slonim ghetto, led by Zerach Kremin. They brought a lot of weaponry with them, which was

---

[60] *Proniagin, pp.40-42*

handed over to the people going out to battle. Among those who arrived was also Lili, the wife of David Blumenfeld, the commander of a small unit in the group.

The command allowed Blumenfeld to meet his wife, who he had left behind in the ghetto when he went to the forest. Then, he had to part from her yet again, and this time, the parting was forever. David didn't return, for he fell in battle.

People went out on their way. In the camp, there remained a guard and a small domestic section. Before the exodus, a parade had been held, where those who were going had been given the battle briefing.

Ya'akov Shepetinski, who took part in this battle as a gunner, says:

"When we drew close to the town, dawn had already broken. Under the command of commander Proniagin, our unit began to take up positions.

"We came down from a hill and crossed a stream. When we were already near the houses on the edge of the village, we lay down and waited for morning light, to start the attack. The signal was a volley from our cannon.

"The other brigades of our troop positioned themselves on the right and the left and ambushes were set up on every road. Our brigade had the task of reaching the centre of the town and taking the police station and the command with a frontal attack. We lay quietly, waiting and very tense – after all, this was the first time that we had been set a real combat task. Our commander, Feodorovitch, crawled from platoon to platoon, allocating tasks, pointing out weak spots and instructing. We, the gunners, had to open fire on the barracks, and pour continuous fire on the openings.

And now the dawn had dispersed the darkness of the night, and you could see the houses clearly. It appeared that we had taken up positions right opposite the ghetto. Following instructions from our command, we entered the outer street of Kosovo.

"The air resounded with cannon volleys. We raced forward as if born up on wings. The cannon is very loud. The people imprisoned in the ghetto are looking at us from behind the barbed wire fence in amazement and fear. We don't stop, and carry on running, and now we're already in the main street. Our people are firing from the right. We take up position and lie down in a chain. Several more volleys, and then, again, we hear the voice of our commander. 'Forward, after me!' We all storm forward, burst into the police building.

Several bodies lay on the floor. Two policemen were standing with their hands up and the rest of them were running away to the German command building, from where they were raining fire on us. The Germans, the Lithuanians and the Belorussian police who were still alive were concentrated there.

"Our troop was attacking from all sides. We again take up a position on our bellies and pour fire on the H.Q. and the church from where they are also shooting at us. Our neighbours let out a cry of 'Hurrah!' and storm forward. You can hear grenades exploding.

"Now we receive orders to shoot at the church. The H.Q. is already in our hands. Feodorovitch gets us up in order to take the church. However, strong machinegun fire keeps us flat on the ground again. We fire back. David Blumenfeld is hit directly and stretched out dead. Another two fighters are wounded. Our artillery men bring up the cannon and aim it at the church. They fire in its windows and its turrets. The partisans burst inside and the opposition ceases.

The youth of the city collect around us, looking at us with admiration and amazement. They're pointing at the police and the collaborators and asking to be accepted into the troop. Several of them have already managed to get hold of some weapons and they won't leave us alone.

"The town is in our hands, a perfect victory. We start to chase after police and enemy collaborators. Somebody lets us know that the Germans and the police are hiding in the hospital. They immediately get what they deserve.

"Maitek Lustig and I fill the disks with bullets from the loot and also fill a gasmask rucksack with them. We need the stock. Our morale is very high. The local residents are telling us how much they trust us – that no traitor will be able to escape the partisan's bullet.

"It's noon, the sun is burning down. We remove the spoils on carts. Our doctors, Blumovitch and Lakomtsev[61], load medicines and first aid supplies and the troop moves out of the town. Our troop, the 51, is now in the rear guard. Most of the people who were shut up in the ghetto come out with us. The young ones who've managed to get hold of some arms are joining the troop, and the rest will live in the family camp."

Other troops, too, which took part in the battle, have wounded. In addition to David Blumenfeld, the Shchors had two more fallen, and the Dimitrov troop, which attacked the municipality building, had lost three men.

Only a few of the young people from the Kosovo ghetto were accepted by the partisans. Most of them had families and the Shchors troop set up the 59 group for them, which was, in fact, a family camp. Most people in this camp were killed in the days of the terrible manhunts, which the Germans carried out in September 1942 and February 1943. They died from enemy bullets, they suffered from starvation, from typhus and the cold, and from being abandoned when they were forced to flee their huts and wander under the open sky in the September rains and the snow and ice of February. A similar fate awaited the neighbouring Biten camp too, the 60 group, after the Shchors troop left them in Volchye-Nori when it was moving eastwards.

Operation Kosovo is reported in the official Soviet history books in these sentences: "From the history of the partisan brigade under the name of P.K. Ponomarenko, concerning the destruction of the German fascist garrison by partisan troops of the Brest strip in the town of Kosovo on 2 August 1942...

17th. August 1944, number 341.

"....Command of the Kosovo operation was entirely taken by comrade Proniagin, commander of the Shchors troop. At exactly midnight, the fighters moved into the assault position...

---

[61] *A Russian doctor, who served with a neighbouring troop.*

"The partisans advanced speedily, despite a shower of lead from the machineguns of the enemy, who had got into fortifications and were shooting continuously. Comrade Pronyagin ordered them to throw grenades at fortifications. A deafening explosion was heard. The partisans behaved with courage and without flinching. The 51 group, in particular, distinguished themselves in this battle. They were commanded by Podorovski and were the first to break through to the town. The comrade Kasian Kalyuni (Kigo) also distinguished himself, demonstrating courage and heroism."

The report states that his role in the operation was minimal and mentions names of fighters of the 51 troop, who led the operation, but doesn't in any way recall or refer to the name of a single Jewish fighter (except for distorting the name of commander Feodorovitch).

The victory really raised the spirits of the Jewish partisans and improved their status in the view of the local population. News of the eradication of the Kosovo garrison spread in the area and fear seized any traitors and their families.

This was a period when the Germans were trying to break through to the Volga. They were still positioned close to Moscow and near to Leningrad, but they had already ceased to be masters of the territory in the rear. Kosovo remained under the control of the partisans for about a month. The Germans collected their dead and made off from the town. Partisan ambushes were set up along the road to Kosovo.

The young Ya'akov Khatzkelevitch tells the story of the battle:

"The fighters were ordered to prepare their weapons, earlier in the day before they left for battle. The camp was buzzing with energy and the knocking of polishing up the weapons. Everybody was happy about the plan to liberate the ghetto, and nobody thought that he would be wounded or killed, even though everyone knew that there were strong enemy forces in Kosovo.

"At 6 am., all the brigades gathered. The chief of staff, Merzliakov, explained the mission which the brigade had been ordered to carry out. The 51 was to attack the ghetto. The message was that the neighbouring troops would come to our aid and attack the enemy from the flank with the two cannon.

"We completed preparations and started marching. Our march went on a whole night, through marshes, fields and forests. All the battalions were arranged in their positions and were waiting for the signal to attack. We were waiting for a long while and then a red rocket lit up the night sky and then we heard the firing of hundreds of automatic weapons and rifles, accompanied by the dull thump of cannon. The police responded immediately with concentrated fire, and the battle heated up. The commander of our group called, 'Hurrah! Forwards!' and then we burst through to the first houses of the town and advanced slowly towards the ghetto.... we broke through to the ghetto, despite the fact that we had wounded. The Jews of Kosovo met us with tears of joy.'

In the camp, on the day of operation Kosovo

On the day that the fighters set out for the Kosovo operation, young Zvi Shepetinski felt very low. He was still without a weapon and was not counted among the fighters. A few people remained in the camp, going around between the pine trees like shadows. The fire that had been burning under the kitchen pot had gone out. Here and there, somebody came to the fire, filled their utensils with the food that was cooking and went off again to their tent or shelter. From time to time, you could hear a whispered conversation. There was tension in the atmosphere, and with darkness, sadness fell upon the camp and gnawed at the souls of the people in Volchye- Nori.

"I prayed in my heart for the survival of my comrades who had gone out on this campaign," says Zvi, "that they should succeed in their task and liberate the Jewish survivors who were imprisoned still in the Kosovo ghetto. I was fearful because this was the first battle for our comrades. It was a night of sleeplessness in the camp. Midnight had long passed, when you could hear in the distance the sound of dull explosions, presumably cannon fire. The fateful battle had begun."

In the morning, silence reigned in the camp. Zvi made use of the opportunity to ask for permission to bring some food for his parents and for the family of his uncle, Yitzhak Shepetinski, who were still living in the "Kommandatura". He wrapped several slices of meat and two loaves of bread and set out on his way. The family received him with joy and fear, as the family of Chana and Yitzhak Shepetinski had three sons in the campaign: Herzel, Yasha (Ya'akov) and the youngest (Reuven). The people living in the Kommandatura said that they had also heard the echoes of firing and had seen the whole sky red from a conflagration. Partisan horseback riders who had passed by a little while previously had told them that the battle was over and that the partisans were collecting up their spoils. Zvi hurried back to the camp to bring the glad news.

In the camp, they were already getting ready to welcome the victors. The kitchen bonfire was burning again and the chef, Imber Snr., and with him his helper, Itzl Rabinovitch, were already working hard by the pot. Imber was a Jew of about fifty years old, heavily built and bald-headed. His big, dark eyes were full of deep sorrow, and he was also very kind-hearted.

Distant voices announced the return of the fighters. The tumult was growing closer. The rattle of the carts was mixed up with the squeak of bicycles and the thump of the approaching heavy steps. Some of the fighters were marching and some of them sitting on the carts, laden with weapons and various other items. The tired faces of the fighters coming home were shining with smiles of contentment, and they scattered with a lot of noise to their shelters - some to rest, some to wash before the festive meal. Now the camp learned of the first Jewish victim of the 51 troop, David Blumenfeld, who had fallen in battle.

Evening fell, and life in the camp returned to its normal pattern. Again, the bonfire lit up the centre of the camp and again, there was a lot of running around between the trees. You could hear conversations in Russian and Yiddish and sometimes with a mixture of Polish words. Here and there, you could hear laughter. The dishes of food were emptied and washed in the water of the well, and hung up to dry. Each person carried their own knives and forks, precious possessions, stuck in their boots.

Bit by bit, people were coming around the bonfire to sit and get together. The conversation revolved mainly around the battle. The commanders were there with their girlfriends in the brigade who had come from the Slonim ghetto. From the neighbouring camps, you could hear the echoes of Russian singing. Helinka Rodenstein was asked to lead the singing and everyone else joined in. The 51 brigade's treasury of songs in Russian was still quite weak, as very few had managed to learn the songs during the Soviet regime in Slonim or in the underground meetings after the German invasion.

The brigade's Komsomol meeting

The next day in the morning, a young person's meeting was announced, to take place at the rear of the camp in a forest of young pines. About twenty young people gathered. From the commander's tent, there emerged a young woman of twenty years old, short, with a chubby face and curly blond hair. She was wearing a khaki Red Army shirt, trousers, and polished boots, and around her waist a broad leather belt with a buckle decorated with a shiny brass star, like the belt of a Red Army officer. From the belt hung a leather holster with a pistol in it. This was Irka Weisselfisch. Her face and appearance conveyed self-confidence and pride, and these were clearly felt when she started to speak:

"Our meeting is dedicated to the foundation of a Komsomol organisation in our brigade. Everywhere that young people are compelled to struggle for the safety and peace of our homeland, the Komsomol must be a pioneering force of the fighters, marching in the front lines and serving as an example to the rest. Our role in these difficult times is to fight to our last drop of blood, to take revenge on the Nazi monsters, who have spilt the blood of tens of thousands of innocent people.'

She continued to speak in this style, 'If I remember rightly,' says Zvi Shefet, who was present at the meeting, 'No questions were asked, and somebody even said that everything was clear. Then Irka registered those present and from that moment, they were members of the Communist Youth Organisation.' Zvi felt quite lonely in the camp. He had no friends or comrades there, apart from his three cousins and their friends. They were all older than him, and they had no reason to become friendly with a lad of sixteen. Sometimes he was attacked by envy and longed to be older. After the Komsomol meeting, he was registered as being seventeen.

Slonim. The bridge over the canal, in front of the ghetto

The Shepetinski's home, at the Michailovski Alley
No1. The underground hideout No2. The hideout and the weapons cache

The forests where the Shchors partisans battalion lived

The Shchara River and 10th Dam on the canal
The arrow shows the direction of the battalion attack

The 10th dam over the Shchara river The upper bridge

The bridge over the canal

Nathan Liker (on the right) and P. Proniagen
Shchors Battalion commander (1942)

Dr. Abraham Blumovitz-Atzmon
Shchors Head Physician (1942)

Aron Bandt (1952)
Troop commander in Shchors

Zerach Kremin (1946)
Shchors explosive Troop commander

Nionia Zirinsky (1956)
Patrol & saboteur in Shchors

Dr. Cheslava Orlinsky (1958)
Shchors Doctor

Abraham Orlinsky (1948)
Patrol & saboteur in Shchors

Aviezer Imber (1947)
Patrol & saboteur in Shchors

Abraham Doktorchik (1946)
Partisan & Gunner in Shchors

Mishka Perzov (1945)
Partisan & Patrol in Shchors

Israel Slonimsky (1945)
Partisan in Shchors

Noah Serviansky (1945)
Patrol & saboteur in Shchors

Zeev Finkel (1945)
Partisan in Shchors

Pesach & Rivka Alpert (sits) w. their daughters, Raya & Hana
Partisans in Shchors

Anshel Delatitsky (1946)
Partisan in Shchors

Eliahu Abramovitz (1945)
Partisan in Shchors

Golda Gerzovsky (1946)
Partisan in Shchors

Yakob Hatskalevitz (1945)
Partisan & saboteur in Shchors

Yakob Gringhauz (1939)
Partisan in Shchors

Lyuba Bandt (1950)
Partisan in Shchors

Grisha Gringhauz (1946)
Partisan in Shchors

Ruben Shepetinski (1939) — Partisan in Shchors
Hertzel Shepetinski (1940) — Squad commander in Shchors
Jacov Shepetinski (1939) — Partisan in Shchors
Fruma Shepetinski (1940) — Partisan in Chapayev
Raya Shepetinski (1945) — Partisan in Shchors
Zvi Shepetinski (1945) — Partisan saboteur in Shchors
Mina Volkoviskoski (1946) — Partisan in Chapayev
Yehudit Shelubski (1946) — Partisan in Shchors
Tania Galerstein (1945) — Partisan in Shchors

First missions of the youngest member of the brigade

The next morning, the store-master of the brigade, Piletski, gave Zvi his first role. Piletski came from a Belorussian village. In the Soviet days, before the war, he was a policeman in Slonim. He fell in love with a Jewish girl from Slonim by the name of Dvora Derechinski and rescued her from the hands of the Nazis, and reached the forest together with her and her brother, Tsadok. Because of his role as store-man, Piletski had built a family shelter near the kitchen. He used to keep foodstuffs for the brigade in his house, and share them out among the cooks. Nearby, the 'butcher's' had been set up, a place where pieces of the animals that had been slaughtered were hung up on a pole. They used to smoke the meat so that it wouldn't go off before time and also to protect it from the flies.

Piletski asked Zvi to go to the brigade's bakery, which was in one of the houses at the back of the village of Okoninovo, and make sure that the bread would reach the brigade by evening. Zvi took the password and was ordered to return with the delivery.

Zvi was very glad of the errand, which gave him the chance to show that he too could be of some use. He went back to his shelter and told his two neighbours about the role he'd received. Zhama Shusterovitch offered him his short leather jacket, as it wasn't fitting for a partisan to appear in the village in shabby clothes. His other friend and neighbour lent him a Nagan pistol. The pistol in fact didn't work because it was missing a certain part, but the handle of the pistol peeping out of Zvi's pocket, was intended to impress more than any polite or friendly words.

Zvi set out on the road leading to the Kommandatura, where his family was still living. Everybody was happy to see him. The handle of the pistol, which was sticking up out of his pocket, made an impression on people in the camp, and so Zvi was embarrassed to reveal the precise nature of the pistol.

After walking for about half an hour, he reached his goal. At the bakery, he approached the man in charge, who was a member of brigade 51. He told him to wait and went to organise a cart to transport the bread. Zvi ate lunch with him and when the cart arrived with the loaves of warm bread, he got on it and took the reins. He returned to the brigade camp and gave the load to Piletski.

Now he was free, but he had to return the horse and cart. How could he do this? His cousin Herzel instructed him: "It's very simple: You take the horse, harnessed to the cart, out onto the road from which you've come, and you giddy him up and the horse returns on his own, along the same tracks, to the place he came from."

In the family camps

The command had carried out its decision to set up two family camps under its protection – the Biteni and the Kosovi. Zvi's parents and his sister Sonia were attached to the Biteni camp. The refusal to accept them into brigade 51 was explained in the following way – that people of an advanced age and children would lower the fighting fitness of the brigade. In fact, this was just an excuse. His parents were aged forty-two and forty-three and at the height of their physical fitness and his sister was nineteen. Soviet citizens and non-Jewish Belorussians were not subject to this restriction. Zvi's uncle and his family were accepted into the group after a while by virtue of their three sons, Yasha, Herzel and Reuven, who were fighters. The last of the people who'd escaped from the Slonim ghetto were also attached to the Biteni camp. The camp was set up on a hill in the forest, not far from brigade 51. The Kosovo camp was positioned on the other side of the dirt path which crossed through the forest. Now the Kommandatura was empty of residents. The H.Q. of the troop promised to help the family camp with food supplies and self-defence, but these promises were never kept and most people living in the family camps perished. Meanwhile, brigade 51 assisted the Biteni camp in supplying some arms and ammunition.

Yitzhak Shepetinski, father of the three fighting sons, worked in a group preparing wood for the kitchen, and his wife, Hannah, served as a cook.

The news reached Zvi that his parents were living in hardship in the Biten family camp. He equipped himself with a little food, asked permission to visit his parents and set out. First, he reached the Kosovo camp. The Jews were living there in small family groups, over a large area between tall pines. There were tents there covered with fabric of all sorts of shapes and sizes, and there were shelters made from logs and branches. At the entrances of the shelters, there were small bonfires, and next to them, the men were working and the women were cooking for their families, baking potatoes in the earth, while the children played with the embers.

Near these shelters stood the farmers' carts, on which small shelters had been set up - another room, as it were, for people living in the shelters. A few young men of National Service age were carrying rifles, which they'd managed to obtain from the townspeople or had taken by force from residents of surrounding villages who were well known as enemy collaborators. They also possessed various useful objects, like sewing machines, which they'd collected on incursions with the combat partisans. Their main role was to hold trials of people who were serving the Nazi regime in Kosovo. After the sentence was passed on the collaborators, their property was confiscated– the partisans took some and some of it was brought to the family camp. The artisans – tailors, cobblers, leatherworkers –had their hands full of work: they supplied the needs of the fighting partisans according to orders they received from their commanders. A large proportion of these orders was intended for the commanders themselves, since there was no organisation in this aspect of supply, and everybody looked out for himself. The artisans received foodstuffs in return for what they supplied. Their wives and children helped them to carry out the orders.

From the Kosovo camp, Zvi carried on to the Biteni camp. Here, he saw fewer shelters, and it was recognisably tidier and cleaner. The residents of the camp were older, and the quiet that ruled here was suffused with sadness. You didn't hear children's voices in this camp, nor the voices of women hushing their noisy children. There were no bonfires burning at the entrances to the shelters and you wouldn't see any craftsmen carrying out their crafts. There were no laden carts standing here and no armed young men walking around. At the centre of the camp was a kitchen which was fenced around with branches and in the pots hung over the bonfire, the meals were cooking for all the camp's residents.

Zvi reached his parents' tent, which was bigger than the others and better fitted inside. Along the length of its walls, three bunks had been set up for the three family members to sleep, covered with radiushkas (Belorussian handwoven folk covers) and in the centre – a small table of unplaned planks and around it several tree trunks which served as seats.

Zvi handed over the food parcel which he had brought and asked questions about their life. His mother was chief cook in the camp and his father took care of domestic organisation. His sister Sonia was attached to the operational detail, which had only a few rifles for guarding, and Zvi went with his father to visit her on her watch. She seemed calm despite all the hardships she had been through. He parted from her with, 'See you again,' but he never did.

In the camp, Zvi ate a meagre lunch with his parents and was there until the bread, which was rationed, was distributed. The family discussed the future. Zvi believed that his parents' right to be partisans would be recognised and they would be armed. However, his parents were right in being less optimistic than he was.

The first watch

Zvi looked for work for himself and volunteered for every job that came up. In the afternoon he was told he would go out on guard for the whole of the next day.

Zvi says:

"I was pleased at the role and I reported to the guard commander. I received a rifle on loan, and I and two older comrades, were stationed at the crossroads of the forest, a distance of about a kilometre from the camp.

"The guard order was always the same: One watches and the other rests while being continually alert and prepared. The third is allowed to sleep. Each one of us was awake eight hours by day and four hours at night. All around, silence reigned and only the sound of birds in sudden flight disturbed the peace. The treetops moved lightly and made a monotonous rustling sound.

"The very fact that I had been set to guard the safety of the camp with my comrades excited me: I felt a burden of responsibility had been laid upon me and all that night, I barely closed an eyelid. I listened to the sounds of the forest animals, to the light rustling of the hares jumping; I tried to distinguish between the normal sounds of the forest and sounds of the footsteps of people approaching. I noticed that the treetops of the pine turned in one direction and their branches on this side were larger and more developed. I told my comrades about my discovery and it appeared that it was well-known that the side to which the more developed branches are turned is the southern side, the side of the sun. I realised, therefore, that we were standing on guard on the east of the camp.

"The captain of the guard visited us several times after he had given us the password for the day, and he exchanged a few words with us and disappeared just as he'd come. The two hours when I stood on guard in darkness seemed like a month to me. I held my rifle at the ready, under my right arm, in order to be able to use it as soon as I needed and that gave me confidence. Nevertheless, I was tense: I pondered how I should behave if an uninvited guest appeared or just anyone who had got lost, and the worst thing of all, if I should suddenly be attacked by the spies who, according to the peasants, were swarming in the area.

"I was very glad when daylight came. The sound of the guard captain's familiar footsteps reached our ears, and he appeared a few minutes later. One of our comrades on guard accompanied him to the camp to bring us breakfast. The day passed more quickly and was less boring. We saw partisans from neighbouring brigades, bringing carts laden with foodstuffs and slaughtered pigs, to the camp. Several of them lay on the carts fast asleep. They looked as if they'd come back exhausted from a long distance. We didn't stop them and just welcomed them when they passed in front of us. In the evening, we were relieved by a new watch and returned to camp.

A problem in the pasture

"I was still getting ready for the evening meal when I was informed that I would have to keep guard that night over the horses of our brigade, who were in the pasture. My job was to supervise them so they wouldn't wander off to the thick part of the forest. Their front legs were tied with short ropes in order to restrict their movements.

"I went to the new guard commander to receive my instructions. The commander was a tall, swarthy young man, who was called Sokolik. He explained briefly what I had to do, and I went out with him to the pasture, again with a borrowed rifle. The place was several hundred metres south of the place where I had stood guard the day before and stretched out over a portion of the forest where the trees had been felled to make a pasture. On the south side, the dirt track on which we'd arrived continued and trees, with wide-branching treetops, which had been deliberately felled, blocked the way for vehicles. Five horses were grazing here, and I had to look after them. They were skipping around peacefully and enjoying the juicy green grass. Several times during the night, I had to check that they were there. I found traces of a bonfire, whose embers were still whispering. I put it out so it wouldn't catch fire and light up the night. I walked back and forth, listening and looking hard. After I noticed that the horses were tired of eating and they began to doze, I did likewise. I lay down for a long while, with the rifle between my legs, its belt attached around my hand, so that I would feel any attempt to touch the weapon. It seems a deep sleep fell upon me because I hadn't slept for several nights. Suddenly, I felt I was shaken hard, but it seemed to me as if I was dreaming. I woke up after a few minutes and then saw that the rifle was gone. I immediately jumped up on my feet and ran towards the road leading to the camp. I saw a figure of a man making off in the direction of the guard. The horses were calm and were still having their night's slumber, but I could find no peace of mind. I couldn't understand this had happened and who could have taken my rifle. I hurried to the guard, and there, I was told that Irka had just passed by on her way to the camp with a second rifle on her. I hurried after her and looked for Sokolik. I found him, and he was sitting by a little fire in the undergrowth of young pine trees and next to him sat a partisan who I didn't know, apparently the inside guard of the camp (Dnievalny). When he saw me, he called me and asked how this had happened. I told him in detail. Only after I realised I had not disobeyed any instructions did I feel easier. But I was still ashamed and I couldn't understand how Irka had succeeded in taking the rifle without waking me. I must have turned in my sleep, which had released the rifle from my grasp. She had used this opportunity to demonstrate to the command her alertness and superiority. From then on, I couldn't stand her.

"I went back and got the rifle from Sokolik, thanked him for supporting me and went back to the pasture. It was still dark, and I told my comrades on the guard what had happened to me. They were very pleased too that the whole thing had finished as it did, and pointed out that I'd been lucky. And I had learnt a lesson that was engraved deep in my memory.

"I couldn't sleep anymore, and I looked at the tranquil animals that were under my command, and was envious of them: what peace and patience, even friendship, reigned between them. Dawn slowly pushed the darkness of night away; the sun rose and the treetops were outlined in their fresh greenery. The night left whitish shadows over the green carpets of the forest's earth, and the dewdrops sparkled with all colours of the rainbow when the sun's rays hit them. The horses, too, woke up and began to frolic and eat the grass.

"Towards noon, I went back to the camp and lay down to rest, having had enough of the upset and anger of the night.

Supplies mission for the family camp

"I awoke towards evening. Just then, a group had been organised to go out on an acquisition mission for the Biteni camp. I asked if I could join them and was granted my request. I was pleased at the opportunity to go back and see my parents and to help people in need. We left for the target village as evening fell, on several harnessed carts. In the village, I met several people from the Biteni camp who had arrived after us, and among them, my father. We only had a short while, and we had to hurry up and collect the goods. We agreed a meeting place after the operation, divided into small groups and scattered right through the village. Each pair of armed partisans from our brigade was accompanied by several people from the Biteni camp. There were people who were looking for clothes from the loot that the Red Army had left behind or from possessions stolen from the Jews. The task was carried out within the appointed time without incident. We marched in single file behind the laden carts. Dawn broke and we were still far away from the family camp, but we arrived there in the late hours of the morning. The people of the camp received us with thanks and joy. We helped them to unload the carts and went back to the camp. I was tired - the lack of sleep for three successive nights was beginning to show its signs."

A few days later, the brigade was called to a new mission to wipe out the German garrison in Gavinovitch.

The Gavinovitch mission (10th. August 1942)

In August 1942, about a week after the Kosovo operation, various rumours were going around the brigade's camp. Commanders met frequently. Partisans were whispering together and trying to guess what the new mission being prepared for them would be. Envoys were sent urgently to partisan units nearby and would come back with their representatives, and reconnaissance groups went out in all directions.

Every day, Jews arrived from the Slonim ghetto and described what was happening there. It was clear that the Germans were on the point of wiping out the remnants of the community and they also said that the Germans were enrolling Belorussian volunteers in the area for an organisation called Samoohova (self-defence) and its role would be to fight the partisan movement and their representatives in the villages.

Zerach Kremin, on one occasion when he came back from a patrol, reported that this organisation already existed in the village of Gavinovitch, where a school for gunners had been set up, which would be able to operate against the partisans. The commander of the school was a Slonim resident and his name was Orlovski, a man from the anti-Soviet gangs. Now, even the private soldiers who hadn't been included in any secret operational plans, caught on that this was evidently to be an attack on Gavinovitch. Zerach Kremin, who was in command of a reconnaissance group, was very keen on the idea. He urged the troop H.Q. to wipe out the organisation while it was still in its infancy.

On his way back from Slonim, Zerach met Captain Fedotov, together with his operational officer. He accompanied them to where the Shchors troop was stationed. This commander, who was called by the partisans, 'the bearded captain,' because of his neatly kept beard, commanded a partisan troop called Tchepayev, stationed by the village of Deloga, near Biten. When he arrived, Fedotov suggested to Proniagin a joint operation of the two troops to wipe out the enemy in Gavinovitch. Zerach remembers that Proniagin wasn't very enthusiastic about this operation. He supposed that this was a matter for the Tchepayev group, which felt threatened by the enemy in Gavinovitch. During this period, each troop operated according to its own needs and its considerations. Collaboration between the troops had not yet been established. But Proniagin did not like to reject the proposal which appealed to Feodorovitch, the 51 commander, and to the rest of the commanders of groups within his battalion.

In a consultation of the commanders, which ended roundabout noon, it was decided to]carry out the operation. At dusk, Proniagin announced that the commander of the 51, senior lieutenant Feodorovitch, would be in charge of the mission. The fighters of the 51, which was designated for this task, were inspected very closely, they and their equipment, by the junior commanders.

That same evening in August, the 51 group was organised with its full weaponry into its platoons and squads. The commanders stood in front of the lines – Feodorovitch, Zerach Kremin, Archik Bandt, Fima Podolski, and Vasya Volkov. The chief of staff, Merzliakov, read the order of the day: the target is to wipe out the Belorussian police school in Gavinovitch. Commissar Dudko read out the text of the oath which the partisans were required to swear and this is the text:

"I, citizen of the Union of Soviet Socialist Republics, am joining the Red partisans in active struggle, my weapon in my hand against the sworn enemy of our homeland – Hitlerite Germany. I swear this oath before the people and the Soviet state: I swear to hit the enemy everywhere without sparing my strength and my blood, and in the hour of need, even my life – for the sake of my socialist homeland, for the spilt blood of our people, for the mothers and fathers, the women and children and for the brothers and sisters who have been tortured to death by the fascist hangman.

"I swear to be devoted to our socialist land, to the Soviet state and to be courageous and of strong spirit in encounters with the enemy; to be decent and disciplined and to keep our sacred military secrets in the partisan struggle; to obey unreservedly the orders of my commanders and political activists.

"I swear that I will fight with weapons in my hand until the complete defeat of the enemy, despite difficulties and losses which will be my portion. If I ever violate this ceremonial oath – may the strict hand of Soviet law punish me."

The commissar read the words of the oath and the partisans repeated them after him as one, and their eyes were moist with emotion.

After the ceremony, everybody dispersed and prepared the final preparations before setting out. The whole camp was under guard. Only the sick and the unarmed remained. Fighters went on the mission from the 51, 52 and 53 groups. They were to meet up with partisans from the Tchepayev troop.

The fighters left in the evening and in darkness, crossed the Shchara. The night march passed quietly, and they surrounded Gavinovitch from the north side, took up positions and waited for the signal.

In the meantime, the Tchepayevs had managed to collect new information about the strike point. It had emerged that the operation wouldn't be as easy as first supposed. The building that housed the German instructors was built of stone and brick and surrounded by fortifications. If the Germans dug in, in the building, it would be hard to take it. The police school was also fortified: all around there were ditches and embankments. In fact, the enemy force was not large, but because of these fortifications, they would be able to inflict serious losses on the attackers.

The fighters realised that they wouldn't be able to win this battle without the cannon that had been left behind in the camp. It was decided to send Zerach with a group of partisans to Proniagin in order to convince him to give them the cannon. Zerach returned and delivered the request to the troop commander. At first, Proniagin refused completely. However, Zerach told him that the operation would be easy to carry out, and he, Proniagain, would go down in partisan history as the commander of the operation. "I managed to convince the hesitant commander to come with the cannon," says Zerach.

Shortly before dawn broke, the 51 group arrived with its commander, Feodorovitch, on the outskirts of Gavinovitch. The fighters took up positions in the sparse woods which surrounded the estate where the school for gunners was situated and cut off the telephone lines in the area. The enemy now had only one line of retreat, and that crossed in front of the Pravoslavi church (Greek Orthodox), in the direction of the Tartatchok marshes and the forests. A reinforced Shchors ambush was set there. Another two ambushes were set up on both sides of the Baranovitch-Slonim road. Fighters of the Molotov troop, which had come from the forests of Kosovo, and the Tchepayev fighters waited here. Fighters from the 51 group lay at the ready, and their eyes were fixed on the target which they were about to attack. The Belorussian police, who lived in the school for gunners, was still asleep.

When the day began to lighten, the order "At the ready!" was whispered, and immediately, commander Proniagin roared: "Fire!" The cannon fired several shells at the building and all weapons thundered. The air resounded with the sounds of explosions of window panes and roof tiles. Fire had not yet been returned from the house on the plot, and the partisans could hear the sound of shouting and cries of pain for help.

Yasha Shepetinski took part in the battle as a gunner. His platoon was placed close to the cannon. The platoon circumvented the estate and took up a position behind a little hill at the edges of the forest. At a distance of several metres between the hill and the farm, lay a field, and beyond it, a vegetable garden, about two hundred metres long, which reached right up to the manor house. The cannon was set up on the mound and aimed for a direct hit on the building. The two machineguns were also set up on the two sides.

Before the signal for attack was given, Feodorovitch personally checked the positions of all the fighters and established each one's goal. Yasha Shepetinski reports:

"Feodorovitch's voice is giving orders: 'For the sake of the homeland, forward, after me, Hurra!' And a chain of his fighters storms after him. We run forward, standing tall and shouting 'Hurrah!' The fast frontal attack immediately broke the police opposition and most of them put their hands up. There was a new Diegtiyerov submachine-gun set in a pit of potatoes, to which I had run with Mietek Lustig, my number two on my machinegun, and next to it, two dead policemen.

Zvi Shepetinski took the machine gun and took the belt with the bullets off the dead man and on the way to the camp, he dragged a double load on his back, his borrowed rifle and the machinegun, which he returned to the camp, to the command."

Zerach Kremin also reports his impressions:

"The enemy opposition was weak; they were confused, and most of them surrendered. There was one sad incident. The chief of the course had fortified himself in the attic of the building and it was impossible to get near him. Vasya Sankov from the 52 group, who was a very brave man, wanted to catch him alive and began to climb up to the loft, but he was hit from a machinegun round in his face and went blind. After this event, we burnt the house and the Nazi in it. After an air link had been created with the Soviet rear, Vasa was flown for treatment in Moscow.

The police who were living in the building, started to flee in a panic through the gate, towards the Tartatchok swamps, and the students on the gunners' course fled, wearing only their lower garments, and even left their weapons behind. The partisans who were besieging the estate split up: Some of them broke into the house and some of them continued to fire after the people who were running away."

Avraham Doktortchik leaned his machinegun on the branch of a tree and emptied one magazine after another. In time, the shooting began to die down, but from time to time, lone shots still resounded from the direction of the swamp, where the police were killed by partisans who were lying await in ambush.

Avraham Doktortchik relates how dozens of police were taken prisoner. They stood in the yard, under partisan guard, only half-dressed, their heads hung, and they didn't dare to look at their captors. Among the prisoners was also their commander, Orlovski, who threw himself at the feet of the Jewish partisan, Moshe Modelovitch, entreating him with pleas for mercy and grovelling: "Moshke, Golovchik, Dorogoy (Moshe, my dear friend), have mercy on me and my family." Moshe sent him a glance of contempt and growled, "Yes, I know you very well - right back in the days of October, I was in the Red Army and you were a Balachovetz Pogromchik."[62] A flame of hate and revenge started up in Modelevitch's eyes and he pinned the body of the murderous traitor to the ground with his bayonet, the ground of the homeland which he had betrayed.

Zvi Shepetinski also has tales to tell of his experiences of the first battle in which he took part, a battle which excited him greatly. He was positioned in the unit of his cousin Yasha:

"We advanced towards the building, alternately making a short run, then throwing ourselves down. Several police were escaping to the vegetable plot and tried to flee in the direction of the village. We opened concentrated fire on them, and they returned fire with bullets which flew over our heads. We fired between the vegetable plants at any suspicious movement. I noticed the black uniform of a policeman who was crawling between the vegetable beds. I told Yasha to send a round at him, but he couldn't see him. I advanced towards the policeman at a crawl, whilst our comrades in the platoon moved towards the building, making a detour to the left, then straight. I waited very excitedly for the policeman who was making off to appear. After a few minutes, I noticed him again. I aimed my rifle towards him and fired. He was still lying down. I

---

[62] *This refers to the October Revolution and to the gangs of "white" rioters, who fought against the revolutioan, and at the same time murdered Jews and and plundered them.*

ran towards where I'd shot and found him dead. I took his rifle and I took the belt with the magazines off him."

The partisans were now in control of the situation and entered the building. Among the police who'd been taken prisoner were many from Slonim. Among them Pesach Alpert recognised his neighbour, who was a murderer. The police were interrogated: those who'd volunteered to serve the Germans were shot on the spot, whereas those who'd been recruited were released to their homes after they had registered their names and their addresses and had been warned not to collaborate with the enemy.

Carts were brought to load up the spoils. Several partisans, in particular, the young women, took part in the operation and sat in the carts, and the convoy returned to camp. Zerach remembers that after the battle his unit collected up about twenty-five Topoliev machineguns and loaded them on a cart, where Liuba Zhagel guarded them.

Meanwhile, partisans from the other groups who had lain wait in ambush and who had taken a small part in the battle, began to demand their share of the loot. They took it by force, despite the opposition of Liuba. She managed to keep only about fifteen machineguns for the 51 group.

The next day, a parade was held in the camp, and the commander called out the order of the day with the results of the operation and its takings. Proniagin and commissar Dudkov made speeches of praise for the part the Jewish 51 group had played in the liberation of the homeland, and then the arms from the loot were fetched and they began to distribute them to partisans who as yet had no arms of any kind. The commander called each man by name and then he left his row and received the rifle. Zvi was standing in the parade and waited for them to call his name too, and then there were only two rifles left: a Karabinka (a short-barrelled rifle designed for horse riders) and a rifle with a broken butt. Zvi, who had brought a Diegtyerov sub-machinegun from the battlefield, was sure that he would receive at least the Karabinka. However, it was given to another fighter and he got the rifle with the broken butt.

To this day, Zvi remembers how the insult burned in his soul: after all, he could have chosen a new rifle for himself, whatever he wanted, and not to have had to depend on the good will of those in charge. But he took the rifle to the camp. Zvi brought it with the broken butt to Shefchuk, the carpenter, who made a new butt, and a nice one, from oak wood for him. The rifle served him faithfully all the time he was a partisan.

The Shchors troop was growing. It already had six groups and each one had one hundred and fifty fighters on average. The 51 brigade was also growing and they had four platoons. Most of the Jewish members of the 51 group took part in every mission and battle, which the group carried out. There were eight hundred people living in the family camps, and more refugees were coming continually from the ghettos of the region.

In the middle of August, three people dressed in uniform arrived at the troop and introduced themselves as envoys from the "Great Land", that is, from the Soviet rear. When they approached the guard of the camp, the commander wouldn't allow them to enter for fear that they might be spies.

After investigation, it turned out that they were telling the truth. These were envoys from the communist party who had come to supervise partisan activities in the region and with them, the Party attorney, Kleschev.

The destruction of the Biten community

There were about eleven to twelve hundred Jewish residents out of the three thousand living in the small town of Biten, in the Slonim district.

The first four Germans entered the town on 25th. June, 1941. The two first days of occupation were days of immediate looting and robbery from the commercial Soviet storehouses. After these two days a Wehrmacht unit entered the town, and broke into Jewish homes, thieving whatever they could lay their hands on, and then a hail of decrees and oppression hailed down upon them, as was the German custom everywhere.

The people of Biten heard about the slaughter of 14th. November in Slonim the very same day, but the Jews of this small town couldn't believe what they heard. The next Sunday, the Judenraat sent a Christian envoy to Slonim, who gave details of the slaughter on his return, but the Jews of Biten still found it hard to digest the bitter truth. They were only persuaded by the sight of the local Belarussians who sped to Slonim with horses harnessed to carts and sacks in order to rob the houses of the victims.

At the beginning of December, ten German gendarmes arrived in Biten, and the Jews were obliged to furnish rooms with the very best furniture, to supply them with all the domestic equipment they needed and to send them ten girls to serve them. The Germans would wander round the streets, breaking into Jewish houses, abusing, beating, robbing and murdering. The management of the region wrung out of the Jews of Biten two kilograms of gold and two hundred thousand roubles in addition to the daily looting of private houses.

After that, demands for manpower were stepped up and every day new demands were invented. On 13th. March 1942 the Germans drove out the Jews of nearby Ivatsevich after they had robbed them in the marketplace of everything they owned. This was a winter's day of bitter cold, about 30° below freezing. About four hundred refugees reached Biten, many of them with frozen faces and legs and broken limbs. The thousand Jews of Biten, who themselves had been dispossessed of their belongings, found themselves required to absorb the four hundred banished from Ivatsevich.

At the beginning of June, the representatives of the Judenraat received an order to move to the ghetto. They were allowed a week to set it up; they were made to go out to the forest, chop down trees and carry the heavy logs for the fence for the ghetto on their shoulders. Using carts for transport was forbidden. Even the scratchy barbed wire for fencing the thirty-nine houses which had been included in the ghetto they were forced to carry on their shoulders.

Now the Jews of Biten, too, saw how their neighbours and friends, the Christian residents of Biten, were pouncing on their houses and robbing them of everything they could lay their hands on. At the end of the week, the gates of the ghetto were locked and they were forced to live in crowded conditions, fifteen to twenty people in one small room.

On 25th. July 1942 the slaughter of Biten was carried out. On the eve of the Action, the Germans, with their Belarussian and Polish servants, undertook the same tricks, distractions and deceptions that they had practised everywhere. They gaily promised to the Jews of Biten that no ill would befall them and they could safely dwell in safety in their houses - but anyone who had prepared himself a hiding place for emergencies went down and hid. The Jewish ghetto policemen went from house to house and warned the Jews not to go to sleep and to be alert to danger, but many Jews who had nowhere to hide were caught and many were also hauled out of their hiding places. Poles, Belarussians and Lithuanians were looking for anyone in hiding and the Germans were merely in command of the operation.

Towards morning the shooting in the ghetto died down, and the thump of the people- hunters' boots and the rattle of cars were silenced. Now carts came into the ghetto and those in hiding could hear how the murderers were taking all the furniture and possessions from their houses and carting them off. Each Jew was numb with pain and only one thought preyed on his mind: are any of my dear ones, my friends, still alive? Through cracks in the walls of the hiding places they saw peasant women who they knew roaming in the ghetto and carrying bundles and baskets. It was as if time stood still, every moment was an eternity.

The next day the Action stopped. Of twelve hundred Jews in Biten, there remained only three hundred and forty. The victims were shot into two pits which had been previously prepared, and those who managed to crawl out of the pits while they were still alive and tried to escape, were handed over by Belarussian and Polish youth who were roaming near the Murder Valley. Murdered bodies were rolling in all the alleyways and yards. The bereaved, orphaned remnants buried the slain and lamented the dead.

Now the gendarmerie gave the "good news" to the survivors that they would leave them alive for another month, and in the meantime news reached Biten about the activities of the partisans in the area and about the victory at Kosovo. The news crystallised the survivors' awareness that they needed to flee and to join the partisans.

Even before that, Jews from had fled from Biten and looked for a way to join the partisans. Most of them had come across difficulties, in the refusal to absorb them. After the first slaughter, a struggle went on in the ghetto between those who wished to leave for the partisans and the rest. The latter claimed that those who flee to the forest endanger the survival of those left behind and because of them, the Germans would take revenge. This was one of the illusions which was widespread in many ghettoes.

The second slaughter in Biten was on 19th. August, most of the work being done by Lithuanians and very few Jews managed to flee to the forest. The last people from the Biten ghetto were murdered on 19th. September and the community was wiped out from the face of the earth. Only in the forests did there still flicker remnants of the Jewish life of Biten but their tribulations didn't end even in the forests. The partisan Moshe Pitkovski[63] says of the history of the survivors of Biten in the forest:

"In the approaches to Volchye Nori, in the Kommandatura, the Jews of Biten, Slonim, Ivatsevich and Kosovo were lying in extremely crowded conditions, on rotten straw which was spread over the floor. Pursued by one fate, they had arrived here with one aim in mind, to take some revenge on the cruel enemy before they died.

"Carts were passing us carrying partisans who had been sent on operations. They were full of life and excitement. They looked at us and went their way. Afterwards, one of the partisans came to us and made a speech in a mixture of Belarussian and Ukrainian. His thick curly hair covered half his face and he was armed from top to toe. This was Pashka Khokhol (a Ukrainian name) in whose company I passed almost two years in the forest. At various periods he was to blame to a great extent for the tragedy of our life in the forest, and these were his words:

'If you've fled from the ghetto and come to the forest in order to save your lives, then there's no place for you here. But if you have come here in order to fight the enemy and avenge the blood that's been spilt, then there is a place for you. However, you must remember one thing, you must get hold of weapons - for how will you operate here without weapons? We have nothing for you; you must get your own weapons by every means possible. Gather information: who are the peasants who have hidden arms in their farms, and we will straightaway get it from them. At any event, you must get hold of weapons.'

"In fact, we were pleased with his speech because after all this was our aim too - war and revenge. We answered him that we were ready for everything and that we would do everything within our power to get hold of weapons."

However, only some of the young people of Biten were accepted into the Shchors battalion. The command organised the 60th. Brigade for the families, which was in fact a family camp. A lieutenant (politruk) was set up over them, a young Russian man called Seryozha Tokarikov, who turned out to be a good man and did all he possibly could in the days of the manhunts to help and rescue the Jews from the clutches of the enemy. The whole brigade was divided into six units (Vsevodi) and the Russian Yefremov Pugachov was their commander. In time, their numbers grew to three hundred and sixty. At first, they had several dozen rifles and one machinegun. The first and second units were responsible for sabotage and supply of food; the third unit was engaged in guarding the camp and numbered fifty to sixty people. The Jew in command of that unit was an ex-Soviet army soldier who had escaped from captivity. The rest of the units were domestic. Their role was to keep order in the camp, to distribute foodstuffs and to prepare the food and so on. Shlomo Shepetinski, the father of Zvi, was appointed manager of the camp.

---

[63] *Moshe Pertkovski, "Azoi iz Untergegangan die Idishe Kehilah in Biten", from the Biten Folder, Buenos Aires, 1954. See below for Pitkovski, and page number.*

The partisans took control of two flour mills in neighbouring villages, where they ground for partisans the grain which was confiscated from villages that were supplying their produce to the Germans. Two young men from the Kosovo Group 59 organised and managed a bakery in the nearby village. In the bakery they baked the bread for the battalions.

Then one morning all the people of Group 60 were called out by their drill commanders. In all the shacks searches were conducted for any useful thing - shoes, money, saccharine - all were taken. After several hours, the people were returned to the camp and took a load of rebuke for not having handed over these things themselves. In the search, money was taken too and many items remained thrown outside where they rotted in the rain.

The burden of suffering of the inhabitants of the family camps was exacerbated in the days of the manhunts and by the many weeks of siege that the Germans imposed on the partisan forests. (This part of the story will be continued later.)

How the young Israel Slonimski from Biten reached Troop 51

Israel Slonimski was sixteen years old when he reached the forest of Volchye Nori. He had been sent first to the forced labour camp in Puzovitch, where Jews from Slonim were also working.

On the night of 20th. June 1942, which was a stormy night, a night when hail and rain poured down accompanied by thunder and lightning, the partisans from Bulak's troop which was near the banks of the Shchara, surrounded the (Puzovitch) camp and shot down the guards, who were positioned in the watchtowers. The German gendarmes fled in half-naked panic, and the Jews prisoners scattered. Israel Slonimski managed to get back to his parents who were still in the Biten ghetto.

After some time, Israel was sent to cut down trees for the Germans who were guarding the Brest and Minsk railway line. There he heard about the destruction of the Jews in the whole area and understood that there was no refuge for Jews other than the forest. During the Action of 25th. July 1942 in the Biten ghetto, he hid with the rest of his family in a hiding place. The enemy discovered them, broke the door of the shelter and started to turn the Jews out with blows from clubs, into a lorry, in which they were driven to the death pits. In the confusion Israel noticed a Belarussian policeman whom he knew, and he offered him his boots in exchange for protection from the blows. This "good" friend took Israel's boots and led him while protecting him from the blows of the other murderers.

"I was one of the last who got on the lorry, and when the Germans gave orders to undress, I didn't hasten to do so" says Israel. The Jews on that lorry had not yet given up; they caught hold of a German gendarme who was guarding them inside the lorry and knocked him to the ground. Israel took advantage of the moment and jumped out. The policemen shot after him but the bullets didn't reach him. He managed to flee and hid in a field of corn between the stalks. From there he saw the terrible sights of the murder of the people of Biten, close to the place where he was hiding.

Israel goes on:

"The rustle of the ripe ears of corn and the blowing of the wind all over the field were silenced by the cries and the heart-rending sobbing which was borne up from the place of killing. Volleys of shots from rifles and machineguns split the cries of pain.

"I fell to my knees and I saw hell on the earth. The Germans and their Lithuanian helpers forced the Jews to strip naked; anyone who didn't obey was shot on the spot. The fathers held the hands of the older children, and the mothers carried the little ones in their arms. The murderers beat the heads of their victims with their rifle butts until they were pouring blood, and then they pushed them into the pits."

Israel's hiding place was dangerous - the field in which he was hiding was very near the village of Zaretcha, and many of the murdering policemen came from there. Some of the young Jews of Biten had studied in the local Polish school with them. If they were to meet him, they would certainly arrest him. When the sun was beginning to set, the sound of running footsteps suddenly reached his ears. Israel was startled, but very soon there stood in front of him someone from his town, Boma Ditkovski, a young man of twenty who was very popular with the young people in his town because of his learning. Boma had escaped the extermination action but a murderer's bullet had hit him in the leg. When he reached the edges of the field where the slaughter was taking place, he fell on the ground and crawled until he reached the place where Israel was lying. Israel bound Boma's wound with a strip of material that he tore from his trousers. Boma told him that he had picked up a stone and beat it in the face of the Lithuanian murderer who was ordering him to undress, and swung his rifle butt on him to beat him.

The two fugitives waited till evening and went out to look for traces of the partisans. Boma had difficulty in walking; at first he tried to overcome the pains that his wounded leg was causing him and dragged his leg, but eventually Israel carried him on his shoulders. They made way very slowly; several times they had to hide between the bushes. In the end they reached the village of Gnoynoye where Boma's father had a flour mill. The guard of the flour mill was in contact with the partisans. He hid the two young men in the threshing floor and supplied them with food and drove them to the partisan camp of Volchye Nori. There, they approached the camp guard and waited.

A group of Jewish partisans had just arrived back at the place from an operation. When Israel heard that they belonged to the Slonim unit, he told them about the massacre in Biten and how the two of them had survived. The commander of the unit ordered one of his men to call a doctor. Quite soon Dr Blumovitch came to the wounded Boma. He took the two young men in his cart and brought them to the 51 troop.[64] Israel was accepted into the troop.

---

[64] *Witness account of Israel Slonimski*

CHAPTER NINE: The Shchors battalion in its march eastwards

The first "Selection" (25th. August 1942) and the expulsion/rejection of the Jews

After the battle of Gavinovitch, news arrived that the Germans were concentrating a large force in the area. H.Q. saw no possibility of standing up to such a strong enemy force. In the Jewish brigade, rumours spread that the troop was about to leave the Slonim district and move eastwards towards the frontline.

Another version said that the area was too small to contain so many partisans and as winter approached, it would be difficult to survive from both an economic and a security point of view. Therefore, they would have to leave the Volchye Nori area and move eastwards towards the marshes where it would be difficult for the enemy to attack partisans. The rumours became reality and H.Q. laid down the framework of the troop which would move eastward. The 51, 52, 54, 55 and 56 groups, which were well-armed, were to depart, whereas the 57 and 58 groups, which had only recently been set up and which comprised many local people plus new partisans, would stay behind. The 59 and 60 groups would, of course, also stay because these were the Biten and the Kosovo family camps, in which there were many people who weren't fit for fighting - women, children and older men without arms.

The troop prepared to move in the meantime to the Yaganov Lake area, east of the Brest-Moscow railway track. The 53 group stayed behind to protect the local population in the partisan Slonim/Biten area and to continue with operations against the enemy. Most of the fighters of the 53 group came from the villages in the area, and they were happy to stay close to their families. The commander of the group was Nikolai Vladimirovitch Bobkov; he turned out to be an outstanding anti-Semite and was to a large extent responsible for the deaths of Jews living in Volchye Nori. His group broke up in the days of the manhunts and many of its people became robbers and murderers, who robbed the Jews in the family camps of the last of their possessions, and killed anyone they chanced upon.

And now the problem of the family camps faced the Jewish fighters in all its severity. Many had parents in the camp, young brothers and sisters and other relatives. Worry gnawed away at them - what would happen to them when the fighters left the area? Who would protect them and help them in their day-to-day survival? The Jewish partisans approached the command and requested to attach the family camps to the troop which was retreating. The answer was that the people of the family camps could also leave, and retreat from the area, but separately from the fighters and under their own responsibility.

Yasha and Herzel Shepetinski, whose parents, their brother Reuven and two younger brothers, had been taken out of the troop and sent to the family camp, put in a request to bring their family back. Commissar Dudko and the chief of staff Merzliakov promised that when they crossed the Shchara, people would be sent back to bring them to the troop. The promise was never carried out and all members of the family perished.

When they left the east, H.Q. damaged the Jewish 51 troop too. Many Jews were turned out of it because, in the opinion of the junior anti-Semitic Jewish commanders, they had been unnecessary in the past and in their opinion they would be a burden on the combat soldiers on the route to the east. Among those who were taken out of the troop there were also longstanding members of the Slonim ghetto underground, people who'd smuggled arms out to the forest and among them Halinka Rodenstein. Doktortchik intervened on her behalf with Commander Feodorovitch. He told him about her past in the underground and her activities in getting weapons out. Feodorovitch was persuaded and Halinka was added to those who were leaving.

Dr. Yasha Kremin refused to go with the people who were leaving because of his parents, his wife and their two year old daughter, who were left behind, and they joined the Kosovo 59 group.

The confiscation of weapons in the village of Chemeri

When the group reached the outskirts of the village of Dobromishl, Belarussian partisans from the village of Chemeri who belonged to the 51 group, told them that in their village, near Slonim, the peasants still possessed a lot of weapons. H.Q. decided to send a reinforced group of fighters who would go through Volchye Nori under the command of Commissar Dudko, strengthen the link with the groups which had stayed in the forest, and carry on to Chemeri. The commanders were tempted by the chance of acquiring personal weapons, particularly pistols which were quite a find. According to the local partisans they were easily come by there.

Zerach Kremin, who was included in this group, says that they left for their destination on 2nd. September. There were twenty-three people in the group, among them Archik Bandt, five partisans from the village of Chemeri, Nionia Tsirinski, Dr. Blumovitch and others. They crossed the Shchara near the village of Dolgoye and at dawn they reached the Tchapayev camp. The next day they carried on to Volchye Nori. Zerach managed to take the opportunity to visit his uncle Dr. Moshe Kremin and his wife who had been integrated into the group. This was their last meeting.

When they reached Chemeri, they were divided into groups and they began to go through the houses which had been identified by their local comrades. Zerach went into one peasant's house and demanded the pistol which was in his possession. The man swore by all the saints that he had no pistol, but his neighbours who were waiting outside said that they had seen a pistol in his house. The partisans threatened to kill him. His wife burst out weeping and shouted: "Give them the pistol. I want you to live and for my children to have a father!" The farmer glanced at his wife, let fly a curse at her and brought the pistol. He asked for a receipt confirming that he had given up the pistol in case other partisans should come and demand his pistol again. Zerach signed the receipt in the name of the brigade.

That night, the fighters obtained another six rifles. They went back to the camp and on the way they received news of the troop's invasion of the village of Chemyeli. There it became clear to them that in face-to-face fighting, the troop was still weak.

The battle of Chemyeli (4th. September 1942)

On 26th. August 1942, the troop departed on its way east. The fighters crossed the Shchara near the village of Dolgoye and the railway track between the Lesnaya and Biten stations. On their way, the troop cut the enemy's communication lines, sawed down telegraph poles, tore down telephone wires along a length of three kilometres and made railway tracks unusable. The movement of the troop which then numbered seven hundred men with its artillery and supply convoy made a great impression on the local population. The Shchors battalion encamped by the village of Dobromishl. This was a suitable place: the Shchara flowed past on one side and on the other, forests and the Telechani marshes stretched out. The convoy was spread out along several kilometres.

After several days the battalion came close to the village of Chemyeli. In one of the forests on the way Proniagin had made contact with the commander of troop 112, Alexei Petrovitch Chertikov, who was encamped in the outlying farms of Samitchin. From him Proniagin heard that in the village of Chemyeli, near the Brest-Moscow road, there was an active enemy police station with fifty soldiers, whose role was to guard the bridge over the Shchara. The command of the Shchors decided to destroy the station and burn the bridge.

In the meantime, several brigades had been sent to obtain food. They gained control over a flour mill without a fight and prepared some flour. The troop rested. During the day they would bathe in the Shchara, visit the villages and make merry. In the meantime H.Q. was working out the plan to eradicate the police station in Chemyeli. The operation was dangerous as a strong German garrison was stationed in nearby Ivatchovitch. Despite this, it was decided to take the risk as the eradication of a local enemy force on a major German traffic artery would leave a powerful impression with the local residents.

On 4th. September two lines of partisans set out towards the starting point: the first line advanced the length of the left bank of the river in the direction of the village, in order to attack the German command. This line comprised the whole Jewish 51 group and part of the 52. The 55 and 56 groups, plus a force from troop 112, were lying in ambush, to stop a possible enemy reinforcement from Ivatchovitch. Captain Victor Guzhevski, who was a unit commander in the Shchors and an ex-officer in the Soviet air force, was in command of the battle.

Yasha Shepetinski, who took part in the attack as a gunner, and was wounded, has described how the battle went:

"It's a dark night. We're marching in the rear guard, holding our breath. Suddenly there's a cry: 'Who goes there?' That was the voice of the enemy guard. He was stabbed several times with a bayonet, before he even managed to fire a single shot. We burst into the yard of the command. I set up my machine gun behind the cowshed, and fire on the building. Our fighters threw grenades, and got in through the windows. My machine gun and Ya'akov Timan's are working well, but we can't see any live target, so we fire at doors and windows.

"Now we hear Guzhevski's order - 'Gunners –attack!' I don't understand the nature of the command. The role of gunners is usually to cover the attackers and silence enemy opposition. But there was no time to think – we had to carry out the order.

"Mietek Lustig and I jump into the yard, to break into the building. Suddenly a massive explosion throws me sideways and tears the gun out of my hands. The Germans had dropped a round of grenades from above, and these had exploded right by the legs of my comrade Mietek Lustig, number two on my gun. I don't even remember how I crawled to the corner, but I heard Mietek's groans: 'Yasha, finish me off!' His two legs had been torn from his body and he was grasping his entrails in his hands. My machine gun lay to one the side.

"The enemy goes on firing. Herzel came running up. 'Are you alive?' 'Yes', I answered, 'but Mietek is dying, and my gun is over there'. I was superficially wounded in my hand and my leg. Our situation is not great. The enemy are not allowing us to move either forwards or back. During the second attempt to break through to the command building our comrade Sibosh was killed. He had been the works manager in the Slonim loot camp, and an active member of the underground.

"The whole brigade is fighting. The Germans are firing full out, dug in behind sandbags. I'm lying there with the grenades in my hands. Various thoughts and strategies are racing round in my head. I can't get to my gun, but neither can the Germans take it.

"After a while our cannon began to make itself heard. Attack. Herzel makes a huge jump and grabs the machine gun. After about thirty minutes the enemy resistance is broken and its command building is taken. We set alight the building and the piles of straw which were covered with tarpaulin. Our two comrades who we had lost in battle, Mietek Lustig and Seibosh, were buried in Chemyeli. Dr. Orlinski dressed my wounds and took a fragment from my leg. The fragment in my hand is there to this day. I was able to walk, albeit with a limp and I stayed in the combat unit.

"The other line wiped out the guards and burnt the bridge. They had no losses. Two vehicles were hit near the ambush which had been set up on the roads into the village. We return to our camp as victors. The inhabitants of the village came to meet us, the partisans, with open admiration."

Now they had to ascertain enemy reaction to the partisan activity in the area. A reconnaissance patrol was sent out. Herzel went out with one of the units. The patrol reported that the Germans were building up a large anti-partisan force. In the Brest district they had unloaded two divisions off the train which was going to the front, and by 10th. September they were already advancing towards the "Shchors" camp. The troop wasn't strong enough to contend with large regular army forces like these – an army equipped with heavy weapons and artillery - and therefore the command decided to cut contact. After a minor encounter, exchanges of fire, near the village of Dobromishl, the troop moved through the swamps towards the islands near the Samitchin farmsteads. Proniagin decide to pause here and clarify the situation.

The atmosphere was tense. Rumour had it that the enemy was trying to surround the partisans. They were getting close to the forest. Later it emerged that the forester in the village had served the enemy as an informer, and had told them where the troop was camped. The command sent people to get rid of the treacherous forester.

Brigade 51 on the march eastwards.

Feodorovich, commander of brigade 51, did much to organise and strengthen the group, and particularly upheld the moral standard of his people. The impact of his personality on his people was positive and his character and moral standard helped protect his brigade from the prevalence of corruption which was widespread in the forest, and to strengthen it against the hostile environment. He succeeded in raising the level of his group above that of the other groups.

Two groups excelled in the "Shchors" troop, which by now comprised six groups: the 51 group, which was still mainly Jewish, and the 54, whose commander was Andrei Leontiev, an officer in the regular Soviet army. The members of the 51 suspected that he was a Jew who was hiding his origins. Andrei gathered into his group mainly selected professional soldiers, whereas Feodorovich accepted the Jews into his group just as they came, without military experience, and including women.

Feodorovich took advantage of even the short period between the decision to move east and the actual departure, in order to train his people. He made sure that his people took nothing from the peasants in the villages through which they passed. It was particularly forbidden to take women's clothes. (There were Jews who learned from the non-Jewish partisans to take clothes from the peasants.)

When the troop passed through the village of Wolka, several of the fighters took luxury items from the residents. ("Luxury" items were considered to be honey, eggs, butter and women's clothes.) The punishment for this was the same as for robbery. When Feodorovich learned of this, he regarded the incident very severely. He insisted that this damaged the whole group, and warned that the Jews would in any case be blamed for offences carried out by non-Jews, and it would be said that the Jews were robbing the population.

There were Jews in the brigade who were critical of Feodorovich, and dared to cheek and "bad mouth" this Jewish commander in a way which they wouldn't have permitted themselves if their commander had been a non-Jew. Not everyone valued their commander sufficiently. It was only after

Feodorovich fell in battle that they realised how much worse their situation had become, and started to appreciate his activity in the past and the great loss to the brigade.

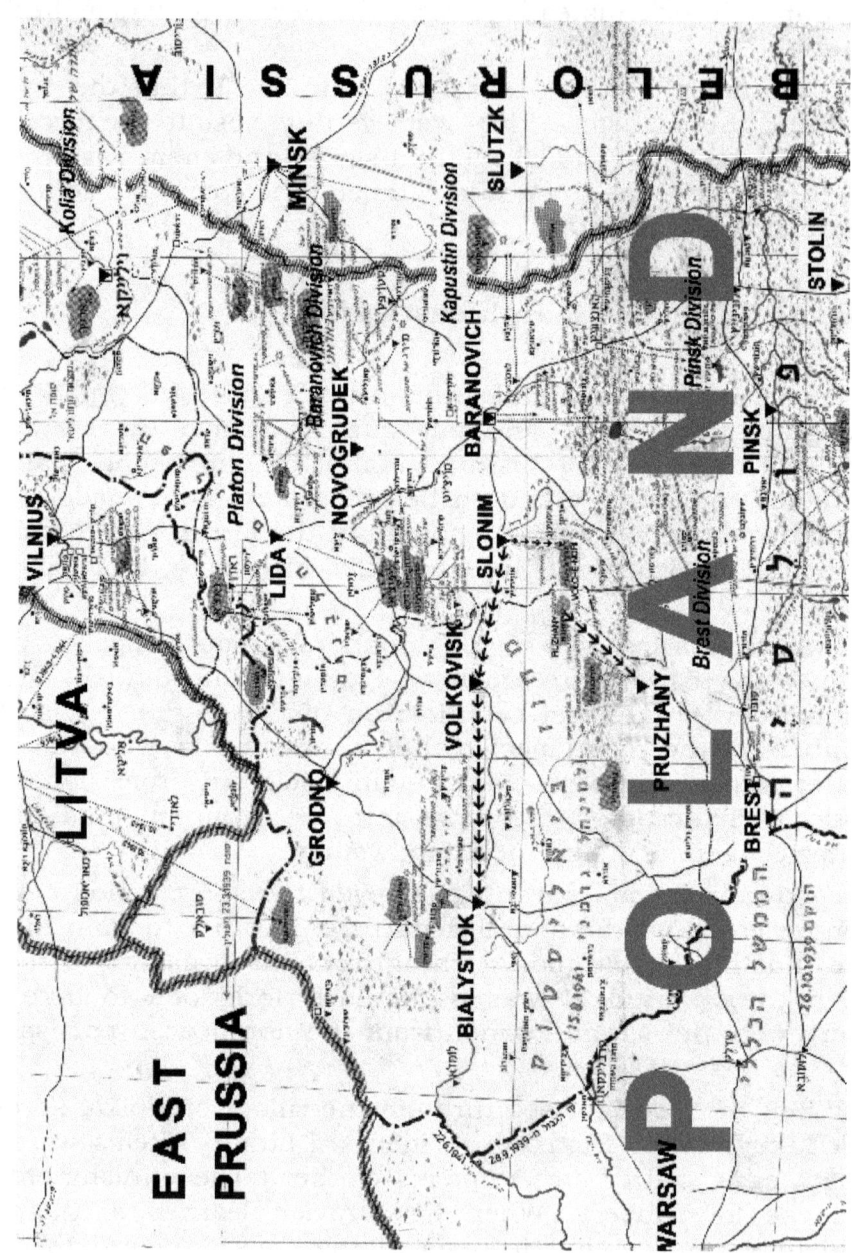

CHAPTER.TEN: In the Days of the Siege and the Manhunt
The battle of Samitchin (11th. September 1942)

The troop's march eastwards was meanwhile very impressive. Lines of partisans spread over several kilometres. The fighters marched two by two, the spaces between the rows being large enough for safety and ease of marching. The commanders rode on horseback, in front of their people, and the liaisons dashed back and forth to give instructions. The supply carts and the equipment, which was transported in army lorries, the two cannon and the vehicle containing the petrol vat, all gave the impression that here was a real Soviet army which had arrived from the front. That sense was intensified by the fact that the German army had been seen in the area a short while previously, and had started many fires in the forest.

As they passed through the forest, the partisans discovered signs of the fires before they had reached the lone farmhouses of Samitchin. Reconnaissance reported that large German forces had disembarked from the train at Ivatzevitch and Domanovo stations. The enemy had got very close to the partisan camp and this time the command decided just to defend themselves. The partisans were in a swamp region, and the tall reeds made it difficult to ascertain the extent of the enemy forces. The Germans were firing machine guns and other automatic weapons and shortly planes appeared overhead dropping bombs. The battle continued until the evening, and then everything fell silent. The partisan command assumed that the Germans had retreated, but they were wrong. Headquarters decided to hold out here until the evening, and then try to cut off contact with the enemy.

Zvi Shepetinski's description:

"We're moving further away from the spot. Once again, there's the murmur of the treetops above and the rustle of leaves at our feet. We can hear sounds of the forest animals running off and the chirruping of the birds, and the tension is growing.

"With dawn, we reached a place to camp – a hill surrounded by swamps. Each group took up the place allotted to it. The horses were unharnessed to rest and feed, and the people in the domestic section started to prepare wood for the fire, to cook a meal for the fighters. Tired people spread out to rest under the trees and on the carts.

"And suddenly shots and cries of "To arms!" made everyone jump to their feet. The news that we were surrounded spread like lightening, and they were shooting from the direction from which we have come. Each group took up a part of the line of defence. Our bit was the edge of the forest facing the swamps. News arrived that our situation was not too good. The onslaught grew all the time. The Germans and their aides were trying to surround us, and we already had casualties.

"We received orders to fire only on what we could actually see, with a certainty of hitting the target. The shower of bullets falling on us without pause was fraying our nerves, and we could now hear the clatter of tanks and motors and that made our hearts sink. I was lying there with my comrades waiting for the enemy to arrive. In front of us lay a swampy area, fairly dry, where the vegetation had been harvested by the local peasants. How long can we hold out against a frontal attack with a limited supply of ammunition at our disposal?

"Overhead some two-winged light aircraft appear, flying low, just over the treetops. We are ordered to put out the bonfires. After a few sorties, the planes started to drop rounds of grenades. Luckily, the enemy was not accurate and the grenades caused no losses. The planes disappeared and shortly after the enemy started to use mortars, apparently following the information they had from the pilots. But the shells only hit the trees.

"It was clear to us that our situation was worsening. With darkness came the order to retreat. We left all the possessions which we had brought in the carts, and the animals. The two cannon were taken apart and hidden in the earth, in the hope that we would be able to come back and retrieve them.

"Everything was scattered all over the camp: loaves of bread were placed on to a cart and pieces of cooked meat laid by the big pot. I put a chunk of meat and a loaf of bread in my rucksack and followed along with everyone else. You could see the signs of the first defeat on the fighters' faces – the retreat.

"We cross a boggy marsh in single file. Our shoes are full of water splashed up from every step. You have to be careful and only tread on sods which are covered with grass, for fear of sinking up to your loins. The march is difficult and slow, but goes on silently – the Germans are close. Instructions and orders are passed from the head of the line by word of mouth.

"It's cold and wet. We've been marching a long time, but haven't got far off yet. Eventually we came into a drier forest. A short rest. I took out my rations to take the edge off my hunger. It turned out that a lot of my neighbours didn't think about food, so I shared out what I had brought and we ate together.

"Troop commissar Dudko passed by us. He told me that they had left the wounded on a small lone island in the swamps with a food supply and several comrades to care for them. The whole night passed in exhausting marching. We marched non-stop so as to get out of the (German) ring around us. Everyone's food supply ran out – we were hungry and thirsty. We had no alternative but to drink muddy swamp water.

"The weather was fine, and during the day, it was fairly warm. From time to time we came out of the marsh into the forest, and gathered small berries which were red and tasted slightly sour. That was our only food during those days.

"We left the boggy swamps and moved during the middle of the day. We seemed to have extricated ourselves from the dangerous ring around us, and from an imminent clash with the enemy. The water problem was becoming increasingly grave. Wherever we camped we dug holes with our bare hands, but only a black mush would appear on the floor of the hole. We would ring the water out of this by means of a dirty handkerchief or scrap of fabric which came to hand.

"Early in the morning, when we had gone through a pine forest, we licked the drops of dew which had collected at the tips of the needles. Towards evening we would pass a village or some isolated farms. The fields were already ploughed, ready for the winter planting, and potatoes had been gathered. Here and there we found little damaged potatoes, which had been left unwanted, and which for us were a real find, and we would eat them just as they were.

"We reached a place where it was decided to rest for a few days. It was a dense forest surrounded by marshes and close to some villages, to which the access was difficult in summer because of the marshes, and only a narrow dirt track with tumble- down bridges linked them. Contact with the outside world took place mainly in the winter, when the bogs froze and one could move across on sledges.

"The more we went on marching, the more I was troubled by worry about my parents, who had stayed in Volchye Nori. My cousins and Archik Bandt were jointly anxious for our relatives. We embroidered plans to organise a group to go back and bring our families to the new place or stay together with them. However, events unfolded differently.

"In order to get out of the (German) ring we had to cross the Shchara. We reached it at midnight and walked alongside. We had heard that you could look for an easy crossing point where the water was not so deep that it would wet the weapons and ammunition. And there was a problem – not everyone knew how to swim. We were waiting for the command's decision."

The battle of the Tenth Dam (13th. September, 1942)[65]

It was 13th. September when the troop reached the banks of the Shchara, about half a kilometre from the Tenth Dam of the Oginski Canal.[66]

The troop stayed a whole day without food or water among the yellowing reeds, which were blighted by the wind and burned by the sun. All around there was an alert silence, broken from time to time by the rustle of insects and the hum of an enemy patrol plane circling overhead. When darkness covered the land the people got on their feet and started to move along the little path between the marsh reeds in single file.

---

[65] *Proniagin barely describes the Battle of the Tenth Dam in his book. Perhaps this was because its planning and execution were faulty, and caused unnecessary losses? Or perhaps because the part he played in this operation was a small one?*

[66] *The Oginski canal, now called the Dneiper-Niemen Canal, was dug between 1767 -1783, on the initiative and supervision of the Lithuanian army commander (Hetman) M.K. Oginski. It is 52.8 kilometers long, and links the Nieman, via the Shchara and its tributary the Yaselda, to the Dnieper, forming a continuous waterway from the Black Sea to the Baltic. The Oginski Canal flowed through the property of this nobleman, and the town of Slonim was also within his jurisdiction.*

Messengers were sent out, and reported that the dam was nearby, and there was a steel bridge tilted over the canal. The command entered into consultation. Differences of opinion broke out between Merzliakov, the chief of staff, and Feodorovitch, commander of the 51 group, concerning crossing the river, in order to escape through the ring around them. Feodorovitch's view was that they should cross the river at any possible point, even if it were not that easy. Exhaustion, tension and a lack of clarity in the deployment plans made for a depressed mood. The 51 fighters noticed that Feodorovitch was not being included the troop staff discussions, and he marched with the men as one of the fighters. On the eve of the battle for the dam Merzliakov came to Feodorovitch, and after a prolonged argument, walked out angrily. Feodorovitch seemed calm. The fighters were not aware of the seriousness of the dispute, and didn't know why it had broken out, except for the fact that Merzliakov, together with the rest of the staff group, had decided that the water of the river was not shallow enough for a crossing, and they led the partisans to the bridges of the dam which connected the Shchara with the River Yaselda.

Here the river split into three branches, and there was a slanted bridge over each one, of twisted iron combined with iron plates. The group lay flat at the edge of the reeds. In front of them stretched out a harvested meadow, scattered with haystacks which looked almost sculptured and were leaning against birch tree poles.

At times isolated shots and also volleys were heard, and bullets flew around like fireflies, burning out as they reached the ground. When the order for night rest was given, Feodorovitch arranged himself in a heap of hay, together with a group of his men. As dawn rose partisans from the 51 began to draw close to the canal through the meadow. A small group of saboteurs, commanded by Zerach Kremin, advanced on the right flank of the troop, which as a whole was moving out sideways, paving a way for itself thorough the thicket and drawing near to an isolated house.

Reconnaissance patrols were sent out. They reported that several Germans were sleeping there, plus an old Belarussian, who was guarding the dam and the bridge. The old man told them that these were SS. men, who had been in wait from the day before for partisans who might cross the canal. The patrol threatened the old man not to wake the Germans or to warn them. Proniagin reprimanded the patrol for not immediately eliminating the Germans with grenades and machine-gun fire. He ordered them to surround the house and set fire to it with its occupants. The task was given to the 51, but as they were approaching the house, they spotted dozens of Germans running towards the bridge.

It emerged that the old Belarussian had deceived them and as soon as they had left, woken the Germans. There were dozens of SS there. The enemy had managed take up positions on the fortified bridge across the canal. As the 51 fighters drew near to the bridge, the Germans rained concentrated heavy machine-gun fire on them. But the main part of the enemy forces was on the dam and in boats on the canal, whilst some had reinforced themselves in the guard's hut.

According to the reports which the reconnaissance had delivered, there should have been just seven Germans there, but in the night a reinforcement of about one hundred SS. had arrived.

The H.Q. gave orders to prepare for attack, and after a short march in the direction of the bridges, the partisans charged to cries of "Hurrah!" The fighters ran some distance to reach the first canal of the dam, but the SS. had already managed to take up positions on the canal crossings and rained down fire on the partisans. The battle took off. The partisans took up a position opposite the wharf of the canal and didn't retreat, since the wharf served as a screen against the enemy's hail of bullets, but neither did they manage to advance. Then Proniagin jumped out on the wharf, twisting and bending over to avoid the bullets. Proniagin remained alone, as none of the partisans followed him, and he went back.

In the course of battle the partisans wiped out the Germans on the first bridge, attacked the first building by the wharf, quickly crossed the bridge over the bodies of the SS., and got on to land which was lower than the river and the canals. Now a pause began in their progress, as the Germans demonstrated strong opposition on the crossing over the river. And then Feodorovitch's voice was heard calling out that there was no other way but to advance, as in retreat the partisans would encounter a much larger force. He shouted "Forward!" and broke through first, followed by the comrades. Suddenly the commander stopped, thrust his weapon into the air saying "Take my P.P.D.!" and fell to the ground wounded. The group raced forward. Some of the men poured fire on the Germans across the canal and overcame them, and some crossed the river from the left side of the bridge. In this battle the partisans wiped out about one hundred SS.

The fighters of the 51, under the commander Feodorovitch, were among the first to storm, and they fought with great heroism. They still remember the course of the fateful battle, as if engraved deep in their souls, and they discuss it, as each one experienced it, from the position from which he was fighting.

Yasha Shepetinski was fighting in the lines of the third platoon, and this is how he describes it:

"The Tenth Dam on the Oginski canal was very easy to defend. It was in an open place. In order to reach the little bridges of the dam, you had to cross a high embankment and two water-blocks of the branches of the Shchara. You could only pass single file over the narrow, small bridges.

"All the groups of the troop approached the start point in complete silence and without being seen. We couldn't see the enemy, but we could sense him very well. The mist helped: it hid us. The feeling that the battle was near gave us strength.

"Our third platoon had the honour of opening the battle. We had to cross the canal and the Shchara with the 52 group. The other groups were on our right. By my side lay Meir Malach. He was very young; he wasn't yet eighteen. Before battle, you can often want to say something, something you would not say in other circumstances, and so Mayorek says to me: 'You know Yasha, I haven't yet kissed a girl, not even once.'

"I didn't then know that this young fighter, who was strong and courageous, would fall at the end of the battle. Did Mayorek feel that the box in which all the years of his life were housed, had emptied and his last hours were running out?

"The mist slowly dissolves, and I can see the shore opposite and the Germans. Two are standing by a machinegun on the dam, and one by the boats. The rest were positioned, evidently, behind the embankment in firing positions. Probably some of them were still asleep in the guard's house. It was obvious that there was no possibility of retreating, not for us and not for the Germans. The battle goes on to the very last fighters.

"A green rocket announced the start of the attack. Our gunners immediately hit the German machinegun crew, and the whole troop opened fire on pre-planned targets. I'm shooting the boats and afterwards, the embankment and the guards' hut. By the time the enemy had come to, some of our fighters had already managed to cross the first small bridge and take up positions, among them Feodorovitch, Doktortchik and Greenghauz. They are shooting, trying to capture the enemy machinegun.

"The Germans open strong fire, but the partisans must cross the two small bridges to the embankment. Our comrades cross, running over the first bridge, and several of them also over the second. Now it's our turn. We cross the first bridge at a fast run and lie to the left of it. For the time being, our unit hasn't had any losses. Our machinegun fire is accurate, all around lie enemy dead from their first line. Our platoon turns to the left, goes away from the battlefield and crosses the canal. You can tell who's firing by the sounds: the Germans don't save bullets and they shoot in long volleys, whereas we, in short ones. The enemy machineguns have a discordant sound, whereas ours, which got from the loot camp, have deep sounds.

"After we've crossed to the other side of the canal, we hit the enemy from the flank. The battle is still at its height. The Germans are resisting obstinately, they're shooting like crazy and hurling grenades. The peat on top of the embankment has caught fire. We shout, 'Hurrah!' and 'Fire!' while running forward. We catch the sound of 'Hurrah' from the other side too. Timan is standing to shoot with his machinegun. In this attack, Mayorek was killed, and Timan was wounded in his shoulder.

"The enemy opposition is weakening. There are battles on all sides, and our group is in the middle. It's dangerous to shoot now as it would be possible to hit our own people. Smoke, which is spreading in our midst, is burning our eyes. The Germans, who've crawled to the guards' hut, are still shooting. We quickly finish off this last enemy nest as well. Victory is ours.

"Our group had heavy and painful losses. Our commander Feodorovitch was mortally wounded.'

"Zerach Kremin also reports from the battle:

"When we reached the crossing place on the morning of 13th. September, weary and hungry after days of wandering through the boggy marshes of Polesia, we were surprised to find a lot of SS.

"We had expected to surprise them, but they had managed to dig in all the length of the canal and in the guards' hut - a large wooden house, which had a big loft which commanded the whole area. The Germans had set up machineguns in its windows and poured lethal fire upon us. Our group, and at its head Captain Feodorovitch advanced at the head of the camp. The heavy mist made our progress difficult. The cruel battle went on for hours and hours, but during the course of this, we managed, thanks to the heroism of the Jewish partisans – Malach, Liker and others – to penetrate the house and set fire to it. The first to cross the dam was Noah Servinski from Augostov, and all of us went after him[67], but there was much loss of life and many wounded. Among those who fell was our admired Jewish commander Feodorovitch.

It became clear afterwards that about one hundred SS. men fell in the battle and only one of them managed to escape and reach the nearby German garrison."

This is the report of Avraham Orlinski:

"I remember that I was drawing closer to the bank at some distance from the crossing. I'm all ready to jump into the water and there was Cheslava, my wife, on my left. And she's short and doesn't swim very well. I caught hold of her with my right hand, and while I was just debating what to do, Shabtai Moshkovski joined me on my left. 'Take her!' I shouted. He grasped her left hand, and together, we jumped into the water. After a short swim, we touched the ground, and we used it to move forward and to get Cheslava out. We went around the bridge and attacked the enemy from the right side.

"When we eliminated the Germans on the bridges, the crossing became free, and the battle drew to an end. We managed to get away from the canal, wet through, and went into the forest in front of us to distance ourselves from the canal and from the large enemy force which was following us.

"While we were still moving away, we heard an order: 'The men are to go back and to help collect up the wounded and the dead.' I went back to the bank with several fighters. A group of partisans was already taking care of the dead. The wounded had already been moved. Ya'akov Greenghauz the younger had fallen, between the bridges; he was eighteen – a bullet had hit his heart. We brought him to the collection point. There, I met A. Imber, who was concerned about the burial: his father was among those who had fallen.

"Sixteen fighters had fallen in the battle, and we also had seriously wounded people, among them, our commander, Feodorovitch, Avraham Doktortchik and Ya'akov Timan. Golda Gertsovski-Doktortchik, who had hurried to help the wounded, had also been hit. The troop's commissar, Dudko, had been badly wounded in his legs.

And this is how Piotr Brinski[68] describes the battle on the Tenth Dam. He was the commissar and the well-known partisan commander, nicknamed, Dyadya Petia:

---

[67] *Proniagin (p.55) makes no mention of the brave fighting of the Jewish partisans.*

[68] *A.P. Brinski, Po tu storonu fronta, p.279-287*

"In mid-September, the Germans took twenty thousand soldiers off the train that was going to the front. They combed the 'Puschyas'[69] of Bialoviezh and Ruzhani. Thousands of partisans clashed with them. Our forests, too, had their turn. Here, the Shchors troop distinguished itself. In one battle, they defeated seven hundred Hitlerites.

"At the Tenth Dam, which blocked the way for the Hitlerites, they completely destroyed a battalion of SS. The Fascists wanted to push the partisans into a trap, to pin them down at Lake Vigonov and the canal. To prevent the partisans crossing the river to the opposite bank at the Tenth Dam (the other end of the canal by the lake), they sent a battalion of SS. against them. It happened at night. The SS. thought that the partisans would reach the dam only at noon, and they went to sleep in the huts on the shore, after they had set up guards. The senior lieutenant, Leontiev, who was in charge of the main group, moved a unit towards the shore in order to take over the boats and block the crossing for the Germans, and with the remaining fighters, he made a lightning attack on the sleeping enemy, took out the guard and surrounded the house.

"Most of the SS. didn't even manage to jump out of their rooms. They were shot at from the doors and through the windows, and those who broke out and ran to the boats encountered the partisans there. Several of them tried later to cross the river swimming. However, on the opposite bank, Kaplon was waiting for them. He had just returned from blowing up a train in which a general had been travelling. Not a single Fascist came out of this battle alive."[70]

In the heat of battle, Zerach Kremin and Avraham Doktortchik, who was fighting under Zerach's command, approached their commander and wanted him to allow them to surprise the enemy from the right flank, where it was still quiet. Feodorovitch agreed, sent the gunner, Agayev, with them, and the three of them disappeared between the bushes. And this is what Doktortchik says:

"We arrived in leaps and bounds at the edge of the forest. At a distance of 100-150 metres, we saw a group of Germans who were emplaced in positions on the other side of the canal, and opened fire directly on them. Zerach was shooting with his sub-machinegun, Agayev with his semi-automatic rifle, and I with my machinegun. I wanted to wait to see the results of the shooting. I raised myself up a little and then up popped the head of a German wearing a steel helmet on the opposite side, and he waved his hand. I felt a kind of bite on my left hand, and as if the sinews in my belly were being gouged out, and I fell to the ground."

---

[69] *Puschya – Dense forests which stretch over large areas of Poland and Beilorus.*

[70] *This description is full of inaccuracies, and the number – 700 Nazis killed - is extremely exaggerated. Brinski took no part in this battle, he omits to say anything about the decisive part the 51 brigade played under the leadership of Feodorovitch, and instead cites Kaplon, who belonged to his regiment, and only chanced to be present and played a very small part in the battle. Proniagin, who commanded the operation, does not mention Kaplon at all.*

Doktortchik's friends, Zerach and Agayev, dragged him and his machinegun between the bushes. Agayev ran to call for medical help and Golda Gertsovski, Dr. Cheslava Orlinski and the nurse, Zhenia Eichenbaum, immediately arrived and dressed his wounded hand.

Golda left the wounded man, gave the bandages to Zhenia, took Avraham's gun and ran towards the embankment, where the battle was still going on. And then she too was hit in both her legs by fragments from the hand grenades that the Germans were throwing. Ze'ev Finkel gave her first aid, and Yisrael Fisher helped her to get out of there. Moshe Modelevitch got her out over the canal, and then they lay her on a stretcher and took her to the first aid camp near the village of Tukovitch.

Dr. Orlinski saw that Doktortchik's pelvis was riddled with bullets. She put his hand down and took off his pullover. Then she saw two wounds bleeding freely. She bound his abdomen and gave him some water, and then she left him there and went back to the battlefield, to carry on and bring first aid to other wounded.

Before Zerach went off, Avraham gave him his two hand grenades and received a pistol. "Don't forget me, Zerach, don't abandon me!" he called after them.

The wounded Doktortchik remained where he was. The battle was still at its height. And then he heard steps coming nearer and was scared – maybe it was the enemy. He gripped the pistol hard and waited, holding his breath, for whoever was coming. When he recognised his comrades, he let go of his pistol and groaned with pain. The fighters had brought a kind of stretcher, plaited from the branches of trees, which they'd covered with some tent sheeting, of the sort that also served the Red Army soldiers as a waterproof garment, and they laid the wounded man on it and carried him off. In order to distract him, they told him on the way how the battle was going, how Heniek Malach, Anshel Delatitski and Noah Servianski had been first to reach the guards' hut, the hut from where the Germans were firing and had set fire to it. Servianski's upper garments were as full of holes as a sieve as he had crossed the bridge first. They told him that Yitzhak Imber, the cook of the group, Mayorek Malach and Greenghauz the younger, had fallen in battle, and he also heard from them about other wounded from the 51 group, and about those who'd been hit in the other groups: about Natan Liker, who had been quick off the mark and shot a German who was aiming his gun at him from across the canal. After the battle, when they crossed the canal, Natan Liker took the German's sub-machinegun for himself. Among the German murderers, there was no-one left alive but one who had fled. A great deal of loot was taken, weapons, ammunition and cigarettes.

The stretcher-bearers reached the 51's collection point completely exhausted. When they put down Doktortchik so as to catch their breath and to change their places, Doktortchik saw, close up, Mitia from the village of Tchemeri, whose perforated neck was spouting blood. Mitia belonged to the underground group in his village, an underground which worked under the direction of Iskrik, and he had joined the troop.

A. Imber and Heniek Malach returned bereaved from the burial of a father and a brother. On their way, they met the reconnaissance patrol, dragging the treacherous old watchman out of the bushes.

"We caught him," they reported with satisfaction to Proniagin, who had come to see them.

"He tried to hide," they said and spat out between their teeth the three-word Russian curse, "The snake tried to get away".

"I have buried my father," whispered Imber with a choked voice, and his eyes were burning with held-back tears.

"I know, I'm sorry," replied the commander, and there was a touch of comfort in his voice. "Well, he's all yours," he went on and pointed at the old man, who stood before them trembling with fear. Imber peeped at the old man and cocked his gun, but the old traitor who was standing before him, all hunched up and trembling, looked so pathetic in his tattered peasant's clothes, that he couldn't pull the trigger. 'Is this the enemy?' flashed through his weary and painful brain. Proniagin glanced with contempt at the young man and shot the old man without restraint, killing him on the spot. [71]

The Death of the Commander

When he reached the forest, Avraham Orlinski came across a number of wounded; some of them were managing to make progress on their own, despite wounds which were pouring blood. They refused to be transported on stretchers. At the side of the path lay the stretcher of Feodorovitch, who was mortally wounded, and by him stood Dr. Blumovitch and Merzliakov. The doctor was despairing of any hope of saving the life of the wounded commander. In his opinion, there would have been no chance, even in normal conditions in hospital. Merzliakov said that they should end his considerable suffering and kill him. The unit commander, Victor Guzhevski, arrived. Merzliakov explained the situation to him and suggested to him that he should cut the thread of life of this man, who was in agony. After agonising over this, Guzhevski answered, "I am not going to lift a hand against my commander" and turned and went on his way.

Orlinski says:

"I went up to the stretcher on which lay Feodorovitch, our commander. He looked silently at his men surrounding him. Several of us had stayed by him; it was hard for us to leave him. He turned to us and said, "Very few of you will survive, but you will be heroes" and he stretched out his hand to us in farewell. My turn came. I shook his hand and forced myself to smile a smile of hope, but inside I felt like stone and tears were bursting in my heart.

Yasha and Zvi Shepetinski were also by the commander in his last moments.

---

[71] *From the memoirs of Avraham Doktortchik.*

"Despite his fatal wounds, Feodorovitch was still fully conscious, he knew his situation and the situation of the troop after the battle and asked us to kill him. The whole group parted from their beloved commander, whilst the fighters were barely holding back their tears".

"His situation was getting worse and worse. At first one of his legs was paralysed and he was very weak, and then he couldn't feel his other leg. He asked his men to go on fighting and take revenge on their mortal enemies. The commander parted from his men with these sentences: "Comrades, there is no chance of surviving, but as Jews we must demonstrate courage and strong spirit and fall in battle without fear as Jewish heroes". He lost consciousness and muttered something. When his consciousness came back, he again begged us to kill him.[72]

After a short debate, it was decided that we should release him from his suffering. But who would do this? We agreed to draw lots among the fighters of the 51 group. The lot fell to Benyamin Rozmarin, but this man – a tough Polish revolutionary, an experienced man of the underground who had been a prisoner in the camp of Kartuz Bereza in Poland which was known for its harsh regime - wailed like a child and shouted, "Even if you kill me, I won't do anything to my wounded commander". So they cast lots again and this time the lot fell to one of the closest friends of Feodorovitch. The stretcher was taken behind a heap of hay, a muffled shot from a pistol was heard, it pierced the head of the wounded man and put an end to his suffering. Our admired commander was buried on the spot.

His friends mourned him with words that came from the heart. The chief of staff Merzliakov also wept and spoke moving words of parting. During his life, Feodorovitch hadn't enjoyed a friendly relationship on the part of the troop chief of staff - whether because of his Jewish origin or whether because he stood up so strongly for the rights of his 51 group. The Jewish fighters couldn't help but wonder if these were crocodile tears.

---

[72] *From the memoirs of Avraham Doktortchik*

The transfer of the wounded (14th. September 1942)

The troop had additional wounded, some of them severely and some less so. Commissar Dudko was wounded in both his legs. Luckily for the partisans, the Germans had become fearful and instead of coming to the help of their aides who were fighting, they packed up their belongings from the nearby villages and made off. At the same time, it was clear that the enemy wouldn't leave the troop alone, that they would tail them, and the partisans would have to face further testing experiences. The problem facing the command was how to transfer the wounded for some time to a safe place and hide them until it was possible to bring them back to the troop.

In the meantime a group had been sent to fetch a little food so that there would at least be food for the wounded. The group came back after about two hours and brought a few potatoes. The peasants in the village of Novosiolki nearby already knew that the partisans had destroyed a whole German unit. They couldn't linger any more. The potatoes were baked on the bonfire and distributed among the wounded only. Golda Gertsovski, who was wounded in both legs, gave up her portion and coaxed the doctor to eat as much as she wanted. "Your life takes priority over the lives of the wounded, for our lives are dependent on you and your health". Dr Cheslava, who was looking after the wounded all the time despite her fatigue and hunger barely stood on her feet. Her wet clothes had already dried on her body. She didn't agree to take anything to eat, but one single potato, for fear that there would not be enough for the wounded.

Drs. Blumovitch and Orlinski came along to care for the wounded who hadn't yet been tended to, and to dress their wounds. They amputated Doktortchik's thumb. After a short rest, Dr. Blumovitch sat down by Doktortchik's stretcher and told him about the wounding and death of the commander. He raised the suspicion which other fighters also entertained that Feodorovitch had been shot from behind by Merzliakov[73].

After a short while, Avraham Doktortchik was separated from the rest of the wounded and taken on his stretcher behind a thicket of bushes some distance from the unit's camp. The stretcher bearers made off without saying a word. The bushes which had been flattened as the stretcher passed sprung up straight and enclosed him. Doktortchik's sensation was weakening and his consciousness was clouding. Consciousness returned to him when his wounds began to hurt unbearably, and then a question started to gnaw at his mind. Why did Dr. Blumovitch tell him about the mercy killing of Feodorovitch when he was wounded? What did he mean by this story? Was it his intention that it would have been better for him to commit suicide with his pistol? Avraham took out his pistol in advance, released the safety catch and put his finger on the trigger, but his whole being rose up against the possibility of this kind of death -

---

[73] *The witness account of Avraham Doktortchik; the memoirs of A. Imber, who also suspected that Feodorovitch had been shot in the back by the chief of staff. There is no proof to this suspicion.*

he wanted to live. At that time it didn't occur to him that he had been hidden among the bushes for a while until they could transfer him to a safe place.

Zerach Kremin was allocated to transfer the wounded to their temporary shelter. Zerach remembers this trek as one of the hardest in his partisan experience, and he says:

"After we had crossed the bridge over the canal with the wounded Doktortchik, I left him under a tree and I went up to the staff group which was sitting not far off. When Proniagin saw me, he asked me if I knew German. I answered that I did, and he took an exercise book out of his pocket and said; "Sit down and translate". This was a diary of the (German) guard unit over the dam which was entered for a whole month and in it there was a list of collaborators with the Germans. This unit belonged to a special division which was based in Minsk and which was working temporarily in the Telekhani area. Unfortunately I found in the list the names of two Jews. On the spot Proniagin and I decided - and I don't remember whether the suggestion came from me or from him - not to mention the names of these Jews, since even without that there was more than enough anti-Semitism in the troop.

"We began to discuss the situation which was really very bad. We knew that the whole area was swarming with SS. soldiers who would definitely rush to help their comrades. We had many wounded who were seriously hampering our mobility and therefore it was decided to transfer them with a few people from the sanitary unit led by Dr. Blumovitch, to an island far from the local villages. Then the whole troop would go in another direction to the forest between the villages of Novosiolki and Razdzialowichi.

"We had found a new German map in the building by the dam and it had an exact description of the whole area. According to the map, we chose a suitable island. I should like to point out moreover that an 'island' in a region of swamps signifies just a raised patch on which trees and bushes grow, and which is surrounded by dangerous bogs. There will be a very narrow path leading across to an island like that, which only the locals know. My unit and Archik's and additional units from other groups received an order to transfer the wounded during the night to the island which had been chosen.

"In the whole period that I was in the forests, I passed many very difficult days and nights, but only a few of them are engraved on my memory. One of these nights was 14th. September 1942, when we transferred the wounded. We prepared stretchers for them from birch tree branches and laid army blankets on them. Every four people carried a wounded person and would change over from time to time. The group which had a rest held the weapons of the four other stretcher bearers and so forth.

"At first we walked on a path between the young birch trees but after a while the path turned into a swamp with many clumps of moss and grasses. The days of wandering, the hunger and the fatigue which had preceded the battle over the great dam and the tension of the battle itself had started to take their toll.

"The rest stops became more and more frequent and when the order was given to rest, people would put the stretcher down on the ground and fall asleep on the spot. I must point out that the wounded too, despite their great suffering, didn't complain. They were aware of the efforts of their friends who, with their last strength, were hurrying to bring them to a place of safety.

"On one of the rest stops, our comrade Ivan Kh. lost the machinegun he'd been carrying. He came to tell me after we had already gone some way. We went back to the place where we had stopped, but we couldn't find the machinegun. I knew that the moment that it was reported to the headquarters, he would be sentenced to death. I gave him a rifle instead of the machinegun and I told him not to speak a word to anyone about what had happened, and so the matter was finished.

"The hours dragged on for an eternity. I imagined that the night would never pass. It was a clear and beautiful moonlit night. While we were walking, I began to forget my tiredness and to muse on moonlit night hikes in the days of my childhood and youth. This helped me a little bit to make progress, and already dawn was breaking through. We knew that we were near our aim, and in fact after a short time we were able to put the wounded down happily and with satisfaction. We decided to rest a little and then to go back to the group which was on the point of moving to the village of Swietitza.

"And suddenly somebody said: 'Quiet, Germans!'. We jumped to our feet and cocked our guns. We approached the edge of the island and we saw at some distance on both sides of the canal SS. soldiers marching towards the dam. They were unaware of us and went on to collect their comrades who'd fallen in battle. When the Germans had moved off, we breathed in relief. We parted for a while from our wounded and their carers, and turned in the direction of Swietitza. Near the village we decided to first go to the lone farms next to the forest to find out where the partisans were camping. The farmer who we approached told us that the Germans had left the village yesterday after a German from the team on the dam had run through the village shouting 'Partisan Deutsch kaput!' and the Germans had made off from many of the villages."[74]

The wounded underwent a very hard time after their comrades were forced to leave them on the isolated island and go back to the unit. They felt suspicious and despondent, afraid they would be forgotten and abandoned. These experiences and fears were sometimes harder to bear than the pains which the wounds caused them. Later, after the manhunt, when the troop was camped in the area of the swamps of Polesia to the west of the dirt road leading from the village Novosiolki to Razdzialovichi, the wounded who had remained on the island returned to the troop. But their suffering was not yet over."

---

[74] *The villages from which the Germans and their aides had fled were: Tukhoviczi, Novosiolki, Zholozye and others.*

In the partisan hospital

After battle, the troop was located near the village of Swietitza which was surrounded by dangerous swamps. The battalion got out of the ring and began to reorganise to continue its movement eastwards towards the village of Khatiniczi. The battalion was divided into several groups and each one encamped separately. The 51 group was located in the forest along the wayside between the village of Razdzialovichi in the south and the village of Novosiolki in the north, and moved camp from time to time.

The group still had thirty wounded, some of them badly hit, who suffered from every movement, and so the command decided to set up a field hospital for them about ten kilometres from the dam, close to the village of Tukhoviczi. They would leave the wounded in the hospital under the supervision of Dr. Blumovitch and several nurses. It was determined that there would be several partisans to guard them, among them Zvi Shepetinski. The guards were joined by some of the lightly wounded who also acted as sanitary workers. After the hospital had been organised, the troop turned its steps eastwards. Yasha Shepetinski too was sent to the hospital since the wound in his leg had become full of infection and he could barely walk. In the hospital he had to take part in guard duties and assist in caring for the wounded.

They made shelters from branches in the hospital. At first the wounded were housed there and later, the team. A bonfire was set up and food cooked on it.

Dr. Blumovitch would operate on the wounded almost without instruments, with a razor or a penknife. He dedicated all his energy and care to his patients. The young women who were nurses also showed great dedication, and among them the youngest was Raya Shepetinski. The devoted care of Dr. Blumovitch, despite his reduced means, made itself felt and the condition of the wounded continued to improve; slowly they all recovered. When night fell, silence reigned here, and they would extinguish the bonfire for reasons of safety.

Ya'akov Timan was badly wounded; a bullet had split his shoulder and he had undergone several operations without anaesthetic. Avraham Doktortchik was operated in the same way. All the wounded of the 51 recovered and eventually all returned to battle duties; even Timan held his machinegun again. But he wasn't lucky enough to see the day of liberation for he fell in 1944, a short while before they met up with the Red Army.

From Doktortchik's memories of the hospital:

"The four badly wounded lay not far from each other: Ya'akov Timan, Avraham Doktortchik, Commissar Dudko and Golda Gertsovski. Dr. Blumovitch is preparing himself to operate on Doktortchik's hand and Golda's legs - all without anaesthetic. Golda is chain smoking German cigarettes which she has kept with her as loot from the battle. Dr. Blumovitch is assisted by Dr. Orlinski checking the sterilised instruments. Adek Schnur, a refugee from Warsaw, is pursing his thin lips and grasping Doktortchik's legs while he is lying on his back. Finkel is holding the patient's shoulders and Dr. Cheslava his elbow and the forearm of his swollen hand.

"Blumovitch kneels by Doktortchik's stretcher and with a decisive and confident movement, passes the blade of a surgeon's scalpel across the skin of the patient, who is gritting his teeth and his lips and muffled groans escape his lips. The surgeon penetrates with the scalpel into a junction of capillaries and slowly cuts with confidence into the live flesh. Orlinski cleans the pus and pushes gauze into the wound. The site of the cut is dressed with rustic fabric and Blumovitch gives his patient a friendly tap on the shoulder and declares, "You're a hero, you are. A hero!"

"Now the doctor has turned to Golda to extract fragments of grenade from the wounds in her legs. Golda's face is paler than ever. The doctor stops for a moment, as if hesitating, and then a fatherly smile floods his face. He wheedles, "A partisan woman trembling and afraid of light medical intervention? That's not right". He tries to provoke her with a nod of his head and with a tender voice and to urge her to agree to the operation. But Golda is fierce in her opinion: "No, no way. You won't succeed, Doctor, in coaxing me". The fear of pain, modesty making her afraid of baring the limbs of her female body and her unshakeable conviction of the ability of her body to withstand the test were battling in her heart. She has carefully followed the operation that Doktortchik had and she has decided against. Dr. Blumovitch, who has acquired the military tendency to order and discipline for himself, struggles to understand her refusal and sees it simply as lack of discipline. But he cannot force an operation on a wounded person and particularly on a young girl. The doctor quickly controlled the irritation which had started to grow. He left Golda alone without telling her off for her refusal and carried on making his rounds of the other wounded with Dr. Orlinski.

"Now he approached Dudko, who had a shot penetrate his left thigh but luckily it hadn't hit a bone. A lot of pus was seeping out of his wound and making a bad smell. The doctor cleaned the wound and changed the bandage. Dr. Orlinski tended to Ya'akov Timan who had a large, deep, gaping wound in his back.

"Dudko was boasting to Dr Blumovitch of the concern that his men showed him and has particularly mentioned Archik Bandt who got hold of a quilt for him which kept his body very warm. But in response, the doctor gave him a lecture, saying that it wasn't fitting for him to be soft like that, frightened and spoilt; he should bear his suffering as befits a Kubanian Kossack and a Bolshevik.

"The autumn was already making itself felt; the skies were turning darker and occasionally rain fell. In the mornings the whole place was covered with thick fog and visibility was poor. The mood in the hospital was low."

Zvi Shepetinski describes the atmosphere in the hospital:

"I don't remember an occasion of laughter or a funny joke as there always was in our camp in the group. Everyone here was serious and sadness prevailed in us. Most of the time I stood guard, and in my free time I would help to go and get food from the nearby village at the edge of the forest. This activity was carried out after reconnaissance and in broad daylight. After a few hours, we would come back laden with foodstuffs, including honeycombs which we had got from the pastor's beehives. (He had fled under cover of the Germans.) We stayed in this hospital with the wounded for a week and a half until the troop sent several partisans and they brought us back to the troop. On 25th. September 1942 we went back to the camp near Tukhovitch. Most of the wounded had recovered except Dudko and Golda who were not yet able to stand on their feet."

The victory of the Tenth Dam was an important victory for the partisans from a political point of view and a psychological one too. The partisans had realised that there was no need to be afraid of elite SS. units; it had become clear that the Germans were frightened of the partisans and they were not in a hurry to come to the aid of their comrades fighting the forest fighters. The various police collaborators had learned their lesson too, that in fact supporting the conquering victors in no way assured their status.

Regular units of German army had fled the area and gone to the front. Only in the cities of Gantsevitch and Kriboshin did there remain a German garrison. But it was of little danger to the partisans. The Belarussian police had entered the big garrisons and fortified themselves there. The Shchors battalion, despites its losses, had retained its battle fitness after the battle over the dam, and enriched its partisan experience. New people came to the troop and filled its ranks; among them soldiers and officers who had lived until then in the villages.

The panicked flight and the wounded are left behind

Only someone who was wounded in the partisan war and forced in the days of siege to be left alone by his comrades, who had to flee for their lives from the enemy - only he can grasp the depth of fear that the wounded felt, and their great dread of falling into the hands of the cruel enemy, helpless to defend themselves or to die at their own hand.

At the beginning of October 1942, the troop was camped in the region of the Polesia swamps to the west of the dirt track from Novosiolki to Razdzialovichi. All the wounded from the battle over the dam and those left in the partisan hospital on the island had already returned to camp. Those who were not yet mobile still suffered.

The people of the 51 group spent only one night here in a cramped ring under the branches of the trees; they'd not yet had time to set up their shelters. Twilight fell upon the camp. Meals were distributed to the group and the watch chief went out with three guards to change the watch. The daily duty person, the 'Dnievalni', was established. A small group of fighters went out to the nearby villages to find food.

It was dark in the camp. Group 51 was lying to rest for the night. Here and there a cigarette was lit, rolled from a scrap of newspaper. You could hear the sound of snoring, mosquitoes buzzing and the cry of an owl scaring the little insects and arousing disquiet in anyone who hadn't yet managed to fall asleep and believed that these calls foretold bad news.

The dawn peeped through. The 51 group awoke from their sleep. The cook Rivkah Alpert set a bonfire and her assistants drew water from the shallow well. The fighters who had gone out two days ago to acquire food came back laden. And suddenly the sound of lone rifles and a volley from a submachine gun from the direction of the Novosiolski-Razdzialovich road broke through the tranquillity of the forest.

The command of the group was surprised and quickly exchanged some words. The organiser of the guard, Yitzhak Gratchuk, was ordered to get the guards back from the watch. Shortly he returned on his own and reported to the watch commander that they weren't to be found in the agreed place. Merzliakov gave an order to immediately abandon everything and retreat to the swamps. The wounded - Golda and Dudko - were on his orders placed among sparse bushes some distance from the camp and left there. Rachel Rozmarin parted from Golda and gave her a scarf which she had taken off her head.

Dudko was angry like an aggrieved child and begged in a weeping voice, "Is that how you behave, 'rebiata' (children), to those who are wounded in battle?" Golda didn't open her mouth, she clenched her lips and her closed face showed stubbornness, contempt and disgust. Everyone retreated in panic, fleeing for their souls.

When Ya'akov Timan and Avraham Doktortchik saw how Merzliakov had given an order to get rid of the wounded Dudko and Golda, they plucked up courage and got up on their feet. Timan was aided by a thick stick, whereas Avraham grabbed a rifle with his right hand and over his nightgown he hung one of the tent sheets which also served as a raincoat. Halinka Rodenstein hastily filled a rucksack with her clothes and Avraham's and took a little food for the pair of them. Avraham, who was wounded in his belly, with his left hand tied in a sling around his neck, and she with a bursting rucksack walked on stumbling feet after those who were fleeing, but the latter disappeared from view among the tall reeds. After they'd gone a few metres and tripped up countless times, they felt that they were at the end of their tether, but the fear of being caught by their pursuers spurred them on to continue and to join up with their friends.

And so they reached the drainage canal. The many footsteps that were there bore witness to the fact that the group had indeed passed here. They sat down on the bank of the canal, slid down into it and crossed it. On the opposite bank they grabbed hold of muddy earth and climbed up with the very last of their strength. Not far from them Finkel came up out of the canal. They called to him and he helped them pull off their boots and pour the filthy water out of them, and wrap up their feet again. And then he parted from them and ran on his way. Halinka and Avraham went on and followed in his footsteps.

Eventually they joined up with the group where it was encamped. Reconnaissance was sent out in the direction of the abandoned camp to the wounded who had been left behind. The reconnaissance patrol came back and reported that as they approached, they heard two lone shots. From that the commander reasoned that the enemy had already invaded the camp and killed the two wounded, and therefore they didn't go on looking for them.

The faces of the commanders looked indifferent. The chief of staff Merzliakov gave a sign to get up and the camp moved on. However, in addition to the wounded, two guards had been left there - Yasha and his cousin Zvi who continued to stay guard and didn't know that the troop had retreated.

Those who were left behind on guard

Yasha Shepetinski says:

"I stood with my machinegun with my cousin Zvi on the distant watch by a paved track and a little wooden bridge over the drainage canal. To left and right the dangerous bog spread out, and in front of us was a straight path about five hundred metres long. At first it passed through a boggy part at the side of which were deep drainage ditches, and from there it crossed to the forest. Visibility in front and to the sides to a distance of two hundred and fifty metres was excellent and the path behind us reached to the forest and was easy to defend. It was impossible to surround us in this place without us noticing. And if we were hard-pressed, it would be easy to retreat.

"With dawn a unit from the 55 group returning from combat passed nearby. Everything was quiet and nothing scared us. The people of the unit who passed hadn't noticed anything suspicious either. But after about an hour Zvi was taken by some discomfort and without letting go of the telescope, he gestured to me to pay attention.

"Then Zvi crawled across the road and gave me the telescope. Now there was no doubt. In the distance men wearing helmets were moving through the forest. It was obvious these were Germans. Partisans wouldn't be hiding in the forest but moving along the roads.

"We decided: if the enemy moves all its troops towards us, we'll immediately open fire; if he first sends a reconnaissance we'll let it get close until we have an easy target to shoot. We had at our disposal a machine gun and three full rounds, a rifle and four grenades. It was forbidden to leave our post. When they heard the sound of the shooting, the troop would send reinforcements of fighters or an order to retreat.

The Germans sent a reconnaissance patrol of four police and they moved in pairs along the side of the road. They couldn't go off the road because on each side there was a canal and a swamp. We lay ready for battle with a finger on the trigger, our eyes fixed on the target and the grenades by us.

"The police moved forward a hundred metres; they stopped and motioned to their men that the way was free. A German officer boldly came up on the path and called out something to the reconnaissance patrol. They continued to move forward towards us. One thought was worrying us: that our machinegun wouldn't let us down. Between us and the enemy there remained only about eighty metres. We were running out of patience and they were moving slowly. Zvi fired the first shot and a second later short volleys came from my machinegun. Three policemen were already stretched out dead; one had fallen into the canal but was crawling back in the water. The Germans opened lethal fire on us; they were shooting but not moving towards us. Zvi shot the policeman who was crawling and the movement in the canal stopped. I had already used a full disc and put the second one in. We're shooting short volleys, each time in a different direction. Enough time had already passed for the troop to send reinforcements, but no one had arrived. As commander of the guard I sent Zvi to the camp. I remained alone with the grenades, one of which was for me.

"The Germans are still firing, but they daren't come out for a full frontal attack. I answer with short volleys. Now the third disc is about to finish. Zvi is back and signals me to withdraw. I crawl to the forest and run to the camp. On the way Zvi tells me that there's no one there.

"We reached it. The fires were still burning, there was food in the pots not yet cooked, and the Germans were still shooting. We looked for tracks of the people who'd retreated, but couldn't find any. We called out to our comrades, but there was no answer.

"And then somebody in the bushes was calling my name. It was the wounded – Golda and Dudko. Golda could only move on her knees. I was upset. I calmed the wounded as best I could, and promised to reach the troop and come back for them. We fetched some more branches and camouflaged them better. Then we ran in the direction Dudko told us, and soon discovered the lines of our comrades, moving through the swamp and the tall reeds.

"The comrades noticed us and stopped. We reported the situation to the commander. I said we must go back and fetch the wounded. It turned out that the guard organiser (the "Razvodiashchi"), who had been sent to bring us back from our position, hadn't noticed us while we were lying on the ground. Probably he had lost his way, or perhaps he hadn't gone close enough to our placement, and had reported that he hadn't found us. Since they had already removed all the watches/sentries, and returned, the guard commander had decided to hide the wounded and immediately catch up with the troop.

"After clarifying the situation, two small groups were sent from the 52 group, to bring the wounded, but they came back empty-handed. When they reached the spot, the Germans were already there. The enemy, who hadn't heard any more shooting from our side, had entered the camp. They saw the tents and the pots full of food and decided that it was all mined. After they threw in dozens of grenades, and shot it all up, they went back to their places, carrying the four police who we had killed. The Germans reported to their commanders that they had wiped out the partisans, whilst in the troop they assumed that the wounded had been shot by the Germans.

The heroism of Golda Gertsovski

However, the wounded were still alive. They had remained close to the camp, all alone, and were sustained for twelve days by the remains of the food which Golda found in the camp.

During that period the troop was around in that area for several days, and passed the German garrison in the village of Khatinichi, then went out to the railway track by Bostin Station. They then crossed the track and encamped in the forest near the village of Novosiolki.

This is the story of Golda Gertsovski, who looked after Commisar Dudko on her own, while wounded herself.

"When panic broke out in the camp, near Razdzhalovitchi, nobody was bothered about our fate. Eventually, Natan Tchertok and another partisan arrived and transferred me with my belongings and Commissar Dudko, to hide us between the bushes. This was done on the order of Merzliakov.

"We heard firing and the rattle of a vehicle. Commissar Dudko said these were armoured vehicles. I could also hear the sound of the farmer's animals and eventually everything went silent. I dragged the commissar underneath a fir tree and we covered ourselves with fallen leaves. I asked Dudko if he had a pistol with him so that we could protect ourselves or commit suicide if we should be discovered. I heard the steps of about five people, probably Lithuanians. They were looking for loot in the camp, and then they left it. From the tension and emotion, I burst into tears.

"The next day, my temperature went up and my body was aching. The thirst tortured us but I decided to wait not look for water, because I was afraid of being discovered. Dudko was thirsty too, and so I decided to move on my knees and search for some water. I found a stock of food and a well, but I had difficulty in bringing food back. From then on, I went out every day to gather a little food in the camp. Dudko was suffering from infection and his wound was aching. I lit a bonfire to sterilise the bandages, and I bandaged him. His wounds were full of pus.

"One day I sensed danger, and I didn't want to leave the hiding place, but Dudko urged me on, and I went out again to the camp. I felt that somebody was in the camp, and then I saw two bearded men. These were peasants who had fled from their village after the Germans had burnt it, and they had come to the camp to look for food. After encountering me, they were frightened and fled, because they thought there were partisans in the area.

"A whole fortnight we stayed in that place. Dudko was ranting and blaming the comrades who had left him in that state. I crawled every day on my knees and fetched potatoes and onion from the stock I had found in the camp. My wounds had started to heal over, and so I was trying to stand up on my feet and begin to walk. This worried Dudko, who was afraid that I would leave him. In the meantime, his condition had improved, and he was able to move.

"On one occasion, I noticed that somebody was around, and afterwards, I also heard footsteps of a number of people. When they became visible, I recognised among them Nyumek (Benjamin) Rozmarin from our brigade. The meeting was very emotional. They had been sent by the troop to look for our bodies in order to bring us to burial. This was the second time they had come with this aim. As it happens, partisans from Andrei's group were returning and had gone into the camp in order to rest."

Andrei's people, who had found them, took Dudko on a stretcher to their camp, and Golda walked on her own. Captain Tschorni[75] was staying in Leontiev's camp at that time, and he investigated their case. Golda and Dudko stayed in Andrei's camp until 15th. (or 20th?) November, and then they were returned to the 51 group, which was camped at that time in Gotsk.

The news reached Gotsk, the new encampment of the group, that Golda and Dudko were alive. A squad to which Ya'akov Khatzkelevitch belonged was appointed to bring them back to the group's camp.

Ya'akov Khatzkelevitch says:

"Izya Boretski, Moshe Sofer, Nyonya Tzirinski and I were in this squad. There were twelve of us altogether. We set out at night. We had to go about 120-150 kilometres on a difficult route. We had to take another route from the one that the troop took, because the Germans had set up ambushes on the way that we had previously taken. After floundering for two days in the swamps, we reached our previous area. We found commissar Dudko and Golda.

"Now we were in a difficult position. We had to transfer two wounded a distance of 250 kilometres through deep swamps, cross rivers and cross a railway track that was very well-guarded.

"Golda could already move around a little on her feet, and we prepared a stretcher for Dudko. It's hard to describe the hardships of our journey. The commissar held a pistol in his hand, ready to shoot all the time, and he was in a very angry state. We marched almost without stopping to rest. I must point out Golda's strength of spirit and character. The whole way, despite her wounds, she walked without complaint and wanted not to be a burden, only leaning on us a little.

A new commander for the 51 group and the arrival of Brinski and Tschorni

When Captain Feodorovitch fell in battle, the 51 group was left without a commander. Negotiations started for the appointment of a new commander. The command consulted with the commanders of the platoons too. Among others, the Dr. Blumovitch and Zerach Kremin were nominated, but they both refused to receive the role. And then they appointed Lieutenant Viktor Guzhevski commander of the group. He was commander of a unit in the past;

---

[75] *From the group of paratroopers who had been sent to the area for special duties.*

he had been an officer in the Soviet air force. The new appointment didn't please some of the people in the H.Q., and Merzliakov was particularly opposed to it. They decided that at the first opportunity they would get rid of the lieutenant. The opportunity arose during the troop's attack on the small town Khatinitchi. It was planned that Merzliakov would shoot Guzhevski, but on the way, the chief of staff was suddenly attacked by stomach pains (perhaps this was his conscience?), and the whole plan was dropped.[76]

At that time, the commissar, Anton Petrovitch Brinski (nicknamed Dyadya Petya) and Captain Tschorni, who belonged to the group which had been sent from the "Great Land", arrived in the area where the Shchors was encamped. They had come to organise partisan activity in the district of Vohlin.[77]

Tschorni and Brinski visited the Shchors camp. During the visit, there occurred an unpleasant but entertaining incident between Brinski and the commander of the 51 troop, Viktor Guzhevski. Brinski was offended that according to him, he said: 'I am the battalion commissar, Brinski, and you will certainly have heard of me.' Guzhevski answered that he couldn't possibly know of every battalion commissar. In response, Brinski protested that Guzhevski was not a commander, but merely 'shliapa' (a hat).[78]

Following his visit, Brinski made public an unflattering description of the Shchors battalion. The unfriendly reception that he had received in the troop from the rank and file fighters was the cause of this. He says:

"At the end of my appearance, I introduced Captain Tschorni, who had just appeared from Moscow, with the chief commander for partisan troop activity…and it seemed to me that in the meeting, in Proniagin's troop, among the friendly looks of the partisans, I saw a lack of solidarity and even hostility in the eyes of one person. And then I heard behind my back:

"Who the hell are you?"

"I am battalion commissar Brinski. Everybody knows what I do."

And then another voice, 'We need to check what sort of a peacock you've brought us here.' These words related to Tschorni – his bright new suit, well-tailored, stood out.[79]

Captain Tschorni didn't organise the partisan troops in the area, but rather Sikorski, commander of the Brest division, which arrived in the summer of 1943.

---

[76] Witness account of Zerach Kremin

[77] Brinski published his memoirs of partisan activity in two volumes.

[78] *This was a pun, since "Shliapa" means both a hat and Shlomiel. Guzhevski used to wear a wide-brimmed civilian hat.*

[79] *Brinski, p.268*

THE BATTLE AT THE 10th DAM

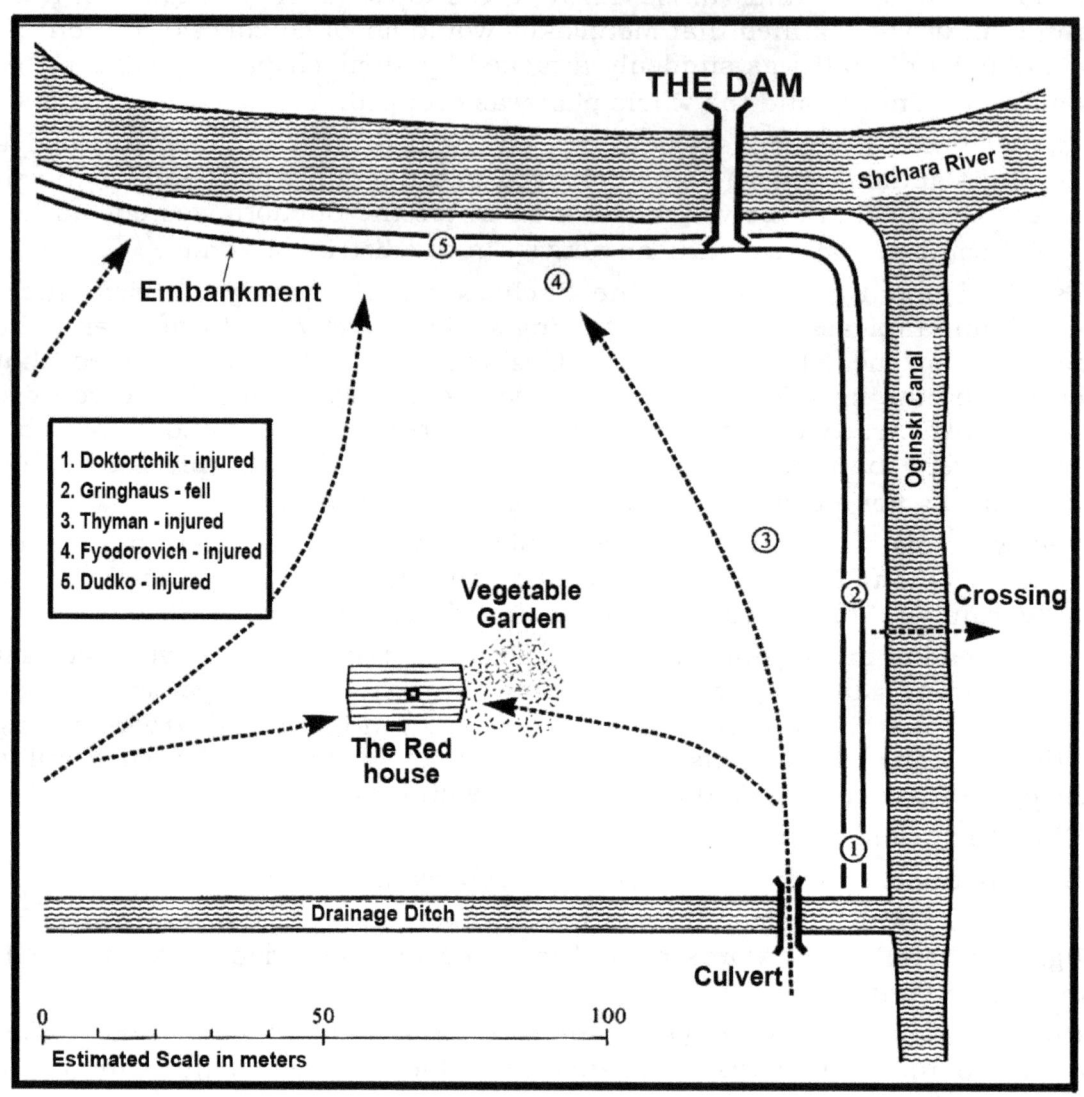

CHAPTER ELEVEN: The Family Camps during the Siege

Left Behind and Abandoned

Half way through September people who had come back from operations in Volchye Nori reported that enemy army units were stationed on all the roads and towns in the area. The Shchors troop, as has been said, had left Volchye Nori, leaving only small groups there. The two family camps – the Biten and Kosovo camps - remained in the area which was now under the control of the Sovietskaya Belarussia troop. When the manhunt broke out, groups from the partisan units which stayed in and around Volchye Nori were hit by enemy forces, and they became rogue[80] groups of bandits and murderers.

When news arrived of the manhunt, the Biten group received an order to burn all the bridges around the forest and to fortify the roads leading to Volchye Nori with felled tree trunks. At the same time they were ordered to set up guards everywhere that they could reach. The reconnaissance reported that the whole area was already swarming with Germans. In the meantime people were ordered to penetrate deeper into the forest and to get near the swamps. The people living in the family camp retreated to a clearing in the forest and started to equip themselves with potatoes which they'd taken from the lone farms in Volchye Nori. They had no chance of reaching farms which were further off in order to obtain foodstuffs. The German army was hemming them in and the echoes of shooting were growing nearer. The Jews didn't realise the size of the danger because their commanders hid the truth from them to prevent panic, and constantly calmed them. On one occasion a group of seventeen people returned from an operation saying that they had been shot at and surrounded by Germans, barely managing to escape by crawling away on their bellies. They had left behind on the roads the carts with the foodstuffs they had acquired.

The whole night of 18th. September gunfire poured down on the camps. Nobody left the forest and only the horseback reconnaissance from the 60 group made sorties from time to time to check the situation. The whole time a German plane was circling above the camp, flying low and checking. The politrok Seriozha Tokarikov gave orders to move to another place in the forest. Suddenly shooting was heard not very far from the place where the Tchapayev troop was attempting to block German penetration into the forest. The commander of the family camp Yefremov gathered the group together and took up a defence position. By now, in the camp, they were speaking openly about a manhunt, but those people in the group who hadn't yet experienced this didn't grasp what it meant.

---

[80] *"Rogue groups" is what groups were called which did not belong to the framework of the established movement, and acted on their own initiative. With the reorganisation of the movement in 1943 these groups were ordered to accept the leadership of the partisan movement and its commanders, and those who refused were eliminated.*

People camouflaged the food stuffs and hid their personal belongings, and everyone was waiting for orders and further instructions. However, they were ordered to still stay where they were and not wander round the forest.

But the shooting wasn't stopping. In fact it was growing nearer and when they started to distribute the food, the plane again appeared above them. Everybody scattered without distributing the food. At two o'clock in the afternoon they heard shooting from the direction where the camp organisers were, about three hundred and fifty metres from the place where the defence was lying in wait. The politruk ordered them to abandon the camp.

They took some of the load, and followed in the footsteps of the politruk who marched on ahead. The group now numbered over three hundred people. They went down into the swamps, crossed the river and went into thick forest where they lay under tree trunks and uprooted trees. When darkness fell, the politrok sent a reconnaissance group to the camp and set up guards.

Moshe Pitkovski says: [81]

"From the direction of the road about twenty-eight kilometres off there were sounds of tanks and cars; the smell of smoke was borne up on the air. Rockets lit up the sky and from time to time you could hear shooting and dogs barking. We didn't know what was happening around us. The feeling was like on the eve of the slaughter in the ghetto. During the six weeks that we had lived in the forest, our morale had improved a little and now despair seized us again. We felt that our fate had been decreed and we were helpless. The night went on for an eternity and we were dreading what was about to happen.

"On Sunday 20th. September a group goes over to the nearby woods. It was the eve of Yom Kippur. They are hoping to find water and digging with their fingers to a depth of about a metre, they reach a little water. They collect about a litre, light a little bonfire in a corner and boil a little soup - and then again the machineguns were opened up on us. A panicked race started through an open area, a distance of about three to four hundred metres, and we reach the dense forest.

"There are five mothers with babies in the group. The politruk sends several people to guard; the babies are hungry and crying all the time and in the evening the crying of other children grows louder.

"Then right by us we can hear motorbikes revving and shouts of "Halt"! The children are crying all the time and there's no more strength to run. The mothers are looking at politruk Seriozha Tokarikov[82]. What can they do? The politruk looked after the children all the time, bringing them milk and everything that he could get hold of. He allowed no one to hurt the children, and now he sat despairingly with tears in his eyes. Then there happened the most tragic event, the worst thing of all: the mothers themselves strangled their babies as if they had gone out of their minds.

---

[81] *Moshe Pitkovski: Azoi iz untergegangan die Iddishe Kehila in Biten, from the Biten Notebooks.*

[82] *Seriozha Tokarikov was from one of the Central Asian minorities, a good and sensitive man.*

"The forest clearing fell silent. The revving of the motorbikes and the shouts of the Germans were quiet. The poor mothers and everyone else burst into terrible weeping. They pulled the hair from their head and the mothers were beating their heads on the tree trunks.

"The enemy planes continued to follow the group. People were running like hunted animals from place to place with no food, no drink. Their strength ran out, and the group which had started as three hundred people was now only one hundred. Many people had been scattered, many had died. Dead bodies were wallowing on all the paths. When we reached a distance of ten kilometres from the camp site we had before the siege, we heard the rattle of motor bikes and the voices of the Germans, and they were still shooting at us from every direction.

"Everybody lay flat on earth without moving, the shooting had stopped, but now we heard the soldiers' voices and we could see their boots. They passed right by us but they didn't notice us.

Politruk Seriozha had decided to go out on his own and check the situation. Several days had already passed and he had not yet come back. People were worried: perhaps he'd decided to abandon them?

"On the Wednesday, the sixth day of the siege, the shooting was further off. The group decided to move on, as here they would simply expire of hunger, and everybody had reached the last of their strength. People envied their dead friends; they were walking slowly and resting every hundred metres. By dawn rose, they had reached the previous group camp - maybe they'd find some water here to refresh their souls? The whole way they had come across signs of the Germans' newspapers, cigarette stubs, cartridges and bullets. The marchers were utterly dispirited – come what may.... they were indifferent to everything.

"It's rained the whole night and we're completely wet to the marrow of our bones. It's hard to move. Several people go out to the abandoned partisan camps to search for food stuffs. In the burnt out camp they find meat, potatoes and a few buckets. "

The Jews of the Kosovo camp were not spared this fate either. Some of them joined up with the Biten camp people, others were scattered in all directions in their search for shelter. They say that their commander Yefremov, who went out to a defence position right at the beginning of the German attack, abandoned the position and fled. Many Jews of the Kosovo camp fell in battle.

Dr. Yasha Karmin, who was the doctor in the Kosovo group, fell in the very first days of the manhunt. His wife Batya, who was carrying her baby daughter in her arms, couldn't find a group that would agree to accept her. The baby was crying all the time because she was teething and the people were afraid to accept her in case the weeping of the baby betrayed their hiding place. Disconsolate and despairing, she wandered around with her child. Many people lost their relatives in the terrible conditions which existed in the forest; hearts became hard and people become indifferent to the suffering of others.

Only a few were still able to rise above their suffering and their dark feelings and offer help to others.

The despairing mother Batya Kremin now looked as if she'd gone out of her mind; she wandered in the forest from place to place until she came across some peasants, but they seized her and handed her over to the murderers.

Thursday, the seventh day of manhunt, passed. They again managed to fetch a little food. In the morning the politruk Seriozha returned which pleased the comrades. Everybody hoped that he would organise the group and unify it. However, the politruk told them that it would be very difficult to retrieve their previous situation, because the partisans had been beaten.

Some people wanted to break through the encirclement and get out in the direction of the Pinsk swamps, but many fell and some of them were taken prisoner. Small groups were wandering around in the forest, afraid that the danger would return. Later they discovered that in this chase which began on 18th. September, two enemy army divisions had taken part and their estimated number was forty-four thousand soldiers. They had sowed the seeds of death and destruction in the surrounding villages. They burnt the village of Okuninovo which is near Volchye Nori and murdered the inhabitants. In the same way the partisan camps went up in flames.

The Belarusian Partisans turn the Jews out of the Forest

Partisan deployment in Volchye Nori collapsed in the days of the manhunt. Now gangs were in control - small groups from the Tchapayev troop which had been beaten, and Bobkov's men, most of whom came from the surrounding villages, and who were anti-Semites without heart or conscience.

The organisation of the Biteni group also collapsed and they had no arms or means of defence. The politruk Seriozha disappeared for a while and came back accompanied by a few Belarussian partisans. He called a meeting and announced that the partisan staff group was ordering the Jews to get out of the forest. The Jews were blamed for bringing the manhunt on the partisans. After him the partisan Pashka Pavlovski spoke. He came from the village of Volchye Nori. At the time of the manhunt the Germans burnt his family alive. He poured out his anger on the Jews. His words were the harshest of all:

"We gave you permission to come to our forest thinking that you would be different. But your Jews gave themselves up to the Germans and brought them to the villages, which were aiding the partisans. Because of you, the villages were burnt and our families were murdered, and so you must leave the forest. Go back to your towns, to Kosovo, Biten, Ruzhani. We need the forest for the fighters, and not for your women and children!"

Seriozha said that he would not send the group to the towns - to slaughter. He would come back and organise them into disciplined groups. They must not wander around the forest. People were divided into four groups and commanders allocated to them. But the hunger forced people to go to the fields and look for potatoes which had been left behind after the harvest.

The Germans renewed the manhunt. Bullets shrieked all around and the dead and wounded were many. Now there remained two groups of seventy to eighty people who were located among the swamps. The hunger was torture. They had no alternative but to go to the village fields to dig for potatoes, and there they would encounter partisans. They would search the Jews and take from them everything that they found on them, even their shoes and clothes, warning them that if they came again they would kill them.

Now the partisans started to hunt the Jews to rob them of the rest of their belongings. They beat the women. Every night there was another assault. Pashka Pavlovski led these bandits, and they would leave the Jews bare foot and almost naked, when the weather was cold and on the brink of winter.

In the forest of Volchye Nori, there were still about a hundred and seventy Jews hiding, but they had no peace - neither by day nor by night. On 6th. December 1942 the partisans decided to gather together the one hundred and thirty-five Jews who were still scattered in Volchye Nori and to get rid of all of them. The Jews turned again and again to the partisans who they met, begging that they would allow them to get hold of some weapons and send them on battle operations. But they were always rejected. The partisans who were encamped in the forest of Huta Mikhalin accepted a few young women into their groups for work in their services, but the pleas of the Jews who wanted to get hold of weapons and fight were rebuffed.

Bobkov Organises his Troop Afresh

Bobkov began to reorganise the partisan groups in the area and was appointed their commander. This was in December 1942. On 6th. December Bobkov reached the Jews, ordered them to arrange themselves in a line (there were seventy-two men and sixty-five women) and started a speech: "Why do you, people who are trained to fight, eat the food that you take from peasants while you do nothing?" One of the Jews answered that the partisans were to blame because they had created a ghetto in the forest. Bobkov replied by again blaming them, saying that the Jews were guilty of the manhunt as the Jews had spied for the Germans.

With Bobkov, a parachutist had arrived who had come from the Soviet rear guard, Fedka 'Polkovnik' (a colonel). He defended the Jews, saying "I am aware that these are empty accusations and that the Jews are capable of being good partisans". Then Bobkov announced his decision to organise them: they had to choose a commander for themselves. They were given four rifles and a few bullets and allowed to go out into the villages to get some food. A role was also allotted to the Jewish group - to go out to the railway track: by 10th. January 1943, they were to saw down the telephone and telegraph poles on the Slonim-Ruzhani road and by 25th. January they were to have derailed a train on the Dormanovo- Lesnaya track. For this purpose they received explosives. They were also ordered to move to the forest of Rafalovka, a distance of eight kilometres from Volchye Nori, by 10th. December.

The last command aroused suspicion in the Jews that the intention was to distance them from the forest of Volchye Nori and hand them over to the Belarussian police and Germans from Biten. It was hard to abandon the warm shacks that only a little while ago they'd finished building with great toil and to go out in the full force of winter and frost and the snow ... but all their pleas were in vain. They were forced to leave. They chose as their commander Noah Polonski and his deputy was Boria Yudkovski. On 12th December a hundred and thirty-five people, among them little children, were forced to abandon their earth huts and go on their way. On the way they met partisans who had only just broken though the German surround, who advised them to return, since there were Germans in Rafalovka. But the Jews were left with no alternative. They divided into two bands: one was to carry out the tasks the partisans had allocated to them, and the other was to build new huts in a place where there was water and the ground was stony.

Seventeen people went to saw down the poles with tools that they took from the villages. They sawed down eighty poles over a distance of only three kilometres from Slonim. Three people were sent to the staff group to report on the execution of this task. The staff group checked and it appeared that the execution in fact exceeded what they'd been required to do.

The Renewal of the Manhunt

They were given a canon bomb for the task of derailing the train. Twice a week representatives of the Jews went to the staff group and on 20th. December it appeared that the staff group had abandoned their position because a new manhunt was approaching. Of course none of the partisans had thought it necessary to warn the Jews. And now they heard shooting all around. The Jews hastily dug shelters in the earth. On 24th. December they were already surrounded by the enemy. The Germans threw hand grenades by every tree that was lying on the ground. One grenade hit the shelter of the Yudkovski family where nine people were hiding. Boria was sitting in the entrance and managed to catch the grenade and throw it to one side. The grenade exploded; all the people in the shelter were wounded but nobody uttered a word. On 28th. December people left their hiding places, tended the wounded and buried the dead. After that, some people were sent out to hunt for food.

On 20th.January 1943 the "Samookhova"[83] from Biten attacked the Jewish camp. Out of one hundred and twenty-five Jews who had survived the manhunts, there remained only seventy. The murderers were Belarussians from Biten, neighbours of the Jews for generations. They stripped the clothes off their victims and took their shoes off. Now there remained only forty-four people, the rest were wounded and sick. In this attack, Mina Gellerstein, the sister of Tanya, was killed.

---

[83] *The civil guard in the Bylerussian villages, who collaborated with the Germans against the partisans, and were armed and trained by the Germans.*

In time the Sovietskaya Belarussia troop was united under the command of Bobkov. The Jews reported the attack and their losses to the staff group of the troop and this was Bobkov's reply: "Now it will be easier for you. You've got rid of so many old rags".[84]

11th. March 1943. In the forest of Rafalovka only a few Jews remained in the family camp when Bobkov allowed them to go back to Volchye Nori. The Jews of the family camp lamented not only their slain but also themselves for still living, as it is said: "Weep not for the dead, weep for the living". They settled themselves in the old Biten camp. After a short while, on 18th. March, thirteen Jews from Kosovo joined them.

Then on 20th. March the Germans again attacked the forests in the area. The family camp grieved for new victims. The whole path to the camp was strewn with bodies. Twenty-five people from the Biten camp fell this time. There were losses from the families of the members of the 51 brigade, among them the wife of Boria Yudkovski, Sheina, and their little son Uri.

At the beginning of April the Sovietskaya Belarusia troop, which had stayed for a while in the forests of Huta Mikhalin, returned. The representatives of the family camp, Boria Yudkovski and Noach Polonski, reported to Bobkov that they would have to rely on the cover of his troop for protection, given their new losses, and again came the cynical and wicked answer: "It will be easier for you now you've got rid of a lot of dirty rags". [85]

Now there were about fifty people left in the family camp. The partisan staff group allowed them to move to the area of the forest by the troop camp, near the village of Koroshcha. A group from the fighting troop ambushed four German vehicles with German soldiers in them. They set fire to two vehicles, killed the Germans and gained a lot of battle equipment. Several people from the family camp took part in this battle and demonstrated great courage. Following the event, eleven people from the family camp were detached and joined the troop for guard duties. The whole group was ordered now to retreat to a distance of four to five kilometres from the troop. The troop took the few rifles from the group that they had, but committed themselves to supply them food in exchange.

The Group of Boris Hyman

At a distance of about thirty-five kilometres from the Biten camp, across the Shchara, there was an independent Jewish partisan group, numbering over forty people, which was active under the command of the Jew Boris Hyman. Nobody knew about them until Bobkov discovered them. They were ordered to cross the forest of Volchye Nori and join up with the family camp.

---

[84] *Moshe Pitkovski, P. 295*

[85] *Moshe Pitkovski, P.303. Boria Yudkovski, who had come to him as a liaison from the family camp, also heard Bobkov say these words.*

Now it became easier for the Bitens. They got hold of a few rifles and became more independent. There was also a certain rapprochement with the fighting troop, since the Jews assisted with guard duties.

Summer arrived. At the beginning of July, they received an order to retreat, expecting a police attack on both sides from the towns of Ivatsevitch and Biten. The troop took up positions. The police went into the partisan camp, looted and burned it, took the horses and the cattle, therefore the family camp retreated to the swamps.

After the manhunt, the family camp was ordered to appoint twelve men from their group for guard duties. They were also required to guard the prisoners that the partisans were holding in a special detention shelter. David Bereskin was appointed the commander of the guard.

At that time, two prisoners were being held in detention. One of them was a brigade commander, Romanov, who had quarrelled with Bobkov and had been imprisoned. But he managed to trick the guard and escaped. The Jew, Greenstein, who was then guarding the prisoners, shot at the absconder, but he missed. Bobkov, boiling over with rage, killed both Greenstein and the guards' commander, David Bereskin. He also took Romanov's wife out of her shelter when she was pregnant and killed her too. Bobkov ran wild all over the family camp like a wild animal, screaming, The Germans didn't finish you off, but I will!'[86]

The report on the murder of David Bereskin, Greenstein and Romanov which Bobkov sent to the battalion H.Q. was full of disgusting lies. Bobkov was trying to excuse the triple murder. He wrote that Greenstein had taken the prisoner some way from this shelter so that he could make off and also wrote that David Bereskin was an untrustworthy man from a socialist point of view and other lies. Bereskin was well known to the partisans as a decent and courageous man who would volunteer for every dangerous and difficult operation.[87]

The continuing story of the suffering of the young women from Slonim and Biten during the manhunts

All the people living in the family camp suffered a great deal in the days of the manhunts. It was particularly hard for the women and the young single girls, who had no relative or protector in the camp. Masha Mukasay says:

R., her sister, who was active in the ghetto in the Slonim underground, went with the 51 troop, whereas she and her younger sister Yocheved stayed

---

[86] Witness account of Pitkovski, who was in that guard detail, p. 37

[87] *The words of this deceitful protocol came to light when the staff secretary, Pashka, lost it in the family camp. It fell out of his jacket pocket when he came to the tailor's workshop in the family camp, to get a suit of uniform they had sewn for him.*

behind in the family camp in Volchye-Nori with the Biten group. The Krupeni family looked after them and helped these two lonely girls.

On 18th. September 1942, suddenly they heard shots in the camp near to their huts. The German forward guard was very near the camp entrance, without the Jews having noticed anything. Panic broke out in the camp, and the people ran off in every direction, without any order or organisation. Masha's legs were covered with sceptic wounds and she ran barefoot with blood and pus dripping from her wounds.

The two sisters lay among the bushes for six days with no food or water. When it seemed to them that the manhunt was finished, they went back to the camp. But in fact, the manhunt was still going on. As a result of hunger and the impossibility of obtaining medical help, there was nothing to even whet the lips of the people burning up with temperatures, and many of them died of their illnesses.

In one of the chases, Yocheved the younger was killed. Masha survived, and after the war, she got married and immigrated to Israel.

The story of Tanya (Tamar) Gellershtein-Imber

When the manhunt broke out, she was in the Kosovo camp. The residents there too fled in all directions, wherever their feet took them. Tanya ran towards the Biten camp, where her sister Mina was staying, but when she got near the camp, she saw Germans there. As she ran, she met a Belorussian girl in the forest. (There was also a Belorussian family camp.) Their residents had also fled, and the two of them ran for their lives.

There was shooting on every side. Bullets whistled over their heads. They heard the groans of the wounded and the screams of pain of those who were hit. Tanya found cover between the bushes. She ran from place to place for three days. It was raining heavily, and the place where she was lying became a huge puddle. The Germans who'd combed the forest, and together with them, their Latvian, Lithuanian and Belorussian helpers – passed very close to her hiding place, but because of the puddle, they didn't approach it.

After it became quiet all around, she tried to move out and scout around for food. She met two Belorussian girls, and together they went looking for food. They met partisans, and among them, the brother of one of the Belorussian girls. The partisans fed them but didn't allow Tanya to stay in their company, because of her Jewishness, and she was again left isolated and lonely in the hostile forest. The wound in her chest where she had been wounded when she'd been hit by a gendarme's bullet was very painful and added to the suffering of hunger and thirst, but more than anything, loneliness preyed on her soul. Tanya says:

"In my flight, I reached the Biteni group camp, but I found only burnt tents and human bodies consumed by fire. In one of the tents, I found a loaf of bread half-burnt, and I bit off part of it. I noticed fresh footsteps of human beings, and I followed them to the Kosovo group camp. I heard voices and hid between tall nettles. I saw Dr. Tzuker, who had looked after my wounds in the past. He didn't recognise me until I identified myself. Dr. Tzuker was on his way to a sick woman, and he passed me onto his wife. Dr. Tzuker's wife looked after me and helped me in the first days. She found some clothes for me to change into and washed me."

Tanya began to recover and also met her sister. In the camp, there was no food, but there were people who shared what little they had. Tanya went back to the Biten 60 group camp, and there she stayed with Masha Mukasay. On one occasion, when she came to the 59 camp for Dr. Tzuker to treat her, she was told that a meeting was about to take place with the command, headed by Bobkov, in order to reorganise the partisans who had been scattered in the days of the manhunt. When she came back to the 60 group, she fell into a German ambush. They had caught a Jewish woman and a child with her. Tanya started to call out, 'Germans, Germans!' so that the people in the camp would have time to escape. As she fled, she fell into a pit that had previously been used as a latrine. After she got out of it, she heard voices speaking Yiddish. These were two Jewish families – the Shepetinski family and the family of Aharon Bandt. Hannah Shepetinski helped Tanya to wash off the filth and also found her something to wear. The family shared with her the little food they had obtained, and Tanya volunteered to go and bring water for the children.

There were a lot of people roaming around the forest, singly and in small groups. Jews were looking for each other. Being in a group gave people a little more confidence and a little more strength in those terrible conditions. However, at every encounter with the enemy, they scattered again in all directions; the groups would crumble, and people would join up with new groups they came upon on their way. Tanya continued to look for her sister, who she'd lost in her flight. She went back to the 60 camp. Everywhere, there were dead bodies and among them, she recognised the body of Yocheved Mukasay, the younger sister. After much wandering and searching, she found her sister, Mina.

At one time, she came to a group of partisans, who had come from the forests of Huta-Mikhalin. The residents of the family camp offered the partisans their water and their services in cooking and laundry and also looked after a wounded man that they had. These partisans treated the Jews well and tried to recompense them with foodstuffs. They agreed to take four young women with them: Tanya, her cousin Zhenia Krupeni and two others. Bobkov, who at that time, commanded the partisans in Huta-Mikhalin, opposed the addition of Jewish girls, but the commander of the group, Fedka, the polkovnik (colonel), who had come from the Soviet rear, condemned Bobkov's anti-Semitic stance.

In the meantime, more Jews had gathered in this place, and among them, Tanya's sister. Tanya, when she saw what a bad way they were in, would bring them foodstuffs.

Bobkov began to organise the partisan groups in the area and was appointed their commander. Of the two family groups, which were in Volchye-Nori, and had numbered about a thousand people before the manhunts, there remained only now about one hundred and thirty people. The remnants built themselves earth huts where they could pass the approaching winter, but it was a great effort.

The partisans suggested to the Jews that they should join them in helping prepare food stocks for the winter. They were required to salt pork and to store it in barrels which were hidden in the earth. Batya Lichtenstein, one of the four girls who had been accepted to the group of Fedka, was sent with the people who were going to hide the meat. Close by, there were two Jewish brothers. They stole the meat from one of the barrels. Bobkov found out and blamed Batya and together with her a young Jewish lad for stealing the meat. He sent them back to the family camp and there executed them.

When the paratroopers arrived from the Soviet rear, the atmosphere in Volchye-Nori changed for the better, but Bobkov wouldn't stop persecuting the Jews. He was looking for a suitable campsite for the troop and wanted to live in the huts, which the Jews had prepared for themselves. When it was pointed out to him that he was not allowed to kick the remnants of the Jews out of their huts, he answered: 'I could get them out of the huts with one machinegun, and it's enough to get rid of a hundred and thirty Jews.'

Zhenia Krupeni, Tanya's cousin, leaked Bobkov's words and his plans to the paratroopers, but Bobkov had organised matters for himself: he ordered the residents of the family camp to move to forests which were sparse and near the town where the German garrison was stationed. The Jews were forced to obey, leave their huts and build new huts. Bobkov gained the place he wanted in the Jewish huts, which were all ready for use.

However, the Jews found no peace in the new place either. A Belorussian peasant called out the Belorussian police to them and again, another fifty-five people were killed. The enemy also took several Jews captive. Among the prisoners was a woman called Shalek, a refugee from Lodz. Several of the prisoners, Shalek among them, managed to escape when the police fell upon a partisan ambush. Bobkov blamed Shalek of espionage , saying that she herself had brought the Germans and the Belorussian police to the partisans, and he ordered her execution. The killing of Shalek was particularly cruel. The wife of an ex-Soviet commissar in Biten, Misova, murdered her with blows from a club. This incident depressed the Jews from the family camp in particular.

Tanya received an order to present at the central partisan clinic, which was near the villages Niekhachevo and Bronna Gora. She was attached to the troop, commanded by Arkadi, Bobkov's deputy. Arkadi went in the role of signaller to the Dimitrov troop, which was stationed on the way to the clinic. He brought her there safely, but conditions in the clinic were poor. There were three earth huts there: one for the wounded, a second one for various kinds of sick people and a third for the team. In addition to that, there was a small shower room, a kitchen and a stable for the patrolmen's horses. Close to the clinic, there was a German garrison stationed. On quiet nights, you could hear the sound of Germans singing in the clinic area. The approach to the clinic was via dangerous swamps, and these could only be crossed with the help of a guide. They also had to be careful not to make any noise, and they weren't allowed to make a bonfire at night.

Tanya worked in the clinic about three weeks, until it was destroyed because of an outbreak of meningitis. The first person to fall sick with the disease was the Slonim doctor, Paretski, and he died within a few days. The carers didn't identify the illness and they were helpless. When two more patients fell sick with this and died, they called Dr. Smolinski, who treated the Tchapayev and Dimitrov troops, to the clinic. He made the diagnosis and ordered them to disperse the clinic immediately. The news was passed to the troop's HQ and Bobkov sent envoys to take the medical crew back to camp. Tanya returned on 18th. March 1943.

And then there was news of a new manhunt. Tanya's group left the camp and moved near to Huta-Mikhalin. During this manhunt, too, most of the fallen were Jews. This time, Hungarian soldiers also took part, and it went on for almost a month. In April, the group returned to Volchye-Nori, to its previous camp, which they found burnt, and which they had to rebuild. Tanya now belonged to the Sovietskaya Belorussia troop. In May 1943, the first and third platoons were sent to the forests of Huta-Mikhalin to prepare a landing strip for planes, Tanya among them. Preparation for the landing strip was carried out at night. The girls worked very hard, and hardly had any time to rest. They also had to fetch water for the camp from the well in the village, and Tanya felt that she was on the brink of collapse. At the beginning of summer, they sent Tanya back to the clinic, and she worked there until August 1943.

In May 1943, the partisan paratroop commander G.M. Linkov, who was nicknamed Batya[88], reached the area. He chose himself a group of distinguished partisans for sabotage operations, but he also investigated and wanted to know about the behaviour of Bobkov's men, and he executed several of the murderers of Jews who were in his staff group.

Thus, in the summer of 1943, far-reaching changes began in this forest. The area moved to come under the supreme command of Sergei Sikorski, commander of the Brest division. He was sent from the Soviet rear by the party and the partisan high command, and the Sovietskaya Belorussia troop, which in the meantime, had grown considerably and become a regiment under Bobkov's command, now came under his authority.

The regiment was divided into two: "Sovietskaya Belorussia" and "The Ponamarenko Brigade". Tanya moved to the second brigade and worked in the clinic under the direction of Dr Lolek Berkowitch. A wave of typhus broke out and Dr. Berkowitch fell ill. Tanya, who was looking after the doctor, contracted the disease, and she fell ill too.

The forces of the Russian traitor, Vlasov, appeared in the area, and several partisan troops engaged in battle with them, among them the Ponamarenko brigade. Tanya took part in the battle as a paramedic. In the winter of 1943-44, Tanya again took care of the sick and the wounded, and together with

---

[88] G.L.LInkov, *Voina v tylu vraga, Moskva, 1951*, "Batya's Book".

them, she was tossed from place to place while still weak from the typhus she had contracted. Her days passed between her own illnesses and the care of the sick and wounded partisans, but she made superhuman efforts to overcome the weakness of her body, going on long marches from place to place, and thus she reached the spring of 1944.

Tanya was lucky and survived to the liberation. She married the partisan A. Imber, went through all the hardships and wanderings of the surviving remnant, embarked on the ship Exodus, and set up home in Israel.

The   Volkoviski

Mina was the wife of Dr. Shlomo Volkoviski, a doctor in the municipal hospital in Slonim. Her experiences in the forest were not very different from those of other Jewish women. The couple left for the forest on 2nd. August 1942. In the manhunt of September 1942, the Tchapayev troop in which her husband served as doctor broke up into small groups. Mina was separated from her husband and ordered to go with a different group.

During the manhunts of that winter, Mina went through a difficult period. The commander of the group to which she was attached made off one night with his cronies and abandoned the group. When Bobkov began to unite them and to gather the scattered groups together, Mina was attached to service jobs in Bobkov's H.Q. She was witness to many acts of cruelty on the part of Bobkov's men against the Jews of the forest and even against their own Jewish comrades. Bobkov, the anti-Semitic commander didn't rein his fighters in.

On one occasion, a group of ten men from the staff guard of Bobkov went out to eradicate a Somoochova unit. The next morning, they all came back safely, save a single Jewish partisan who had gone out with them. The partisans disarmed the enemy and burnt their house. Mina was told that at the end of the operation, they ordered the Jewish lad to go into the house and set fire to it. When he was on the point of leaving the burning house, they shot him dead and left his body to burn with the house.

Throughout the whole period of the manhunt Mina never saw her husband. She finally met him, but they couldn't find the Tchapayev troop to which they should have been attached, as had been agreed at the start of the manhunt. They had some very difficult times, of loneliness and wandering around the forest.

Eventually, with the unification of the scattered groups, Bobkov appointed Dr. Volkoviski as doctor to the staff group, and Mina stayed with him in the troop clinic where Tanya Gellerstein was also working.

The troop had many wounded in the manhunt of February 1943. Mina was sent to the clinic by request of Dr. Berkovitch, the clinic director. When the brigade was split into two, Mina stayed with her husband in Bobkov's unit, while Dr. Berkovitch transferred to the 'Ponameranko' regiment.

The Volkoviski couple survived to the liberation and established a home in Israel.

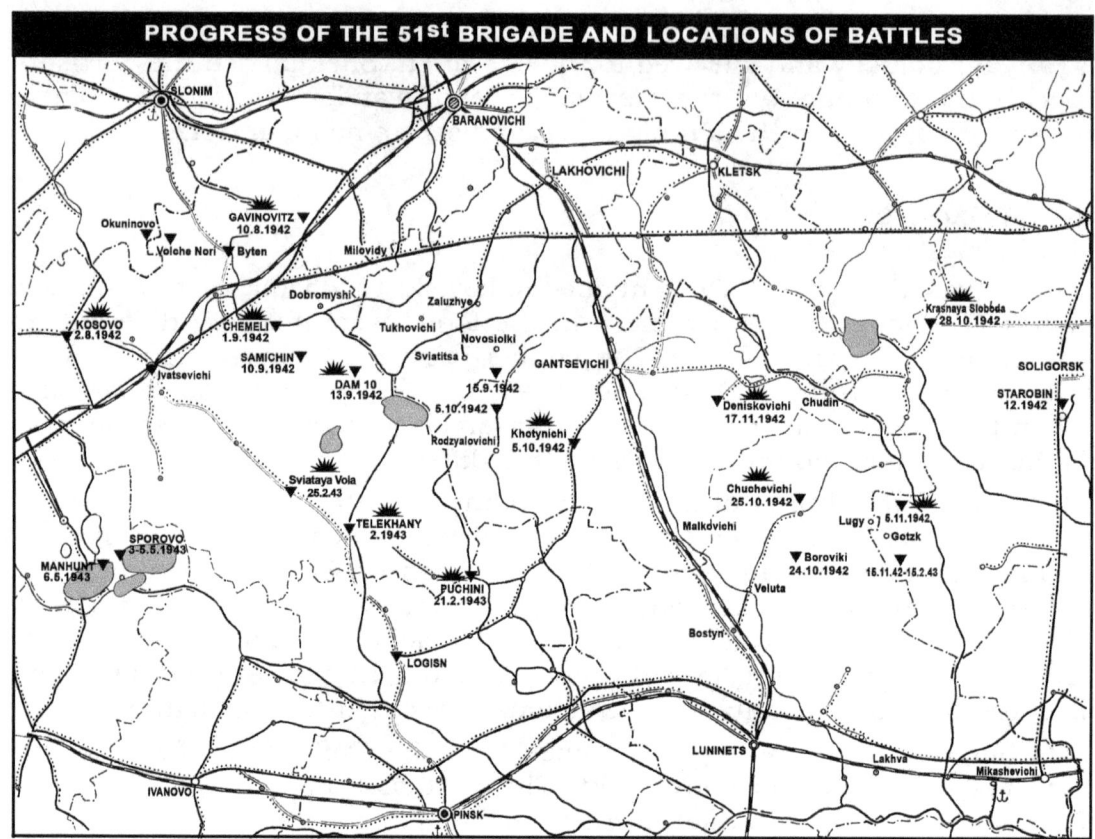

THE BRIGADE'S CANNON - THE SHCHORS TROUP

CHAPTER TWELVE: The Shchors troop in the autumn of 1942

We return to the story of the Shchors battalion, which was on its way east. Despite changes in the situation on the fronts of the war, and despite its objective in remaining as a partisan troop in the rear, the troop went on eastwards.

The journey to Kribushin

As winter drew near, the 51 group needed to furnish itself with food and clothing. In the villages of Svietitza and Bezaluzhye, the comrades took several carts with horses and went out to the small town of Krebushin. Before they went in they sent a patrol and reported that there were no Germans in the place.

Krebushin was once a typical small Jewish town, but now there were no longer any Jews in it.

"It's hard to describe what I felt," says Zerach Kremin. "That night when I wandered through the houses, in the depth of my soul, I expected that somebody would come out of a house, some Jewish granddad or child, but to my sorrow, a miracle like that never happened. The Jews of Kribushin had all been turned out, after they had been tortured, into the ghetto of Baranovitch, and there they died with the local Jews. Only a few were saved among them – Dr. Sayet and Dr Strinkovski. The two of them settled in Kribushin in 1939 as refugees, and before the expulsion they had fled to the forests."

The next day, Zerach went to visit his wounded comrades in the 51 group who were in the hospital set up on an island between the marshes. He brought them some supplies. Contact between the members of the group and their wounded was kept until they recovered and the hospital was demolished.

On one occasion, when he came back from a visit to the wounded, Zerach came across a group of Jews, among them two doctors, Dr Sayet and Dr Strinkovski. They told him there had been a larger group of Jews, refugees from the surrounding ghettos, but on one occasion when they went to requisition weapons, most of them never returned. The doctors had two rifles in their possession and were accepted into the 51 group. They knew the area very well and were a great help to the troop in food supplies and finding weapons among the peasants.

Loss of life among the comrades – The killing of Natan Sapirstein

In that period, when the troop was encamped between the villages of Radzhalovitchi and Novosiolki in the second half of September, a distressing incident happened in the brigade which cost the life of members.

One evening, a group requisition unit set out for an area where some strong German army units were camped. The commander of the mission was Vassily Volkov, one of the veteran fighters. Near the Baranovitch-Luninietz railway line where wealthy farmers lived, the fighters heard several shots from some farmhouses as they passed by. The unit spread out and prepared for attack, but the fighters couldn't find the enemy. Volkov refused to let the incident pass without a response. He decided that the shots had come from a particular house and proceeded to burn it. Only then did the partisans go on their way, although the burning of the house led to fires in the neighbouring houses, whose owners were not guilty.

When the partisans reached the villages where they were about to collect food, Volkov and the lieutenant, Vasya, began to look for additional foodstuffs and this took precious time. At ten o'clock, a convoy of loaded carts left to return to the place where the group was camped. On the way, a peasant came out to them from one of the houses that were on the edge of the village and asked help for a wounded partisan who was nearby. Volkov ordered the convoy to stop and sent several partisans with the farmer to bring the wounded man. They returned without him and said that the condition of the wounded man meant that he couldn't be moved.

Aharon Bandt spoke to Volkov and suggested sending several fighters to visit the wounded man and to talk to him. It turned out that the wounded was a Jewish paratrooper from Moscow, one of the group of paratroopers under the command of Captain Tschorni. The wounded man told them that he was in a group of six men. The arrangement between them had been that one would stand guard and the rest would sleep. It happened that the one who was standing guard killed his sleeping comrades and called the Germans. It emerged that he was a German spy (more of him later).

The peasant who had called the partisans to the wounded man had heard the shots of the spy from his nearby farm. He found the dead, and among them, this man who was badly wounded. The partisans decided to collect the wounded man, despite his serious condition and called Dr. Blumovitch.

However, meanwhile, the supply unit had lost precious time. A partisan, Natan Sapirstein, decided to make things a bit easier for himself and put his cocked rifle on the cart which was full of a live load. There was a sheep with its legs tied near the rifle. On the way, due to the shaking of the cart, the sheep's foot fired the rifle. A shot escaped and pierced the chest of lieutenant Vasya, who was walking by the cart and killed him.

The commander of the mission, Vassily Volkov, decided to bury the dead man by a single birch tree on the road. They wrapped his body in a sheet and put it into the grave, with other objects which he collected during the operation.

This disaster distressed the partisans a great deal and caused another delay, while they were still in open and dangerous territory. Suddenly, a German army unit appeared behind them and opened tank fire. In panic, the partisans abandoned the convoy with the goods and hurried to take cover in the forest. The Germans were still pouring fire into the forest. The partisans retreated in two groups, one of them with Vassily Volkov, and the other under the command of Aharon Bandt, each one of them reaching the camp separately.

The day was drawing near to its close. When Bandt's group crossed the river, they saw Dr. Blumovitch with his escorts approaching the wounded man.

The next day in the morning, Bandt was told that Volkov and his group were already in the camp, and on the strength of his report, they were about to execute Natan Sapirstein. Archik hurried to stand as defence for Natan. He told the staff group that the accident had happened because of fatigue and begged them to listen to other witnesses. He claimed that they had lost time because two men of the command, including the lieutenant who had been killed, had been requisitioning food for private purposes, and also because of caring for the wounded paratrooper. But the staff group executed Natan Sapirstein.

When Volkov reported the death of the lieutenant, Captain Tschorni, unfortunately for him, was in the staff group. He did in fact instigate the death sentence of Natan Sapirstein, but he also listened attentively to what Bandt had to say about the incident and the reasons for the loss of the convoy. In the end, he passed the death sentence on Volkov for having been responsible for the failed mission. Now Volkov was sentenced to death and shot by a partisan in the 54 group. In total, the failed operation had cost the lives of three dedicated fighters. The Jews of the 51 group were very sorry about the death of Vassily Volkov. Between him and the Jews there were decent and respectful relationships and he always looked after his men. This was a hasty death sentence, and there was no thorough investigation of the accusations.[89]

The venom of anti-Semitism simmers[90]

Now it emerged that the troop was near the end of its journey, since the supreme partisan command would not allow the partisans to cross the front line and ordered them to return to their previous field of deployment. Evidently, this restriction aroused bitterness with certain commanders who were sick of the partisan life and with anti-Semites like the chief of staff, Merzliakov, who, from time to time, would look for a pretext to pick on a Jewish partisan and an opportunity to get rid of Jews from the 51 group.

The troop was still stationed in a temporary camp around a forest clearing green with tall fresh grass. The group had some cows which were milked by the young women in the group and the milk urns stood by the staff group dugout.

Avraham Doktortchik, who had not yet recovered from his wound, happened to come nearby. He saw how the chief of staff, Merzliakov, lifted the lids, checked the contents of the urns with a glance, closed them with a bang, and burst out with vicious resentment: "What are they thinking of? Who's this enough for? Parasites, greedy mouths who've fallen upon us. We should get rid of them straight away!"

---

[89] *Witness accounts of Zerach Kremin and Avraham Doktortchik.*

[90] *From the memoirs of A. Doktortchik*

"The greedy, gluttonous parasites, comrade, chief of staff, are definitely the wounded; look, they eat and they don't work,' Avraham Doktortchik called out from a small distance.

Merzliakov turned his head towards the voice:

"Is that you, Avraham? My God, empty words, you're talking rubbish! How did such an idea get into your head?' And a sickly smile spread over his pock-marked face.

"A rabble is trailing after us," continued Merzliakov, "riff-raff whose only wish is to find shelter behind our backs to save their souls. The problem of them is getting worse, particularly as winter is coming on. These cowards are a millstone round the necks of the whole group. A handful of people who are daring and resourceful will have to look out for their maintenance and act as a shield for their contagious faintheartedness. We must act with toughness and quickly to cleanse our ranks of this scum, to choose only brave people with strong spirits, who can withstand the difficulties of the season.'

Merzliakov finished his ranting and went off to the command. Avraham understood something was about to happen, something that sprang from vicious hatred of the Jews. They would probably 'cleanse' the serpents of anti-Semitism in the guise of partisan fighting.

And in fact, Doktortchik was right in his suspicion. Merzliakov soon had an opportunity to get rid of the Jews, who were too numerous in his opinion, when the troop was encamped near Boroviki.

The Khatinichi operation (2nd. October 1942)

Khatinichi is a small town on the Razdzhalovitchi-Hantsevitchi road, where a German garrison and Belorussian police were stationed. There were also strong German garrisons in the two towns of Telekhani and Hantsevitichi. The place where the Shchors troop was camped was on the Razdzhalovitchi-Svyetitza road. The command decided to clear enemy forces out of Khatinichi, as the requisition of foodstuffs was dependent on eliminating the enemy on the road along which the partisans could move to whichever district they wished.

The troop approached the goal by means of a narrow and difficult path over dangerous bogs, through which it was possible to pass only by leaning on sticks. They chose this route so as not to be seen in advance by civilians who were prepared to warn the Germans. Avraham Orlinski has this to say about their experiences:

"The partisans were divided into two branches. The first had to sabotage telephone communication and take control of the nearby dairy, whilst the other one, the larger, was to get control of the German garrison and police station. The roles were explained only when the group was camped in the forest.

"Everything went according to plan. The partisans wiped out the garrison and the police station. They took control of the town and took a great deal of spoils. The difficulty arose on the way back, as we couldn't return the way they'd come through the swamps, and had to go along the road over the little bridges above the canal. However, when we reached the canal, we saw that the bridges had been destroyed, so we had no alternative but to go off the road and cross the canal."

The route was full of Germans and the danger of bumping into them made the fighters edgy. They agreed to abandon their convoy with its load, and eventually they arrived safely back in camp. Only later it emerged that the lack of coordination that prevailed in various groups had meant that in parallel to the 51 group, another group was moving in the same direction and that was the one which had destroyed all the bridges on the Khatinichi-Razdzialovitchi-Vigonovitchi road, the route along which the Germans moved.

From Khatinichi, the troop moved to the area of the villages of Boroviki-Kormozh.

The German spy Ragimov and the battle on 5th. October

The Germans didn't only carry out manhunts, they adopted other methods in order to defeat the partisans, who were giving them a lot of trouble and wrecking their transport lines to the front. They began burning the forests and the villages around them. The fires sometimes reached the places where the partisans were encamped and they had to move off and look for new places to camp.

They also sent spies against the partisans. These envoys, in the service of the Germans, pretended that they were Soviet partisans and sought to gain acceptance into the troop. Their remit was to report to the German command on partisan movements, their encampments and size of their forces, and on the people in the towns and the villages all around who were in contact with the partisans. Frequently, women were also sent, whose role was to poison senior partisan commanders. The spies were trained in special schools. There was a school like this in Minsk and in other conquered cities. Spies were enrolled from the Russian, Belorussian and Ukrainian populations. In particular, attractive young women were enrolled in this activity, and they would seduce the partisan commanders to engage in intimate relationships with them. The partisans caught more than one of these spies, and after interrogation, they would execute them.

The Russian Ragimov was just such a spy. He had been recruited by the Germans early in 1942 in a prison of war camp. After training, he was admitted to the Brinski group, took part in its operations and battles and with them, reached their camp near Lake Vigonov. On the way to one of the missions, he shot at his comrades and made off. However, one of the partisans who had been thought dead was only wounded and survived (See above). Ragimov, who thought that none of his comrades were still alive, returned after a few days to the troop and told them a fictitious story that the Germans had attacked the group, killed all of them and he was the only one who had managed to escape. But the wounded paratrooper who had survived had told them about his betrayal and Ragimov was executed.

Ragimov's betrayal hit the partisans hard. The Germans had received information from him as to where the partisans were encamped, and they went out on a manhunt. The head of the Baranovitch Gestapo led seven hundred German soldiers and a supporting force of Latvians and Lithuanians.

A group of paratroopers who had come from behind the Soviet lines was encamped with the Shchors troop in the village of Zablotye, and the Germans wanted to hunt them down. The enemy advanced in three arms. One of them came from Khatinitchi from the south, the second from the northwest, from the crane-bird swamps, and the third from the village of Borki from the northeast.

The partisans set up two watches: one from the direction of Razdzhaloviczi, with Avraham Orlinski and the other - from the Novosiolki and Swietitsa side with Yasha and Zvi Shepetinski . Zvi became aware of the Germans who were coming from the northwest and alerted the camp. The Germans reached Zablotye, near the Shchors troop, and were led by a forester who was an enemy collaborator.

They discovered the partisan hospital. Those who were superficially wounded managed to disappear into the swamps, but those who were badly wounded, and among them the paratrooper, Krivoruchko, who had been wounded by Ragimov, were murdered. The Germans threw the paratrooper's body into a well. They also murdered the two doctors Krushelnitzki who had served the hospital faithfully, and subjected the female doctor to abuse. The Shchors troop managed to retreat and located itself on the bank of the River Lahn.

Charges against Jewish Partisans

While the partisans were marching towards the Pinsk swamps, Zerach Kremin and Nionia Tsirinski were sent out to reconnoitre. They crossed the Baranovitch-Hantsevitchi railway track. The track was guarded by peasants, whose role was to inform the Germans when the partisans appeared (in partisan slang, they were nicknamed cuckoos).

The partisans entered the plantations of Novosiolki and went on to the villages of Boroviki-Kormuzh.This was the swampy area around Pinsk. The road was built like a ramp of tree trunks and sand. During the years, the ramp had become a narrow path intersected by ditches of water. Crossing on this road was very difficult and from time to time, the partisans, who were marching in single file, would slide into the canal, but in this way, they managed about eight kilometres, until they reached Boroviki. Zerach and Proniagin went out in the morning to reconnoitre in the village, and found it completely deserted – all the inhabitants had fled.

Towards evening, the brigade entered the two neighbouring villages, Boroviki and Kormuzh. The partisans were divided among the village houses; each unit was allocated two houses in which to eat. Each partisan was only to go into the house that had been allocated to his unit. These villagers were very poor, and their staple diet was dried fish.

Two incidents happened to four of the Jewish partisans from brigade 51 – Waxman, Zvi Shepetinski, Burshtein and Natan Finkel. In the first incident, Waxman went in, against orders, to a house which had been dedicated to Zerach Kremin's unit. He sat at the table and ordered them to prepare food for him. His bad luck was that Proniagin and Merzliakov came into the house and found him eating. They immediately asked him what he was doing there and why he wasn't with his unit. The commanders decided to judge Waxman and Merzliakov wanted the death sentence for this lack of discipline.

A worse event happened to the three others, Burshtein, Natan Finkel and Zvi Shepetinski. They were sent to a hidden watch in the forest, between Kormuzh and the small town of Chuchevichi, where Belarussian police were stationed. The charge against them was that they had entered peasants' houses to ask for food. This was a serious offence again orders for the secret watch and a non-fulfilment of duty. Zvi Shepetinski describes the incident. The person responsible for the three of them was Burshtein. Zerach was then responsible for the guard duties. He led them on the forest paths, across the road which led to the village of Chuchevichi. The German command, which controlled the whole area, was stationed there. The boys took up a position a few dozen metres from the road, between the trees and the dense bushes, from where they could command a view of the road and the whole area. For many hours, they noticed no movement at all, and they only heard isolated voices from the nearby village.

Noon approached and they decided that two of them would watch and one would sleep, alternately. People were hungry and thirsty and longing to be replaced, but the change of guard didn't come. From the field to their right, they could hear voices of peasants. Burshtein decided to find out who those voices were. He followed the field and went up to the famers. Finkel and Zvi Shepetinski stayed where they were. Burshtein came back after about quarter of an hour, satisfied, and brought a little food and drink. He told them that when he followed the farmers in the field, he bumped into one of them and stopped him and interrogated him. It emerged that he was a resident of the nearby village and lived in one of the outer houses. Burshtein accompanied him to his house in order to check out the truth of his story, where the peasants fed him and gave him a drink. Burshtein told him that there were several other hungry comrades with him, and offered him a piece of soap in exchange for bread. The peasant gave him bread and dried fish and also a jug of water. The men decided not to report this to the staff.

Evening approached and there was no sign of the relief nor of the officer in charge of the watch. It had begun to grow dark.

"They seemed to have forgotten us." Mused Zvi

After a little while, the watch officer appeared and called them to come back to camp. Burshtein reported on the events of their watch, but concealed his visit to the village. Zvi Shepetinski joined up with his section and took out of his rucksack the bread and dried fish and offered them to his comrades. Anshel tried to investigate him – where had he got this booty? 'If you want to eat, eat, if you don't, don't,' answered Zvi. 'And what does anything else matter?'

However, reconnaissance returned to the camp and reported on Jewish partisans who had gone into a peasant's house to ask for food. Not long passed before Shepetinski was called to the command. Proniagin and Merzliakov interrogated him about the events of the previous day. Zvi told them every detail, save for Burshtein's visit. When they couldn't get a single word out of him, they asked him if he knew that all the men of the watch would be held responsible for an offence of one of them. Zvi answered that he was always on the spot and that he carried out every instruction of his superior and was absent from there only in order to relieve himself, and his comrades did the same. He also told them that no one had come to relieve them until the late hours of the evening. Zvi was released but not for long.

After him, Finkel was called to an interrogation. Zvi suspected that somebody was wanting to take vengeance on Burshtein, who had acted as a policeman in the ghetto, but he didn't know if Burshtein had actually committed an offence against his own people while in that job. Zvi was again called to the command, and his rifle was taken from him. He was told that he was under arrest, until it was clarified whether yesterday's watch were guilty, a watch that had committed a serious offence when it had left its position and engaged in plunder in the village.

Zvi understood then that there was a matter of an informant. He was ordered to sit on a tree trunk, under guard. After a little while, he was again called to the command for interrogation. He was told that reconnaissance from another brigade, which had visited the village yesterday, had heard complaints against partisans of brigade 51. The villagers told them about looting under threat of weapons that had been carried out by non-Russian partisans. According to their description, the guilty person was Burshtein. Zvi insisted that he knew nothing about this, and that Burshtein had only gone once to find out who the people were who were talking loudly nearby them and had come back within a short time. Under guard, he was brought to a place where Burshtein and Finkel were already sitting. The situation looked very serious. Zvi told Burshtein about the evidence that he had given, and Finkel had also asserted the same.

The command of the troop and the commanders of the brigade went off in the forest for a discussion. Zvi suggested to Burshtein that he should get out, since he had nothing to lose and since they would almost certainly execute him. Finkel was very depressed. Burshtein found the right moment and disappeared into the forest. He asked several times permission to relieve himself, claiming that he had a diarrhoea attack, and he didn't come back. The guard told the command and they started to search for him, but without result. Burshtein disappeared with a rifle he took from a partisan, one of his friends. Burshtein had a death sentence passed on him in his absence, and the whole affair hit the Jews of Brigade 51 very hard.

The first expulsion/ rejection (20th October 1942)

Zerach Kremin was called to the command. At headquarters, Proniagin was talking about two incidents in which Jewish partisans had committed offences and said that among the Belarussian partisans of Brigade 51, particularly the people from Chemeri, there was beginning to be some agitation. Many of them wanted to leave Brigade 51, just as had happened in the early days of the troop, in the forest of Rafalovka. Accordingly, he, Proniagin was suggesting throwing out of the group and the troop, the people who were causing the lack of discipline and were likely to be a stumbling block to the troop on its way eastward. Proniagin showed Zerach, who was a member of the command, a fairly long list of Jewish partisans that he wanted to leave behind when the troop went to conquer the village of Chuchevitchi. Zerach agreed, since Proniagin had relented over the execution of Waxman and the two comrades on the previous day's watch, who had failed through lack of discipline.

In the early hours of the evening, a parade was announced. The brigade lined up, according to its sections and squads, and their commanders in front of them. Chief of staff Merzliakov, read out the order of the day. After he'd gone over the rules of the partisans, and then their duty in the war against the enemy and in helping the Red Army in the liberation of the homeland, he announced that Brigade 51 was about to carry out two difficult missions, while continuing on its way. Accordingly, it was decided to leave behind people who were an obstacle in the advancement of the brigade and in its fighting. Then he read the names of more than thirty Jewish partisans, whom it had been decided to throw out of the group. And they were: Yitzak Osak and his wife Sarah, Yitzhak Boretski, Yitzhak Gratchuk and his sister, Musia, Tzadok Derechinski, Adolf Waxman, the two Weintraub brothers, Kuba (Ya'akov) Zilberhaft, Dov Yevshitski, Moshe Modelevitch, Yisrael Slonimski and Gita, his sister, Israel Sokolik, Feitel, the brothers Natan and Ze'ev Finkel, Nachum Tchertok, Mendel Rubin, Yehudit Shelubski, Ya'akov (Yasha) Shepetinski, his sister, Raya, and his cousin, Zvi Shepetinski, David Gringhauz and his son Ya'akov, Yitzhak Zilberman, Baruch Burshtein, Sonia Abramovski, Avraham Pitovski, Yitzhak Pinski, Yehudah Brakner, and his two sons. The four last were from Biten.

Among those elected to be expelled there were also A. Imber and Halinka Rudenstein, but they were allowed to stay. After Merzliakov had finished reading the list, he announced that the partisans whose names had been read out would stay on the spot with their weapons. They were to set up a separate group and continue the war against the enemy. Later in the parade, a second order of the day was read out, which related to the incident with the secret watch, and in it was stated:

"On...a secret lookout was set up on the Kormuzh-Chuchevichi road, where a German garrison is stationed. The task of the lookout was to discover any suspicious movement and to inform the command. It appears that the person responsible for the position, Burshtein, abandoned his position, and with the help of another man, who was under his command, went off to a nearby village and looted honest peasants, peaceful citizens of the Soviet Union, who were suffering from the Nazi yoke and were living under great privation. The investigation has found without a doubt, that Burshstein was the person who looted the village during the carrying out of his role. Together with him, two other comrades on the watch are guilty, Finkel and Zvi Shepetinski. They took part in the offence, because they didn't prevent him leaving the lookout and didn't inform the command about the incident.

"In accordance with the seriousness of the offence and the rules of war, the command has decided to execute the three of them by fire. But with consideration of the clean past of Finkel and Zvi Shepetinski, in demonstrating discipline and courage in the fulfilment of their roles in battle, the command has decided on pardon and to expel them from the troop. Burshtein, whose past is dubious, since he was a policeman in the Slonim ghetto and he fled from arrest, has been sentenced to death by fire, anywhere and at anytime. This instruction will be conveyed to all partisan commanders in the occupied territories."

The commander finished and the blow sunk in. Group 51 was given an order to prepare to move. The comrades started to run around in an attempt to find somebody who could influence the command and set in motion the cancellation of the sentence, so that they wouldn't be expelled from the group. Imber, who was mourning his father from the battle on the Tenth Dam, and was a machine gunner in the group, received authorisation to join, that is, stay in. Avraham Doktorchik intervened with Proniagin on behalf of Halinka Rudenstein, who had continually looked after him. He told them about her past in the ghetto underground and her activities in getting weapons out of the loot camp. "If she's necessary, to care for you, then let her stay" Proniagin agreed. Herzel Shepetinski announced that as a sign of protest over the expulsion of his brother and sister, he would stay with them. Many comrades and friends parted privately, and the rest were going around like strangers, as if they had not known each other all this time and as if they had had no common fate up till now.

Everything was happening so fast that the people who had been expelled didn't have time to recover from their shock. Group 51, and at its head, the troop command, organised itself into single file and disappeared between the trees of the thick forest of the Polesia swamps. Those who remained stayed quiet, with the insult burning in their hearts. A distinct portion of those who'd been expelled had no arms and among them were women and men whose fitness for battle was limited. Everyone was depressed, not speaking, and there were those who lost their emotional equilibrium and wept, particularly the women, whose personal security as partisans was disadvantaged in a combat group. The people gathered together around the fire. Those who had no weapons tried to place themselves close to people who were armed and kept watch on them, lest they should go farther afield and leave them alone.

The group was no longer tightly knit, capable of enduring the difficult conditions in which they found themselves and carrying out missions which required great effort and courage. Neither was there the active social closeness from the days of the Slonim ghetto underground, and the common suffering, which had connected people. Some of these people had come to 51group at other periods and from other places. So now the links were unravelled which had linked the people of the Slonim group, and their hearts were empty, for they had lost the thing which gave some point to their life and struggle.

Evening fell and darkness covered the forest. Up till now, it had seemed to people that they were fighting for a great and holy purpose, for freedom of mankind and for equality. Now everything they believed in had been wrecked – friendship, belief in the partisan mission, the link with the 'motherland', for the liberation of which the members of the communist party had been fighting without regard for their lives. Everything now sounded like empty promises.

They discovered that they had made a great mistake, and in fact, everyone was fighting only for their own survival. Friends from the time of the Slonim underground experienced a particular pain, because their comrades didn't stand by their side during that fateful time and they accepted the decision and abandoned them. Only A. Imber the younger made an effort for the rejected people: he hid a machine gun for them among the bushes.

Those who had been rejected felt that a new enemy had been added: the commanders of their past troop, officers in the Red Army, refugees from German prison camps, who, until now, they had seen as a symbol of solidarity. However, they had to organise themselves and carry on living. A small group of arms bearers, with, Herzel Shepetinski at its head, went out to look for food. Those who stayed behind set up watches around the place where they were encamped. However, after a little while, the parcel came undone. Those who had weapons left the women and the unarmed people behind and went off. From that point, each one of the veterans of the underground had his own story.

Integration into the Vasiliyev troop

During that difficult period, the people who had been banished from the 51 met with partisans from the Vasiliyev troop. This troop was organised in March 1942 in the region of the town of Volkovisk, which is in the Bialystok district. The organisers were Soviet officers and soldiers who had been caught in the German surround, but hadn't been taken prisoner. In July, they moved to the Minsk region, and there, additional groups of the defeated Soviet army joined them and together they retreated to the Pinsk region. Their commander was Vasili Alexandrovitch Vasiliyev and the commissar was Ivan Vasilievitch Ziborov. Until June, their chief of staff was Kalyuyev, and later, Kistyunin.

This troop, too, was commanded to return to the rear and to continue partisan fighting. They retreated to the Polesia region and were integrated into the Pinsk division, which was under the command of Komarov, (also called Korzh).

The expelled people told their story to the Vasiliyevs, who promised to bring their matter to their commanders. They welcomed the Slonimers with bread and meat and dispersed their fears. The Slonim people marched with the Vasiliyevs, until they reached an inhabited area and went into a granary to sleep the night. The Vasiliyev's men and the Slonim people sorted themselves out separately. When they woke up in the morning, to their amazement and dismay, they found that some of the Vasiliyevs had disappeared and taken their weapons. The people who had been robbed insisted on having their things returned to them. The refugees of the 51 group marched after the Vasiliyevs, until they reached their troop's lookout by a river. Vasiliyev's men crossed the river and disappeared into the trees of the forest, together with a promise that they would make sure that their commanders would come to them.

And in fact, in the afternoon, Captain Vasiliyev and the commissar of the group arrived, and with them, a representative of the High Partisan Command, who, only a little while before, had been parachuted into the area in order to bring some organisation into it. After the commanders had introduced themselves, the Slonim people told them their story. The commanders had a discussion and announced that they had decided to only admit the people who were armed into the troop. The rest would be received after they had obtained arms for themselves. And moreover, they promised to prepare an interrogation and if it became clear that their complaints were justified, their weapons would be returned to them. Those who were accepted now were taken to the troop's camp.

The order which ruled in the camp made a great impression on the men of the 51. From now onwards, the way of the Shepetinski brothers and of the other rejected people who had now been received, parted from the others who remained in the Shchors and belonged to the Brest division (which was set up later), whilst the Vasiliyevs fought within in the framework of the Pinsk division.

The hardships of Yehudit Shelubski

The people who had been rejected from the Shchors who hadn't yet been accepted into the Vasiliyev remained in the forest isolated and in pain. In fact, after a fairly short time, the rest of them were accepted, but the women, even those who had been accepted into the Vasiliyev troop, found that their situation didn't improve.

The young Yehudit Shelubski, in describing her hardships, tells how she was thrown from unit to unit, how she was accepted and then abandoned by turn, and tossed from despair to hope, until she reached the day of liberation. In her story, the pain and sorrow are obvious, even in relation to her friends from Slonim, who abandoned her.

"They left us in the forest, in the fierce cold, and went off. In the Shchors, there were also Belarussian families, who hadn't fought and had done nothing in the troop, but they didn't turn them out, only the Jews. One day after the people who were armed had been accepted into the Vasiliyev troop, several people got up and took the submachine gun, which A. Imber had left us, said goodbye and went. And I even said to one of these people, who I'd known from school in Slonim, "What are you doing? We'll be left behind defenceless." One person only stayed with us, with a rifle. At night, we would go into the farmhouses and beg for food. In the end, the farmers complained to the partisans that there were Jews wandering around here who were coming to take food, and then our situation was extremely bad."

In time, everybody was accepted into the Vasiliyev troop, but Yehudit's suffering didn't end with this. They attached her to the fourth section, whose captain was Kistyunin. He was a corrupt anti-Semite. Yehudit says:

"We had quarrels between us, for personal reasons, from the start. He constantly tried to take revenge on me, and turned me out of the group. I managed to reach the commissar and asked to speak to him openly. He ordered the people who were present to go out, and then I told him everything that had happened between me and Kistyunin. He sent me back to the group and said: 'You say, child, in my name, that you have a right to be in the fourth group.' When Kistyunin saw me in the group, he was boiling with anger and shouted: 'Who gave you permission to come back here?' I lifted my head and said: 'According to the commissar's order, I'm staying here.' Kistyunin understood that the commissar had intervened. I stayed there until 1943 and then I left for another group."

In spring, Yehudit was sent to a new troop, the Krasnoslovotski, which had been set up in Eastern Belarus. She was the only Jewess there. She worked in the services and stood guard. When a command was received to retreat westwards, then they threw her out, she and another Jewess, and left them on their own, in hostile territory. They gave them a little food and told them to wait, that they'd come back, but they were tricked: no one came back to them. Then they decided to go back to the troop themselves. They walked a great distance and reached the troop's lookout, but they weren't allowed to come into the camp. Yehudit managed to creep inside and reached the same good commissar, Ziborov. It was her bad luck that Kistyunin was also in the headquarters, as in the meantime, he'd been promoted and appointed chief of staff. He ordered them to turn her out of the camp.

And again, Yehudit was shoved from place to place with nowhere that would accept her. For a while she lived in a hut that belonged to a Belarussian peasant, and then envoys arrived from the Soviet rear. They called her and she told them her story and complained of anti-Semitism. They told her to forget all about it and didn't help her.

On one occasion, she met a group of partisans, and with them was a Jewish partisan, whose name was Shulman, a refugee from Poland. With his help, Yehudit was received into the group. The group worked around Bobruisk and belonged to the Burevestnik brigade, under the command of Marmuliov. In the headquarters of the brigade, there was a writer, who was writing the chronicles of the partisan fighting, and Yehudit, who was well-educated, received work in the headquarters and served as the writer's secretary.

In May 1944, the brigade was subject to a siege. The enemy aimed to surround the partisans so as to clean up the retreat routes for the German army. The partisans marched through the swamps, and Yehudit almost drowned there. When she came out of there, she saw Marmuliov. She was pleased, because she always felt safe around him, and she went with the partisans who had teamed up with him. Marmuliov was anti-Semitic, and Yehudit tells of a conversation she had:

"Once, it was before the liberation, we were sitting in a little group, and Marmuliov began to speak against the Jews, that they didn't fight. Somehow, I dared to point out to him that you have here two Jews, what have you got against them? Doesn't Shur fight well, and doesn't the other one fight well? Why do you make generalisations against the Jews, saying that they're hiding and don't want to go to the front?"

With the liberation, Yehudit reached Minsk. Eventually, she also received a commendation, not from her commander, Marmuliov, but after two months in partisan headquarters. In 1946, she reached Poland, and in December 1948, she immigrated to Israel, and there, she set up her family.

The Chuchevichi operation (24 October 1942) and an incident in the reconnaissance

The removal of most of the Jews changed the Jewish character of the 51 group. The troop continued with its activities and went out on the Chuchevichi operation. The reconnaissance was sent to check out the situation in the area. Among those who took part were: Binyamin Rozmarin, Eliyhu Abramovski, Moshe Yankelevitch, Shabtai Moshkovski, and two Belarussians from the village of Chemeri, Yasha Iskrik and Nikolai Rovsani. Aharon Bandt, the commander of the reconnaissance, ordered them to advance secretly so that the police and the local residents wouldn't discover them.

The reconnaissance advanced in the direction of the village on a path that went through a thick/dense forest. After they'd been several kilometres, they suddenly noticed a farmer who was ploughing the soil near to the forest. The farmer was aware of them, and therefore, they decided to make a detour around the place in a wide arc.

The path was difficult and it went through thick vegetation and dense bushes. The marchers were hungry and thirsty. They reached a place where a pine tree had been felled, blocking the road and they camped there. In the meantime, Aharon Bandt was cleaning his pistol. The pistol let out a shot, and the bullet went through Aharon's hand and the two feet of Yankelevitch and stayed stuck in the thigh of Nikolai. Now, the unit had three wounded and couldn't progress any further to carry out their mission.

The wounded were bandaged and a stretcher was prepared from two wooden poles, on which they lay Kolya and Yankelevitch and transferred them to a hiding place among the bushes. Eliyahu Abramovski and Iskrik went out back to the troop in order to report to H.Q. what had happened and to ask for help.

The people who stayed behind waited two or three hours and then Shabtai suggested that he should go to look for the group, and Binyamin Rozmarinand Archik Bandt would stay put with the wounded. After he had gone a certain distance, he came onto the Chuchevichi group and met the partisans from the Shchors, who informed him that the troop hadn't waited for a report from them and had attacked Chuchevichi, and now they were returning from the mission. In the battle the 51 and 55 groups took part. The partisans had won and they had taken loot and military equipment and even an 80mm mortar with a full set of bombs.

Merzliakov approached Shabtai and demanded a full report on the incident that had happened to the patrol unit. The two patrol soldiers who had been sent to get help had reached the troop and they had informed them of their wounded comrades, so Dr. Cheslava Orlinski had gone out with escorts to the place where the incident had happened, but they hadn't found the wounded. It emerged that those who had stayed behind, when they saw it was already becoming dark and no help had arrived, decided to transfer Moshe Yankelevitch, who couldn't stand on his feet, to a safer place and to send Archik and Binyamin to call for help. They transferred Yankelevitch about the distance of a kilometre. Benyamin stayed to look after him, and Archik went back with the wounded Kolya and the two of them began to advance in the direction of Chuchevichi. With dawn, they knocked on the door of a farmer. His wife fed them and they lay Kolya down in hiding. Archik and the farmer went out with a cart to collect Yankelevitch and Rozmarin. When they found them, they put the wounded man on the cart and went back to the village. Then they took Kolya and carried on to the troop's encampment.

In the camp, when Cheslava couldn't find the wounded men, Merzliakov ordered Avraham Bandt to look for them and not to return without them. On the way, Avraham met Jews who had been separated from the Boroviki troop. They had reached the place where the wounded men had been left and met the patrol, and then, he learnt that the wounded had returned to the base under their own steam. After the expulsion of the Jews from the 51 group and the Chuchevichi operation, the troop continued on its journey eastwards.

The battle of the river Lahn (5th November)

Winter was approaching. The command of the troop consulted and debated where the troop should spend the winter. There were differences of opinion. It was decided to cross the Baranovitch- Luninietz railway track and reach the dense forest, where it was possible to set up sheds with food for the winter months. The 55 and 56 groups led the way, and after them the 51 and 52. After the withdrawal from Chuchevichi, they moved onto the village of Lugi and advanced to the junction of the roads to the villages Lugi-Gotsk-Gavrilchitsi. From there, they turned in the direction of the river Lahn. On the edge of eastern Polesia, in the swamp region, the centre of this area was the small town of Starobin. The partisans began to set up the camp in the midst of a forest of non-fruit bearing trees. Each group chose a place and started to build shelters from branches and bunks for sleep. The whole length of the river, they found bunches of neatly arranged kindling, which the Russians had prepared back in 1940-1. This wood saved the partisans work, and they used them for kindling and lighting bonfires. The river wasn't very wide and an ancient oak tree which had fallen across it served the fighters as a bridge to cross the river.

The Jewish members of the 51 group reached the place exhausted in body and soul. Some of them had neglected themselves to the point where lice spread over their whole bodies. People had become indifferent to their fate and their condition and didn't battle against the damage that these wounds had done to their bodies. The events of the last few days, the anti-Semitism in the troop to which they had been witness, the expulsion of their comrades and friends with whom they had gone through years of suffering with in the ghetto, and the joint activity in the underground, all these, and the loss of their families, had broken their spirit. Their comrades, who were still holding on, were forced to look after them and wash their bodies and clothes, until they returned to a normal condition.

A brigade composed of various groups was sent out on a mission under the command of Shura, a commander of a unit in the 56 group. At a distance of only about one kilometre, the secret guard unit of the troop heard shots. The commander Shura, a careful man, commanded to return. In the camp, they found their comrades ready to move under the command of Merzliakov. Zerach Kremin says.:

"On the fine morning of 5th. November 1942, we awoke to the sound of rifle and machine gun fire.Everyone started running around, and Proniagin directed everyone to take up a position at the edge of the forest, opposite the path which led to the junction. I had a sore foot and I couldn't get one of my boots on, so I hung it on my shoulder, and while I was wearing only one boot, I ran with the unit to take up deployment. In my unit, there was no gunner, so I took the gun as well, and as a number two, Moshe Yankelevitch, with two discs.

"We reached the edge of the forest and took cover. We couldn't see anything and we were just shooting in the direction of what we could hear. After about a quarter of an hour, we saw a red rocket from the direction of the enemy. Merzliakov thought this was a sign of a German attack, and therefore, he shot a rocket, a white rocket, as a sign of retreat. This wasn't a retreat in the usual sense of the word, but a flight. Everyone ran back as if a devil had got hold of them. I began to run too, and when I saw that Moshe Yankelevitch had left me the two discs with the bullets, I hid the spare boot and the discs in the bushes, and I began to march. Because of the weight of the machine gun and the submachine gun I was dragging, I couldn't run. After about a kilometre, it became evident that the Germans weren't chasing us at all, and then a short rest was declared, after which we again moved eastwards, deeper into the forest.

"Before noon, another rest was announced, and then Proniagin called me and ordered me to choose several partisans who would stay in the camp as liaison because several groups were now outside the camp, and among them the groups of Archik Bandt and Moshkovski. When they came back, they wouldn't know where the group had disappeared to. All the rest went out now to patrol in the Deniskovichi region, and from there they would make contact with us.

"I chose Liuba Zhagel, Heniek Malach, Natan Liker and Shimon Snovski. We separated from the group and went back to the camp. We found it desolate but intact. There was plenty of food in the kitchens of the group. We organised for the night and decided to stay in the camp at night, at dawn to cross the Lahn and sit among the piles of straw that were scattered over the bogs and to lookout in case the Germans came back. It turned out that the shots that we'd heard in the morning were shots that a Latvian support unit had fired on the guards in our secret guard unit, which was placed on the path opposite the forester's cottage at the entrance to the forest.

"The battle took place by a lone farm, near which the secret guard unit was positioned. Two groups, the 51 and 55, which were lying by each other, heard these shots but they didn't go to see what was happening with the guards and to offer help. After a while, silence fell. The Latvians had retreated and collected their dead. However, the 51 group lost two comrades, Yeshua Busel and Israel Rabinovitch, who were in the secret guard unit and fell from enemy bullets.

"And moreover, the next day, it became clear that the white rocket of the partisans had confused the enemy, who had thought that the partisans were coming out to attack and began to retreat hastily and in disorganisation. The Latvians were a punishment battalion, which came from Gantsevitch to wipe out the partisans.

"We recruited a number of villagers from the area, and they collected up for us 320 kilogram of seeds, supply for the winter. We also cleared out the beehives and took the honey of plantations of collaborators, who had killed members of the 55 group. After a few days, we met the Finkel brothers, who had been wandering about the area after the first rejection, and also Moshe Modelevitch. We took them into our group. I also met a Jew from Baranovitch, whose name was Berkovitch. Before the manhunt, he had belonged to the 113 group, but had lost them and was now wandering alone around the area. I brought him too into our group.

"One evening, Shabtai Moshkovski reached us and with him were several partisans who had been envoys with Komarov. After I'd informed them roughly where the group was, I went. We were informed that the Germans had ordered the village of Gotsk to supply a thousand kilogram of corn and bring it to them in Gantsevitch. We made contact with several farmers and worked out a detailed plan. After the all the corn was gathered in, and collected in the school, we would mobilise carts and take all the kernels to Gavrilchitsi. We would grind all of it in the windmill, which was working there, and bring the flour to our bunkers. And we went to Gavrilchitsi to organise the grinding.

"The time came to gather in the corn. We came to Gotsk at night and we called the head of the village and insisted that he grind the corn within two days. Obviously, we came to collect the flour several days later for fear he might set up a trap for us. We brought the flour to the bunkers, and we had a full supply for the winter."

Organising intelligence in the area

"The days passed and became colder. There were difficulties with the guarding, and so I decided to try and organise some intelligence among the farmers of the surrounding villages, intelligence which would inform us of any suspicious movement of the enemy. We began with Lugi. We had been informed that in the village there lived a past representative of the Supreme Soviet in Belarussia. One night we went to him and insisted that he take up his place again as a representative of the Belarussian national council. We claimed against him that he had betrayed the Soviet principle: the whole state was fighting the invader and bleeding and he was sleeping in a warm bed at night and doing nothing. It was shameful that he, the elected by the people, should behave in this way. The man was very frightened and promised to do what we commanded him.

"We asked him to organise an underground cell of activists, who would be in touch with us. The 'deputat' told us that there was one young man in the village who was very pleased when the punishment brigade attacked us and also, at the time of the Chuchevichi massacre, had caught two Jews who had escaped and handed them over to the Germans, and they were murdered. We took revenge on this 'guy'.

"We had to wait for our group to arrive and we moved to live in the houses of the farmers, where we used to receive daily information on what was happening in the district, and also what was happening with our group. The group, in the meanwhile, had conquered the saw-mill in Deniskovitchi and burnt it. This was one of the biggest saw-mills in Poland. The Shchors troop didn't come back to our camp, but instead, moved northeast in the direction of the village of Gavrilchitzi. On 16th. November, they paused in the place where, before the war in 1939, there had been a Polish border guard position."

The Deniskovitchi operation (17th. November 1942)

Now the troop was preparing a new mission to wipe out the German force stationed locally, sabotage of a major railway line and destruction of the sawmill near it. It was also in the plan to sabotage the narrow railway track, along which the Germans transported wood to the station in Gantsevitch. Most of the troop were recruited to this operation and only a few groups were sent to the villages to acquire food and clothing for the winter, which was already beginning to make itself felt.

Orlinski went out with one of these groups. In one of the houses, they found sheepskins. To the partisans, who spent most of their time outside, and frequently had to sleep in the snow, sheepskins were an extremely vital commodity. The owner of the house agreed to give him the sheepskin and said that it belonged to her son who was serving in the Red Army. Her words disturbed Orlinski and he didn't take the sheepskin, even though the cold was giving him open sores on his back and hands, and they caused him a great deal of suffering. "This incident," pointed out Orlinksi, "taught me an important lesson in the life of the partisans. From now on, I would not be so delicate and considerate." At that time, the group returned from a mission in Deniskovitchi, and Milikovski brought a sheepskin for the wife Dr. Orlinski, so he had the old sheepskin of his wife. The troop continued from this temporary station to the Gotsk area.

CHAPTER THIRTEEN: Shchors in the Pinsk division

Shchors while stationed at Gotsk

The Shchors troop reached Gotsk on 18th. November. That night, snow fell and covered the partisans who were sleeping outside with a pure white sheet. The troop decided to pass the winter there, and stayed until 13th. February 1943. The wounded Dudko and Golda, who had been staying in the partisan field hospital, were also brought to Gotsk, but their wounds were not yet healed. Partisan command units were set up in the nearby villages. In the Pinsk region, there were already active partisan troops, some of them functioning alone, and some of them united under the command of Korzh, (also known as Komarov)[91].

At the end of 1942, the representative of the communist party, Alexey Yefimovitch Kleshchev, was parachuted into the region, and on his initiative, at the end of November/early December, the isolated troops in the region (that is, troops Komarov, Kirov, Vasilyev, Shesh, Tchapayev, Dombrovski) were united with the partisan division of the Pinsk region. Korzh's H.Q. was camped in the village of Horostov, and Kleschev was appointed commissar of the division. They invited Proniagin to their H.Q. and suggested that he should join the Pinsk division, to which he agreed. Before long, Korzh and Kleschev visited the Shchors camp. This visit decisively affected the fate of Brigade 51, because in their view, the percentage of Jews was still high.

The partisans went into earth huts for the winter. Every dugout of this kind was home to a squad of twelve people. The walls of the huts were supported by tree trunks about a metre high and covered with a sloping roof built of branches and covered with birch bark. A gangway was left right along the length of the dugout. At the rear it reached a height of 1.80 metres. Stoves were set up in the huts, most of them in metal barrels, and a chimney was set up on the upper side for the smoke to escape through the roof.

The winter had advantages and disadvantages in the lives of the partisans. The winter cold and the snow enabled the partisans to move around on sledges, and travelling around on them was easier and faster than on carts, and so they could go out on missions further off. But footprints showed more clearly in the snow, and could lead the enemy right up to the camp, and therefore, it was better to go out on days when it was snowing to cover the footprints. The long winter evenings, when the partisans were free of tasks, were used by the command for political indoctrination.

---

[91] *Korzh was a veteran communist, and had fought in the International Brigade in the Spanish Civil War. When the Soviets retreated in 1941, he stayed behind to organise a communist underground. From the start, he had managed to organise a partisan unit, numbering sixty men, from which the Pinsk division eventually sprang.*

Iz istorii partizanskovo Dvizhenya Beilorusii, P.21

The Berkovitch incident (December 1942)

The Jewish fighters of Brigade 51 now really felt the lack of their commander, Feodorovitch. Incidents of anti-Semitism and discrimination were frequent and now they had no beloved commander standing up for them, who would protect them from the outbursts of the anti-Semites. Their new commander, Viktor Guzhevski, was in fact an intelligent man, but revealed himself to be someone, who, first and foremost, was preserving his position and too clever to argue with those above him, or to scold the anti-Semites when they fell upon the Jews.

And so there occurred a very serious incident: three reconnaissance patrolmen, and among them Berkovitch, the Jew from Baranovitch, who spent most of his time in reconnaissance tasks, and so was less well known in the brigade, were sent out to take care of a Belarussian peasant who was suspected of collaboration with the enemy. Fedya was in command of the reconnaissance detail. The partisans nicknamed him commissar because of his tendency to flaunt various stripes on his shoulders. (In the same way, some commanders hung a bag of documents on their shoulders as well as individual arms). Fedya belonged to the 56 group and was well known as an habitual drinker and corrupt type, and incidents of rape of women in the villages and charges of looting were attributed to him. But the man was not punished, because his commander, Zhuravliov was also addicted to alcohol, and neither was his moral standard of the highest. And so he protected Fedya because the latter used to supply him with spirits every time he came back from a trip.

The reconnaissance patrol interrogated the suspected peasant and Fedya commanded Berkovitch to shoot him. Unfortunately, it appeared that the peasant was a relative of Korzh and trusted by him. A furious Komarov and Kleshchev came to the H.Q. of Shchors and insisted that those guilty of the killing of the peasant should be punished. Even though Berkovitch only carried out the order of his commander, he was blamed for this and arrested.

Officially, Berkovitch belonged to Avraham Bandt's unit, so Avraham was the one who took care to bring food to the prisoner and to talk to him where he was detained. Berkovitch expressed fear over his fate because of the presence of Komarov in the troop. In bitter despair, he even offered Aharon his gold watch to remember him by, so that it wouldn't fall into the hands of strangers. Archik wouldn't accept it and encouraged the prisoner, promising that his comrades would defend him in a trial and no evil would befall him. Archik still believed that a fair trial would take place.

However, that very evening, Bandt heard a shot from the side of the camp, where Berkovitch was imprisoned, and he went there to see what had happened. On the way, he met Merzliakov, who told him there was no need to go there, everything was fine, and he could go back. Merzliakov turned towards to the kitchen, but Archik's suspicions were aroused, and he went on in order to see what had happened to Berkovitch.

On the way, he met the prisoner's guards, who told him that Merzliakov had taken the prisoner from where he was held, some distance away, and had killed him with a shot. And then he had taken his gold watch. Archik was upset and hurried off to inform Dr. Blumovitch that the prisoner had been executed without a trial and without hearing witness accounts, while the person who had given the command, Fedya, had come out of the whole thing clean.

What happened after that is told by Avraham Orlinski

"At that time, a group studying the history of the communist party, under the leadership of commissar Dudko, was centred in the dugout of the 51 group. The group would meet in Avraham Bandt's dugout, where the lecturer also lived. That evening, I went into the hut for the first time. I was sitting and thinking that the time to start the study session had already passed. The lecturer wasn't there, and very few of the people had come in when Aharon Bandt burst into the hut and in an angry voice, ordered everybody to collect on the hill with their arms. I hurried there with my weapons, and found a group of comrades agitated and angry. Dr. Blumovitch leapt to the top of the hill, and with a furious challenge, flung out the sentence, "And who's coming with me?" Opposite stood the commander of the group, Guzhevski, embarrassed and begging for restraint and calm, because the division commander Komarov, and Kleshchev, the member of the Supreme Soviet in Belarussia, were in the H.Q. After an exchange of hard words and words of protest from Blumovitch, the two of them went to the command hut, where Komarov and Kleshchev lived.

"It appeared that Berkovitch had fallen victim to a mistake, and his commander, Guzhevski had not protected him like Zhuravliov the drunkard had defended Fedya. Guzhevski had chosen not to intervene.

"When they brought Berkovitch's shoes back for the group, all the Jewish commanders were aware of the crime. They were shaken by the wrongdoing and the injustice, which had been carried out by the anti-Semites, and therefore, Aharon gathered the Jews on the hill while they were armed. When H.Q. became aware of the demonstration of the Jewish partisans and their fierce protest against the carrying out of the death sentence without investigation and without trial, they were stunned. In particular, the scathing and forceful protest of Dr. Blumovitch hit them, and they behaved in the accepted Stalinist manner of that period – hiding every wrongdoing and every one of their failures with excuses and ideological explanations."

Dismantling the Jewish 51 brigade (end of December 1942 – early January 1943)

Next morning, after breakfast, an order was given to line up in a clearing of the forest. People lined up along three sides of a rectangle. The fighters presented in three arms and Kleshchev stood before them and started his speech, hurling criticism and blame at them as follows:

"A representative of the Mensheviks, of the counter-revolutionary, strangers who have stolen into the ranks of the partisans and Soviet patriots; an enemy of the people, who intrigues and subverts the solidarity of the Soviet people, brings danger to the ranks of the freedom fighters and damages their struggle against the Nazi enemy for the liberation of the people and the homeland. We must pull this hostile element out from the roots of the ranks of the partisans."

It was obvious to everyone that these words were directed at Dr. Blumovitch. The blaming and the distortion of the truth made the hearts of many comrades tremble. Everyone was debating how to behave and act against the scheming of Kleshchev and his supporters. There was a notion that the Jews should just immediately leave the troop with their weapons, but the Jewish fighters were aware that behind them, outside the forest clearing, were positioned armed partisans from other groups, who were prepared to act in the case of opposition from the 51 group. Now the commander of the unit, Aharon Bandt, sought to make himself heard and he spoke decisively: 'Dr. Blumovitch is not a stranger and has not infiltrated us. I am the one who has looked for a doctor for the partisans of the Shchors group, to help us and to meet our needs. He was the only one who responded to our request to join us and help us. In those days, Dr Blumovitch was the only doctor, and therefore, now I beg you, take account of the fact that we, the fighters of the 51 group, are not fighters waving a baton of clearance ('Shompol') against the rural population.[92]

'We are fighting against the Nazi enemy, the enemy of our people and of the Soviet people and of all humanity - with the quantity of arms (he pointed towards the large and varied quantity of arms of the group) which we took from the Germans. These are the same weapons which other men of the Soviet armies left behind for the Germans. Please look for criminals among the anti-Semites, and not among us.'[93]

Archik's claims were reinforced by his second in command and other Jewish fighters. Everybody supported his words defending Dr Blumovitch. Among the speakers was Zhenia Eichenbaum, and she said: 'When I came to the Komarov's H.Q., they called me 'Zhidovka' (a derogatory nickname for a

---

[92] *This is a reference to the behaviour of certain non-Jewish partisans, among them Fedya, who used to beat the peasants with the cleaning stick of a rifle when they refused to meet their demands for food supplies.*

[93] *These quotations are from the evidence of Avraham Orlinski, archives of Lokhamei Hagetaot.*

Jewess). Do I need to say more?' All the speakers were protesting against the signs of anti-Semitism in the troop.

The last of the speakers was Proniagin, and his words were quiet and conciliatory. Summing up, he said: 'We must acknowledge that expressions of anti-Semitism are widespread in our environment.' The commander of the 51 group, Guzhevski didn't interrupt, didn't open his mouth, as if the whole matter had nothing to do with him. He looked after his skin very well, even though, in the depths of his heart – and his men knew this – he was against the regime.

Klashchev's disappointment was obvious. He had supposed, as he had been used in the past, that all the commanders would support him and agree to get rid of Dr. Blumovitch. His disappointment led him to decide to break up the 51 group, most of whose members were still Jewish. And the explanation, again, was ideologically camouflaged. It was 'not done' to set up national groups in the Soviet partisan movement. The command had turned a blind eye to the history of the 51 group because of the fact that the Jewish group had arisen when non-Jews had left, saying, 'Look after yourselves.'

Following the instructions of Kleshchev, the fighters of the 51 group were dispersed among the groups 52, 55 and 56. The two latter groups were smaller and had been set up before the group had left Volchye-Nori. Their commanders were from the Soviet army, but men of a low moral standard. The 51 group was divided in the following way:

To the 52 group (Later Shchors troop)	To the 55 group (Later Kotovski troop)	To the 56 group (Later Bodyoni troop)
Abramchik	Eichenbaum Zhenia	Imber A.
Liker Natan	Abramson Lonka	Abramovski Eliyahu
Dr. Liepak Yitzhak	Berger Yitzhak	Orlinski Avraham
Moshkovski Shabtai	Berezin Archik	Ogushevitz Yehosua
Mukasey R.	Buzin Abba	Olanski Yehoshua
Malakh Heniek	Blumenfeld Lili	Abramchik Leah
Kunitza Rivkah	Bublatski Avraham	Alpert Pesach
Shusterovitch Zhama	Guterman Shmuel	Alpert Rivkah
	Gertsovski Golda	Alpert Chaya
	Doktortchik Avraham	Alpert Hannah
	Zhagel Liuba	Bandt Avraham
	Mishelevitch Yitzhak	Bandt Aharon
	Mishelevitch (Akerman) Mania	Bandt Liuba
	Moshkovski Hillel	Delatitski Anshel
	Snovski Shimon	Khatskelevitch Ya'akov
	Dr. Strikovski	Yankelevitch Moshe
	Smolinski Miron	Modulevitch Moshe
	Servinski Noah	Mishler Feivel
	Dr. Sayet Avraham	Mishler Esther
	Feldman	Sofer Moshe
	Podolski Fima	Finkel Ze'ev
	Pok Mordechai	Finkel Natan
	Kremin Zerach	Tsirinski Nionia
	Korsh Yitzhak	Rav Yitzhak
	Rozmarin Niomek (Benyamin)	Rodenstein Halinka
	Rozmarin Rachel	Shefchuk Karpel
	Stein Sima	Shabtai Yehoshua
	Shnur Adek	

In the troop H.Q.	The troop clinic
V. Irka	Dr. Orlinski Cheslava
Kagan Guta	Dr. Blumovitch Avraham

Proniagin continued to command the troop; the role of commissar was allocated to Artiom Samsonovitch Avestisian, in place of Dudko, who was wounded, and after him Sergei Yegorovitch Yegorov, who, before the war, had graduated from the Soviet Institute for political science. The Jews in the group nicknamed him the 'white hat', because of the white fur hat which he was accustomed to wear. The Jewish partisans put no trust in him and had reservations about him. A man of the NKVD, Pavel Grigoryevitch Kovaliov was appointed commander of the special group[94]. After the dispersal of the 51, the ex-members of the Slonim underground

---

[94] *The role of this unit (Osoby Otdel) was to take part in intelligence and matters of security, and to supervise the political correctness of the partisans and the people from the surrounding villages who were linked to the troop.*

fought in the ranks of his group and afterwards also in other troops to which they belonged, each one on his own battle and life path. [95]

The 51 group had aroused the fears of the anti-Semitic commanders. They were afraid that its fighters, most of whom were still Jews, would rise up against certain anti-Semitic commanders and denounce their deeds, which were in contravention to declared partisan ethics, to the high command. With the renewed organisation of the partisan movement, after the arrival of new envoys from the Soviet rear, the situation changed for the better and some of the commanders, who had acted corruptly, were punished.

The people of Slonim, the fighters of the 51 group, whose group was broken up, who were forced now to separate, each from his friend, and to transfer to other groups, bore the insult in their souls to the very end. But they continued to fight with bravery and with dedication to their goal, even in the ranks of the new groups. The separation and the dispersal did not damage the texture of devotion and loyalty, which had been woven in the years of suffering in the ghetto and dangerous underground activities in Slonim. Their past continued to unite them. However, some of the members, particularly the women who had been abandoned, could not forget the behaviour of certain comrades, who, in the hour of hardship, failed to stand by the members who were in distress. In their hearts, there remained pride at having been in the Jewish Slonim 51, even in the period when they were fighting in the ranks of other troops and after the liberation in the ranks of the Red Army.

The failure of the Starobin operation (end of Dec 1942)

Before the breakup of the 51, groups from the Shchors and other troops set out to eradicate the German garrison in Starobin. A hundred and fifty to two hundred men went out from the Shchors. The whole 54 group was sent under the command of Leontiev with fighters from other groups and two troops from the Pinsk division. The fighters of the 51 didn't take part in this operation, and the Jews took it as a burning insult, since on all previous missions, they, and the fighters of the 54, were among the main operators.

However, in this battle, the partisans suffered a defeat, and in particular, the fighters of the 54 group, for they sustained heavy losses. They had received no support from the group who were required to support them. The fighters of the Leontiev's group emphasised that if only the role had been allocated to the 51, the outcome of the battle would have been very different.[96]

---

[95] *Proniagin mentions the dispersal of the 51 group in just two sentences in his book, with no explanation for the dispersal. "Following the suggestion of Kaleshchev and Korzh we solved a number of organisational problems. The 51 group was disbanded and dispersed among the other groups." (Proniagin, p. 60).*

[96] *Proniagin justifies himself in his book (p.61), saying that he was not involved in the planning of the operation, and he is therefore not responsible for the defeat. According to him, the chief of staff of Pinsk Division, Rayevski, commanded the operation. Proniagin does not state the date of the Strubin operation.*

Coming to the camps of Kovpak and Kapusta

At the beginning of January 1943, they reached the area where the Brest and Pinsk divisions were encamped - the big partisan camps of the famous commanders Kovpak, Sevorov and Fyodorov. Sidor Artemyevitch Kovpak was the most admired partisan commander in the Soviet Union. He was born in 1887, in the village of Kotalva, which is in the Poltava area. He fought during the Bolshevik revolution on the side of the Soviet regime and had been an officer in the Red Army. Before the outbreak of WW2, he was chairman of the workers' union of the town of Putival. When the front moved nearer to his town, he organised the partisan base in the surrounding forest, and he was then 56. His brigade was set up in the months of August – September 1941, and it gained in strength in the course of battles with the enemy. In the summer of 1942, he moved with his troop to the region of the Briansk forests.

His troop grew quickly, becoming a brigade and finally a division. Kovpak's division was mobile and became famous for its daring incursions (called 'raids' by the partisans) into the whole breadth of the enemy conquest. In the days of 25th. and 26th. October 1942, he set out for the big invasion, which was called the Stalin invasion. On 8th. – 10th. November, he crossed the Dneiper, and at the beginning of January, the Pripiet, and reached the operational territory of the Belarussian partisan movement, that is, Polesia and Wohlin.[97]

Kovpak's band went out to the Prince's Lake and were stationed in the villages on the south bank of the lake. His H.Q. was camped in the forest of Liachovichi, with one battalion in the village of Pukhovichi and so on. He met up with Captain Tchorni and with 'Batya'. This last was Gregory Matveyevitch Linkov, a parachutist, a commander of 'the special services troop'. Kovpak invited the commanders of the Pinsk division to meet him and also visited the H.Q. of Korzh, which was in the village of Khorostov. The large division of Sevorov, who was the commander of the Zhitomir division, moved in parallel to Kovpak's camp.

At that time, the German army was being wiped out near Stalingrad. It was already obvious that the advance of the conqueror had been blocked and retreat was near. The Germans were then preparing their attack on the Oriol-Kursk line, and the Soviet army asked the partisans to sabotage the transport lines and to intercept the enemy supplies on their way to the front, in order to prevent the enemy from quickly getting reinforcements to rescue their beaten army near Stalingrad.

---

[97] *The second most famous route-march of the Kovpak camp was the 'raid' on Kraftim (12th. June – 5th. August, 1943). During his invasion of the breadth of Wahalin, Kovpak took on Jewish partisans, and on his march to Kraftim he liberated the Jews of the Skalat ghetto, who formed the basis of the Seventh Platoon. Kovpak was twice decorated Hero of the Soviet Union. From 1947 – 1967 he held the office of chair of the Supreme Soviet of the Ukraine. He died on 11th. December 1967, at the age of 80. He is buried in Kiev.*

The Zhitomir division moved a distance of five hundred and thirty-four kilometres. During their march, they conducted sixty-seven battles, blew up seventeen bridges, blew a German train off the tracks, destroyed two enemy planes and killed seven hundred and fifty-four Hitlerites.[98]

In March 1943, the troops of A.P. Fyodorov, who was nicknamed the Tchernigovi, after the town in the area in which he operated, set out for the invasion of western Ukraine. The mobile Ukrainian divisions of Y.A. Melnik., M.A. Naumov and others set out with them. They operated in Polesia with the Belarussian partisans, and in Polesia and Wohlin they developed a huge strip of territory under partisan control. The Sevorov division set up a landing strip for planes there (near the lone farm of Dovnitskoya) where they would fly in partisan organisers, activists and military equipment from the Soviet rear. Similarly, the wounded were flown back to the rear. Robert Stenovski's Polish division and the Moldavian groups received battle supplies via the landing strip.[99]

Later, in September 1943, the Slutzk division, under the command of V.A. Semutin and Major General P.P. Kapusta set out. This was a division that had developed from a large army unit. It hadn't laid down its arms when it had become encircled and so wasn't captured, but rather, organised for partisan fighting. They founded the Bialystock division and their goal was the Bielovezh Pushcha, and the Bialystock district. The division passed through five districts: Minsk, Pinsk, Brest, Baranovitch and Bialystock. On the night of 29th. October, they crossed the Baranovitch-Volkovisk railway line in the Slonim Zelva strip. They sabotaged the railway track and then entered Lipchani Pushcha, of the Baranovitch district. From there, they went on through battles to their goal. They came up against roadblocks of the enemy forces and were unable to base themselves in the Bialystock district. Therefore, they were divided: some of them remained active in the Lipchani Pushcha and some of them in the Ruzhani part. Only small groups reached the forests of Grodna and there they absorbed Jewish rebels from Bialystock, Grodna, Miyadel and the surrounding area. In November 1943, the Polish brigade by the name of Kastos Kalinovski was founded within the Kapusta framework, under the command of the Polish N.K. Vitchekhovski.[100] The mobile Ukrainian units, which were active on Belarussian land, helped the partisan movement in the Republic considerably to intensify its attacks on the enemy and to flourish.

In the days of the manhunt and the siege of February 1943

Invasions of the large Ukrainian (partisan) divisions, the battles they conducted and the landing strips which they had organised, also stimulated the enemy to intensify their activity. On 9th. February 1943, the Germans attacked the forests of Orliuk and Ruzhani (where the brigades from Kapusta's

---

[98] *"visheha shkola", izd.* **Partizanskie Soyedinenia Ukrainy**, *Starozhilov, 1983, p.90*

[99] **Istoria velikoi otechestvennoi voiny** *Sovetskovo Soyuza, tom 3, p.35*

[100] *Op cit., p.45*

division were camped) from the direction of Krasnaya Sloboda, Smazevo, Morotch and Gantsevitch. They held out for two days and on the night of 11th. February, they retreated into the depths of the forest, towards Gotsk

On 10th. February, the enemy attacked the partisans from the Pinsk division. The first to engage in battle was the Vasiliyev group. The battle swept through to Gotsk, where the Shchors troop was camped. On 11th. February, the Germans also attacked the partisan positions of the Kirov troop, in the area of Starobin, Lenino and others. On 12th. February, the other troops of the Pinsk division - the Shesh, Tchapayev, Dombrovski and the Shchors troop, entered the battle. But the enemy forces were far superior to the forces of the partisans, who ran out of ammunition, and they decided to retreat.

The first to abandon camp was the Shesh troop. The rest of the troops gathered by the forest of Vila on the night of 14th. February, and retreated through the swamps in towards Logishin and Telekhani. When the enemy closed the circle on the 15th. of the month, they couldn't find the partisans.

It was a stormy night and a snowstorm covered the footprints of the retreating partisans. They marched through the night and on the night of 16th. Feb, the division crossed the Baranovitch/Luninietz railway line, north of Bastin station, and with daylight, reached the village of Plotnitza, which is in the Logishin area. There, they took up a position for a three day rest. Afterwards, the H.Q. of the Komarov (Korzh) division and the Dombrovski troop moved to the village of Rodnaya, in the Telekhani area while the rest of the troops took up positions in the lone farmlands in that region.[101]

The exit from the trap

The Shchors troop broke through the trap on the night of 13th. February 1943. Before the breakthrough, Avraham Orlinski was lying in ambush with the detail headed by Kuzmitch Lapitchev. When the unit returned to the camp, they found it abandoned.

Orlinski says:

"We turned to follow the emergency route that the partisans had left in case the enemy surrounded them. All the partisans of the division, who numbered about two thousand, were moving along this route. The Shchors troop, and within it, my 56 group, marched behind as security.

"It was a winter's night, and a difficult route. The partisans scattered among the trees and bushes in order not to be seen as a convoy by the pursuing enemy. German planes were patrolling the territory. We were moving all the time, and occasionally rested in the open air, despite the fierce cold. On 14th. February, we reached an agricultural area, where the forests were sparse. We lay around a bonfire. We found a little straw and spread it over the

---

[101] *Iz in: Korzh O.Z., Narodnaya borba protiv nemetsko-fashistskikh okupantov Pinshchine, Istoria Partizanskovo dvizhenia v Belorussii, p.228*

snow, and I lay facing the bonfire. However, after about fifteen minutes, I jumped up on my frozen legs."

The killing of Kandelshtein

On guard, they used to work in pairs, one guarding and one resting. On one occasion, Kandelshtein, who came from the city of Bidgoshtch in Poland, and his partner, a veteran Belarussian partisan, were on duty together. Kandelshtein was a tall young man, handsome and strong. He didn't have shoes and so he used to wrap his feet in rags. The chief of staff, Merzliakov, found the two of them asleep on guard. This time, it had been the turn of Kandelshtein to sleep, but the Belarussian claimed it was his time to rest. Merzliakov barely wavered at all and decreed Kandelschtein's death sentence. He allocated execution of the death sentence to the commander of Kandelshtein's unit, Pshenitchnikov, but he refused to carry it out, saying: 'I'm not shooting one of my fighters.' Then Merzliakov ordered Sofer to carry out the execution. Sofer didn't have the courage to refuse the order, and he carried it out and shot him.

Fleeing in panic from the village of Putchini (21st. February 1943)

There were not only heroic chapters of courage and dedication in battle in the lives and wars of the partisans, but also shameful incidents, which the Soviet historiographers do not care to relate. An incident of this kind happened to the Shchors troop in the village of Putchini.

When the partisans reached this village, they settled down in peasants' houses and were received in a friendly way and given good food. People rested and the horses rested too. A patrol was sent into the area and H.Q. waited for a report. The reconnaissance patrol came back, with one of them stretched over his horse drunk. They reported that everything in the area was quiet, and there were no Germans. But it emerged later that the patrolling soldiers had drunk far too much and did their work deceitfully. A convoy of partisans started to move towards the forest along the main street of the village, being sure it was safe, because of the reconnaissance report. And suddenly a sleigh convoy came out of the forest, from the same direction in which, just a little while ago, the patrol had emerged, and fire was opened on the partisans. Germans and Belarussian police were sitting in the sleighs.

Panic burst out in the partisan convoy. Some of the sleighs galloped forward, dragged by frightened horses unable to keep any order in their movement. Carts overturned, knocking over other carts and hitting the passengers, who flew out of the vehicles and were dragged along the ground. The troop had a lot of wounded. It was an embarrassing and depressing sight, not at all in keeping with the partisan spirit.

Orlinski, who was also one of the injured, says of this stampede:

"A convoy of toboggans suddenly appeared from the nearby forest, and they were moving fast and shooting at us. These were German soldiers and Belarussian police. Somebody gave the order 'Move out to the sides!' meaning 'Go out quickly to the nearby forest in the same organised way, vehicle after vehicle.' But the result was a complete disaster. The order was disarranged as there would suddenly be a row of one, two, three or four vehicles, all of them galloping forward as if in competition, each throwing forward and dragging his neighbour. A cart passed me on my left like lightning and hit the toboggan in which I was sitting, lifting up its left side. I was thrown out like a bow from an arrow from this toboggan. It's hard to describe how quickly I thought, because even as I was flying out through the air, before I hit the ground, I'd already made my decision not to hang around on the ground, because two rows of vehicles were galloping along on the right. I knew that I had to roll over to the right from the road to the canal.

"Horses' hooves were flashing above my head while I was rolling and reached the canal, and then I jumped up on my feet. The rifle was with me still and also the cartridge of the submachine gun, which had become a part of my body. I was pleased. I didn't feel my wounds.

"The road before me had emptied in the meantime and here on my left there was galloping a fantastic, huge grey and white horse, and behind it, a cart without a driver. I jumped onto the road, a second jump, and I was in the cart, which continued to fly in the storm. I calmed down. I trusted the horse to bring me to my comrades. The cart was holding a considerable load of foodstuffs; it must have belonged to the domestic people. Nobody was chasing me. The horse and cart continued to gallop until they reached the troop. I'd been hit in the head.

"In the meantime, Cheslava appeared, and I went over to her for her to take care of me. It turned out that my wounds weren't deep, but a lot of blood covered my face, and the first impression was scary. While she was looking after me, my wife told me that she had also suffered in the tumult. The cart in which she was travelling had been sucked into the mad race. She had been thrown between the horse and the toboggan, and because of her first aid bag, she had been dragged along with the toboggan. Luckily, the driver noticed it in time. He stopped the horse and this allowed her to get up. The whole thing ended in a heavy blow to her head, and she felt that for a long time. I returned to my unit with my head bandaged up."

The partisans succeeded in stopping the Germans, who were forced to retreat. The troop returned to the village to look after the wounded and bury their fallen. This time, the Jew Zimnavoda from Lodz had fallen, and the Russian Mitka was among the wounded. He remained lame and took up the role of camp manager. Korzh, commander of the Pinsk division, describes the flight from the village of Putchini in these sentences:

'On 21st. February 1943, the fascists again fell upon the Shchors troop, which was encamped in the village of Puchini. The troop was forced to retreat to the village of Rodnaya, because of lack of ammunition. The Hitlerites were trying to break through to the village at the height of their chase. However, when the partisans hit back hard, they retreated to Logishin.'[102]

Shimon Milikovski falls in battle

And now it became apparent that the Jewish partisan, Shimon Milikovski was missing. Several partisans were sent out, among them Ya'akov Khatzkelevitch to look for Shimon. They found him stretched dead on his rifle in the village from which they had retreated. Milikovski was buried that same night in one of the lone farms along the way.

The killing of Zhama Shusterovitch (22nd. February 1943)

Zalman (Zhama) Shusterovitch was born in Slonim in 1920. He was a keen communist back in the days of the Polish regime, and an idealist. He was very active in the ghetto underground, smuggling weapons and ammunition from the loot camp store. He was among those who had been turned out of the troop in the first rejection. Zalman was a weak young man from a physical point of view and his comrades feared for his fate and tried to support him. They managed to bring him back to the 51 group, and after the dispersal, he was transferred to the 52 group.

During the panic-stricken retreat, Shusterovitch lost his rifle. In fact, the rifle was found, but the command decreed the death sentence, even though it wasn't exactly known whether he'd lost his rifle or the weapon had been taken from him during the flight. A partisan from the 54, Volodia Voronov, killed Shusterovitch with a bayonet. This man was proud of his effective method of stabbing a man to death with a bayonet. The Slonim comrades carried on fighting with a heavy heart. The injustice which had been done to their longstanding comrade emphasised unbearably the anti-Semitic relationship of the troop and it hurt and insulted them. The drunken patrol soldiers who had misled the troop with their deceitful report and caused needless death were not punished.

---

[102] *Iz istorii partizanskovo dvizhenia. P.229. The Soviet historiography does not mention this panic flight. Proniagin writes in his book that the troop retreated "in order not to endanger peaceful citizens" (p.63).*

CHAPTER FOURTEEN: Parting from the Pinsk division and the end of the March Eastwards

The battle of Svietaya Volia and return to Lake Vigonov

After Putchini, the troop stopped for a short while in the village of Rodanya, where Korzh's troops had also arrived. On 23rd. February, the troop set out for the village of Bobrovitchi and from there towards the village of Swetaya Volya, where a strong German garrison was stationed.

The division command decided to attack this garrison on 25th. February, but the Germans soon brought in reinforcements, and the partisans were forced to retreat. The commander of the troop, Anton Dombromski, the head of staff of the troop, Ivan Dmitrevitch Bobrov and other partisans fell in this clash. After the battle, the Shchors battalion parted from the Korzh division. Their journey eastward came to an end, and they turned towards the old familiar places in the direction of Lake Vigonov.

This place had several advantages and disadvantages. Supplying food was difficult, for the Germans had burnt the villages adjacent to partisan territory, and in order to obtain food, they were forced to go a long way. But from a security aspect, it was a suitable place and not least because the regular German army, which had been called to wipe out the partisans at the beginning of the manhunt, had in the meantime gone to the front. The fighters had left their vehicles in and around their previous encampment in the swamps, and they had thrown off their loads, which they couldn't carry on their backs, and let the horses loose.

The Orlovski incident

Back at the beginning of February, before the manhunt started, three Jewish lads had been sent - Natan Liker, Zerach Kremin and Aharon Berezin - to the village of Meshoki, in the Gantsevitch area. The Shchors troop was short of ammunition and its commanders had been told that in that area, they could obtain weapons and ammunition which had been left behind in the days of the Red Army retreat.

According to Zerach Kremin:

"We reached Meshoki just before evening and went into a peasant's house - an acquaintance of Berezin. The peasant had served the Germans as a forester. He shuddered when he saw us, and begged us to get out of the area, for the next day, the whole place would be crawling with Germans. And he knew this because the Germans had enrolled about two hundred peasants in the village for a hunt, which would begin the following day. The patrol knew that in the local forests, a special group of paratroopers was stationed under the command of the polkovnik Kiril Prokofievitch Orlovski. He was a much older man, a veteran of the Spanish Civil War, one of the International Anti-fascist Brigade. The patrol decided to warn the paratroopers about the Germans. The lads went on their way and coming across the group's guard were taken into the paratroopers' hut. There were nine of them, and with them was one local resident, who was hiding from the Germans, since he had served as a forester, in the period of the Soviet regime.

"Orlovski didn't believe the story about the hunt. He thought it wasn't a suitable season for it because the snow was falling and covering animal footprints. The forester thought the same. Orlovski suspected that the enemy was preparing a manhunt. The paratroopers decided to set up an ambush for the Germans and the three Jewish reconnaissance soldiers joined them. The forester chose the place for the ambush, where, in his opinion, the enemy would have to pass.

"At the start of 9th. February[103], the people, now numbering thirteen, went out to the place where the ambush was to be. Orlovski, a very brave man, was delighted to operate against the enemy. He ordered the men to spread out sideways, a distance of twenty-five steps from each other, in order to cover a greater area. The partisans dug themselves camouflage positions in the snow, and as dawn broke, they were all ready to face the enemy.

"After about an hour, they heard the shouts from the peasants coming out of the forest, and some shots, but they hadn't yet seen a single German. Before noon, the voices went quiet, and the peasants sat down to rest. Orlovski was disappointed, and decided not to wait anymore, but to draw nearer to the Germans. The partisans got up out of their positions and began to move in the forest in the direction from which they had previously heard the voices. They reached a forest clearing where there was a bonfire burning. Around the bonfire stood Germans and behind them, the peasants. The partisans were very near, but they couldn't shoot for fear they would hit the peasants. The Germans sat in sleighs and went off to continue the hunt. To the disappointment of the partisans, they passed right by the place where previously, the lads had lain in ambush. Downcast and angry, the partisans went back to their previous positions and waited for the Germans to come back.

"Evening was drawing near. Orlovski decided that, if Germans didn't come back within half an hour they must have left the forest by another route. Then they heard the sound of sleighs coming nearer. According to the plan, they had to allow the enemy to pass along the length of the ambush track, until the first enemy horse was opposite the last partisan. Then he had to shoot the horse and block the way forward for the Germans. And this is what happened. After the first shot, the partisans opened concentrated fire on the sleighs, which were, as it were, 'arranged' in front of them. Twenty Germans were hit already in the first volley, but several managed to shoot at the partisans.

---

[103] *According to Soviet sources, this took place on 17th. February, 1943. A.E. Kleshchev, Pinskoy oblassti v borbie s fashistskimi Zachvatchikami in: Niepokorennaya Belorussiia, p.260*

"And then a disaster happened. Orlovski, who was standing as it happened by Zerach, had previously prepared pieces of TNT, ignited a Bickford delaying fuse and on a call of 'Gunners, fire!' he threw the explosives at the Germans. But the explosion went off too near Orlinski's hands and his right hand was torn to the upper arm and his left hand was hit. Zerach was stunned and couldn't help his commander, who was badly wounded. One of the Germans, who lay opposite Zerach, didn't allow them to raise their heads and rained fire on them all the time. After Zerach recovered, he threw a grenade at the German and killed him.

"The Spaniard, Justo Lopez, Orlovski's comrade from the days of the Spanish Civil War, and his second in command, hurried towards him. He gave the wounded man first aid. The rest of the partisans went onto the road and began to advance in order to take loot - papers and weapons of the dead Germans. And that's how they found photographs of the mass murder of Jews in the area. The burning question now was what to do with the commander who was badly wounded. It was impossible to bring him to the Shchors, to Dr. Blumovitch, because a manhunt was already going on in the surroundings, and the way to the troop was blocked by German forces. Zerach Kremin remembered that a partisan troop was camped near the village of Swetitsa, and Dr.Lekomtsev was working in it. The young men immediately set out and arrived late at night at the village. They contacted the local partisans and before dawn, the doctor reached the wounded man. He decided that they would have to amputate Orlovski's right hand and remove the palm of his left hand. The partisans had no anaesthetic drugs and had to fetch some alcohol in order to keep the sick man drunk. Orlovski's men had some medicinal alcohol by their hut, but that night, it was impossible to get there. The next night they brought the spirit, found a rusty saw at the blacksmith's at the village, and with these Dr Lekomtsev carried out the operation."

In the meantime, the partisans heard shots from the direction of the Shchara. The men placed the wounded man under the care of the local partisans, and went out in the direction of the shots in order to defend the place. They found that there were several Germans positioned on the other side of the river, by the village of Zaluzhye. When the partisans showered them with fire, they made off.

The Jewish lads went back to the local brigade, but they couldn't find the wounded Orlovski. The local partisans, when they heard the shots, had wanted to get away from the village, and they carried the wounded man on a sleigh. On the way, they spoke to him, but Orlovski, who was still dozy from the alcohol, didn't answer. The partisans decided that the wounded man was dead, so they laid him on the snow and went off. The Jewish patrol found him stretched out on the earth and brought him to Svietitsa to Dr. Lekomtsev, who continued to care for him and saved his life.

(From Zerach Kremin)

"Natan Liker took part in the battle at the village of Medviyeditchi, the battle in which Orlovski was seriously wounded. He and the other partisans fought for his life and brought the wounded man, unconscious, to the village of Svietitsa, to the well known doctor, Viktor Alexeyevitch Lekomtsev. There, a complex operation was performed on Orlovski, and was crowned with success."[104]

Apparently, one of the dead Germans was the Governor of Western Belarussia, Fentz. He had been preparing to go on home leave and wanted to hunt some animals in order to bring them to his house in Linz. Among the dead were also his second in command and officials from the police in Baranovitch, the chief forester in the service of the Germans and other high-ranking Nazi officials.

Orlovski managed to come through the war. He returned to his village and died well into old age, at the age of eighty, being the head of an outstanding collective farm, decorated with a gold medal and honoured as a Hero of the Soviet Union.[105]

Anti-Semitism and parasitism in the troop

At that time, many partisans who previously had served the enemy as police and in various other roles had joined the Shchors battalion, and various other troops. They were saturated with the spirit of anti-Semitism and poisoned the atmosphere in the groups. The anti-Semitism distressed the veteran Jewish fighters a great deal, for they were without protection. These new 'partisans' used their weapons in order to set up a comfortable life for themselves, at the expense of others. They lived in the camp and drank and gorged in the villages which they visited. They would get drunk and take everything they wanted from the peasants by force, laying the blame on others, mainly the Jews, who could not defend themselves against it. This situation was possible because these characters, many of whom had military rank, were given the command of the units. They ruled with neither restraint nor conscience, were not held responsible for their actions by their superiors, and enjoyed great autonomy in their units. Obviously, these commanders also defined the character of the behaviour of those beneath them. Not even the commissars or the politroks were free of the disease of drunkenness and corruption. They did nothing to stop these expressions of anti-Semitism and parasitism of their men.

The partisan high command in the 'big land' became aware of the state of the partisan forests of the region, and decided to put an end to it. And so, a delegation from the Soviet rear arrived in the Brest area, to which the Shchors battalion belonged, with the task of stopping this rampage, reorganising the

---

[104] *Proniagin draws attention in his book to the part Natan Liker played in saving Orlovski's life, but does not mention Zerach Kremin.*

[105] *Vsenarodnaya borba v Belorussii, tom 3, p.398. This source does not cite the date of the battle in which Orlovski, whom he calls 'a legendary hero', was wounded.*

partisan movement on more healthy foundations and leading it into intensive activity against the enemy.

In March 1943, the commissar Yegorov, who was also an anti-Semite, was informed that the special staff command was due to arrive in their forest and would take command of the partisans in the area. Yegorov decided to prepare for the coming of his commanders - to 'cure' the troop, as it were, to bring it to battle strength.

What this meant was that he was first of all going to expel the Jews from the troop, among them veteran partisans who had taken part in all the battles and all the troop missions. Every commander was asked to bring a list of people, who in his opinion, should be sent out of the unit. Thus, corrupt types, like the 56 commander, Zhuraliov the alcoholic, had to decide who would stay and who would be turned out. One imagines that the decision to turn the Jews out of the troop was taken also with the thought that they should get rid of witnesses, who might describe the behaviour of the corrupt commanders.

In mid- March, a group of ten elite fighters set out under the command of Zhuraliov, on a mission which wasn't intended for all the comrades of the 56. What happened to them, and in particular to Zhuraliov, Avraham Orlinski recounts:

"Kahar Abdurozkov was with the ten, a Kazakh in origin, a handsome boy with pleasant manners, a strong body and a quiet temperament. I had become friendly with him. He had arrived at the Shchors with Zhuraliov's group. After a few days, I found Kahar coming back to the camp alone. I asked him what had happened. He told me that the ten had been allotted the task of checking out the chances of crossing north of the Brest-Baranovitch railway. On the way, they bumped into some Germans and this made them run off in panic, so they were coming back to the camp in disorganisation one by one. Kahar was the third to return whilst the commander, Zhuraliov, was still missing. In his report, Zhuraliov told H.Q. that there it was impossible to cross the railway track at all. Almost every bit of it was guarded by about forty guards - Germans, French and people of other nations who were in the service of the Germans. But this report was false.

"The 56 group didn't have their own doctor, only a nurse, who was the girlfriend of Zhuraliov, and he was interested in transferring my wife, Cheslava, who was serving as doctor in the H.Q. under Dr Blumovitch, to his group. I knew the character of Zhuraliov very well. He was an ignorant man, a cruel drunkard, and had a negative approach to anyone educated, so I suggested to Cheslava that she shouldn't leave her work in the H.Q., and in fact this is what happened. I had to pay for that advice of mine, and from then on I knew no rest in the group. It was usual when a unit or a group of fighters returned from a prolonged mission after they had been away from the camp a number of days, to receive at least a day of rest. However, this custom wasn't applied to me. They would transfer me immediately to another task, particularly to a guard task of twenty-four hours. At the end of the watch, and sometimes also before the twenty-four hours were finished, they would put me in another group which was going out on a local mission. And so it happened that they barely saw me in the camp and I didn't know what was going on there. Since the reason for this treatment of me was obvious to me, I was able to withstand it and carry out the duties that were imposed on me. I didn't complain and didn't protest, in order not to give my superior a pretext to accuse me of lack of discipline."

The second and third rejections (27th. March & 1st. April 1943)

On about the 20th. March, a unit from the 56 group set out for Svyetaya Volya, which is in the environs of the town of Telekhani. The unit walked for several days and nights and carried out operations, in which Avraham Orlinski also took part, close to German garrisons. When the unit came back after several days and nights of wandering and activity, the group was sent to rest, but not Orlinski. After about half an hour Zhuraliov sent him, and three others, on a distant twenty-four watch at the crossroads of the Razdzhialovitchi-Novosiolki roads, near the canal. The next day, even before the end of the duty, a partisan came riding through the camp with a bucket of food for the guards. Before Orlinski could eat this messenger told him to return immediately to the camp, and he would take his place.[106]

Orlinski rode back to the camp and found a group of Jews on parade. He was told he must join the group which was leaving for Volchye-Nori, to set up a base for the troop. When Avraham examined the group, he realised it was made up mainly of men and women who carried no arms. They told him that their weapons had been taken from them and given to Ukrainians who had come from captivity and had been accepted into the troop without arms. Among those from whom their weapons had been taken was Avraham Bublatski. His rifle had been given to a Russian, who had been accepted a short while ago without arms. After the interventions and efforts of Archik Bandt, who was about to lead the rejected group out, Bublatski was given a German rifle and just three bullets.

Orlinski remembered the Kahar's report that ten of the best partisans hadn't been able to cross the railway track and had been forced to return. And now, they were sending men and women without weapons.

The plot was clear as day. Orlinski's wife, Dr. Cheslava, wanted to join her husband. However, he persuaded her to stay where she was. Fedya, commissar from the 56, who was well known to be corrupt, was commander of the group who were going out to Volchye-Nori, supposedly to set up the base, and Archik Bandt was to function as his second in command.

The group set out for Svyetitsa. It was a cloudy day and cold, and many of the crossing places were covered with water. And these are the Jews who were sent:

Dr Avraham Sayet, Mordechai Pick, Golda Gertsovski, Avraham Doktorchik, Natan Finkel, Ze'ev Finkel, Manya Mishelevitch (Akerman), Yitzhak Mishelevitch, Fima Podolski, Lili Blumenfeld, Feldman, Rappaport,

---

[106] *Eventually, Zhorbaliov was punished and demoted to the rank of corporal.*

Yitzhak Korsch, Rachel Rozmarin, Archik Bandt, Liuba Bandt, Hillel Moshkovski, Sima Shtein, Liuba Zhagel, Adek Schnur, Avraham Bublatski, Avraham Orlinski.

But there were still 'superfluous' women in the troop and the command sought to get rid of them. And indeed, a few days after the second reject group left, a third expulsion group was composed, which was supposed to go to Gotsek, and in this group were:

Irka Weiselfish, the girlfriend of Proniagin, Pesach Alpert, Rivka Alpert (his wife), Hanna and Chaya Alpert, Pesach's daughters, R. Mukasey, Krusi Abramchik, Leah Abramchuk, Guta Kagan, Dvorah Derechinski. Dvorah Derechinski was the wife of a Belarussian, Volodya Piletzki, who had saved her life in the ghetto and come to the 51 group, where he had served for a long time as storekeeper. When he saw that they were sending his wife away, he joined her.

There were Jews from all groups in the reject groups. They were very dispirited. Everyone understood that they were simply being turned out of the troop for an ugly reason. But there were also others who believed in this 'mission'. The Jews knew that Zhuraliov's faithfuls, Fedya, 'Commissar' from the 56, and Grishka, the commander of the 56, who were sent with them, were extremely negative, and they had absolutely no reason to trust them. Walking, they had to cross the Brest-Baranovitch-Minsk railway lines close to Lesnaya station. Around that area there were enemy army camps and prisoner of war camps, a very dangerous place for the partisans to make a crossing. [107]

Before the group reached the crossing place, they camped in a lonely agricultural area from which there was one crossing to the railway track. When they were just about to leave/set out, they realised that Grishka and Fedya had disappeared into thin air, and the Jews were left without a commander and without a single Russian. There was no one to give instructions for the rest of the way.

Orlinski and Hillel Moshkovski went out on to reconnoitre the railway track at the edge of the forest. And they found that on both sides of the track, to a length of about three hundred metres, the trees had been cut down, so the partisans wouldn't be able to get near the track without being seen. Only in a small section, the nearest to the station, did the forest reach the track. They decided to cross there, despite the danger of getting close to the station, which was guarded by the enemy.

The next night, the group set out to cross the track. At their head marched Orlinski and Moshkovki and behind them, everybody else. They approached the station and crossed the track, under the sound of passing trains. After they'd crossed, they realised that not only the non-Jewish commanders were present, but their Jewish deputies had disappeared. Nobody was surprised at the disappearance of the non-Jews, but where had the Jews Bandt and

---

[107] *The end of Fedya "Komissar" was execution as punishment for his criminal acts against the local population. This sentence was carried on the order of the Brest Division staff group.*

Doktortchik got to? Archik was the only one who knew the area, and he was sorely missed by the group.

After consultation, it was decided to return and to check out where the Jewish officers were. Orlinski and two comrades went back to the railway track, to the place where they'd last stopped before they crossed, and there they found Archik Bandt and Doktortchik! They explained that they saw the non-Jewish commanders turn back, and they were so surprised that they remained where they were, without knowing whether to go on or come back.

Orlinski told them that the whole group had crossed and was waiting for them, and now they must take on the command, so they went back, crossed the track and found the group. From now on Aharon Bandt led them. On the way, they were told that they should be careful of local partisans who hated Jews. The scheme of Commissar Yegorov, on whose orders they had been thrown out of the troop, and of other commanders, was now clear to everyone. They had to weigh up what they had to do in future. Everybody understood that being poorly armed, they wouldn't be able to survive in a hostile environment, surrounded by the enemy - Germans and their supporters, and anti-Semitic partisans. Therefore, it was decided to ask their comrades who had remained in the Shchors, to leave the troop en masse with their weapons and join them. Together, they would constitute a force which could survive and fight. But who could pass the message on? They didn't know the password, and partisans were forbidden to go anywhere when there were fewer than three of them.

The mission of the reject group to the Shchors troop

Orlinski suggested that he himself should go back to the Shchors and deliver their decision to the Jewish comrades. Rachel Rozmarin, whose husband had remained in the troop's camp, joined him and the partisan Yitzhak Korsch.

They crossed the railway track, passed through forests and fields, and on reaching the house of a Polish family whom they knew, went in for a short rest. Orlinski went out at night to explore the route. It was in his plan to enter the forest in the morning, on the other side of which there were lone farms belonging to Baptists, which they should reach by the evening. He went back and brought his comrades out to the forest. With evening, they reached the farms of the Baptists and there they felt safer. Rozmarin and Korsch went into one house and Orlinski into another. The owners fed them and even gave them something for the road. The owner of the house where Orlinski stayed agreed to serve as guide up to the next village. He even took them to the house of his friend, who continued to lead them on and gave instructions about the rest of the route. With morning, they reached partisan territory, and this is how Orlinski describes his route:

"Spring was in full swing. The wide open spaces and the sweet smelling air and the gentle and pleasant rays of the sun calmed our spirits. There was no one around and we settled into a nice corner in the forest, near a lonely path.

We ate and got up the strength to carry on. It's hard to convey the effort we needed to get up and carry on after we'd already done sixty kilometres on a route that wasn't really a path.

"We drew near the Shchara. The long bridge, which used to be in that place, hadn't existed for a long time. There were only some pillars which stuck up from the water and had been used as a foundation for a temporary bridge, but that too had been destroyed in the meantime. On our bank, we found a boat. We crossed to the opposite bank in it, and from there a surfaced path went on to the forest, which we could just see in the distance. At the end of the path, at the entrance to the forest, there was set up an advanced guard post of a group of Zhorkints [108], who hated Jews. If they knew that we were from the reject group, it was doubtful if we would come out of their hands alive. This was also the reason for the order of the partisan H.Q. not to walk around with fewer than three men together and without the daily password.

"I didn't let my comrades know my fears. We advanced in the direction of the guard. Near the forest, I heard a shout, 'Who goes there?' I answered, 'From the Shchors troop.' At a little distance, there appeared the figure who'd asked and then other partisans began approaching. When we reached the guard, I found them armed with rifles and a submachine gun. I learned from them that our troop had left its place for fear of a German attack on the camp. The news was not at all nice and we didn't want to believe these Zhorkints. I overrode my desire to be rid of them straight away and continued a short friendly conversation with them, and so we left them. We continued on our way, and when we reached the Shchors camp, we found the place abandoned. There was no sign of anyone and no sign at all to indicate where they'd gone.

"The main problem now was how and where to find the troop. We were tired and decided to pass the night in the abandoned camp and the next day, to divide into two units. Korsch and Rachel Rozmarin would move forward with one, and I in the other. The first unit went off to one of the previous camps, to the right of the Razdzhalovichi- Novosiolki road to the lone farm, where Rachel Rozmarin hoped to receive some news of her husband, as had been agreed between them. And I turned towards a remote island, in the middle of the swamps – the same island to which we had at one time transferred the hospital and the wounded, under the supervision of my wife.

"After a night's sleep, and having arranged a meeting place, everyone went on his way. When I reached the island, I found it was empty of any human being, and as I continued to search, I found no sign of either man or horse having been there. And so, I turned towards the lone farms, where I had arranged to meet my comrades. Then, in the distance, I saw two figures, who looked to me like Rozmarin and Korsch. However, this was a line of Latvian soldiers in the service of the Germans, and they were advancing towards me. I just managed to jump off the road into the bushes in the forest. I ran a little and stood behind some fallen tree trunks, with my weapon ready in my hand.

---

[108] *They were called by the name of their commander. There were many tales among the Jewish partisans of the murder of Jews the Zhorkints chanced upon.*

Some time passed quietly and after that, the sound of prolonged firing reached my ears from the direction of the abandoned camp.

"When the shooting stopped, I went on again towards the lone farms. As I drew near, I saw that the grass was burning. I went on to the camp, which Rozmarin and Korsh had been going to visit, but that was abandoned too, and I met no one. I reached the farms of Svietitsa and I found a lot of signs of men and horses having passed. It seemed that the Germans had passed here. The huts were all empty and in one hut, I found some kindling ready by a stove. I lit a little fire to dry my clothes and then there was a knock at the door: I was overcome with fear: maybe someone from the Germans? I quietly drew near the door, aimed my rifle and opened the door quickly. Opposite me was a young peasant, who paled at the sight of the weapon trained on him. I addressed him in Russian and asked him to come in and he calmed down. He told me he had come to check if his family had returned, as from a distance he'd seen smoke coming out of the chimney. He knew where the partisans had gone and led me to the guard of the 54 group, which was under the command of Andrei Leontiev. And there I had to wait until the commander appeared."

Andrei enjoyed a high degree of autonomy in his operations. He looked after his men and was known as the best of the commanders. His group always used to camp at a certain distance from the troop camp, and one had the impression that he was seeking to distance himself from the influence of the men from the other groups.

Andrei received Orlinski courteously, and Orlinski told him about the task of setting up a base for the troop in Volchye Nori that had been imposed on them, and about the difficult state of his group. He also pointed out that he was supposed to go back to his commander and ask for help. Andrei promised to help him reach the district he wanted, that is, the 56 group, but that he would have to wait patiently. Andrei instructed his men to leave Orlinski on the guard's hill and feed him, but didn't allow him to enter his group's camp.

Some days passed and Orlinski was still stuck with the guard and waiting. Groups were going in and out of the camp but still there was no solution for him. He was already beginning to be doubtful about the value of his staying there, and on one occasion, he bumped into a nurse from the 54 group, who knew his wife, the doctor. He learnt from her that Cheslava had left the troop's H.Q., but she didn't know where she'd gone - it seemed, to the Gotsk area. The news hit him with dismay: he'd come to her and she'd gone off, and he didn't know where. Several more days passed and there was no news from Andrei. Orlinski felt that he was superfluous.

He decided to go out to the drainage canal near the camp and to check out the area: maybe he could reach the 56 group under his own steam. While he was standing on the hill, looking around, along came a horse rider, and he recognised Dudko. Since he had been wounded, Dudko hadn't been given a role of any standing, and Orlinski didn't know what he was doing now. The Jews saw in Dudko a friend and therefore Orlinski didn't hesitate to approach him and tell him about his situation. However, Dudko answered him curtly: there was no point in his going to the 56 group; they wouldn't accept him there, and he couldn't help him. He said, 'Leave it,' and went into the 54 camp. The frosty manner and indifferent answers of Dudko gave Orlinski a shock. He agonised over the question as to whether he should be wary of the people of the 56 group to which he belonged. Where would he go? He went back to the hill and sat down, broken in spirit, without being able to concentrate his thoughts.

"It was quiet all around, a fine day, the sun was shining, the air was fresh, and I was sunk in my thoughts," relates Orlinski, "and suddenly I heard someone calling my name: "Where are you? Commander Andrei has informed us that you must get ready, a group of partisans is coming, and you have to join them on their way to H.Q."

Orlinski joined the group of partisans, who were carrying receivers, transmission instruments and a typewriter for the use of the staff group which was about to arrive from Moscow. The question still gave him no rest: would he be allowed to enter the 56 camp? Maybe an order had been given to arrest him?

The men paused by the Shchors guard post, which was just at the entrance of the forest. The chief of the guard was well known to him; in the past, he had been a policeman in the employ of the Germans. The group went into the forest, and Orlinski with it. When they reached the troop camp, Orlinski went on the internal path to the 56 group, passing Zhuraliov's tent. When he passed the H.Q. yard, he heard the voice of Merzliakov calling him to approach.

Orlinski approached and saluted. In answer to Merzliakov's question, 'What's been happening?' he laid out the explanation that he had prepared for his commander Zhuraliov, about the help which was essential for the group. As he was talking, Proniagin approached. He'd heard Orlinski's words and burst out, 'That's nonsense, there's no point in you talking to Zhuraliov.' But Merzliakov said that he should go to his immediate commander and tell him everything he'd told Merzliakov.

Orlinski went on to Zhuraliov, who was sitting in front of his tent and saluted as usual and started to say that he had come to ask for help in setting up a base in Volchye Nori. Zhuraliov heard him silently and asked, 'Where have you been roaming around for the last ten days without permission?' Orlinski began to explain to him that he had been with the 56 group but he couldn't come earlier because of the ban of walking around on your own. However, Zhuraliov blamed him for vagrancy and said that he should take his punishment. And then he heard behind him the voice of Marzliakov saying, 'Leave him, he's come a long way. First of all, give an order to feed him and have done with it.' Marzliakov had followed him as he went to Zhuraliov and came to his help. He ordered the camp manager to take him and feed him. Zhuraliov said nothing and that was the end of contact with him. Orlinski remained in the camp, but was given no role and he had a bad feeling. The day passed without contact with his Jewish comrades

Only now did Orlinski learn that several days after he had gone another group of Jews had been sent, the third reject group, to Gotsk, again camouflaged with the excuse that it was to set up a base for the troop. This troop was mainly women, and the men possessed no weapons. Among those who had been sent out were the Jewish girlfriends of the commanders Proniagin and Merzliakov. The sending of the commanders' girlfriends was intended to separate the couples, a scheme which was evident in that period in general, in other groups and divisions, apparently under the instructions of the supreme command, but it was the Jewish women who were affected most by it.

Most of the partisans already knew about Yegorov's initiative in distancing the Jews from the troop. The anti-Semitic commanders supported him. Among those turned out was also Dvorah Derechinski, the Jewish wife of the Belarussian Piletski. Volodya Piletski decided to join his wife and go with her to the forests of Volchye Nori, which he knew well. When Dr. Cheslava heard this, she joined the Piletski couple in order to reach her husband. She approached Commisar Yegorov and begged permission to go with the group to Gotsk, claiming that the group had no doctor. Yegorov agreed, but emphasised that they weren't sending her away from the troop

The group that was sent to Gotsk left the camp on 1st. April, but instead of turning southwards to Gotsk, they carried on eastwards to the Babin farm. On the way, Commander Proniagin caught up with them, looking for Piletski and Dr. Orlinski, because he had discovered that they intended to go to Volchye Nori. He entreated Piletski not to carry on, and disclosed to them that it was impossible to get there. It was hard to cross the railway line and it seemed that the first group hadn't reached Volchye Nori and had gone to Gotsk. Only after he had received their promise that they wouldn't leave the group and carry on to Gotsk, did he return to his HQ. And this highlighted the plot of the anti-Semitic commanders, in sending the second reject group to Volchye Nori.

When they went on their way from the Babin farm, the Jews who'd been turned out met the patrol group under the command of Zuyev (commander of the 52). Natan Liker and the Armenian, Artiom (from the 53 group) were with the patrol. Zuyev and his men saw how poorly these Jews were armed and decided not to go back to the Shchors camp, but to accompany the group to Gotsk in order to ensure their safety. And in this way Dr. Cheslava reached Gotsk.

Two tasks now remained before Orlinski: to get the message, which his comrades who had been sent to Volchye Nori had given him, to Dr. Blumovitch, and to reach Gotsk and his wife. In the meantime, he learned that Natan Liker had returned from the patrol. Orlinski went to the 52 group, found Liker and asked if he could join the reconnaissance patrol in order to reach his wife. When Dr. Blumovitch heard that Orlinski was staying with the 56 group, he came and heard from him what had happened to the group, and the decision of the group, which had stayed near Lesnaya station, that all Jewish comrades should leave the Shchors battalion with their arms and come to their help. Blumovitch answered that the Jewish comrades in the group thought the same thing, but news had reached the command about their intentions and now they were being closely watched. In addition to that, they were waiting for the arrival of the envoys from Moscow and the comrades had decided to approach them when they arrived and ask for their help in bringing back the people who'd been expelled from the troop, and only after that would they decide on their next steps.

Disintegration of the reject group and the murder of Avraham Bublatski

The representatives of the group which had been sent to Volchye Nori - Orlinski, Rachel Rozmarin and Korsch – returned to the Shchors, and meanwhile, the second reject group was advancing to the west. They had encountered a group of partisans belonging to Bobkov's battalion, which was controlling Volchye Nori and the locality. The commanders of the group, Archik Bandt and Doktortchik, reported to Bobkov, but he refused to accept them and ordered them to get out of the forest under his control. Without options and without leadership, the group broke up. Those who had arms - Fima Podolski, Lili Blumenfeld, Yitzhak Mishelevitch, Manya Mishelevitch-Akerman, Hillel Moshkovski, Mordechai Pick, and the Finkel brothers and others, left Golda Doktortchik, Rappoport, Feldman, Sima Shtein, Liuba Zhagel and others and went off. After a while, Avraham, Doktortchik and Hillel Moshkovski came back to them, and they turned towards the lone farms of Basin. There were a few Jewish families already living there. They hadn't been accepted into any troop and had wandered round the area.

Archik Bandt and Bublatski went out the village of Bastin to clarify what was happening there. Following the guidance of Archik, Sima Shtein, Rapaport and Feldman also set out for Basin. Avraham, Doktortchik, Hillel Moshkovski and Liuba Zhagel went out one dark rainy night towards the railway line in order to go back to the Shchors, but because of the danger of crossing, they didn't cross. Trees had been cut down all along the track, and enemy posts were guarding it. They too went back to the Basin group.

Archik now decided to look for members of his family who had been left behind in Volchye Nori when the troop moved eastwards. He found his mother and his sister, Matla, and her two children with her, living with an elderly widow, who lived in the village of Skolditch. His father had starved to death, back in 1942. Avraham took his family and his girlfriend, Liuba Abramchik, who eventually became his wife, and went with them to the forest of Prushkovo. In the forest, they prepared a hiding place. Avraham Bublatski joined them and there they lived the life of hunted animals

Avraham Bandt was born in 1914, in the village of Skolditch. When he finished elementary school, he went to work in Slonim. He was a member of the Shomer Hatza'ir movement, and in 1935, he went on pioneer training, in the town of Novogrudek. Like many pioneers of that time, he didn't manage to immigrate (to Israel). In October 1936, he was recruited to the cavalry of the Polish army. After his discharge, in the autumn of 1938, he returned and went on preparatory training in the movement's kibbutz in Rovna. In March 1939, he was called up to the reservists and with the start of tensions between Poland and Germany, he was transferred to Warsaw and sent to the east Prussian border.

With the outbreak of war, his unit managed to clash several times with the German army, but it was ordered to withdraw southeast. On 9th. September, his unit reached Siedlietz, and there, they encountered the red army, which was coming to confront the German army. All the soldiers of his unit were taken captive in a prisoner of war camp. In his unit, there were twelve Jews, and among them, eight from Slonim. They persuaded the guard to let them go home, got on a train and reached the station in Domanova. At the station, they met relatives and acquaintances who put a cart at their disposal, and that was how they travelled to Slonim. Archik returned to his family, who were then living in the village of Skolditch, and began to work as a mechanic. When Germany attacked the Soviet Union, he was recruited into the Red Army, but hadn't yet been placed in a unit, and he remained in Slonim, trapped in the ghetto, one of the outstanding activists of the underground organization. On 29th. June (see above), he set out with a large group and joined the partisans. He was accepted by them and became the commander of a unit in the 51 group. His expulsion from the troop in the second reject group hurt him badly.

With his wife and Bublatski, he reached the forests of Volchye Nori, but the local partisans, under the command of Bobkov, wouldn't let them to stay in forests which were under their control. Consequently, he went to the nearby forests of Skolditch, where his family were hiding. When Sikorski took command, and demanded that all the expelled people should return to their units, Archik refused to return to his brigade, having been humiliated and abandoned by the anti-Semitic commanders. At this point he was declared a deserter and sentenced to death, this sentence being conveyed to all the neighbouring troops. Now he also had to hide from partisans who wanted his life. Archik built many hiding places and would move among them frequently. Bobkov's partisans continued to look for him. On one occasion, they passed very near to a pit in a potato field, in which he was hiding with his group. The next day, they all went to the village of Skolditch and hid for a few days with the same old woman, Philimonikha. After that, they went back to the forest.

At the end of March, 1944, Avraham Bublatski and Archik's sister, Matla, went out to look for food. They were caught by local partisans who demanded that they take them to Archik's hiding place. Matla suggested to them that she should go to look for him on her own and call him, otherwise he would be likely to open fire. They agreed, but held Bublatski. Matla ran to the hut and called out o the family to leave the place. They managed to hide. Bublatski, who was held by the partisans at a distance of about a hundred metres from the hut, managed to call out: "They're going to kill me!" The partisans led him a little way off and shot him in the head with a pistol. Bublatski was buried right there, on the slope of a hill, between the villages of Skolditch and Tushevitch. Archik and his family continued to hide in the forest, until the Red Army arrived on 11th. July 1944. However, Archik's hardships were not yet over; more of this at the end of the book.

Golda Gertsovski, and the people with her who had been abandoned in the forest, also went through a very difficult time. Two partisans came from Volchye Nori, and led them to their forest, according to Bobkov's command. They took the rest of their belongings and put them in an underground hut, where they found a little food. They were told that this was where the

Shepetinski family had formerly lived. They were afraid that Bobkov's men were preparing to murder them, but the arrival of Sikorski saved their lives. [109]

Golda was transferred to the medical unit on a remote island in the swamps, the island where the partisan hospital had been set up, and there she looked after the wounded. Rumours reached them of a new manhunt. The partisans retreated to the Svarin region, on the other side of the Dnieper-Bug canal. There was a division supply base there. They took Golda and other young women with them, and they were allocated to prepare food stores for division H.Q. which was encamped in the village of Sporovo. The girls would salt the meat and store it in barrels, which were hidden in pits in the earth. The supply base was under the command of the Shchors troop and had been set up on the 52 group (to which Golda later belonged) base. She was liberated in March/April 1944, with the arrival of the Red Army, married Avraham Doktortchik and immigrated with him to Israel.

The fate of Pesach Alpert's family

On one occasion, as Zvi Shepetinski and his comrades were returning from carrying out a mission, they bumped into an older couple and a young girl. The man was carrying a rifle, and he was unshaven and his clothes were in tatters. The woman and the girl also looked neglected, like him. As he drew nearer, he recognised, to his dismay, Pesach Alpert, his wife and their daughter, Hannah.

The meeting was emotional. Pesach embraced him and was tearful. Zvi didn't want his Russian comrades to be present during their conversation, and so he told them he had met someone from his town, a dedicated veteran communist, who had been among the first of the partisans in the 51 group. He asked them to go back without him and to tell his commander, Lomaiko, about the meeting, and that he would stay for a short conversation with his fellow townsman.

When the Russians were further off, Pesach told him all about the second reject group. Zvi knew nothing of this, and when they told him about Irka being thrown out of the troop, despite her links with Proniagin, Zvi felt some satisfaction. The young woman who had appointed herself as commander of the Komsomol and supervisor of the partisan fitness of the Jews was well-known for her arrogance and unfriendly manner. It turned out that none of this helped her as she too had been turned out.

He wanted to help the Alpert family, and led them to the Vasilyev battalion camp by a roundabout route, so they wouldn't encounter any guards. At the entrance to the camp, he asked permission from the commander of the guard to bring his friends into the camp, to feed them and to allow them to rest for a few days. His request was granted. The next day, he approached the battalion commander and told him about the family's past and about their tribulations

---
[109] *The witness account of Liuba Avramchik-Bandt; evidence of Archik Bandt.*

and asked to attach them to the troop. Lomaiko agreed. Pesach was attached to the domestic unit, and his wife began work in the kitchen.

The vicissitudes of Mishka Pertzov

Not only from Slonim and Biten did Jewish partisans reach the 51 group and the Shchors troop; they also absorbed Jews from various and far-off places at different times. Among them were intellectuals, experienced and talented craftsmen, businessmen and simple labourers. Some came from the small towns of Wohlin and Polesia, people who previously had been wandering alone in the forest in small groups until they met Jewish partisans who took them into their group. There were some whom fate had moved about from place to place, far off to the cities of the Soviet Union, and they reached the troop as refugees from German captivity.

One day in February 1943, a young Jewish man, called Mishka by the partisans, came to the Shchors group. He was one of six in a non-Jewish detail, who had brought an urgent letter from their commander, "Dyadya Vasia", that is, commander Vasilyev, to the commander of the Shchors, Proniagin.

Mishka's real name was Mikhael Pertzov, born in the village of Osovah in the Pinsk region. He had joined up in 1940 and been sent to the Red Army barracks in Leningrad. With the outbreak of war against Germany, he reached the Novgorod front, where he was wounded and taken prisoner. In the prisoner of war camp, he suffered hunger and abuse and was witness to the death of tens of thousands of the prisoners. With the help of some kind men, he managed to remain alive. Mikhael was absorbed into a unit where most of the prisoners were Ukrainians and Russians. The Germans began to transfer the Ukrainians to a separate camp in order to recruit them and train them for service. His two Ukrainian friends, with whom he had become friendly in the army and with whom he had reached the camp, had an alternative: they could enrol in the service of the Germans and stay alive. In the memoirs which Mikhael wrote after some years in Israel,[110] he says:

"Anyone who considers himself to be Ukrainian, stands in the queue and gives his personal details to the recorder, who is one of the Ukrainian prisoners of war, appointed to do this by the camp commander. The candidates undergo a 'fitness' examination in the presence of a German guard and carried out by a special team of Ukrainians from among the prisoners of war. Many of them are discarded, whether because of their external appearance or their accent, which wasn't pure Ukrainian enough. Since my friends were genuine and pure Ukrainians, they passed the test, and they had put me on the list as well, without my knowledge and without me having to undergo any examination. How they managed this, I didn't know, and I didn't ask them. For me, it was important that we weren't split up. Their belief in me touched my heart.'

---

[110] Mikhael Pertsov: *The Lad from Osovah: Life Experiences*, duplicated.

Those who were chosen were taken out of the camp and put on a train and transported for three days without water or food, and reached a prisoner of war camp in the town of Shabli in Lithuania. Many died on the way. Those who remained alive suffered whiplashes from right and left. In the camp, Mikhael was sent to work.

One of the Ukrainian guards recognised that Mikhael was a Jew and took him to a doctor to certify his Jewishness. The doctor sent him with the Ukrainian taskmaster to the sergeant who was responsible for him, in order to get permission from him to murder the Jew. But on the way, the German guard, who had accepted Mikhael for work, met them, and saved his life.

This is how Mikhael describes his rescue:

"As if he had dropped on us from above, the German guard who had taken me on for work is standing in front of us. He grabs the taskmaster's hand and orders him to go away. The latter tries to explain, but the German guard doesn't want to hear his words, and commands him, in no uncertain terms, to go off, and calls me to follow him. I didn't know what was happening here: is this Nazi doing this because he resents the privilege of murdering a Jew being fulfilled by a Ukrainian? He's marching with quick steps, and with my stumbling feet, I'm trying not to fall behind him. From time to time, he calls to me, 'Kom, kom!' in German: 'Come, come!' - and glances all around. He's surely looking around for a place where he can vent his rage on me, without anyone disturbing him.

"And so we've reached one of the camp's huts, and the guard comes to a halt. He's looking all around, here and there, and after that, his gaze rests on me. He's speaking to me and my ears are taking in words which my heart can barely accept.

"'Listen, young man,' he says, 'as you can see, I'm already an old man. I've seen a great deal in this life, but an obscenity like this, I have never seen. And now my son's recruited, and who knows if he's still alive. And what is all this?' he goes on. 'For Hitler, the shit, yes, my young man, it's all shit, Hitler's shit, the war's shit, everything's shit.'

"'I don't want you on my conscience, I don't know what will happen to you, but I don't want in any way to take part in your murder. I've brought you to the sick hut. I've risked myself and I've done what I've done. Now you go into this hut and lie down wherever you lie and if someone comes into the hut, make sighs and groans, and then you can be sure no one will come near you. They'll think you're in your death throes and they won't be interested in you. Whatever else you do, or what will happen to you, even in another moment, I won't know, but I will be the one who saved you from certain death. I've played my part, and now, please, take this little bit of bread I have on me and some cigarettes and have done with it.'

"That's what he said, and again, he looked all around and went off."

The next morning, they called the sick people out to a parade. Everyone was required to present, except the Ukrainians. Mikhael presented there and they transferred him to the main prison in Shabli. From the prison, he was sent to work. For several days, nothing had touched his mouth and now he received boiling water and one rotten potato, and under a rain of blows and whiplashes of young Germans, whose eyes were burning with contempt and hate, he went out with other prisoners to work.

And here's another thing which is worth pointing out:

Mikhael's boots were torn and his toes were peeping out. During work, a German guard murdered a young Jewish man who had offered himself as a translator. On the feet of the dead man were undamaged boots. Another guard, older, with glasses and an intelligent face, called Mikhael to take the boots off the dead man for himself. Mikhael refused. He would on no condition put on the boots of a victim. The older guard looked at him and asked where he was from. Mikhael answered that he was a Jew and he came from Pinsk.

"Why won't you take the boots?" he asked. "Look, you're not guilty of his death. It's silly to refuse."

"I knew in my heart that he was right. However, these boots, I couldn't bear the sight of these boots. No, absolutely not!"

The older guard suggested to Mikhael that he should join the work group which he was escorting. Mikhael managed to get across to it, and the guard brought him to the house of a nearby peasant where two Jewish engineers from the Shabli ghetto were working on setting up a sewer. The Jewish engineers suggested that Mikhael should come with them to the Shabli ghetto, but Mikhael refused their offer. According to him, he couldn't bear seeing the yellow badge of the Star of David, which the Jews wore on their chests and backs.

Mikhael was integrated into the group which Fedka, the chief interpreter in the camp had organised, a group, which was preparing to escape from the camp. Fedka trusted him: "You're a Jew," he said, "so you won't betray us." The conspirators dug a tunnel underneath the floor of the sick hut, and on 10th. May, 1942, they escaped through it to freedom, after first getting rid of the camp commander, whom they hated.

Before they went down into the tunnel, the escapees divided into small groups. Before their flight, Mikhael had revealed the secret of the escape to the son of a Belarussian peasant from the Kobrin area, and included him in his group, and in this way, saved his life. The peasant, whose name was Andriosha, was very moved and swore to Mikhael that his home would be Mikhael's home.

They marched along the paths of Lithuania for three months, walking at night and hiding in the day, and eventually, they reached Andriosha's farm. However, here the young man forgot his vow and went into his house and left his comrades on the plot of land and didn't come out to them again. Mikhael managed to talk and soften the heart of the farm-owner, Andriosha's father, and he took them to a place where he had hidden two rifles. So now Mishka and his friend, Vanka, were armed with two rifles, and they went on their way to look for the partisans. After much wandering and various adventures, a number of other people joined Mishka and his comrade.

In the autumn of 1942, they met a patrol of the Vasilyev battalion. The patrol soldiers took their rifles off them and led them to their "Kommandatura". They were thoroughly interrogated about their past and how they'd reached the forest. After the interrogation, eight men from the little band were attached to the group, but they refused to accept Mikhael and another young lad from their group, called Pashka, who had lost his rifle while fleeing from policemen. They left them in the "Kommandatura" and came back the next day to interrogate them again, and this is what Mikhael has to say about this:

"From time to time,'Diadia (Uncle) Vasya' (Vasiliyev) and his companions stop me and ask again about my escape from captivity, about the tunnel and so on. I answered everything, but I tried to be as factual and to the point as possible. At the end of the investigation, Vasiliyev exchanged glances with his escorts, and afterwards, turned towards me and Pashka, with these words, 'I would gladly accept you among our ranks. You certainly deserve it, but I just haven't any room to integrate any more comrades. And so this is what we'll do. We'll escort you to another camp, not far from here, and I wish you all the best.' Pashka didn't reply to this. However, I got up on my feet and I declared, 'No way am I moving from here to anywhere. I've come such a long way together with Vanka the Moscovite [111], and now when we finally reach a partisan unit, you're on the point of separating us. And what's more, you have my rifle, and I'm not giving it up, not at all, no sirs, I'm not moving from here.'

"I saw that my words had an impact on 'Uncle Vasya' and his escorts, and they went out to confer. After a few minutes, they came back and Uncle Vasya turned to Pashka and said, 'You, comrade, you go with these two comrades of ours, and they will accompany you to your new place. However, you,' and he turned to me, 'leave us tomorrow, after your weapons have been returned to you.'

"Vasiliyev left with the "Kommandatura", with two of his escorts and Pashka and his two escorts also went out. I remained alone and my heart sank. Something bad was going to happen here. I was aware that these interrogators had come after having already interrogated our comrades, who had now been accepted by them, and who knows what they had said about us? It was obvious that they blamed Pashka for dropping his rifle carelessly when we happened upon the policemen. As for me, it was hard for me to come to terms with the idea, but they simply wanted to get rid of me because of my being a Jew."

---

[111] *Vanka the Muscovite escaped from the P.O.W. camp with Mikhael, went the whole way with him, and even swore that he would not leave him. It was for him that Mikhael obtained the second rifle.*

In the meantime, a group of men had arrived at the "Kommandatura", soldiers who had been in the Red Army, who, up till now, had been sitting around doing nothing in the villages, and whom Vasiliyev had now attached to the partisans in his group. Mikhael exploited the situation and on his own initiative, set out with them for the troop's camp. The new men were split up into squads and units. Mikhael recognised one of the unit commanders as the partisan who had accompanied Pashka. Now he was wearing Pashka's pullover and his boots. It was obvious that they had executed Pashka.

Mikhael was attached to unit A, squad B. He was given a rifle, but not the one that had been taken from him. He demanded emphatically that they should return him his rifle and even reported to Vasiliyev, despite the danger in doing so. Mikhael's stubborness and his devotion to his rifle in fact pleased Vasiliyev, and after several days, his rifle was returned to him. Mikhael was placed in a patrol squad.

The days of the February 1943 manhunt arrived. Mishka, as has been said, reached the Shchors camp by virtue of his reconnaissance role. And then his comrades made off and abandoned him in the Shchors camp. The manhunt was at its height and Mikhael wasn't able to look for his unit. In the meantime, he was attached to Proniagin's troop as a runner, a liaison, with the rear guard. Riding on a horse, he was constantly moving between Proniagin and the rear guard. Here, now he became a true partisan, and after the manhunt, he was transferred to the command department. No liaison men from the Vasiliyev troop arrived, and Mikhael was declared by them a deserter, and a death sentence was passed upon him.

Mikhael Pertzov completed his partisan service in July 1944 and was sent to work in a town in the Brest region. Here he met his comrades from the Shchors battalion. In Brest, he enrolled into the Red Army and continued to fight.

The ninth of May 1945 found him near Berlin. His unit was called out to a parade, and he heard the good news of the defeat of the Third Reich. His war against Nazi Germany was over, and Mikhael Pertzov too, like his Jewish partisan comrades from the Shchors and the Vasiliyev, was eventually able to set his feet, weary from wandering and from the storms of war, on the soil of the State of Israel.

CHAPTER FIFTEEN: Under the command of Sergei Ivanovich Sikorski

Establishing the Brest division

On 30th. May 1942, the central H.Q. of the partisan movement, under the leadership of Ponamerenko[112], was established near to the Supreme Command of the Red Army. In September of this year, the H.Q. of the Belorussian movement was also set up, and subsequently those of the partisan movements of the Soviet Republic in other conquered lands.[113]

From now on, partisan groups were not able to act under their own initiative. They were combined into larger units - into battalions (otriady), these into brigades, and into divisions (soyedinienye). From now, they functioned according to the instructions of the political commanders and the commissars of the divisions. Representatives of the Bolshevik party also sat on these, and they supervised the operations of the partisans and passed onto them orders and instructions for their missions. Reports were written on the partisan operations and transferred to the high command in the rear. The troops were no longer allowed freedom of movement. They were forbidden to wander from region to region, and each one was fixed to a particular area. It was permitted to leave their place only during manhunts, in order not to end up being surrounded. With the retreat of the enemy, they were required to go back to their regular place of action.

Neither was the number of people in the troop set. A troop whose number of fighters grew would be divided into two or three. Sometimes a group of people would be separated from the troop, and was allowed to grow through integrating further people and becoming a new troop.

In 1943, the appointed representative of the Bolshevik party centre arrived in the Brest area, together with his escorts. He was responsible for reorganising the partisan movement in the Brest area and was to include under his authority the independent partisan groups, which up till now had been operating on their own initiative, without supervision and without authority. This man[114], whose name was Sergei Ivanovitch Sikorski, set to work straight away. The H.Q. of the Brest division was encamped meanwhile in the forests of Sporovo, near the Black Lake in the district of the town of Kartuz Bereza. In the process of reorganisation in the Brest district Colonel Sikorski

---

[112] *Istoria velikoi otechestvennoi voiny, tom II, p.122.*

[113] *On 30th. June 1941, the "Operative Group" was founded by the Ukrainian Bolshevik Party, headed by the party secretaries - Kharuschov, Burmistenko and Korotchenko – in order to speed up the establishment of the movement in the Ukraine. In this group was T.A. Strukatz, among others, who eventually became the partisan chief of staff of the Ukraine. Shem, vol. III, P. 465.*

[114] *Partizanskoye formirovanye v Belorusii, razdel III, P.122.*

also reached the Shchors H.Q., which belonged to that district. The Jewish partisans raised the issue of the rejections with him, and Sikorski ordered them to be returned to the troop. His envoys also reached the Vasiliyev battalion envoys in this operation

Some of the banished people came back, but there were Jews who refused to return, because they had been badly hurt by the attitude of certain anti-Semitic commanders in the Shchors. The Alpert family were among those who refused to go back. They had been absorbed into the family camp which was under the protection of the Vasiliyev battalion. Pesach's wife remembers how well they were treated there.

In July 1944, the Red Army reached the swamps of Polesia, and the partisan units were dispersed. The Alpert family returned in a military lorry to Slonim, and from there immigrated through Poland to Israel. In the Shchors, a group was organised to go to Gotsek under the command of Guzhevski. Natan Liker went out with them and took it on himself to look after Dr. Orlinski on the way and make sure she got back safely. Meanwhile, Sikorski set about the job of reorganising the partisan movement in his command area. The H.Q. of the Brest district division was set up and headed by Sikorski, commander of the division. His deputy was Ivan Ivanovitch Bobrov, and the third in command - podpolkovnik (colonel) was Nikolai Nikolaivitch Drozdov, ex- NKVD commander for matters of intelligence. They attached Proniagin as the head of the division staff group. This was a considerable promotion in rank for Proniagin. Dr. Avraham Blumovitch was appointed chief medical officer of the division and Yegorov was given the role of the division commissar for party matters.

And now, each group in the Shchors battalion, which then numbered seven hundred men, became the kernel of a separate troop which was required to enrol new people and grow. The commanders of the groups were elevated in rank to troop commanders, and the troops were now called by other names.

The 52 troop inherited the name "Shchors", and Zuyev remained its commander.

The 54 group became a troop which was called "Suvorov", commanded by Andrei Leontiev.

The 55 group now went by the name of "Kotovski" and Lapitchev was its commander.

The 56 group received the name Budionni, and its commander remained Zhuravliov. Kovaliov was appointed commissar of the troop, and Merzliakov was appointed the battalion chief of staff.

The Budionni troop became the staff troop of the division.

The commanders of the troops and battalions were required to act according to the instructions of division command and to report back on their activities. From now, the story of members of the 51 troop, "Shchors", ended, and became that of the people who'd come from the ghettos of Slonim and Biten, who were dispersed all over the troops of the Pinsk and Brest divisions -

a wide area between the forests of Polesia, the swamps of Pinsk and the banks of the Shchara.

The troops moved to their new encampments. They marched twenty kilometres south of Ivatsevitch, reached the drainage canal east of the lake at Tchornoye (the Black Lake) and up to Lake Sporovo. On the eastern bank of the lake, they met the guard of the Major P.M .Kovalski's troop, which was later called the Kalinin troop. In this troop too, the ex-51 people met other Jewish partisans. Kovalski was an intelligent man and had been operating in the area for some time. At the time of the reorganisation, his troop was affiliated to the Brest division.[115]

After they'd marched about an hour, the troops reached the place of their new camp, on the two banks of the drainage canal, in forest surrounded by swamps. The same day, groups were sent out to new territory to patrol and find food. The river Drogobuzh, which links Lake Tchornoye to the river Yaselda, flowed through the territory. The villages in the area still lived in peace and economic prosperity, and the partisans had no difficulty here in obtaining food. The territories around were well-worked, and a sense of safety prevailed in the villages. The Yaselda is a broad river, whose banks are verdant, with stretches of meadow and forests. The bridge over the Yaselda no longer existed and only the tips of its pillars stuck out of the water, so the partisans were forced to bring the food which they had collected to the camp in boats.[116]

The fighters set to work building earth huts and spacious wooden shacks for establishing the H.Q. and the clinic and to provide shelters for the soldiers. When the organisation of the troops was completed, Sikorski transferred some of his faithful men to new places, to broaden the division's control. For that purpose too, the Suvorov troop was sent under the command of Leontiev into territory which was under the control of Bobkov, to Volchye Nori, to create order there and to integrate the troop into the division. In order to add validity and authority to Leontiev's mission, Sikorski's deputy, Bobrov, went out with him. Afterwards, the Kotovski and Shchors troops set out south of the Brest-Minsk railway line and positioned themselves south of the Dnieper-Bug canal[117], amongst the Pinsk marshes. In the area where the Shchors troop was encamped the Brest division set up an airfield under the supervision of Viktor Guzhevski.[118]

---

[115] *This is according to Proniagin (P.67). According to the official book – "Vasenarodnaya", vol. 2, P.184 – there were only 447 men in the troop.*

[116] *Since administrative divisions in the U.S.S.R. are not identical with those of Israel, we will translate the term 'Oblast' as 'district', and the smaller unit 'Rayon' as 'area'.*

[117] *The Dnieper-Bug canal, formerly called the Krulevski canal (King's Canal), was built in 1732-1848, during the reign of the Polish king, Stanislav August Poniatovski. It links the Dnieper with the Visla by means of the River Pina (a tributary of the Pripiet) and the River Mukhavietz (a tributary of the Bug).*

[118] *Proniagin, pp. 72-77; 79- 84.*

Envoys were sent to the distant troops in the whole region, and they accepted the authority of the division's HQ. Any commander who refused was got rid of and new commanders were sent to his troop. Moreover, any commanders were changed who had delayed their reply for a long time and sought to maintain their independence. Finally, envoys were sent to the underground organisation in the city of Brest, in order to check out the situation in the capital city of the district.

Before the outbreak of war, Colonel Sergei Ivanovitch Sikorski, and with him the military unit that he commanded, was stationed in Brest. His family - his wife and three children - also lived there. When war broke out, he left with his army for the front, and managed to retreat and reach the Soviet rear. His family remained in occupied Brest, and he knew nothing of their fate. When, in April 1943, he reached the Brest district, he sent envoys to the town, and they brought him the good news that his family was alive and whole.[119] In time, they managed to get them out of the city and bring them to the forest. When the building of the landing strip was completed in the division, Sikorski's family members were sent to Moscow.

The arrival of G.L.Linkov

In the last third of May 1943, the paratrooper colonel, Linkov, arrived in the Brest district. He had been sent from the Soviet rear for special duties. From the beginning, there appeared signs of a certain tension between Sikorski and Linkov over their authority. And, in fact, after clarification at the beginning of June, they decided that organisation of the partisan movement, and its command, following the instructions of the supreme partisan command in the rear, would be under the authority of Sikorski, whereas assignments and the special roles imposed on the paratroopers according to the instructions of the regular army command, would be under the authority of Linkov.

Deployment of troops of the Brest division

With the division of the Shchors battalion into four troops - the Shchors, the Budionni, the Kotovski, the Suvorov - each of them left for their allocated area. They left the Baranovitch district, where they had camped up until now and transferred to the Brest district.[120]

---

[119] *S.Y.Sikorski, Komunisty brestkoi oblasti v avangarde partizanskoi borbi, in: Nepokorennaya Belorussia.*

[120] *The Jews called Brest "Brisk d'Lita". There was a fortress in the town, which was defended with great courage and daring by the Jewish officer Efraim Ben Mosheh Pomin. The defence of the Brest fortress became famous in the history of the Second World War as one of the most heroic episodes of the Red Army's war in the difficult weeks of its retreat. Efraim Pomin fell into enemy hands on 30th. June, 1941,*

The Kotovski troop went to the southwest, towards the small town of Antopol, and took up a position, after crossing the Dnieper-Bug canal, among the treacherous marshes of the Pinsk region, close to the village of Roditch. In the winter, the partisans moved to live in the houses of peasants in the villages.

The Shchors troop was positioned further south, near the village of Svarin. Later, the partisan landing strip was established within its boundaries. The Budionni troop remained where it was, as the staff troop of the division, and camped around the Tchornoye Lake, near the H.Q. The Kommandatura, the forward partisan command, and staff guard, was set up in the village Sporovo.

The Suvorov troop was sent to Volchye Nori (see above), to the area under the Bobkov's command. The Budionni troop, under Merzliakov, escorted the men going to the Brest-Baranovitch railway track and stayed to cover for them until they reached the track. Orlinski and a local Belorussian partisan was sent to accompany the marchers up to the track and when they had crossed it, they had to fire a rocket as a sign that they'd crossed safely, at which point the Budionni would be able to go back to its base.

The Belorussian who was sent with Orlinski fell back halfway along and refused to go any further from his troop. Orlinski went on escorting the men of the Suvorov on his own, waited until the people had disappeared into the forest across the railway track, and then he fired the rocket, as agreed, and turned back. However, when he reached the place where the troop should have been waiting for him, it emerged that Mzliakov hadn't waited for the agreed sign, and the troop had gone further off from that place. Orlinski had to guess in which direction they had gone and hurry in order to catch up.

An improvement in the condition of the troops

Before the division was established, the troops were short of ammunition, and neither were there any more existing supply sources for military equipment. However, now, after creating the links with the 'great land ', military equipment and ammunition arrived by air, and intelligence about what was happening in the area and on the fronts improved, since radio communication worked every day. At certain times, radio transmissions were received from Moscow, reports were sent on partisan events, and requests were conveyed.

Discipline and responsibility for missions had also improved. A special unit was functioning (Osobi Otdiel) and every offence was relayed to its consideration and judgement. Now there were no longer acts of punishment and arbitrary executions by the commanders, as there had been before.

The Brest division, which eventually numbered twelve to thirteen thousand fighters, was an organised and disciplined force. This situation forced the Germans to also raise their level of activity and to undertake various methods to defeat the partisans. The enemy set up schools for intelligence and

---

badly wounded and paralysed, and was shot. His portrait is displayed in the War Museum in Minsk, and streets in Minsk and Brest have been named after him.

espionage. Russians and Belorussians who graduated from these schools were sent to the partisan troops, disguised as volunteers, and their aim was to spy and wipe out the partisan command. Women, too, were frequently sent. Spies like these also reached the Brest division and the Budionni troop, but information was received about them in time, and they were captured and eliminated.

From June 1943 to April 1944, the following brigades were established in the Brest district: Ponomarenko, Sovietskaya Belorussia, Stalin, Dzerzhinski, Sverdlov, Tchapayev, and Lenin. The divisions had eleven brigades and thirteen separate troops, living in the north and south of the region. From February 1944, Major Piotr Mamertovitz Kovalski commanded the brigades in the south.

The reorganisation in Volchye Nori

Bobkov's 53 group, which had crumbled in the days of the September 1942 siege, was reorganised into a battalion with the name of Sovietskaya Belorussia. Many of the peasant people and residents of the small towns in the area joined them. These were unmistakably anti-Semitic people. Among them were looters of Jewish property and some who Jews had entrusted with their property when fleeing from the massacres. They sought to get rid of the Jews so that, after the war, no Jew would be able to come back and claim his property.

On 23rd. July 1943, when the number of partisans in his troop had reached four hundred, the troop became a brigade, and Bobkov, its commander (Kombrig). Senkin was appointed commissar. Over time, many ex-collaborators were absorbed into this brigade, Belorussian and Ukrainian policemen, who up till now had been doing the dirty work for the Germans and had taken part in the destruction of Jewish communities in the area.

After Sikorski gained control of affairs in his district, he set about organising them in the forest of Volchye Nori. In addition to his troop, the brigade now included the troops: Kirov, Dimitrov, Gastello, Tchekalov and Suvorov (under Leontiev).

In the summer of 1943, the brigade grew and took in additional groups and troops, and therefore, it was divided on 28th. August into two: Sovietskaya Belorussia, over which Bobkov continued to command, and the Ponomarenko brigade, to the command of which Senkin had been appointed. This brigade camped in the forest of Huta Mikhalin.

Now the murderous rampage of anti-Semitic partisans stopped. The Jewish family camp was again established n the forests of Volchye Nori, and hope revived for the survival of the remnants of the Jews in the forest.

In 1944, there commenced another development in the life of the family camp in Volchye Nori: a group of people, mainly weapon-bearing men, was separated from the family camp, and was attached to the Sovietskya Belorussia brigade, as a unit whose role was to serve the staff group and be responsible for supplies of food and other needs. The unit, which numbered forty-six people, was commanded by Boria Yudkovski from Biten. Fifty-six people remained in the family camp, including, twenty from Biten.[121]

Both the hope of remaining alive and the hope of seeing revenge on the Germans and their Belorussian helpers were reawakened among the remnants of the Jews. These were days of tension and expectation. On 10th. July 1944, a reconnaissance patrol of the regular Red Army reached the forest and that very night, they were already released.

The troops of the division were spread over an extremely wide area, and they had overrun the railway tracks and the main roads on the Brest-Baranovitch and the Brest-Minsk lines. Dozens of sabotage groups were active on the railway lines and on the road, and they sabotaged both transport and transit and caused heavy losses in men, military equipment and supplies. Jewish partisans from the Slonim ghetto also took part in the sabotage activities - Nionia Tsirinskyi , Zerach Kremin, Natan Liker, Avraham Orlinski, Malach, Korsch, Milikovski, Guterman, Mukasay, Rozmarin and Yankelevitch.[122] Natan Liker commanded a squad of saboteurs in the Shchors troop, and later, in the Kotovski troop and was distinguished for his courage.

The actions of the Budionni troop: the battle for Antopol (4th. July 1943)

Antopol is a small town, situated on the main Brest-Gomel road. The Brest division staff group decided to attack the German garrison and its helpers, who were stationed in Antopol, and to wipe it out. Several troops were recruited to this operation, among them fighters from the Budionni and Kirov troops. There were Jews, past residents of Antopol, in the Kirov and the troop's doctor, Dr Tcherniak, also came from the town.

Some of the fighters were to take up positions facing the towns of Drogichin and Kobrin, while the others were prepared to attack the town and take control of it in order to wipe out the enemy garrison and the Belorussian collaborators. The medical unit, under the leadership of Dr. Tcherniak, was to take a position at the entrance to the town.

At midnight, volleys of tracer bullets were fired from the direction of Drogichin and Gorodietz. This was the agreed signal for attack and the fighters swept through the town. The enemy combat points were eliminated in a relatively short time and a great deal of loot (weaponry) was taken from enemy houses. However, some of the garrison force had 'dug in' in the police station in the middle of the town. Partisan fire and the grenades which were thrown at

---

[121] *After the war Boria Yudkovski immigrated to Israel, raised a new family and was active in Kibbutz Lochamei HaGetaot and the Kibbutz Hameuchad. He became ill and died on his kibbutz in 1969.*

[122] *They are mentioned in reports of the official partisan command: Vsenarodnoye Partizanskoye Dvizhenie, vols. II and III.*

the building didn't cause much damage, though the fighters burned one building from which the enemy was firing. In one of the houses, the Jewish fighters found pages of Pentateuch and scraps of parchment from Torah scrolls. These finds were witness to the nature of the people living in the house, and the Jewish partisans, who were seized with anger, treated these residents as they deserved.[123]

The operation in Peski

Peski was a large farm on the shores of Lake Tchornoye (The Black Lake). It was working for the Germans. There was an enemy barracks stationed there, most of which were support forces - Ukrainians, people from Vlasov, and Belorussian police. They were attached to a German army unit, which was encamped in Bronna Gora, at the crossroads of the Brest-Baranovitch track and the Brest-Slutsk road. This garrison interfered a great deal with the activity of the partisans and would set ambushes for them and open fire on the camp of the Klinin troop, which was commanded by Major Kovalski.

The Major had devised a plan to attack the village and defeat the garrison. This suggestion appealed to the commander of the division, Sikorski, and he laid the responsibility for planning the operation on Proniagin, who was now the operations officer of the division. His view was that fighters from the past Shchors troop should take part in the battle because they were now elite brigades in the Budionni and Shchors troops. Proniagin knew them and was able to trust them. Fighters from the Kalinin troop also took part in the operation. This decision was reached largely on the basis of information from Danila Solima, the commander of the reconnaissance patrol of Kalinin, who assured him that he had reached an agreement with the police in Peski, and they had promised to attack the Germans from the rear. Merzliakov commanded the whole battle, and the Budionni fighters were commanded by Zhuravliov.

The partisans set out for the operation when darkness fell, under cover of the tall trees growing there, and they reached the farm buildings, but it became apparent that the expectation that the police would attack the Germans from behind was in vain. The commander of the patrol who had promised the help of the police had disappeared. During the battle, it became clear that the enemy was not at all surprised and received the partisans with hellfire from automatic guns. They were firing from all directions, and the partisans were forced to lie flat. Merzliakov was wounded and Dr Cheslava got him out of the battlefield.

As the commander of the operation had been wounded, the partisans waited for someone to take on the command and lead them in a renewed attack; however, no command was heard. The Budionni fighters were waiting

---

[123] *From the memoirs of Avraham Orlinski, who was a patrol man in the Budionni-troop (Lochamei HaGetaot Archives)*

for instructions from their commander, Zhuravlov, but he was neither seen nor heard, and then Proniagin commanded to retreat.

"When we came out of the forest to the shore of the lake,' says Orlinski, who took part in the battle, 'we suddenly saw Zhuravlov lying on a slope by the edge of the lake, with his deputy Grishka. We passed them silently and continued to withdraw. We couldn't understand why they hadn't been seen or heard in the hour of need in battle."

It was one of the examples of fearfulness and corruption of a commander, which the literature of Soviet partisan memoirs passes over in silence[124]. During the retreat, Orlinski was carrying a wounded man. He met Delatitski, who had come to collect the wounded with a cart, and handed over the partisan whom he was carrying.

The next morning, the Budionni troop advanced to the village of Nimerzha, which had become a centre for concentration of supplies for the H.Q. stationed in Sporovo. Budionni troop had organised a reconnaissance patrol, which was commanded by Avraham Bandt, and included Nionia Tsirinski and Ya'akov Khatskelevitch.

The bombing of the forest and activity on the airfield

The Germans had acquired information as to the whereabouts of division H.Q. and the Budionni troop. German planes would come from the German landing strip in Ivatzevitz and bomb plot after plot in the forest. The partisans had sussed the method and would move to parts of the forest which had already been bombed: then the Germans came back and got wise to this. They would disappear and come back with their engines silenced so as to surprise the partisans, who would come out of their hiding places after the planes had disappeared. The partisans got hold of this method too and became adept at being cautious, and thus, there were hardly any people hit from the bombings. There was an incident when a bomb fell by the tent of the Orlinski couple. The doctor managed to salvage the stock of medicines from the tent which had caught fire, but their personal belongings were burnt.

The Budionni troop relocated its camp to the shore of Lake Tchornoye and crossed with division H.Q. to the western side of the canal. H.Q. now had four communication units: one unit served the division commander, Sikorski, another was at the disposal of the commander of the security forces, Colonel Drosdov, and the third was for conducting propaganda in the villages. It would disperse leaflets to the population and included a printing union, which had published the newsletter of the party in the underground, 'Zaria'. They would distribute this in the villages and in the small towns roundabout.[125]

---

[124] *Proniagin omits mention of Zhorbaliov's action in his book.*

[125] *Memoirs of A. Orlinski*

No planes landed on the airfield by the H.Q. They were only marked as a place for dropping sacks of supplies from the rear. Sometimes envoys would parachute in, sent by the rearguard partisan supreme command.

They would fix the times of the drops via the radio, and they would prepare the markers from birch tree bark, which they would arrange according to a pre-agreed sign, and set alight. The bark burned very well. On the radio, they would announce the number of parcels which they were about to drop. Sometimes a certain sack would drop outside the marked area and then it had to be located so as not to fall into enemy hands. The parachute silk would be handed over to the hospital, where they would prepare slips from it, and sometimes bandages, or even cover the walls of the sick room with it.

On one occasion, twelve parcels were announced. They searched all night and found only eleven of them. Only the next day was the missing 'parcel' found, and it was Lizhin, secretary of the communist youth organisation, who hadn't felt secure in the place that he had dropped and hid with the parachute. He brought orders to blow up the railway track of the Brest-Minsk and Brest-Pinsk lines on 8th. August 1943.

The need now arose to prepare a landing strip. After some searching, they identified a suitable place, near the village of Swarin, south of the Dnieper-Bug canal, near the place where the Shchors troop was encamped. The planes that landed there would bring materials and equipment which couldn't be dropped by parachute. On the way back, the planes would fly out the severely wounded, who couldn't be treated in partisan conditions and those whose disabilities didn't allow them to carry on in the forest. Vasia, who had been blinded in the Gavinovitch operation was flown back in this way. The partisans would offer the pilots some piglets for their personal needs, for the food supply in Russia at war was very difficult at that time.

Activity along enemy transport lines

The partisans were now taking control of additional territories at a decent rate. The Germans were concentrating on guarding the main roads and railway lines near the territories under partisan control. Despite this, they couldn't prevent sabotage along their lines of movement. The partisan squads of saboteurs would reach the main roads, set up ambushes and successfully sabotage the railway track and telephone lines.

The Germans would check the lines and repair the damage, so then the partisans started to hide explosives under the railway lines. The explosives were mainly a sabotage brick with a spark plug. A cable was attached to it, stretched over the ramp, and its other end held by a saboteur. It was not easy for the soldiers guarding the railway tracks to find this installation. When the train arrived, the saboteur would pull the cable, activating the spark plug and causing an explosion on the railway track. The engine and usually the carriages would come off the track. If the rampart of the track was high, the carriages would roll down at the sides of the rampart, and a great deal of damage would be done.

Not long passed before the Germans discovered the partisans' method and they had to change it. Now the explosives were hidden in the earth and the spark plug would be in the appropriate contact with the tracks. At the moment the train passed over it, the heavy weight of the engines or the carriages would press on the spark plug and activate it.

In time, the enemy recognised this method too. But this time, the partisans were cleverer and found new methods: they would lay the sabotage charger in the short time between the guard checking the railway line and the passage of the train. The explosive was attached to a stick, which would be caught in the engine and cause the explosion. Eventually, the Germans started to send a number of carriages laden with stones in front of the engine in order to activate the charge before the engine reached the place which was mined. However, the partisans found a response to this German trick too. The war of the railway tracks was going on all the time. The partisans would develop new methods, and the enemy would try to discover them and invent an antidote. The sabotage caused the enemy a great deal of damage, as sometimes essential shipments to the front were delayed, and at times, the railway tracks were blocked for hours and days, delaying supplies which were decisive for the outcome of battle.

The partisans were active on the roads too. They would wipe out enemy cars and prevent the enemy transferring supplies to their garrisons and sending farm produce to Germany. Ambushes on the road gave the partisans important information. In the rucksacks of dead soldiers and officers and in the pockets of their clothes, they would find military documents that were very valuable for intelligence. Sometimes the documents included information of value to the army at the front, and then they would forward it to the 'great land'. In the letters which they found on the corpses, there was also important information about the situation in the German rear guard about the morale of the population. And they found photographs, many of which had been made during the massacres in the conquered territories, photographs of hangings, Actions and mass annihilation by the pits.

And it happened that in the letters there would be intriguing information: a soldier about to come on holiday to his family after a long absence would find that during his absence, a child had been born to his wife. There was also information in the letters about secret armaments (V1, V2), which the Germans were developing, weapons which they hoped would be decisive in the progress of the war to their advantage. All this correspondence was checked with a fine-toothed comb, and the important material was transferred to the rear. Avraham Orlinski, who functioned both as reconnaissance and as a saboteur remembers several episodes from this period of his service:

"This was the time when they started to place a charge with explosives under the railway lines in a method where the explosive charge would be activated by the weight of the engine. After they explained the method to me and showed me on the map the place identified for the sabotage, I would make me a sketch of the environment, and I planned the journey to the identified place.

"In our group, there were six people and Viktor Bistrov commanded it. He didn't trust the new method, and so he ordered us to carry a reel of cables so that we would be able to do the work in the old method. Viktor ordered a young Belorussian from our group to carry the reel, which was heavy for me, when I needed to patrol the movement in a dangerous place. At first he refused, but he had to obey. We crossed the road safely and quickly. As morning came, we came to a place close to the target. The place was open and only a little copse of low bushes grew by it. We waited in the forest, lying down until evening, so that we could go out to work at night. During the day, we saw a movement of residents and police. In our group, there were three Ukrainians from the Soviet army, who had been captured by the Germans at the beginning of the war. They fled the camp and reached us a few days before the rejection of 27th. March 1943, and they received weapons which had been taken from the Jews. Now the three were very frightened because of the coming activity and were all prepared to run back with the fall of darkness. Viktor sensed this and asked: 'Who is in favour of continuing this mission and who is against?' I was amazed. The three Ukrainians and the young Belorussian who had refused to carry the reel were against continuing and against sabotage of the train. They claimed that it was dangerous to remain in the open spot where we were staying and asked to go back immediately with darkness. Bistrov responded to them and decided to go back. He would not agree that the two of us, he and I, should carry on to the railway track and carry out the mission.

"The task was not carried out. I know of no similar incident in Jewish saboteurs group. It emerged that the head of the Ukrainian group, who had previously accepted into the group a man who was called Scrifnik, sorted himself out very nicely as manager of a stores in the village of Nimerzhe and lived comfortably until the end of the partisan activity without ever taking part, even once, in an operational activity, and without ever using the weapon that had been taken for him from a Jew."

The partisans, who had taken control over wide areas, prevented the Germans from taking out the farm crops from the villages. And so, the Germans started to come with reinforcements to the villages in order to take the quota of crops which they had imposed on the farmers.

The partisans also organised large mobile supply units. Small partisan units would wait to ambush the Germans on their way and delay them until the large supply units arrived. On one occasion, a large partisan unit surprised the Ukrainians who had previously encamped in the village of Peski and had been transferred from there. One of our partisans suggested negotiating with them in order to bring them over to the partisan side. Three partisans went out to confer with them, among them the man who suggested this. During the conversation, the Ukrainian 'democrats' murdered the man who had made the suggestion and wounded the two others and made off on their horses.

There was another incident which occurred in the course of guarding the crop: the H.Q. of the Budionni troop received an order to send a small unit to help the Molotov troop guard the crop. The unit went out. Among their fighters was Orlinski, and as evening fell they reached the Molotov camp, where they organised a night's stay. With dawn, they went on their way and came close to the village of Heidaki, which is in the direction of Nikhatchevo, where a unit from Molotov was waiting in ambush. The partisans from the Molotov troop told them that a small unit hadn't honoured its obligation to delay a unit of Germans which was coming to take the crops, and had retreated before reinforcements had arrived. The Budionni fighters advanced to the place where the German unit was expected to pass and took up a position suitable to ambush them among the tall, dense bushes. They lay there until they were informed that the Germans had changed their mind about taking the crop and retreated from the area. The commander of the gang who hadn't carried out his task was punished.

Orlinski continues in his memoirs and recounts the punishment:

"Tuesday. We're on the edge of the forest, which is at the top of a hill and waiting for a commander to appear, who will gather us together and give us instructions, and suddenly, he appears, accompanied by his men. A drill was organised and the order 'Silence!' was given. The commander told us about an investigation into the incident and blamed three of the fighters, among them, Shtchukin, the commander of the gang which had let them down, and with him, the medic of the small group.

"Shtchukin was called out to stand in front of the drill, was reprimanded and demoted to the rank of private. The other guilty party, the medic, was considered to have a greater responsibility. He had left the unit during the battle and had fled to the village of Heidaki and stayed there until his unit retreated. He was sentenced to be executed by firing. At the end of his speech, the Politruk ordered the medic, who was stunned, to turn round, but the sentenced man froze on the spot and shouted with all his strength, 'My brother!' However, he was shot with a bullet, and only his shouting and the sound of the gunshot reverberated in the air.

They took out his body to behind the bushes to where he'd been standing and the parade remained silent in order that the fighters would have time to think about what they'd seen and heard. The parade was then dispersed and the Politruk went back behind the bush and in his hands were the shoes of the dead man.

This death sentence was not carried out according to the order of a commander, but according to the decision of the special unit attached to the H.Q. of the division.

The rescue of Jews by Jewish partisans

The Jewish partisans should be credited with making efforts to rescue Jews who were wandering without any shelter from place to place and hiding in earth huts that they dug in the forest or with kind farmers who offered them shelter. Jewish partisans invested great efforts in trying to persuade their commanders to absorb at least young people who had combat sickness into their units. They also hastened to help orphaned children and solitary young girls, organising better conditions for them so that they would be able to survive. The mitzvah of saving Jews frequently presented itself to the Jewish patrols, as they were often moving around the territory and had the opportunity of meeting Jews who were hiding, or meeting farmers who told the partisans about them.

As the Shchors troop moved eastwards, the Jewish reconnaissance men met three doctors and another lone Jew, and they managed to integrate them to Troop 51. They were Dr. Strikovski, Dr. Avram Sayet and Dr. Itzhak Liepak.

It should be pointed out that Jewish partisans, who had been born in the Soviet Union, and its supporters who had served before the war in the Red Army and had escaped from captivity to the partisans, would often hide their Jewishness and didn't tend to intervene for Jews who were saved from the ghettos. A patrolman, Ya'akov Khatzkelevitch, says about rescuing a Jewish family:

"Nionia Tsirinski and I had never hidden our Jewishness. On the contrary, we were proud of it, and so we were able to save other Jews. In one village, after a conversation about the fate of the Jews with the farmer who was hosting us, I said to him that I too was Jewish. The farmer didn't believe me. He stressed that he understood Yiddish and wanted to test me out. When I answered him in Yiddish, he revealed his secret to me. In the forest, near to the village, there was a Jewish family hiding who had a little child. I went to see them. They were husband and wife, his sister, and a little boy of two or three. They looked like shadows of themselves. They had been surviving on uncooked potatoes which they rinsed in melted snow. We were very happy to see Jews, for every meeting with a Jew who'd been rescued was a joyous event. But it broke our hearts when we saw their condition. We brought them to the village of Nimerzhe. We found them a place to stay and got hold of a cow for them. The man started to work for the partisans as a tailor and the women knitted. Eventually, they were integrated into the family camp."

There was another example of this. Jewish patrolmen became aware of a young Jewish girl who was alone, and her name was Lida. This time too, the farmer was hesitant to disclose the secret to us, because he was afraid that the anti-Semitic partisans would hurt the girl. Eventually, he was convinced and led the Jewish patrol to an island among the marshes. There, Lida and the farmer's daughters were shepherding sheep. The patrol group brought the girl to their troop.

274

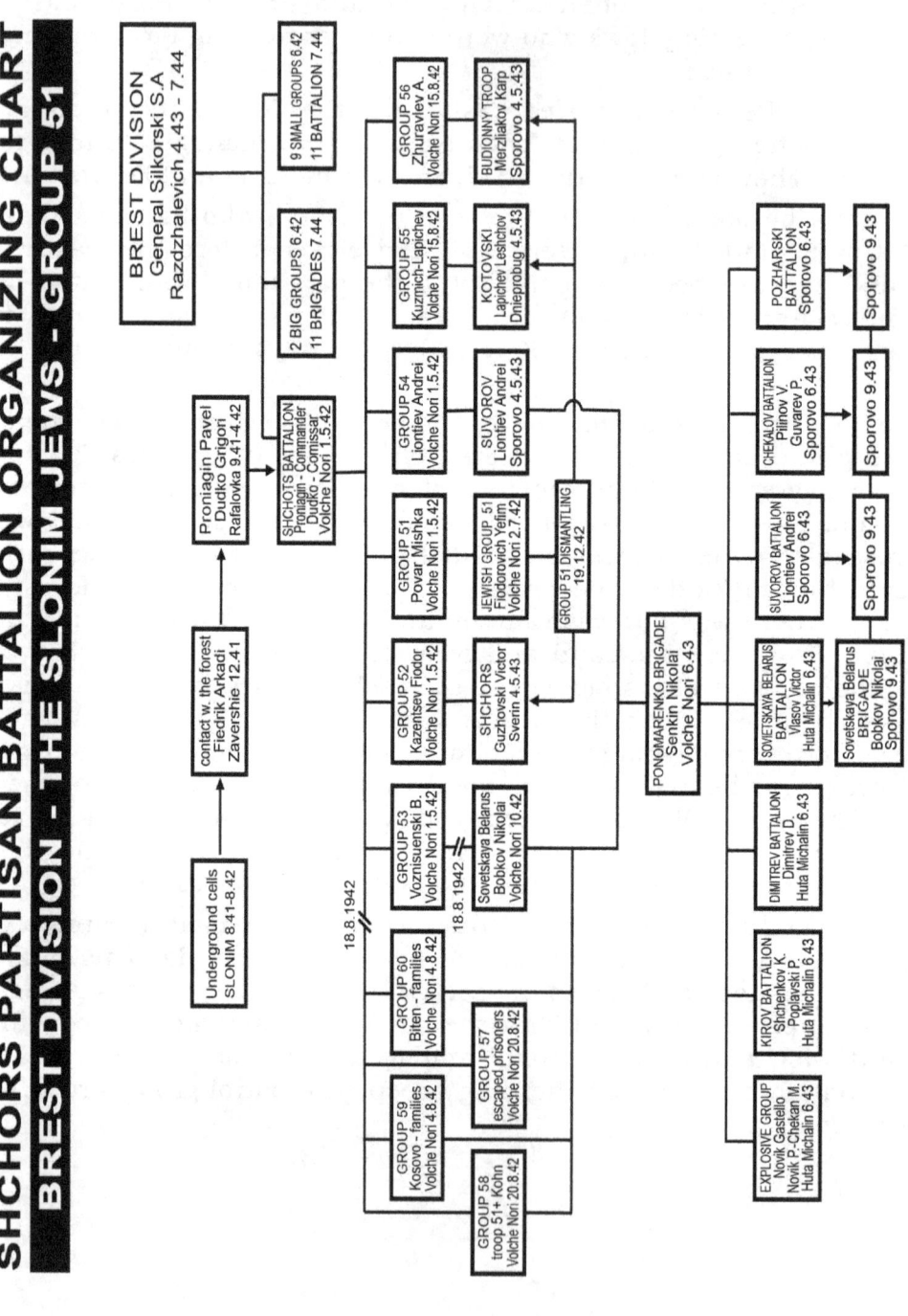

CHAPTER SIXTEEN: The War on Enemy Communication Lines

'The war of the railway track' and 'the concert'

The activities' organiser of the Komsomol (communist youth organisation), Nikolai Mikhailevitch Lizhin, arrived at the Brest division H.Q. His role was to supervise sabotage on the railway track. Planes were dropping T.N.T.-(High explosive) bricks, which weighed a hundred grams each. This was insufficient material for the projected operations, so partisans went out to look for unexploded bombs from which to produce explosives. This activity was very dangerous, and more than once, partisans who were doing this work were torn to shreds when a bomb blew up in their faces.

Operation 'Rail-track War', as it was called, was set for the night of 3rd. August 1943. The Brest/Minsk, the Brest/Gomel and the Brest/Kovel lines were sabotaged on that night, over a distance of dozens of kilometres. The Shchors troop and the Budionni and Kotovski troops took part, and among them were ex-fighters from the 51 group.

On the night of 18th. September, the Brest division carried out another organised mission over of dozens of kilometres. The mission was called 'Concert' and other divisions took part as well. This time, too, Jewish saboteurs from the 51 took part.

In two reports commanders have said:

"The Shchors troop set out for a stretch of the track on the Zhabinka/Kobrin line. The Troop chief of staff, V.P. Guzhevski, was in charge of this mission. The battalion commander was Morat Gadzhayev. Enemy machine guns rained down heavy fire on his fighters, and he hastily contacted Natan Liker, commander of the saboteurs unit, who sent several more men to help him and ordered, 'Silence the focal points of enemy fire; we will cover you.'

These brave men were divided into two groups and when they crawled right up to the reinforcements, we immediately heard loud explosions. The enemy machine guns fell silent. Among the courageous who succeeded, in a few moments, in covering the enemy bunkers in grenades, with Natan Liker, were the brothers Nikolai and Grigorai Stalkov, Pavel Guzhinov.....

'The partisans of the Shchors troop sabotaged three hundred and ninety railway tracks. Working alongside them was the Kotovski troop, whose fighters also had every reason to be pleased. They sabotaged three hundred and thirty tracks. [126]

Another official report says:

Kotovski troop, commander Zerach Kremin: They derailed ten enemy trains, and moreover, Kremin and his group obtained for the troop eighteen submachine guns, sixteen automatic rifles and many rifles and explosives. [127]

---

[126] *Proniagin, P.124*

[127] *Vsienarodnoye Partizanskoye Dvizhenie, vol. 3, p224*

Zerach Kremin, who was in charge of a group of saboteurs, says:

"The summer of 1943 was a season of great activity on the railway lines, but frequently we had to produce our own explosives for this activity."

Avraham Orlinski says of his experiences in the rail-track war:

"A short time after the arrival of Lizhin, whose role was to run the Komsomol in the Brest division, the command announced an alert for carrying out a special mission, without defining it in advance.

"It happened on 8th. August 1943, when a group under the command of Grisha Yarmolenko, the commander of a battalion in the Budionni troop, set out for the lines accompanied by Merzliakov, Lizhin and Dr. Cheslava. On the way, the group paused at the camp of Kirov troop, who controlled the Antopol region. The partisans made camp in a relatively young forest. Here, Orlinski met Dr. Tscherniak from Antopol, who was serving as doctor of the Kirov troop.

"The next morning, the group received a briefing on the aim of the mission to blow up the railway line at midnight that night. Every saboteur received four T.N.T. bricks, to which was attached a detonator with a delaying fuse. Each of the saboteurs had to put the charge in the middle of four parallel lines and light the four delaying-fuses, which were attached to the detonator and to run off. The task was carried out as required.'

"The Soviet history books note the great difference between the war of the tracks and the "Concert" and sabotage missions that were carried out up till then. In the years prior to the summer of 1943, they would send small groups of experts out on missions against the German transport. Now, with the integration of the means of sabotage and the broadening of manpower, men not trained for this would go out on missions. Brigades and troops of all the districts in Belorussia took part in operation Concert, and they sabotaged almost a hundred and fifty thousand tracks of which over ninety-thousand were in Belorussia. In addition to that, the Belorussian partisans blew up one thousand and forty-one trains."[128]

---

[128] *Vsienarodnaya borba v Belorussyi vol.II, P. 239-240; Razvitie vsienarodnovo partizanskovo dvizhenia, vol. II, P.21 (Order no. 0042)*

From the experiences of Jewish saboteurs: A sabotage mission in which A. Imber took part

Imber had reached the Budionni troop, which was commanded by Zhuraviov and attached to a squad of saboteurs under the command of Galaztsev. He was a simple and kind-hearted young man. There were seven people in this squad, of whom Nionia Tsirinski was one. Not one of them had any experience yet and knew nothing of how to put a mine together or how to lay it.

When he worked in the loot stores in the ghetto, Imber would go out with Sergeant Mutz to blow up explosives. Mutz used to get him to prepare the T.N.T. bricks, stick the detonator in them and place them under a pile of bullets. With the help of an electric detonator, which worked off a battery, they would blow up the heap. On the basis of this small knowledge, Imber went out with the gang to derail a train. They marched along the stretch of track near the Bronna-Gora station, which is between the towns of Kartuz-Bereza and the small town of Ivatsevitch. Zhuraviov ordered them not to return empty-handed and to sabotage only a train that was going to the eastern front. It was about thirty kilometres from their camp to the target.

The saboteurs were dragging explosive material weighing about seven kilograms. They reached the target at night and lay in wait for the train. The station was hectic - lamps were shining and lighting up the whole area. The Germans were shrieking and shooting all the time in different directions. Imber describes the operation:

"We were waiting for the train to come. The German guard was marching back and forth all the time and checking the stretch of track. We were forced to wait until the very last moment before the train's arrival, so that the guards wouldn't discover our mine. When we saw the lights of the engine from a distance and the track-checkers had moved off, two of our comrades sped up on to the tracks, and buried the charge. We always tried to bury the mine by a telephone pole, because you can see a pole from a distance, and when the engine passes it, you know that the moment has come to pull the fuse.

"And indeed, that's how it was this time. The engine that had been hit pulled the forward carriages, which were laden with tanks and cannons and the rear carriages were full of soldiers who were going to the front.

"The soldiers on guard opened hell-fire in all directions. We exploited the confusion for a hasty retreat, since the Germans would generally comb the area using dogs.

"We reached the camp just before morning. The commander of the small group, Galaschev, presented to the command with us and reported on the mission. However, Zhuraviov already knew of our success. He had been told that about eighty Germans had been wounded and killed and there was extensive damage to their battle equipment.

"This was the first sabotage operation on a train in which I took part."

The second sabotage mission in which Imber took part, and how he was abandoned on the battlefield.

A few days later, another order was received to go out to a train. The group was given the choice as to where to blow it up. They chose the Niekhachevo station, near the town of Ivatzevitch. Here, because of the dangerous swamps near the railway track, there was no sharp-eyed guard, since the Germans supposed that the partisans would not be able to reach the track.

The partisans who lay in wait for the train had to defend themselves against the mosquitoes, which swarmed upon them to suck their blood. They waited the whole night. The Germans lit up the area with rockets every few minutes, and the partisans began to fear that the night train might not arrive. Maybe the enemy had become aware of something suspicious and stopped all movement, and maybe other groups of partisans were active in the area, and maybe the train wasn't coming because of them?

Eventually, they heard the familiar clatter of a train approaching. The commander, Glazatchev, ordered Imber and another partisan to advance to the track. Imber says:

"We crawled through the mud very slowly. The train was near to us now, and there was no point in waiting. A last leap onto the tracks, and we manage to attach the detonator to the mine, which weighs about seven kilos. The long fuse which attaches to the ring of the safety catch must be stretched out on the ground and free, so that it can't be set off by accident before time. We retreat and wait a few seconds for the engine to approach the charge, and then a pull on the fuse and a big explosion, accompanied by a mighty flash, splits the silence. The engine started to roll down, dragging the carriages with it."

It was not easy to retreat, for in the meantime, morning had broken. The patrol soldiers went out and began to pour fire down towards the forest. The partisans had to go quite a long and dangerous way to the main road, where there would probably be a German ambush waiting for them. As usual, the road was full of military vehicles. The saboteurs found an opportune moment and crossed the road to reach their squad.

Glazatchev decided that not only would they blow up the train, but they would also cut the telephone wires in several places. In the squad, there was a nimble, light-footed young man, who climbed the poles like a cat and cut the wires with pliers.

Going back to camp, they marched by daylight, as the road passed through a friendly village. They sent a liaison, to gather wood for kindling, as it were, but actually to check what had happened to the railway track, and they themselves returned to the forest to rest. The liaison returned and told them they'd seen many ambulances standing by the line and carriages overturned in the canal. As evening approached, the group returned to camp and was welcomed with much jubilation and rejoicing. Their group of seven people developed into a tightly knit group, which carried out its missions fearlessly.

The Germans supposed that the partisans would not come back to sabotage the same place where they had already been active once, for fear of an enemy ambush. And so, they were less careful to guard these places. The partisans knew this and decided to return to carry out a second sabotage, near Bronna-Gora station. The station was near the Brest line and was the largest in the region, with many trains passing through it laden with soldiers and military equipment. But this time, Imber had a very difficult set of experiences:

"I was waiting, my comrades were asleep. Suddenly, I heard the clatter of a line-checking trolley, which was going by with the German guard, who were checking the line with the help of searchlights. I understood that soon a train would leave the station. I waited until the trolley went back to its starting point, but suddenly, the Germans lit up the whole place and opened fire from automatic weapons. Since that same evening, Tsirinski and I had to go up onto the track, I started to wake up the comrades from their sleep, but to no avail. They only scolded me for disturbing them and they went back to sleep. I had no alternative - I took the charge, started to crawl to the track and waited for the train. From a distance, I could already see the faint lights. I jumped on the track, managed to stick the detonator in and run away, as the engine was only a few dozen metres from me.

"Without waiting any longer, I pulled the fuse wire and as usual there was a loud explosion. The Germans opened a heavy bombardment towards the forest with everything they had. I reached the place where my comrades had been lying to cover me and found not a soul there. The same moment, I thought that maybe I'd not reached the right place, and I tried, despite the German fire, to go back and forth, but in vain. I was bewildered. It was dark all around me, I had no compass, and there was not a single star in the night sky. The trees around were bent over and behind me there was shooting without pause. I got further away from the place in order to reach the road. The forest was between the road and the railway line. The more I marched, the more the forest became more dense, and I sensed that I had lost my way. After walking for hours, I returned - I had got back to the railway track. In the darkness, I had thought that that was the road.

"I was in shock. I had no alternative but to retrace my steps, but in the meantime, dawn had broken. I cocked my submachine gun and stepped towards the road. Now the noise of vehicles indicated the direction. I waited a while, and took advantage of a pause in the traffic, then ran across the road in broad daylight and into the other side of the forest.

"Now it was easier for me. I reached the village Sokolova and went into the first house which was on my path. I asked if they had seen or heard partisans going by. The farmer, who was, by chance, one of our supporters, confirmed that in fact, partisans had passed through there on their way back from a mission and told him that their comrade had been killed or got lost. I didn't tell him that I was that man, but I asked him to show me the way to the partisan area. The farmer replied that it was too late, it was swarming with Germans there all the time, and it would be better for me to hide during the day in one of the woods on the edge of the village or to go into the cornfield. I had no alternative - I went into the cornfield in the middle of the village and lay down between the ears of corn. But I hadn't noticed that there was a road on the edge of the cornfield, which was constantly buzzing with movement, and the shouts of the Germans could be heard very clearly. A small movement on my part, and I would be found.

"The sun was boiling hot and burning my body, and thirst tormented me and made me despondent. I couldn't get comfortable for suffering. I wanted to get to sleep, but couldn't; the clattering of carts near me wouldn't let me sleep. That day I would have been prepared to give up half my life for a sip of water. Towards the evening, I got up out of the cornfield. The Germans had made off, and I entered the forest on my way to the camp.

"After marching a little while, I heard voices and saw figures approaching. One of them shouted out to me 'Don't move!' I called out the password, and they ordered me to come closer. I was amazed when I identified partisans from my group, the 56. Viktor Bistrov, the sergeant major, was walking at the head of the group. When they saw me alive and whole, they started to shout: 'How can it be? Sergeant major Glazatchev reported that you'd been killed!' I told them what had happened to me in the last few days, and despite that, the group commander, Viktor, who had led them to the ambush on the main Brest-Moscow road, asked me to accompany them, because their machine gunner was inexperienced. I asked to rest a little while and for a little bit of food, since I'd reached the limit of my strength.

"After I'd rested, we continued walking down the road in order to mine it. We tied the fuse wire to the detonator and gave the end of it to David Sofer, who had been asked to pull the fuse wire when the first vehicle reached the place where the charge was laid.

"This ambush had been planned following information brought back by the reconnaissance patrol, that the heads of the regional Gestapo were about to have a meeting that very day in the town of Kartuz-Bereza. We laid wait for our prey. And then we heard the chugging of cars. The tension rose and a small lorry appeared which was apparently intended to open up the way for the cars following. It passed over the charge undamaged. We didn't know the reason. Whilst arguing about the reason for it, we heard the rumbling of a car. Sofer pulled the cable and the car shot up in the air, turned over and rolled down into the ditch where we were sitting. Many other vehicles were advancing behind the car, and Germans jumped out of them into the ditch and took up positions. We opened fire the length of the ditch. They returned fierce and well-aimed fire, since they had seen the direction from which we were shooting. And then they got to on their feet and tried to surround us.

"There was nothing left for us, for Viktor and me, but to retreat. On the way, we met the whole gang who had retreated without me. Viktor was boiling with fury and threatened them with a military tribunal for running off and leaving us. Thirty partisans took part in the ambush, some of them from the Major's troop, and the rest from our troop. On the way, the Major's men returned to their camp, and we went on to ours. My return to camp astonished everybody, since they were sure I'd been killed. I was called to the chief of staff, Merzliakov, to report how it had happened, that the commander responsible for me, Glazatchev, had left me alone. I defended him: I said that I was very near to the spot of the explosion and my commander thought that I'd been killed and there was no point in carrying on. The matter ended with a scolding for several partisans.

In the company of the paratroopers

In October 1943, fourteen paratroopers reached the Budionni troop's area of activity for sabotage duties and political indoctrination. Their commander was Captain Shumilin, a man of about thirty, who came from Irkutsk in Siberia. The paratroopers were not familiar with this foreign region and asked Sikorski to loan them two local partisans, one who knew the methods of sabotaging the trains and the other, a veteran communist, who would serve the paratroopers as a leader in ideological propaganda. A. Imber was sent to them as a saboteur.

He was happy to work with and keep company with them, since the paratroopers were free of prejudices against the Jews and of anti-Semitic feelings. They had brought with them the latest materials and methods of sabotage. They decided to operate in a sabotage sector that Imber would choose, and he decided to go to the places which he knew from previous operations.

All the paratroopers, except for their commander, were young men. At the rear, they had been trained in the use of arms and in sabotage operations, but they lacked practical experience. They had brought with them an instrument for laying mines which looked like a frog, and was called in Russian Liagushka (frog) and was made of metal. When the engine pressed on the track, the "frog" would activate the charge, which was buried under the lines.

At that time, the Germans used to saw trees all along the length of the railway track, to a depth of thirty metres, and that made it very difficult for the partisans to get near the track without being discovered. Imber took the paratroopers to the Kartuz-Bereza district. The Germans continuously lit up the lines and would open fire, whilst their guard patrols checked the track all the time, forcing the saboteurs to lie close to the ground.

Time went by and the train had not arrived. The paratroopers were tense and nervous, but couldn't go back to base without carrying out the task. Eventually, they heard the clatter. Captain Shumilin asked Imber to go with one of the paratroopers to the track. However, instead of a train, a checking trolley arrived. The saboteurs waited until it had gone back, leapt onto the tracks and set up the 'frog'. Then they made off and lay down, watching. The engine reached the charge, the explosion reverberated and the carriages rolled down.

The Germans opened heavy fire. The paratroopers, for whom this was their baptism of fire, were alarmed. But Shumilin, who was a brave man, calmed them and explained that they had a great deal of work ahead of them: they had been charged with easing the pressure which the enemy was exerting on the Red Army at the front.

The paratroopers were a group united around their commander. He radiated authority and instilled courage in his men. Shumilin was a handsome-looking man, and his outward presentation also charmed his men. As they withdrew from the place of the explosion, he told his subordinates about his life in Irkutsk, how he had enrolled into the special group.

At dawn, when the paratroopers were already out of the danger area, they sat down to rest. Then one of the band drew out a bottle of vodka, and everyone had a sip of it. Imber didn't know how to drink and refused a sip. The paratroopers looked at him as if he were from another planet. They didn't want to offend him, but they pressed him from time to time to have a sip. Once for the sake of the homeland, once to honour their leader Stalin and once in honour of their successfully completed task! As evening approached, they reached their base. Shumilin reported their successful operation to Sikorski. The group had a shortwave transmitter, worked by a young Tartar man, and he would report the success of their activities to army H.Q., which by now had reached Gomel.

Shumilin took care that his men should behave appropriately. He would not allow them to take goods from the peasants, as the partisans were accustomed, but only to barter in exchange for soap or a silk scarf, which they sewed out of parachute fabrics. Some of the men in this group, would go out to the villages on political indoctrination missions and propaganda on the roles and activities of the partisans. Neither would he permit them to stay in base longer than necessary. "He would always urge us on," recounts Imber, "saying, 'The more trains blown up, the nearer the day of victory is.' From now on, we would go out to the railway tracks particularly in the direction of the front.

"Once, we decided," recalls Imber, "to set out for the Brest-Pinsk track, along which the trains moved to the Ukrainian front. It was a long way. We crossed many rivers in small boats, in the direction of Lake Sporovo, and also, the big lake towards the village of Nimerzhe, where the reconnaissance patrol of the Budionni troop was stationed, under the command of Avraham Bandt. The troop's stores and H.Q. were also in the same place.

"We left Nimerzhe in the evening and marched through the villages towards a big station on the Brest-Pinsk road. This territory was not forested and so we were marching right across, completely visible. In the distance, we could see the small town of Yanovo. Once, a large Jewish community resided there, but its residents had been completely annihilated. When we were near to the station, I said to Shumilin that I wanted to get up on the track in order to hide the mine in it. It wasn't my turn this time, and so Shumilin asked what I meant by my request. I told him that as a Jew, I wanted to take revenge on the Germans for all they did to my people. It turned out that Shumilin knew almost nothing about the Holocaust. In the city of his birth in Siberia, there were hardly any Jews living, and the residents didn't know about the Holocaust in Europe.

"When we got near the station, we saw a lot of shadows moving along the railway track in the darkness. We understood that these were soldiers of the German guard. We decided to allow them to continue. We followed them until they went off and then we leapt up onto the track. We connected the frog mine, and withdrew to a distance from which we could see how it worked.

"After a while, the train appeared in the dark, its lights shining, and drew near to the mine. We heard a loud explosion, and the whole area shook from the force of it. The Germans were pouring out heavy fire and firing shells, and the whole area was lit up like daylight. We ran off some distance, as we didn't have the force to conduct a battle in an open territory, and we kept throwing ourselves down on the sticky ground. We got back to the village through which we had passed on our way to the track, and asked the farmer who had guided us to our target, to clarify, as soon as possible what the outcome of the explosion was. After a few days, he reported to us that the train had been taking fuel to the front, and everything in it had been destroyed, though there had not been a fire, and the military escorts of the train had been killed.

"Three months passed. According to the agreement with the commander of the Budionni troop, to which Imber belonged, Shumilin should have returned him to the troop. But the captain approached Sikorski and asked him to free Imber and transfer him to his disposal. Imber was happy to remain with the paratroopers, as relationships in the group were like those of a tightly knit family. He continued to fight with the paratroopers until his liberation in the summer of 1944."

The death of commander Shumilin

The activity on the railway track became increasingly difficult owing to the reinforcement of the Germans and their supporters, who guarded them, and also because of the cruel reprisals of the enemy, who were in the habit of setting fire to the houses of peasants who supported the partisans and murdering many of the village people., The Germans would frequently set ambushes on the partisan route to the railway track, and they escaped with difficulty and suffered losses. Despite this, almost every day German trains were blown up.

In May 1944, Shumilin's group was working close to Antopol. The group had crossed Lake Sporovo in boats so as to rest a little in the village of Nimerzhe and from there, to go on to the track. Close to this place, a German garrison and a Hungarian support force were stationed. The peasants lived there in constant fear, as a German reprisal brigade would come almost every day into villages of that area to burn houses and execute people who they suspected of supporting the partisans.

The Shumilin group went into the village to check it out for Germans. Later, it turned out that there were Germans there, and they had entered a house which stood on a hill overlooking the area and held the owner so that he would be unable to warn the partisans. The band of saboteurs didn't know about this and arranged a place to bury the mine. Shumilin felt ill, complaining of severe headaches and his men persuaded him not to go out this time to the railway track himself, as usual, but to wait for them at an arranged place. Shumilin handed over command of the operation to Imber and wished his men success. The group went out to the track, and managed to blow up the train, but as they withdrew, they ran into heavy fire from an ambush. The saboteurs tried to rescue their commander who had remained in the village, but they couldn't find him in the place which had been fixed. They found him in another place, badly wounded in his stomach and his legs. The partisans took him to a yard behind a house and told him not to shoot, so as not to reveal his location. They took up positions in the cemetery and protected themselves behind a heap of stones. But Shumilin opened fire all over. The Germans captured him while he was in a mortal state and transferred him to Antopol. In Antopol, he died, and the Germans buried him in the yard of their headquarters.

After the liberation of Antopol, his fighters found his grave, disinterred his body and buried him with a full military ceremony. This is what A. Imber says about the beloved commander:

"We went back to the base, broken and exhausted from this huge loss. Shumilin was not only a commander, but he was also a faithful comrade to everybody. Everyone who knew him mourned bitterly his untimely death."

During the battles which preceded the liberation, Imber and his friend, Ya'akov Khatzkelevitch, found themselves near the town of Kobrin, where they met up with a reconnaissance patrol of the Red Army. Imber was liberated on 24th. July 1944.[129]

From the memoirs of Ya'akov Khatzkelevitch

Nimerzhe is a small village, not far from the towns of Drogichin and Antopol, small towns where there was an enemy presence. The village lies next to a river, which was the border between the partisan troops and the Germans.

"The base of our unit was in an isolated lone farm a distance of half a kilometre from the village, which served as a base for supplies for the troop and H.Q. for the division. I stayed in this base for about half a year, without visiting the troop's camp. From the base, we would go out to operations, and afterwards, come back to it. We had food in abundance and also alcohol - Samogon (home-made, unrefined spirits made from seeds or potatoes), which we produced from apparatus which we had on the spot.

"Once I was wounded in my leg. They informed me that the Germans had arrived, but they were wearing different uniforms from the usual ones. They appeared looking very spick and span. We lived at that time in houses very close to each other, on the bank of the river. When the 'Germans' came near the houses, we saw that these soldiers were wearing yellow uniforms. It turned out that they were Hungarians in the service of the Germans. Exchanges of fire started between them and us. As I skipped from one house to another, I was hit by a bullet in my thigh. The Hungarians got right up to the river, but they didn't cross it. Apparently, they were afraid. In the meantime, the news had gone round the camp that I had been killed. The comrades

---

[129] *From the memoirs of A. Imber*

dragged me to one side and called a doctor from the camp. The doctor arrived and was very angry that he had been called for my non-serious wound.

"They transferred me to the partisan hospital forty kilometres away. I stayed in the hospital about a month and returned to the unit in March 1944.

"We were three Jews in our unit, Avraham Bandt, commander, Niounya Tsirinski and me. Altogether, our unit numbered nine fighters. Generally, Yermolenko, who was an excellent commander, would come out with us to operations. In our group, there was also a partisan who had come to us from the Ukrainians, who was an alcoholic and raped girls in the village. He ended up being executed. Once, when we were lying in ambush on the Brest-Moscow road, our goal was to capture "Lashon" (tongue). [Lashon (*Hebrew: tongue, language>information* - refers to prisoners of war from whom information might be extracted about what was happening at the front.) refers to prisoners of war from whom information might be extracted about what was happening at the front.] We waited all the night. Quite suddenly, we saw in the distance, a vehicle covered in tarpaulin. Yermolenko ordered us to open fire. When we stopped it, it turned out that this was a mobile workshop. We took some of the tools and the three German captives and went back."

A saboteur unit, in which Khatzkelevitch worked, remained active in 1944 too, and took eleven German trains off the track during the first three months. His saboteur squad got stuck in the marshes and was in a very difficult state, without food or drinking water. They stayed there, cut off from the H.Q. and surrounded by enemy forces, and then one morning, the sounds of canon thunder reached them. When a patrol band went out to check who was firing, they saw to their amazement, a long convoy of Red Army soldiers. Khatzkelevitch was liberated from his partisan activity in July 1944.

Zerach Kremin in the Kotovski troop

Zerach Kremin was one of the most active partisans in blowing up enemy trains. As the commander of a squad of saboteurs in the Kotovski troop which was founded on 26th. April 1943, the blowing up of twenty-two enemy trains with live freight and military equipment is credited to him.[130] He recounts something of the part he played in the war of the railway tracks in the burning summer of 1943 and the experiences of his life until he was liberated until the spring of 1944.

---

[130] *The number of trains which were blown up is cited in the official list (boevaya kharakteristika) which was awarded him after the war by the partisan command.*

1. My new submachine gun

"In the summer of 1943, I was attacked by very bad toothache. I decided to contact the dentist, Dr Liepak, who was serving next to the H.Q. in the forest of Sporovo, about a hundred and fifty kilometres from where our troop was stationed across the Dnieper-Bug canal. I received permission and set out with a few comrades. At HQ, Dr Liepak decided to take the infected tooth out.

"He sat me down on a tree trunk and began the work of extraction with tongs, without any anaesthetic. Partisans collected around me to see how I would react. They were waiting for me to shriek with pain. Of course, I didn't utter a sound.

"The Komsomol envoy, Lizhin, reached H.Q.. Representatives of the troops were called to a meeting. Since some of the troops of the division which were encamped on the other side of the canal had no representatives at the meeting, they asked me to represent the Kotovski troop. The paratrooper told us about life behind the front and about the task which had been imposed on the partisans. Soviet intelligence had been informed that the Germans had no rail line stock here and most of it was west of Warsaw, and therefore, we had to blow up the railway tracks. There would be a pause in the transit of the trains to the front and back from it until they could bring new lines.

"Lizhin brought T.N.T. material in the shape of eggs, each one weighing seventy-five grams. In the middle of the 'egg', there was a hole for the detonator, and that was worked with the help of a Bickford fuse. On this festive occasion, he distributed new submachine guns made in 1943 to all the commanders.

"Sikorski presented me to the guest as a partisan who had managed so far to blow up ten trains, and the paratrooper gave me a new submachine gun. I knew very well that in the troop, the commander would take this new weapon from me, and so, I asked Proniagin, who was already acting as division chief of staff, to give me a letter confirming that this weapon had been given to me as a personal gift.

"I hastened to return to the troop so that they would have time to organise for the operation, which was to be carried out by all troops on a particular night. On my return, we got organised together with the activists from the surrounding villages, for the whole length of the Brest-Pinsk railway track, and went out on the designated evening. We took up positions by the railway lines and began to stick our charges to the lines. On a command, we set alight the fuse wires and distanced ourselves from the place. Everything worked. We heard explosions, and lightning split the whole sky, which could be seen by the neighbouring brigades. That night, the railway line was blown up from the front to the Polish border, The Germans were astonished. They didn't know what was happening. There were garrisons which abandoned their positions for fear that the Russian army was parachuting in.

"We continued to blow up the rail track every evening for about a month. After several days, the Germans understood what was happening at night, and would quickly repair the railway track. Nevertheless, we hit hard at the smooth running of their trains."

2. Alone in the rye field

"On one of the summer days in 1943, we went out, a group of five saboteurs with a mine, to blow up a train on the Brest-Moscow line, at the Bludien station. The forests in this area were sparse, and we had to reach a distance of two kilometres from the target and spend a whole day in the bushes. We crossed the Brest-Moscow road and reached the place where we were to camp, but towards morning, shepherds appeared around us, and although we moved around so they wouldn't discover our location, they did discover us. We held them until evening so they wouldn't be able to inform the Germans about us, and we let them go when we went out to the railway track. Opposite our position, there was a tall building, and to us, it looked abandoned. When we got close to the lines, we heard an approaching train in the distance. We unrolled the cable quickly. I left my comrades by the end of the cable, and I ran to the lines with the mine. I managed to lay it between the tracks and stick the detonator in, then I ran back the length of the cable to my comrades. I told them to withdraw and to wait for me when they heard the sound of the explosion. In order to make the running easier for me, I gave them my gun, and I left myself only with a pistol and a hand grenade. When the train arrived, I pulled on the wire and heard the explosion. Then I rolled up the cable and ran back to my comrades.

"The Germans who were asleep in that building woke up, and began to rain lethal fire in my direction. They lit up the whole area with rockets. I lay flat on the ground and moved further off crawling. When I reached the place where my comrades should have been waiting for me, I couldn't find anyone.

"I began to march southwards according to the compass, so that I could cross the Brest-Moscow road. I walked about an hour, but I couldn't see the road. I sat down to rest and put the steel cable down. Then I noticed that the compass was showing a different direction. I realised that the cable had distorted the compass, and instead of walking south, I'd been going west the length of the whole road.

"I changed direction and reached the road, but it was a place I didn't know. Across the road was the green of an unfamiliar forest. I turned south and reached the edge of the forest. Before my eyes there stretched out a large village, and in the distance, there was no forest to be seen.

"Dawn had broken long ago, and it was a bright clear day. I reached the first house, knocked on the door and asked for water to drink. The startled farmer refused to open to me, because partisans hadn't yet been seen in this area. I knew that not far from the village was a police station. I decided to go in the direction of the station, and about half a kilometre from it I went into a rye field, and lay down there to sleep.

"At noon, I heard the voices of peasants around me. Suddenly a dog came up to me. I offered him a piece of bread, which I had received from the farmer, and he made off. This day stretched out like an eternity for me. In the evening, I left the field. I approached an isolated house, told the farmer that I was a partisan fighter, and asked him to harness a horse and cart and bring me to a territory which was under the control of the partisans. We travelled all night. Just before morning, we reached my brigade. The boys told me that they had fled when fire had opened on them, because they thought I'd been killed. It turned out that the explosion had been crowned with great success: twenty-four carriages laden with Ferdinands (mobile canon of the Ferdinand brand) had gone off the tracks.

3. How they taught me to drink

"In the autumn of 1943, five of us again went out to get a train off the tracks in the Drohitchin region. When we drew near to the target, we had to wait until darkness, because here too, trees had been felled a width of a hundred metres from the railway tracks, and we could have been seen. I saw that the area was muddy. All along the track, there was an embankment to a height of about four meters. When darkness fell, I went up to the lines, buried the mine and rolled out the cable. At the other end, I stood two men. The others waited at the edge of the forest.

"And then we heard the sound of train approaching. I stuck the detonator into the mine, and I began to run along the cable to its other end. I released the two partisans to run to the edge of the forest, and I stayed on the spot to wait for the train. When the engine came near, I pulled the cable. I heard a loud explosion, and began to run to the forest.

"The Germans lit up the area with rockets and were shooting hard in the direction of the forest. I advanced at a crawl, and reached the place where I had left the comrades, and again, found no-one.

"I despaired searching, and began to walk south with the help of the compass. When I left the forest, I noticed the light twinkling in the window of a solitary house. I approached carefully and peeked inside. And then I saw my band sitting round a table, eating and drinking. I was furious. I burst in and shouted, 'You leave your comrade *and* you're drinking and getting drunk!'

"They hurriedly invited me to the table and explained to me that they were drinking to the eternal memory of my soul, because they were sure that I had been killed. I was very indignant about it, but they were already tipsy and they filled me a cup and pressed me to drink. I refused. I explained that I had never drunk alcohol in my life, and then the commander took out his pistol and shouted, 'Drink, or I'll kill you!' I was very angry, but I drank, and I immediately became drunk. The next day, they brought me to the camp, and that's how I learnt to drink spirits."

4. How we closed the Brest-Warsaw railway line

In honour of the celebration of October 1943 (see above), we decided to blow up two trains on the Brest-Moscow track. Again, we were a group of five men, and this time, Zhenia Eichenbaum came out with us on the mission. We arrived near the railway track by the Orantchitsi station and were given hospitality by a farmer known to us. On the night of 7th. November, we approached the target and blew up a train that was going east, and then that same night, we went westward and blew up a second train that was travelling east with a cargo of cement. It was a rainy night, and snow fell mixed with rain. The open carriages, which fell off the track, became wet and a lump of concrete formed on them, and it closed the two lines. The local Germans couldn't move the lumps of concrete off the track. By the time they'd brought the cranes from Warsaw, the track had been blocked for seventy-two hours.

5. The war of the pennants

"In January 1944, the partisans from the Kotovski troop carried out operations to torment the Germans. They would stick small flags with words like: 'Death to the German conquerors' on the railway tracks, and mine them. The Germans who went to pull off the flags off the track would step on the mine and be blown to bits.

"But sometimes, the flags were deliberately not mined, so the enemy, having learnt from bitter experience, would stand and shoot and shoot at the flags from a distance, to get rid of them, and the partisans would watch and burst out laughing."

Memorial tablet to those who fell in the Gantsevitch area, next to the monument, among them Herzl Shepetinski R.I.P

CHAPTER SEVENTEEN: Members of the 51 in the Vasiliyev troop
Good integration

There remained about thirty people in Boroviki. Their weapons hadn't been taken, but they hadn't been furnished with any information with which they could have become orientated to this unfamiliar area, and neither had they been given any instructions on how to operate in the future. Yasha Shepetinski was wounded in his leg from the Chemieli battle and not yet fully recovered. He was the gunner in his squad, but with his injury, his machine gun had been passed to someone else. Herzel made sure he got his gun back. After the meeting with the Vasiliyev people, they agreed, as related above, to accept some of the people who'd been abandoned.[131]

The Vasiliyev troop was organised in June 1942, out of men from the Red Army who had been cut off behind the German lines in the Gansevitch and the Krasnaya Sloboda regions. The troop commander was Vasiliyev, who was nicknamed by his men, Uncle Vasya. He was a tall, slender man, who elicited respect and gave off authority. He had a warm smile. Vasiliyev was accustomed to dress in Soviet army officer's uniform, and he was a well organised man who demanded neatness and discipline from his men. The commissar of the troop was A.M. Ziborov, a well-built Russian with the face of a learned man. He also took care to dress in Soviet army uniform, and he would strap on a pistol and submachine gun and always accompany the commander.

And these are the ex-members of the 51 brigade who were accepted into the Vasiliyev troop and integrated into a small group: the brothers Herzel and Ya'akov Shepetinski, their sister Raya, their cousin Zvi Shepetinski and three Polish refugees:Feitl, Tchertok, and Kuba Zilberhaft, who had become citizens after the fall of Poland in Slonim. The others included were Tsadok Deretchinski, Yitzhak (Ilya) Gratchuk, his sister, Musia, and Boris Yevshitski - they were some of the people freed from the Kosovo ghetto.

Ya'akov served in the small group as a gunner, and Raya, who was only fourteen, worked in the facility. She had a sweet voice and loved to sing. Tschertok was a plumber by profession, about thirty years old, stocky and a good worker. Feitl was a tall young man in his mid-twenties, formerly a student at Warsaw University, who came from a good family and was a little spoilt. It wasn't easy for him to get used to the partisans' living conditions and physical work. You could see how he felt about it in his eyes, which were always sad.

Tsadok Derechinski was a swarthy young man, quite short, reflective and disciplined. His sister, Dvorah, stayed with the Shchors troop, with her husband, Volodya Piletzki, the Belorussian who had rescued her and Tsadok from the ghetto. Yitzhak Gratchuk was a tall and somewhat thickset young man, one of the veterans from the Slonim underground and one of the people

---

[131] *From the memoirs of Ya'akov and Zvi Shepetinski*

who had been active in the German loot store. His sister, Musia, who was short and plump, was in her mid-thirties, a seamstress by profession, and she worked in the services in the camp. Boris (Dov) Yevshitski was one of the older people in the Jewish partisans' group and almost thirty and was an accountant and son of a wealthy family from Ivatzevitch. He was a quiet and delicate person who would faithfully carry out anything required of him, but would never push to be among the first. Lastly, Kuba the "Radist", that is, Ya'akov Zilberhaft. He was also a refugee from Poland, a sad, introverted young man, a radio technician and signaller by profession. After links were created with the forest, he was among the first sent out, at the request of the Shchors partisans. Kuba did not stand out as a fighter.

The people from the 51 brigade were absorbed easily into the Vasiliyev troop, and their physical and emotional condition improved.

The battle for Krasnaya Sloboda (28th. October 1942)

A German garrison was stationed in Krasnaya Sloboda, formerly Vizna, and a functional active Belorussian police station, so there was a concentration of many collaborators. The H.Q. of the troop decided to defeat the garrison and to turn the police out of the town.

An order was given to prepare for a combat mission. The order surprised some of the fighters, although it might have been expected because the reconnaissance patrols had been stepped up lately. Everyone was ordered to present on parade and the commander ordered preparation to move out. The way to the destination went without incident. The 51 men were among the marchers and in the camp there remained only the service workers, the sick and the guards.

The partisans marched all night through the forest, in territory a long way off from the villages, so as not to be seen or to arouse suspicion among the peasants. Smoking was forbidden. The 51 members observed complete silence and were deep in thought.

Dawn broke at about four o'clock, when they halted and had a briefing on the target and the aims of the operation. And these were: to conquer the German garrison command building and that of the Belorussian gendarmerie and police, to take the military hospital and the guard that was in it, and finally - to clear the town of collaborators. For that purpose, a small unit of patrolmen was identified headed by the commander of the troop's special department. Some of the troop lay in ambush on the approaches to the town to prevent reinforcements arriving and to prevent the enemy and the collaborators escaping

A flare signalled the start of the operation. The attacking squad had to pass almost half-way through the town in order to reach the hospital. Zvi Shepetinski was active in that unit and Yasha was in the unit that attacked the command.

It appeared that the command was situated not far from the hospital. This was a single-storey building in which guards resided, and they started to return fire. The partisans fired on the guards and wiped them out. The German military doctor was shot while he was trying to run away, and the German soldiers were wiped out, among them, pilots who were lying in their beds. Some of them were taken for interrogation. The Belorussian collaborators were shot on the spot. They weren't treated with mercy, for the partisans were full of rage at these traitors. Several German guards went up onto the roof and were shooting from there. The saboteurs who were on the offensive, had prepared a charge of explosives, and one of them crawled to the building and laid the charge by the door. When it exploded, a wide hole gaped in the door. The partisans burst inside and eliminated the enemy fire. After this battle, they saw that inside there were many more Germans than they had originally supposed. The search revealed an underground tunnel, which led from the building to the fence bordering with the fields. There, there were several reinforced bunkers, which had been used in defence operations against partisans coming from the forest. After clearing the building, they set fire to it.

The police command was eliminated with very little opposition. Some of the police escaped through the yards. The rest surrendered.

The unit which had attacked the garrison command approached the bunkers. There were five in all. The Germans returned lethal fire, concentrated and precise, from the apertures of the shelters. Some of the attackers were wounded. This was a battle of uneven conditions. The men on the offensive were completely visible, and the defence were sitting hidden in their bunkers. After the battle had gone on over an hour, it was decided to lay siege to the Germans and to "bother" them from time to time, so that none of them would be able to get out. The enemy was cut off, since the telephone communications had been sabotaged too.

The food and medication store was next to the hospital. Some of the partisans set about emptying the store. A partisan driver went up to a Soviet lorry, from the loot which the Germans had taken in the war, and called out, "Load it on, guys, as quick as you can!" The store worker, who had opened to us, stood there stunned, unable to utter a word. The driver waved an improvised red flag from the lorry, and after about half an hour, moved off towards the town. Another lorry was laden with various essential goods, including petrol.

The partisans burst into the houses of police and enemy supporters and put their whole contents at the disposal of the population. At noon, the partisans retreated towards the forest. Several of the fighters went by the priest's house. He had apiary. They poured buckets of water into the hive, which neutralised the bees, and drew out full honeycombs.

The squad to which the Slonim people belonged would go out frequently on operations to acquire various foodstuffs to prepare a stock for the winter months, which were approaching. They brought to the forest mainly flour, salt and slices of pork, which they took from the farms of peasants who supported the enemy. Salt was a very sought-after commodity in the villages, and on this excursion, a whole load of sacks of salt fell into the partisans' hands. They also used them to bargain with the peasants who supported the partisans and their helpers.

Winter 1942-1943: Daily life in the troop

The days and nights were already very cold. One had to make sure of warm clothing, which was confiscated from enemy supporters in the villages. The troop was preparing to move to a new place, where they could dig out underground shelters.

One day in November, the order was given to prepare to move out. Carts were enrolled and the belongings and equipment of the brigade and the store were loaded on them. The lorry, which had been taken from the enemy loot, was taken apart and put completely out of use. The convoy moved towards the marshes of Pinsk, where there was a concentration of about two thousand partisans. This was also where the troops were unified into the Pinsk Division, under the command of Komarov.

The Vasiliyev battalion was located in a dense pine forest. The camp was set up on a hill, so that rainwater wouldn't penetrate into the shelters. Each unit received its place to erect a shelter and the building went on for about a week. The battalion, to which 51 people belonged, had two platoons, and each platoon had two squads. The partisans brought the necessary tools for building the earth huts. They would go out to the nearby villages to look for abandoned shacks and take the doors and doorframes out, and any other parts for their 'houses'. Zvi Shepetinski was among those who dug and sawed the trees. He was used to this work from the days of his parents' house and from his frequent visits to the sawmill in Slonim. He would load the heavy logs on his shoulders and carry them to the designated place. He wanted to prove to his non-Jewish comrades that he didn't fall beneath them in terms of manual labour. His comrades in the unit were mainly from Siberia and had never before met a Jew where they lived, and had only heard legends about them. In these stories, the Jews were described as black devils with horns and they believed these stories. Eventually, when they came to know the Jews, friendly relationships were established between them and their Jewish comrades.

In each earth hut, there were four bunks, built from tree branches and padded with hay and hand-woven, rustic-style blankets. Eventually, they managed to add to their huts stoves of tin or iron, which served to warm up the place or to prepare an evening meal: fried potatoes or fried cow's liver, freshly prepared. In every hut like this, there lived about six to eight partisans. Generally, the Siberians and the Jews had separate quarters. Zvi lived in the fourth and last hut in the row, with Tschertok, Feitl, and Yevshitski and three Russian partisans. They belonged to the first platoon. Partisans from the second platoon lived in the huts opposite them, and behind them, in a small, separate hut, lived the commander of the troop and his wife. The troop's command building was a few dozen meters away and next to it, there was a domestic unit. All the brigades were placed around the central command.

Winter came. The snow covered the huts until it was impossible to see them, even from quite near. Relationships between the Jewish partisans and the non-Jews in the Vasiliyev troop were usually reasonable, but here too, the Jews occasionally found evidence of hostility and contempt. Zvi recalls this particular incident.

Standing up to challenges

The months that Zvi lived in the conditions of the forest, constantly in the open air, toughened his body and raised his fitness. He was young and healthy. The partisans' conditions and the constant movement outside, had a good effect on him. After months of hunger and lacking everything in the ghetto, he felt that he had become stronger and that he was no less fit, physically, than his non-Jewish friends. This sense gave him self-confidence. On one occasion, he was faced with the need to prove that a Jew, too, can have self-respect, no less than a non-Jew. And this is his story:

"Once, when I was serving as a guard in the unit in the camp, between the huts I came across Vas'ca, the Belorussian, and he was doing something that is not acceptable to do in a public place. I reprimanded him for that, but he answered with a juicy curse, and said that he didn't take orders from a Jewboy like me.

"This happened at noon, and so there were witnesses to it. I answered him that if I were not in my role and bearing arms, I would teach him the lesson he deserved. He laughed at me in front of everybody and said that in a while, when I finished my watch, he would wait for me in the square to see what a strong man I am.

"This Vas'ca demonstrated his anti-Semitism at every turn: he would imitate the halting Russian of some of the Jews, whose gutteral 'r' stood out, and was also accustomed to tell tasteless and humiliating jokes about Jews. My Jewish comrades tried to convince me not to take on this Belorussian, because he was bigger and stronger than me, and not to arouse any more tensions than those that already existed in relation to the Jews, but I persisted, and at the appointed hour, I presented in the square opposite Vas'ca. Our comrades from the unit had collected there to watch this unusual event, that is, wrestling for honour, with shouts of encouragement. We were both wearing winter clothing, which made movement heavy.

"Vas'ca stood in front of me, certain of his strength, and with a mocking smile, provoking me: nu, nu? I was burning with anger, but tried not to let my feelings overcome me so that I wouldn't fail and make my Jewish comrades fail with me. He pushed me with his shoulder, to laughter from his comrades. When he tried to do this a second time, I punched his face with all my might. He was stunned and swayed from side to side, and then I sent him another punch on the chin, and knocked him to the ground, with blood pouring from his nose. I asked him if that was enough for him, or did he want to go on? Now his friends intervened. They brought him a snowball for his nose, to stop the bleeding. They helped him get up, and insisted that we shake hands. That's what we did, and everybody dispersed to their huts.

"The troop commander heard about this. I was afraid that they would make me a discipline problem, but everything went safely. The troop commander, when I met him by chance, said to me, 'Grishka Molodietz ('good fellow') and said no more. In the eyes of my comrades from Siberia, I had changed from a quiet Jewish lad to a good chap and their friend. Respect for the other Jews was raised and anti-Semitic mocking in our presence ceased.

"My friends from Siberia tried to persuade me that Russian blood flows in my veins. I explained to them that they don't know Jews. The Jews, if they only have the chance, surpass the Russians in courage and daring. At this time, the comments about Jewish fearfulness from our arms-bearing comrades decreased, comments that had hurt us a great deal and were demoralising.

Producing "do it yourself" TNT in the troop

During this season, the troop was active mainly in the acquisition of food and other essential goods. Sabotage operations in the winter were few, and one reason was the lack of the explosive T.N.T., which they used to drop for the special paratroop unit, and for their use alone. To obtain explosives from the German stores, like we did once, was very difficult. We had no alternative but to create it from bombs from planes and unexploded shells, which it was still possible to find in the fields or neglected store sheds. They would bring them to the camp, take apart their mechanisms and smelt their explosives in a primitive and dangerous manner. They would suspend the bomb at an angle above a small bonfire without the flame reaching the material, but only heating the outer casing. When the material became warm and liquid, it would drip into a square wooden dish. When it cooled, it would become a TNT brick and they would set the detonator in that. More than once, while they were attending to the bombs, disasters occurred. The bomb exploded and those involved with it were torn to shreds.

Jewish artisans in the troop

The ex-51 group members met other Jews in the Vasiliyev battalion. One of them was the butcher, Mendel Rubin, a well-grown and masculine-looking young man, a Polish refugee. He was engaged in his profession in the troop. With his great strength, he would knock down a beast with a quick turn of its head and slay it, open the skin and prepare the meat, quickly and efficiently. Sometimes he would give the fighters the liver and the spleen, and the partisans would prepare with this a festive evening meal, with the addition of a sip of vodka.

The partisans met Rubin when he was walking with the two Weintraub brothers, who were barbers by profession. They were accepted by virtue of their two rifles. In their free time, the Weintraubs would work as barbers.

In the brigade, there were several partisans who were good singers and played the accordion. They used to make the boring time when we were stuck in the huts in the long winter evenings more pleasant by singing and playing. In the unit, there were also several 'professional' dancers, experts in "Kazatchok" dances. However, we had to absolutely implore them before they would see fit to move their feet in their national dance.

The days of the manhunt of February 1943

The Rifle Incident.

At the start of February, Zvi had a very bad experience, which almost cost him his life. He was on guard in his unit, while several brigades from the troop went out on a major acquisition mission, to equip themselves with foodstuffs for the freezing months which awaited the partisans. His cousin, Herzel, stayed in the camp, because he was sick and in bed with a temperature. On occasion, Zvi would go into his hut to put some more kindling on his fire and to give the patient some "tea", as they called boiling water.

The warmth of the hut made him sleepy. Then suddenly, a cry from Herzel woke him. He also heard the voice of the brigade's quartermaster calling his name. The first sleighs had already returned from an operation, and the quartermaster already blamed Zvi for non- fulfilment of his role as guardsman and sleeping while he was on duty. He asked Zvi to give up his weapon. Zvi justified himself, saying that he was in the sick Herzel's hut in order to give him a drink and presented as soon as he heard the quartermaster's call. However, his pleading didn't help at all. The quartermaster and the troop's commander took his rifle from him by force and even though the time that Zvi was slumbering in the hut didn't last more than a quarter of an hour, he was in for a severe punishment, and very worried about his situation.

The acquisition operation had not succeeded. The partisans who had gone out on this mission had found enemy reinforcements in the villages and had come back to camp empty-handed. The reconnaissance reported that the Germans were in control of all the roads in the area, and they were preparing a manhunt and aiming to surround the partisans.

A command was given to prepare to move. Zvi was preoccupied by his problem. The commander of his unit went to the troop commander to ask that his weapon should be returned. The reply was that the weapon would be returned to him in time, when he demonstrated excellent behaviour. In the meantime, he found out that his rifle had been given to a new partisan who lived in his hut and had been accepted to the troop a short while ago without arms.

The partisans set out in sleighs, loading only what they absolutely needed, like foodstuffs, which were distributed among the units, so as not to weigh down the horses. The stores and kitchen equipment were loaded on a special sleigh. On the way, snow began to fall, which was a blessing for the partisans, because it covered their footsteps. On the way, they met up with various partisan units, who were also moving towards the Pinsk marshes, in order not to be surrounded.

On their way, they passed a partisan unit which was marching mainly on foot. This was a group from the Sovietskaya Belorussia troop, who operated in the forests of Volchye-Nori. Zvi knew a neighbour from Slonim among the marchers, Max Astrinski, a well-off Jew, who had been well-built. Now he looked shrivelled, dressed in rags. The man embraced Zvi and tears rolled from his eyes. When Zvi asked how his parents and brothers were who had stayed in the forest, the man stammered and said nothing clearly. He knew that they were dead, but he couldn't tell their son. The children of the Shepetinski family never saw their parents and their little brothers again.

The death of the Jewish violinist

Every time the situation in the partisan camps became more dangerous, the situation of the Jews worsened. Not long before, a Jew from Baranovitch had been accepted into the Vasiliyev troop, and he had arrived at the brigade with his violin. The man had fled from a labour camp, wandering in the forests and the villages, and he would play for the peasants for food. He was an excellent player. In the camp, he had played for the Germans and his death sentence had been postponed and he managed to escape. When he came to the troop, they interrogated him for a long time and wanted to know how he had stayed alive when other people had died. The partisans were suspicious of him because he had survived and also had managed to rescue his violin.

The man was not armed, and so he was engaged in various domestic jobs. In the evening, he would play for the partisans, Russian folk songs. Now, during the flight, he had been made responsible for a sack of salt. It seems that this man had fallen asleep on the sleigh and had lost the sack of salt. It was not known if the sack had fallen from the sleigh or if his partisan 'comrades' had stolen it in order to do business later on with peasants and to exchange it for more sought after goods. However, the brigade quartermaster and another partisan asked him to accompany them, and they shot him with a pistol in his head.

In the Gotsk region

On 12th. February, the Vasiliyev troop reached the Gotsk area and stopped between the villages of Gotzk and Vasino. They were bombed by enemy planes, but suffered no losses. After a few days, some other troops from the Pinsk division clashed with the enemy. On 14th. February, the division managed to get out of the encirclement and reached the Logishin and Telekhani area. On the night of 15th. February, they crossed the railway track between Bostin and Malkovitchi stations and stopped near the village of Plotnitza. They stayed here briefly.

On 5th. March, the Germans again started a manhunt. They attacked the Shesh and Tchapayev troops, after those troops had initiated a distraction attack on the German garrison force of three to four hundred men in the village of Swiataya Volya. Even though the Germans had received reinforcements, the partisans managed to get away across the Vigonov Lake. However, as has already been said, the division had losses: the commander of the troop, Dombrovski, and the chief of staff, Bobrov, both fell in battle. The partisans were in a bad way - they were lacking in ammunition, and they had no food. The many wounded received no attention because of the lack of medical equipment and bandages. Luckily, spring came early, the snows were melting, and the swamps in the region provided them with a protective belt. On 9th. March, the troop again crossed the rail track on the Luninietz-Baranovitch line, and camped near the village of Novosiolki, where the Brest division had previously been active. Now they felt more confident and could turn again to fighting the enemy. In fact, on 9th. March, they attacked a German military train, which was travelling to the front to Diatlovitchi.

In this difficult period of the manhunt, the wounded suffered a great deal. So that they wouldn't hinder the troop's movement, and to get away from the enemy, they were left on a lonely island in the swamps, under the care of one or two nurses. The Vasiliyev troop also reached the banks of the river Lahn and positioned themselves on a hill in dense forest, protected by rivers and swamps.

Herzel Shepetinski falls in battle (14th. March 1943)

On 13th. March, a patrol group in which there were ten people from the unit of Ya'akov Shepetinski set out from the troop. They went to the village of Chudin and other villages. Yasha stayed to guard the entrances to the forest with his machine gun and his second in command, Volodya, from the village of Kolki. Herzel went with the patrol. The next morning, only seven of them returned. In the camp, the commander of the unit, Vas'ka Kotchiriganov, who was also commander of the reconnaissance patrol, told them what had happened in the village. Three volunteers had entered the village of Chudinu: the lieutenant, Volodia, Kolka, who came from a local village and Herzel, who went with them. When they came near to the village, heavy fire opened up on them, and hand grenades were thrown. The two first men in the group were killed on the spot. Their bodies were smashed. Herzel was wounded in his leg. He bandaged it himself and crawled along to get away from the village, but he hit an ambush of Latvians, who had noticed him and wanted to catch him alive. Three Latvians came up to him and ordered him to get up. Herzel said that he was wounded in his leg and couldn't stand. Then they ordered him to throw his weapon to them. He obeyed. Two Latvians approached him in order to pull him up, and then he let off two grenades, which killed him and the two Latvians together with him, the third one being badly wounded.

Yasha went out with another partisan to the place where this had happened. They found the two first men who had been slain near the outer village houses, and Herzel's crushed body thirty metres away. They collected the bodies with the help of local peasants, who were Baptists, and they brought them to bury them with their own, near the local cemetery.[132]

Founding of the Lenin brigade (4th. April 1943)

In March 1943, the Vasiliyev troop crossed the railway track near Lushcha station on their way back to their old locations in the region of the Chuchevitchi and Novosiolki villages. Now, the partisans had a short breathing space, since the regular enemy army forces, which had carried out the manhunt, had been gathered together and sent to the eastern front. There still remained German support forces - Latvians, Ukrainians, Lithuanians and Belorussian police – in the areas close to the partisans.

The partisan troops began to reorganise. Their ranks were being filled with new people, who flowed to them from the villages. This situation put a strain on supplies of food and clothes, because many of the villages had been burnt by the enemy, and the partisans were forced to go further afield to equip themselves with essential supplies.

On 4th. April, with the pioneering growth of the partisan movement, the following troops within the Pinsk division were combined and attached to the battalion that went by the name of Lenin: Vasiliyev, Kutuzov and Tchapayev. Commander Vasiliyev was now commander of a battalion (Kombrig) and Commissar Ziborov was appointed commissar of the battalion. Kluyevs was appointed chief of staff and from July 1943, Kistiunin replaced him.[133]

The plan to visit Volchye Nori

The days of the spring 1943 manhunt passed. The region was relatively quiet. Since the Shepetinskis had parted from their families, who had been left in Volchye Nori, worry for the fate of their dear ones had given them no peace. From time to time, they planned to return there and to help them, but in the meantime, the manhunts of the autumn 1942 and spring 1943 befell them, and the question of going there was postponed. Now that they had a breathing space, the Shepetinskis were looking for a way to visit their families.

At that time, a lack of weapons and ammunition was felt in the troop. Hundreds of partisans without weapons were being accepted into the troop and into the division, and the need for more arms was pressing. So Yasha Shepetinski approached the commander and suggested going to Volchye Nori.

---

[132] *Yasha heard the details of Herzel's death from a peasant from the village of Chudin, who had driven the Latvians who took part in the battle to Daniskovichi. The peasant heard this description from the Latvian soldiers.*

[133] *Partizanskoye formirovanie, P.600-601*

He told them that he knew of some weapons which were hidden in the area. Yasha received permission to go to Volchye Nori. Four partisans went out under the command of the Russian, Petrovitch. Zvi, Yasha's cousin, was also one of the four. When they were near the small town of Gantsevitch, they stopped for a short period and Petrovitch went to visit some acquaintances from the days when he was staying in a local village. The next day, he came back and told them he had created links with a local policeman, who was ready to collaborate with them and offer them weapons. Petrovitch went out the next day again to that village, and the rest of them waited for him in the forest. Several days passed, and the partisans saw that Petrovitch had not returned and there was no point in staying in the place. They found out where he was, and were informed that he was staying in the policeman's house, having a good time with his sister, and there was no chance of gaining any weapons from there.

Yasha says: "We decided to put an end to the waiting and carry on towards Slonim, as planned from the start. Petrovitch didn't like this. An argument broke out between us, and in the heat of the quarrel, he aimed his rifle at me, but immediately heard, behind his back, the sound of a rifle being cocked. This was my cousin, Zvi. Petrovitch understood the hint and he put his rifle down and said, 'I was only joking.'

"We went back to the camp because he refused to go on to Slonim. I thought that they would allow us to organise another group, but I encountered a refusal, and so we didn't succeed in reaching Volchye Nori to find out what had happened to our families".

A few years later, a partisan commander, a Hero of the Soviet Union, Linkov, wrote about what had happened to the 59 and 60 Jewish groups who had been left in Volchye Nori, and he relates in his memoirs:

"In the second half of August 1942, the Hitlerites hastily organised a big reprisal operation. Three German divisions, which were on their way to the Eastern front, were set down in Slonim and Baranovitch. Thirty thousand soldiers and officers began to comb the forest from west to east and from south to north. They managed to, almost completely wipe out the Jewish partisan troop based in Volchye Nori, which was caring for families."[134]

Linkov doesn't say anything about the part the Soviet partisans played in wiping out the Jews from the family camps. The Jewish partisans from Slonim knew nothing about the fate of their families until the end of the partisan fighting.

1st. May Festival

In honour of the festival, a large saboteur group of volunteers was put together to derail a German train. The volunteers were allocated a stretch of track between the Bostin and Malkovitch stations on the Baranovitch-

---
[134] L. Linkov, *Voina v tylu vraga*. P. 325

Luninietz line, where they were to blow up a train. There were five people in the band and they were given an explosive charge weighing two kilos. Zvi Shepetinski, who was wearing peasant sandals plaited from tree bark and a coat and hat in peasant style, volunteered to patrol the road to the track. When he drew near the rail track, he noticed an enemy bunker which had machine gun emplacements, aimed at the railway track. He waited, and watched what was happening in the station and its surroundings from a hiding place. Not long passed and slowly there came a cargo train along the track. In front of the engine were two trucks. The first was full of labourers and the second full of Germans. After the train appeared, a team of labourers arrived to rake the edges of the track and check for suspicious objects. After half an hour, they went back to the station, and Zvi went back and reported.

While it was still light, the partisans left for the target, marching one by one, at a distance of ten metres from each other. They arrived without incident and laid the mines.

Zvi had to lay a mine on the track, whose height was two metres. In order not to leave any marks, he spread out a blanket and climbed up. The commander of the band, Zeitzev, remained at the foot of the track and put the explosives in the mine. When he reached the place, Zvi dug a shallow recess with a knife underneath the base. The earth from there, he put on the blanket, and the gravel on the sack which he was carrying. When the hole was ready, Zeitzev gave him the mine without the mechanism, in order to check if it fitted the hole. After a number of adjustments they laid the mine, with the mechanism, in the hole. A short rope was attached to the safety pin, which they had to pull out after the final setting. The distance between the tip of the mechanism and the lowest level of the base would have been about ten millimetres, the thickness of a finger, so that the mechanism would be set off only when the engine depressed it on the railway track and the bases, and not under pressure from the safety trucks, which travelled in front of the engine. As the train approached, the small movements would get larger, but only the engine would cause a large enough movement of ten millimetres and cause an explosion. Zvi filled the dug-out hole with earth that he'd taken out, returned the gravel stones to their place and swept the dust off the base with the sack. With the help of a splinter of wood, he repaired the marks of the rake, so that no sign would be left of the work that he'd done. And then he got off the track and got his rifle back. He and Zeitzev put the branches the Germans had scattered back on the path.

The band went back to camp and waited for an announcement that their work had been crowned with success. Before noon of the next day, there came an announcement that the Germans had found a mine on a track. It turned out that this was a mine that another group had laid. Zvi was depressed, since he was afraid that his work had not succeeded, but in the evening, the reconnaissance patrol came back and reported that a train, laden with equipment and military staff, had gone up with a mine, just before the Malkovichi station and ten trucks had been derailed. The next day, in the parade, the operation, which had been carried out under Zeitzev's command, was singled out and praised.

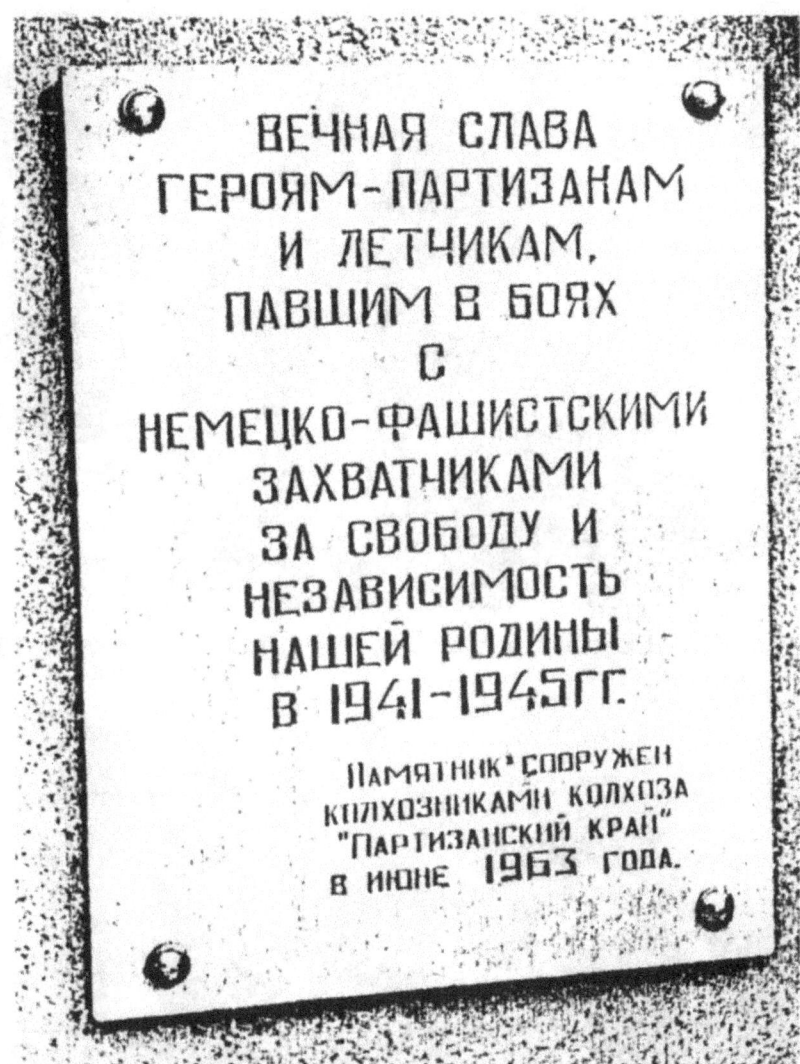

Memorial tablet for the partisans heroes and the pilots who fell in battles against the German Fascist conqueror, for the sake of freedom and the independence of the motherland, during 1941-1945

The Great Synagogue and the "shulhoyf" (square) - 1989

Paradna - Street view - 1989

CHAPTER EIGHTEEN: Vasiliyev fighters from the Lenin brigade in the 'war of the railways'

Sabotage on the railway lines

In July 1943, the partisans began to train in the preparation of delaying fuse wires with detonators and in using explosive bricks made of "Tol".[135] They were taught by professional saboteurs who were parachuted from the Soviet rear guard. On 14th. July, the order "War on the Rail-tracks" was received. All the divisions took part in this operation, right almost up to the front line, each troop on the strip which was allocated to it that night, 3rd. August.[136]

Firstly, reconnaissance patrols were sent out to check out the approach to the section of track where they were supposed to operate. After that, the fuse wires and the charges were carried to the target, while still unconnected. After the second check and preparation of the place for laying the charge, they were connected and lit by two partisans from each squad, with the help of a lighted cigarette and a small puff. Each partisan who had finished laying the charge had to wait by the last charge till the person who was igniting arrived, in order to show him where the charges were. The "igniters" would run the length of the track and ignite up. Those who lay the charges had to count the explosions in their section to be certain that every charge had blown up, and then report to their commander.

Zvi Shepetinski took part in this operation as an igniter. The unit to which his relatives belonged was near the bridge and the station. When the first explosions were heard, rounds of bullets were fired in all directions. Mortars were set into action from this station and from the enemy bunkers and their bombs fell and exploded near the bridge. Suddenly, an explosion like thunder was heard. These were the charges that the partisans had laid to blow up the bridge. The Germans fired with everything they had, including anti-aircraft weapons, because they thought the explosions had been caused by aerial bombing. Several people were wounded in their legs in the unit which blew up the bridge. After they'd been bandaged, they walked independently and only one of them had to ride a horse.[137]

The revenge of Avraham Hirschler

The Polkovnik Linkov[138], who operated in the Brest-Baranovitch region, recounts with amazement an act of vengeance upon the enemy, which a Jew by the name of Avraham Hirschler carried out. He had been imprisoned in a camp in

---

[135] Translator's note: "Tol" refers to trinitrotoluene, the substance from which T.N.T. is prepared.

[136] *Vsenarodnaya borba v Belorusii, vol. 2, p.234-238*

[137] *From the memoirs of Zvi Shepetinski*

[138] *L. Linkov, Voyna v tylu vraga, p.332. There is no confirmation of this from any Jewish source.*

Slonim. The relatives of every Jew in the camp had been executed, among them, Hirschler's wife and son, though he did not yet know this. One day, he was called to the command of the German camp and entertained with a meal, the like of which he had not tasted since. He was told that they wanted him to take a mine off the tracks which the partisans had hidden. At that time, the partisans were successfully preparing mines which the Germans didn't know how to remove without first exploding them. The explosion would wreck the railway tracks and stop movement on the railway line for some time. Hirschler was an electrician by profession and the Germans promised him, that in exchange for this service, he would have good food and that his family would survive.

The suggestion elicited a difficult struggle in Hirschler. On the one hand, he didn't want to serve the enemy and cause damage to the partisans, on the other, he wanted to save his family. He was brought to the railway line and succeeded in removing the mine. The Germans stood at a distance and watched what he did. From then on, the mines on this track stopped exploding.

On one occasion, Jewish slave labourers passed along the road. One of them threw a note in Hirschler's direction, in which he was called a traitor, serving the murderers of his family. Now Hirschler knew that the Germans had deceived him. When he was brought the next time to the railway track to get rid of a mine, he called the Germans, who were standing close by to look at what he was doing, because there was no danger in it. When the murderers approached, there was a terrific explosion. The four Germans who stood around him, and Hirschler himself, were torn to shreds. Before his death, this man had also made a sketch for the partisans of a mine which the enemy would not be able to remove.

German sympathisers

The Italians

Several times in the summer of 1943, the partisans came across Italian soldiers, who had abandoned the front and turned westwards in order to return home. They went through the villages, asking for food. Sometimes they bartered: food in exchange for weapons. The Germans couldn't stop them, but didn't supply them with food or any means of transport. Lone Italian soldiers also joined the ranks of the partisans. The fighters bought personal weapons off them, pistols[139], in exchange for bread and meat, but before long, the

---

[139] *Among the partisans a pistol was considered a personal weapon, which the commanders were not authorised to remove from a partisan. They were mainly acquired privately. The pistol was important for a partisan, and especially for a woman, for self-protection or to commit suicide so as not to fall into enemy hands if they found themselves with no way out.*

Germans began to hunt the Italians and to imprison them in special prison of war camps.[140]

The Hungarians

In the rainy autumn months of 1943, Hungarian support forces were seen in the territory of the Pinsk division, accompanied by convoys of carts, which were pulled by prisoners or enforced labour slaves. Hungarian soldiers, who accompanied these convoys, rode on horses.

The partisan commanders tried to establish relationships with the Hungarian soldiers in order to persuade them to join their ranks. The Hungarians would agree only to relationships of coexistence: the partisans wouldn't trouble them and they would ignore the presence of the partisans until they left the area.

However, as the command had not succeeded in drawing the Hungarians to their side, it was decided to hit them. After the first round of firing, the Hungarians crumpled, got on their horses and rode off, leaving the whole convoy of carts where it was. And now the partisans understood that the men dragging the carts were Hungarian Jews. They spoke not a word of any other language except Hungarian and a little German and didn't understand what was happening to them. After it emerged that they were Jewish forced labour, it was suggested that they join the partisans. The Hungarian Jews refused and argued that they feared for the fate of their families who had remained in Hungary, lest they suffer reprisals. The partisans confiscated some of the carts and went back to their camp.

The Belgians

Near the village of Deniskovitchi, where there was a German garrison stationed, there was a saw-mill that supplied construction logs to the Germans. They set up watches in the saw-mill and around it to prevent sabotage, and had even built bunkers on the side facing the forest. A narrow railway track went between the monastery and the railway station of the small town Gantsevitch, and transported the chopped trees from the saw-mill to the train. A Belgian military unit guarded the saw-mill.

The partisans made contact with them too, and suggested that they move to the forest or clear off. The Belgians delayed their answer for a long time. In order to warn them, it was decided to attack the narrow train and also to catch a few Belgians. Maybe that would persuade them?

The Vasiliyev troop set out for the task. The distance from the forest to the track was about ten kilometres. A mine was hidden under the track and the

---

[140] *After the rebellion of the Italian General Badolio, (September 1943), who got rid of Mussolini and made a peace treaty with the Allied anti-Nazi states, the Germans started imprisoning Italians in P.O.W. camps.*

saboteurs waited until the engine was passing them and pulled the detonator. An explosion was heard and at the same time they fired hard on the closed carriages. The train stopped and the partisans burst into the carriages. Several passengers jumped from the train to the other side of the track and disappeared into the forest. The rest of the passengers were taken prisoner and interrogated. Several partisans started to check out the contents and loads of the carriages and suddenly the train started to move backwards down the hill. The engine driver, who they hadn't been guarding, had set the engine in motion and the partisans were forced to jump from the carriages. The interrogation of the prisoners didn't take long. It emerged that among the passengers there were also Russians, born in the Soviet Union, who were collaborators with the Germans, and they were eliminated.

This operation didn't help negotiations with the Belgians and the Germans reinforced their guard and their defence installations of the saw-mill. Later, the saw-mill was taken too.

The war of pamphlets and manifestos

The war was fought not only with weapons but also with words. Both sides were dependent on a propaganda and information war, both by word and writing. The Germans flooded the conquered territories with various manifestos and hoardings. While they were winning, they would stick numerous proclamations appealing to the population on the walls of houses in the towns and villages where they passed on their way eastwards. At the beginning of the war, they boasted that Moscow was already in their hands, and that Leningrad would soon fall, and on the day of the revolution, Hitler would make a speech in the Kremlin. They promised that they were not fighting the civilian population, who could calmly and safely return to work, and their daily concerns. They were fighting only the Bolshevik commissars and the Jews, and they, the armies of the Third Reich, were not coming as oppressors but as liberators from the communist yoke.

In time, when their progress was stopped, their planes showered down coloured proclamations. On one side, there were drawn luxury houses and spacious autostradas - the outcome of the friendly arrangements, as it were, that the Germans would conduct in Soviet territories. On the other side were drawn burning villages and heaps of bodies, mass marches of skeletons - and the slogan: "This is what the Bolshevik regime will bring you." (Proclamations like these were found by partisans and brought to their camps on the banks of the Shchara.)

Neither was the other side quiet. Teams of partisans would visit the villages and set up meetings with the peasants in which they would conduct debates and explanations and pass on information about what was happening at the front, and about the need to enrol to the Red Army which was liberating its homeland. In the partisan printing presses in the forest, they printed partisan newspapers and pamphlets, which were distributed by underground activists in the cities and the villages. Later, particularly in 1943 and 1944, when Soviet planes were circling above Belorussian territories and bombing the enemy, they also dropped pamphlets in which they recounted the victories of the Red Army and called on the residents to enrol to the partisans and help the army liberate the homeland.

In one of these proclamations which were found on the ground by the banks of the Shchara, there was printed something which bore witness that in the Soviet rear, they knew very well about the collaboration of many of the local people, Belorussian and Polish, with the enemy:

Prosti menya, mat rodnaya	Forgive me, dear mother,
Tchto ya tebya bombil	For bombing your house.
Moya zhena sniemcem spala	My wife was lying with a German
Ya eyo razbudil.	And I woke her up.

Raising the level of discipline and party indoctrination

Changes had come about in their internal life and in relationships with the commanders too. Now they began to be more exact and to investigate the past of partisans, and people were given roles, not only for their abilities, but for their fidelity to the regime, according to the opinion of the commissars and the politroks. If there were breaches of discipline, they would be sentenced to imprisonment and also transferred to the punishment battalion, where they were allotted the most difficult and dangerous roles of all. Parades were conducted where the heads of staff appeared who represented the Soviet regime in the conquered territories, and they explained the importance of discipline and conduct to the partisans. At one of these parades, a young partisan, a peasant from the local area, was brought to the Vasiliyev camp.

His hands were bound behind his back and he was terrified to death. He was accused of looting items of female clothing for his girlfriend. The sentence was execution by firing. The young man burst out weeping and begged for mercy. He was shot and everybody dispersed silently to their huts. It was felt that the security forces of Soviet Regime (NKVD) had again gained the upper hand and hope faded that after the war the internal regime in the Soviet Union would change.

There were incidents where partisans who had contracted syphilis were executed so as not to infect others. Criticism of the regime, gossip about the collective farms and about exile, which had been heard before from time to time in the huts from veteran partisans, ceased.

Close relationships and friendship, which had prevailed before among the partisans, and intimate revelations and mutual trust were also damaged. Now, everyone was afraid to speak and to express what was in their hearts.

On a mission for Komarov

Zvi Shepetinski, who was then seventeen, always wanted to be a fighter like all the rest. He didn't want anybody to treat him like a youth. Indeed, he would from go out from time to time with the partisans on various operations. And on this occasion, a special task was imposed on him, a mission which raised his morale and his image in the eyes of his comrades. One evening, a letter was delivered to him, and in it, he was commanded to hand it over personally to the division commander, Komorov, or his deputy.

Zvi hid the letter on his body under his clothes. He was given a horse, but without a saddle, and was ordered to carry out his mission as fast as possible. He left in the night, going through the forest to the division command and reached the advanced guard. After uttering the password, he said to them that he had to deliver a personal message to the commander and he was allowed to continue to the centre of the camp. The guard accompanied him to the command hut. Zvi was brought in front of Komarov and reported on his mission. Komarov asked him how old he was, praised him for the speed with which he'd arrived and asked for the letter. After he read it, he let Zvi go to return to his unit. Zvi asked the commander to confirm that he had received the letter and Komarov wrote on the envelope in which the letter had been brought, 'I was impressed by your envoy. He's young, but he's an exemplary partisan.'

When Zvi got back to his squad, he showed his comrades what was written, so they would see and treat him as he deserved.

The battle for the Deniskovitchi saw-mill

Zvi was appointed deputy to the gunner of the squad, Vas'ca the Siberian. Vas'ca also shared Zvi's bunk in the hut. He was a well-built young man, smiling and likable, a soldier from the regular army, who had fled from captivity, hidden two years in a village, and a short while previously, had reached the troop.

The winter was at its height and snow covered the ground and the trees, and then an order was received to present at the troop parade. At the parade, the partisans were informed that they must be ready with their weapons to go into action. Vas'ca lay sick and so they transferred his machine gun to Zvi and set him as number two to a young Chuvashi man from Khazakstan, whose nickname in the troop was Shulik. He was a young man of conscription age, whom neither Zvi, nor his other comrades, knew. Zvi used to chat with him about life in the Chuvashi tribe, which roamed in the wastes of Khazakhastan. His main characteristic was fearfulness. A shot would freeze him to the ground and paralyse his body. Zvi was not experienced with the machine gun; he knew how to take it apart and put it back together, but had not yet fired it. When he was given such a hopeless number two, he was afraid of the consequences. After all, they'd been told they were going out on attack, but the target had not yet been disclosed.

Zvi examined his gun, took it apart and polished the parts. Two of the paratroopers who saw Zvi doing this work gave him a special oil which didn't freeze, and he spread it all over the parts of the bolt. The troop had got hold of winter carts and they made most of the journey in them, up to a distance of about an hour's walk. At their last stopping place, the fighters had been commanded to load their machine guns and be prepared to shoot. Up till now, Zvi had carried the machine gun without the cartridge. He checked the working of the mechanism and his eyes clouded over: the trigger was creeping as if it was covered in tar. Zvi caught on that it was the oil with which he'd spread all the moveable parts. He was forced to take the mechanism apart immediately and polish it up. The frozen metal parts he put into his clothes, to warm them with the heat of his body and get the oil off them. A number of times, he was obliged to repeat this action until he managed to get rid of the oil. He did, in fact, tell his commander about this, but all the time, he was afraid that his gun wouldn't work.

With daylight, they heard the first shots near the gate. The role of the squad to which he belonged was to take the hill of sawdust from the saw-mill and to give cover to the lads, who were assigned to blow up the machine rooms and burn them. Another troop attacked the bunkers of the Belgians who were guarding the saw-mills. The Belgians fired in all directions and made it impossible for the partisans to get nearer. Zvi's squad scattered on the hill of sawdust and when Zvi tried to fire his machine gun, he found that it wasn't working. In vain, he tried to get it going by hitting with his fist on the handle of the bolt, but the gun wouldn't work.

A wooded tower rose above the saw-mill building and Zvi noticed that from time to time, someone would appear on it and send a volley of shots towards the attacking partisans. They already had wounded men. He gave Shulik his machine gun and asked him to work the mechanism continuously, in the hope that it would start to work. He took Shulik's rifle and started to shoot at the tower. He told the attackers on his right about the figures shooting from the tower so that they could silence them from the side. And now he saw Shulik, clinging to the ground as if frozen. In the full light of morning, he could clearly see a soldier wearing a peaked cap and a black uniform aiming his machine gun at them. Zvi fired and the soldier disappeared behind the wall. He carried on firing into the entrance to the tower, as did the comrades. The firing from the tower stopped and now the attackers could move more freely and carry out the task.

A tough battle took place next to the enemy bunkers. One of the courageous partisans took his life in his hands, and equipped with a number of hand grenades, he ran to one of the outer bunkers, threw himself against the firing aperture and rolled a hand grenade inside. After a moment, a dull explosion was heard and the partisans broke through into the bunker. The enemy fire was silenced. Silence reigned - the bunkers were taken. However, the brave partisan who had opened the way for the attackers was also there, wounded in every part of his body, and after a short while, he breathed his last. In the evening, the commanders investigated why Zvi's gun hadn't worked. His commander praised his courage and the resourcefulness which he had shown in battle.[141]

The dispersal of the Vasiliyev troop

In spring 1943, during the broadening of the partisan movement, the Vasiliyev troop became a brigade - 'Lenin', but even after that, the brigade and the Vasiliyev troop continued to grow.

During the spring of 1943, one of the battalions of the Vasiliyev became a separate troop under the name of Dzerzhinski. The commander appointed was Ivan Vasiliyevitch Shevchenko, and in 1944, Naum Dimitrevitch Lomeyko replaced him. Most of the people from the Jewish 51 battalion were absorbed into the troop: Raya Shepetinski, the brothers Herzel and Yasha, their cousin Zvi, Yitzhak Grachuk and his sister Masha, Tzadok Derechinski, Nahum Tschertok, Feitel (a refugee from Warsaw), Dov Yevshitski, the two Weintraub brothers, Mende Rubin and Kuba Zilberhaft.

In May 1943, one unit (two squads) was split off from the Dzerzhinski troop, about fifty people, and they founded two new troops: the Ordzhenikidze troop and the Funze. Yasha and his sister Raya were sent to the Ordzhenikidze and all the rest remained in the Dzerzhinski. In June 1943, the troop clashed several times with the Hungarians who were serving the Germans. In December, a mounted reconnaissance patrol of eight men was founded in the troop, which functioned until January 1944. Its commander was Shevchenko.[142]

An incident near the village of Lushcha

There was a drunken anti-Semitic partisan, whose malicious thoughts were no secret. Yasha had become aware of it when he'd come back from a patrol assignment in the Logishin region and visited a partisan envoy in the village of Lushcha. This man told him that he'd seen a group of armed men dressed in civilian clothes walking in the direction of a forest. This aroused Yasha's suspicions, since the partisans were accustomed to walk in open roads in the areas over which they had control. He decided to inform the command about it.

In the meantime, another unit of their troop entered the village, under a partisan called Zachar. The unit had returned from an acquisition assignment. Yasha warned Zachar to check whether there might be an ambush. Zachar, who was very tipsy, had his eye on Yasha's horse. He replied that Yasha was a coward, causing needless panic, gave the order to carry on and the unit fell

---

[141] *From the memoirs of Zvi Shepetinski*

[142] *Partizanskoye formirovanye, p.60*

into the ambush. When the policemen opened fire, Zachar's men abandoned the carts with the goods and fled in panic. At the same time, Yasha got up on his horse and rode with his comrade Volodya towards the troop's camp. When he reached the little bridge, he noticed that his horse was showing signs of anxiety. They only just got onto the bridge and the horse reared up on her hind legs, and Yasha was thrown from her back and from the bridge. Immediately, there was firing. It was obvious to the patrol that they had walked into an ambush. Yasha crawled among the bushes out of the range of fire. The police in the ambush didn't search for him, but just continued to fire from where they were and he survived. After a long detour in this territory, he got back to the camp. It turned out that his horse had not been hit and had also returned on her own. His friend, Volodya, on hearing the firing, had also turned aside and returned to the camp without a scratch. An investigation was held and Yasha recounted what had happened. The unit commander, Zachar, was relieved of his post.[143]

On completion of their assignment, Yasha returned to the Dzerzhinski troop. Two groups of paratroopers who had crossed the front line had arrived in the troop: one group was expert in sabotaging rail track and the other group was in intelligence. The troop served protection for them.

On the night of 8th. August 1943, the fighters of the troop took part in "Mission Concert", the code name for the second concentrated operation on the rail-tracks, almost as far as the front. At the beginning of November, the troop returned to the forest, where its brigade, the Lenin, resided. They had to march long distances for sabotage operations.

---

[143] *From the memoirs of Yasha Shepetinski***Error! Bookmark not defined.**

CHAPTER NINETEEN: Winter and spring of 1944

The capture of 'Lashon' (Tongue)

In the winter, the Lenin brigade left on a mission to blow up the Luninietz-Baranovitch train on the section between Malkovitch and Lusino. On the train there were wounded German soldiers who were being transported to their rear. One of the aims of this operation was to capture "Lashon". Lashon (*Heb:tongue, language>information*) refers to prisoners of war from whom information might be extracted about what was happening at the front.

Zvi Shepetinski says:

"Our battalion was located in a forest of young birch trees. Our role was to immobilise the Germans if they should demonstrate opposition and come to the support of the attackers in the hour of need. I heard one of the partisans from the other unit, to which my cousin Yasha belonged, saying to his comrades: 'At the start of firing, we'll knock out our Jew and take his machine gun from him.' I understood that he meant Yasha, because there was no other Jewish machine gunner in the unit.

"Yasha was positioned with his machine gun at the edge of the forest, and with him, other gunners. Without thinking much, I approached them and said, "If you shoot our partisans, I will be the first to send you a bullet in return." And in order to show them that I meant what I said, I stuck my rifle into the back of one of them. From a distance, you could already hear the sound of a train approaching. Our main charge blew up only partly and didn't activate the second charge. You could hear the friction as the train came to a halt. We heard a command, "Forward!" The unit burst up and covered the carriages with a hail of bullets. Fierce fire was returned from the carriages. The battalions on the offensive ran to the train and Germans jumped out of the carriages, apparently a unit of regular army. They engaged in a counter offence.

"The partisans didn't manage to get near and to break into the carriages, and we already had wounded. We heard the command to retreat and to gather up our wounded. I was in the rear guard. Next to me was a partisan who had not long joined our ranks, stood leaning against a tree not moving. The unit commander decided that he'd had a heart attack from fear and took his rifle and left him. After the battle, some way off, when they checked who was missing, the head of the unit told commander Lomieko, about the man who had apparently had a heart attack. The commander ordered immediately to go and fetch him. It turned out that he had been hit directly in the heart and died on the spot. This failure stung us all."

"The winter passed without particular incident for the partisans. The economic situation was much better than it had been the previous winter, and now, older people began to appear from the rear, armed very well with brand new weapons. The fighters understood that these were party envoys who had come to prepare the Soviet regime, and impose it after the enemy had been pushed back. Hopes bloomed in the approaching spring.

Ukrainian spies

In March 1944, the unit in which the Shepetinskis served on guard duties was stationed in the village of Budtchi. In February, an airstrip for the division was set up by the village of Lenino. Zvi was sent to the guard unit for the airfield.

The troop advance guard were located several kilometres from the small town where the German garrison and police were stationed. On one occasion, an attractive young woman appeared to the advance guard. She had come from the town and told them she had fled because they had begun to take revenge on her, as she had connections with peasants who supported the partisans. The young woman remained with the guards until they were relieved. The commander of the guard heard her story and ordered them to hold her somewhere until they could find out who she was. The young woman remained with the guard another two days and several partisans of the guard enjoyed her favours in the meantime. After the partisans' liaison men had interrogated her, it emerged that she had been sent to the troop in order to spy, and not only that, but she had a venereal disease and she had been ordered to get friendly with the partisans and infect them with the disease.

There was another incident. Partisans who had returned from an advance guard came back with two handsome, tall and slender young men, who looked like educated people. They spoke Russian with a Ukrainian accent and they claimed that they had been recruited for forced labour in the Ukraine, but they had fled in order to join the partisans. One of them played the accordion and the other sang very well. The guardsmen killed a cow and then one of the guests offered to help prepare the meat and did it with great expertise. This aroused the partisans' suspicions: how could a young urban and educated man have this experience? After a few days, the members of the guard came to the camp with the two guests and put them under guard. After an interrogation, it became clear that they were graduates of the Germans school for spies. They were executed after they admitted to their offence.

Again, there was sabotage of the enemy railway lines, clashes with German units and their supporters, attacks on the trains - missions which had become the norm in that period. In the meantime, the front was growing nearer, and the day of liberation for the whole of Belarus was approaching.

Doubts of the liberation

On 5th. July, the Lenin brigade met a Red Army rescue unit from the infantry brigade of the Guardia, no. 55, which had reached the Lushcha/ Bostin region, but the partisans were not yet liberated. They were called upon to help the regular army drive the enemy out of the region. The fighters of the Lenin brigade were sent to the rear of the enemy, westwards, to the Logishin area.

On 15th. July, they again met a Red Army unit that had advanced westwards. The brigade, and within it, the Shepetinski family, and other fighters who had come from the Jewish 51 brigade, now completed their partisan fighting.

However, Yasha Derechinski was to have yet other experiences. Together with Tsadok Derechinski he was recruited to the (Red) army. Tsadok fell in one of the battles, whereas Yasha reached Berlin in 1945. He served in the Red Army until 12th.April 1946. He was arrested for the offence of an attempted escape from the borders of the Soviet Union and exiled for ten years to the Urals. In 1956, he was released and transferred to Khazakhstan, where he stayed until 1958. From there, he reached Riga in Latvia, married his wife, had a daughter and immigrated with his family to Israel on 15th. June 1966.

His cousin Zvi continued to fight the rail-track war until June 1944.

The troop was continuously on the move and never rested for an instant. In the last weeks of the war, there were many casualties in the troop. In one of the battles with the German garrison in the Bostin station, the elder brother Weintraub fell when a mortar shell exploded in the top of a tree under which he lay.

In July 1944, the partisans in his unit met up with some Red Army reconnaissance. That whole day, regular army troops flowed in - engineering corps and artillery, who set up cannons on the hill, behind the village of Valiuta, where there was a meeting place. The engineering corps built a phantom bridge on the river Tsna. The next morning, the partisan reconnaissance briefed the regular army forces on how to get to Bostin station, which was on the opposite bank of the river. Suddenly, there was a terrific explosion and two of the troop's reconnaissance were killed by a sprung landmine which the Germans had buried.

The partisans received an order to conquer Bostin station. This time, the soldiers of the regular army and their artillery also took part, with Soviet air support. The station was conquered, but the war was still not over for the partisans: they were expected to retreat to the enemy rear and to continue to fight. In the end, Zvi was liberated from the partisan ranks, but his hardships were not yet over.

After several days of rest, the partisans were called to a parade. Several speeches were heard where they were informed that they were to take part in a victory parade in the town of Pinsk with a regular army unit. Indeed, they were now liberated, but in the heart of the Jews, there was no joy of victory, but sadness and pain for their comrades' loss of life just before the end of the war, and also great fear and anxiety for their families, whose fate they did not yet know.

The victors were marching in the streets of Pinsk, but what was in the heart of a young man from Slonim in that same parade?

"The day was flooded with sunshine. The military band was playing. Red flags fluttered from several houses. The residents stood on the pavements and watched us with astonished looks. I'm looking at them and trying to read what's on their faces: did they watch like that quietly with no reaction when tens of thousands of Jews from Pinsk were led to the death pits?

"I lower my eyes and I see a gravestone with the Hebrew letters Pe, Nun, under their feet. They had used it to lay the pavement. I carry on looking and notice fragments of headstones. I look at these 'unfortunate' citizens, who suffered under the Nazi jackboot until we liberated them. And now, they're walking on Jewish headstones, as if it were the obvious thing to do."

After the parade, the troop's fighters went back to their base in the village. A day or two passed, and they began to disperse the partisans to different destinations. A parade was held for the troop according to their units. One group was recruited to the army and left the place. Zvi was taken in a lorry, with nine other partisans, to Pinsk, where they were placed at the disposal of an internal security (NKVD) unit. In one of the houses, they found a vacant apartment, which had apparently belonged to a collaborator, who had fled for fear of the Soviet regime, with beds and bed linen in it, which seemed very strange after two years of living in the forest.

"At night, says Zvi, we took our clothes off for the first time and lay down to sleep in comfortable beds with spring mattresses. I couldn't fall asleep. I got out and lay on the ground where I slept the sleep of the just. Several other comrades did the same. It took me a whole month to get used to sleeping in a bed again."

Zvi Shefet in his home town of Slonim

Zvi was posted in a police station as a policeman on the beat. He fell ill and ran a temperature. The Polish doctor who examined him said he was sick with spotted fever. But Zvi suspected that the diagnosis was incorrect and that the Polish doctor had given the order to hospitalise him in this unit in order to infect him with typhus. He succeeded in escaping from the unit despite the opinion of the doctor, who refused to discharge him, and when he felt better, he received permission to visit Slonim. He still hoped to find someone from his family. He set out, armed with a submachine gun and a pistol. The journey was hard because of the many changes of train.

He reached Slonim after various strange adventures, including arrest by the military police, who suspected him of being a deserter from the army, and maybe an escaping war criminal?

Eventually, he was in Slonim, standing at that same railway station through which Jews had passed from Germany and Austria on their way east to slaughter.

Zvi remembers:

"When one of us, Jewish labourers, warned them that they were being taken to their death and suggested that they should flee, they looked at us, the Ost-Juden, with contempt and argued that they were German citizens going to work near the front. After the war, they would return to their homes."

After Zvi saw the ghetto in its destruction, his parents' house and his relatives' house, of which there remained only heaps of wreckage, he began to look for somewhere to sleep. Night was approaching, and there was not a single person in his hometown who could take him in. Luckily, he met a policeman who was a partisan in Volchye-Nori who directed him to an apartment where the Jewish partisans used to meet. When he reached this hostel, he met Golda Gertsovski and other Jews. Now he found out that no one from his family remained. They told him that at the start of 1943, they had killed his father and his uncle Isaac. The local villagers complained that the Jews were coming and taking food from them, that they were vandals and vagrants who had brought all the problems on the peasants. The rest of the family, the women and the children, had been murdered by local policemen.

Zvi wanted to collect their bones and bring them to a proper burial. No one was able to direct him to the underground hut where death had found them. In Slonim, he also met the Alpert family, several of the young women from the 51 group and his cousin, Raya. Zvi borrowed a hoe and went to Mikhailovski Lane, to the house of his grandfather, where they'd had the shelter from which they had left for the forest. He tried to dig but found nothing save a few coals from the kindling, which had camouflaged the entrance to the hideout. Zvi felt about the wreckage of his burnt house, what most of the Jewish partisans felt when they stood in the place where once their houses had been and not a single one of their dear ones could come out to meet them returning from war:

"I dig with tears choking my throat and they refuse to wet my eyes. I cannot cry, even after years. All the sorrow and humiliation – because Jews were murdered by partisans in the forests of Volchye-Nori, because many of the murderers were walking free in the street, respected citizens - sting in my throat and burn in my soul. I didn't yet know then that the murders were with the full knowledge of the local commanders."

Zvi returned to Pinsk and gave himself up to searching for anyone who had helped in the slaughter of his people. However, his commander told him off and said he was exaggerating. He went to Minsk, completed a course for intelligence officers, returned to Pinsk and registered secretly to migrate to Poland, and with him, his cousin, Raya. Now he was forced to hide, since they were looking for him as a deserter.

Raya and Zvi reached Lodz. There, they knew activists from the pioneer movement, who were engaged in helping people get out. They furnished them with documents, and these enabled them to reach Berlin. Yasha Shepetinski was serving in East Germany as a translator in an army unit of the security service. Zvi looked for a way to immigrate to Israel. There were more adventures crossing borders, adventures in which they had to be very daring and nimble. Zvi moved to the American sector of Germany, and there met his girlfriend, Gita. The two of them were married on 20th. April 1947. In the displaced persons camps in Bad Reichenhall, Germany, Zvi worked as a technician and studied in an ORT. technical school, so he would have a profession when he came to Israel.

Finally the day arrived when he was about to immigrate with Aliya Bet. The couple embarked on the ship Exodus. They set sail from the coast of France full of hope, but suffered the same treatment as many of the illegal immigrants on the Exodus. Despite opposition and a struggle, they were returned from the port of Haifa and forcibly taken off in the port of Hamburg, then transported to a detention camp in Peppendorf, near Bremen, and from there to the Emden camp on the shore of the North Sea. In April 1948, an illegal immigrant group of Aliyah Gimel set out and Zvi and Gita, who was pregnant, were transferred to the camp of Bergen-Belsen. They reached Israel via Italy in the ship, "The Argentina" on the day that the independence of the State of Israel was declared, 14th. May 1948.

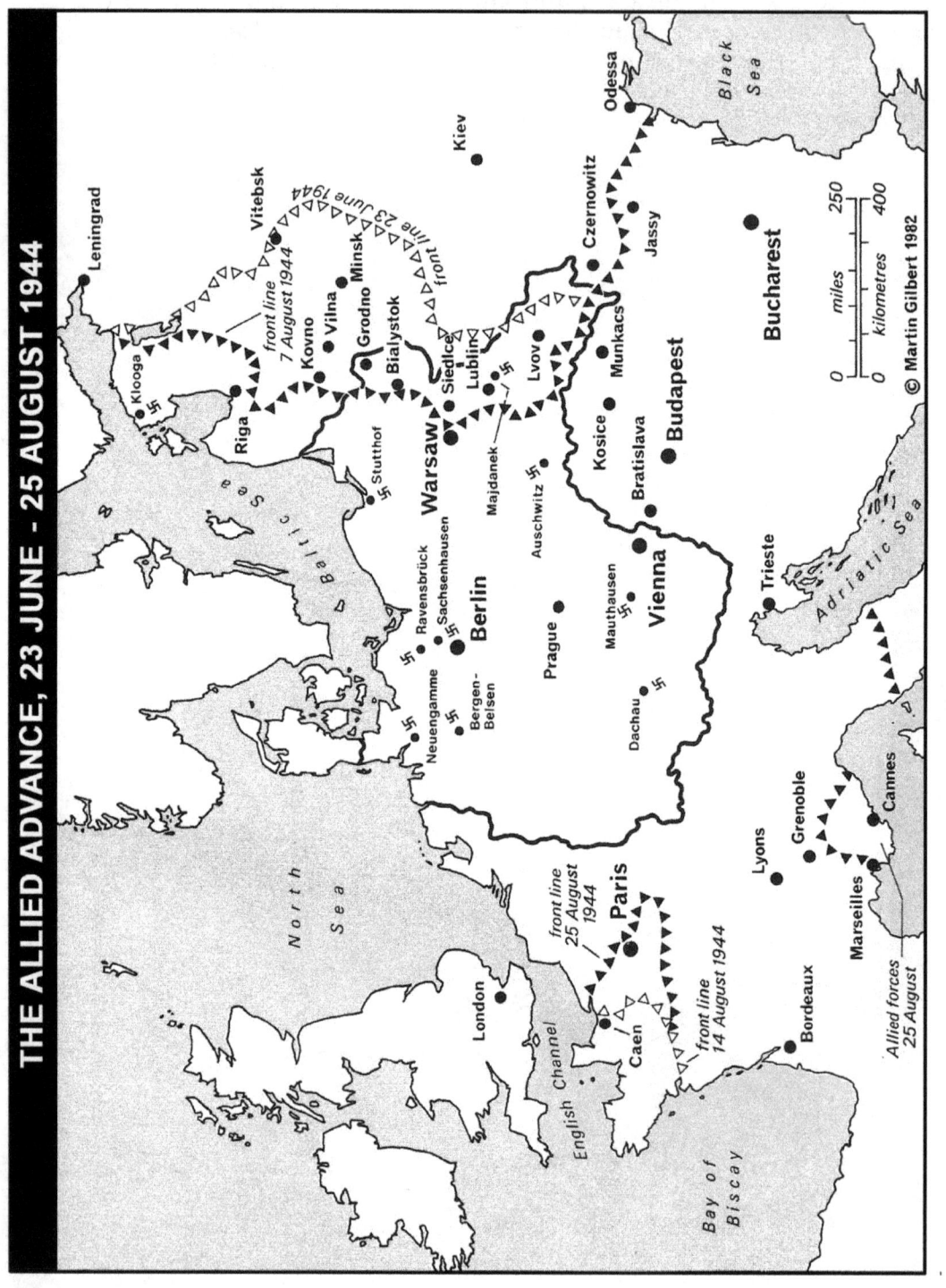

From the ATLAS OF THE HOLOCAUST by Martin Gilbert - Courtesy of Yad Vashem

CHAPTER TWENTY: The Brest division on the road to liberation

Spring 1944

In spring 1944, the front was situated near Kovel and nearing the borders of the Brest region. The Brest division, too, went through difficult battles in the spring. The area in which the division was active was flooded with German soldiers, and they made partisan activities more difficult. In February, the Germans exerted heavy pressure on the southern troops of the division, on the Shchors and the Kotovski troops. These troops, with units from the Pinsk division conducted fierce battles under the command of Major Kovalski, who was formerly the commander of the Kalinin troop. In the period between 21st. February and 30th. March, battles were conducted in the area around the Dneiper-Bug canal. On 31st. March, the two troops drew back in the direction of Shechitinskaya Volya and crossed the river Pripiyet on ferries which they had built.

The partisans who had operated on the south of the canal now had a steady link with the command of the regular army, and operated on their orders and directions. The Shchors and Kotovski troops moved to territories where the H.Q. of the division was stationed, defended by the Budioni troop and the Dzherzhinski and Sovietskaya Belorussia brigades.

On 28th. March 1944, Proniagin was sent an instruction from the H.Q. of the Soviet Infantry Division 160 to maintain regular contact with H.Q. of the division. P.D. Ponamarenko, chief commander of the partisan forces, notes in his letter to Sikorski on 7th. April the difficult conditions in which the partisans were now forced to fight, and sends them good wishes for success.

After tough battles from 3rd.-10th. April, the partisans stopped the German offensive near the village of Zditovo, on the river Drogobuzh, which links the Black Lake to Lake Sporovo. After a brief respite, the partisans started to filter between the enemy units. They used sabotage and fought open battles. They blew up supply vehicles, and destroyed lines of transport - all in order to prevent the enemy removing residents and their property from territory not yet liberated. The partisans moved the residents to the forest so that they wouldn't be taken to forced labour in Germany.

When the Germans reached the River Pripiet and realised that they would have to retreat completely from Belorussia and the Ukraine, they decided to withdraw their navy, which was sailing the Dnieper, from the borders of the Soviet Union and transfer it to the Baltic Sea. They transferred their warships and their commercial ships through the Pripiet river to the Pinsk area - to the Dnieper-Bug canal - and from there, planned to sail them westwards.

The troops from the Brest and Pinsk divisions and the Suvorov troop, and a Jewish battalion from the forests of Farchev, which had been joined by some of the rebels from the extermination camp in Sobivor who had managed to escape - their task was not to allow the Germans to carry out their plan. They chopped down trees the length of the canal, cast them into the water and mined some of them. Those responsible for the transfer of the German navy to the Baltic Sea were Hungarian army units, which were concentrated in Minsk.

The Kotovski troop was then in the corner between the Dnieper-Bug canal and the Beloye Oziero (the White Lake). Zerach Kremin remembers that they didn't know what was happening in the area, but they sensed that the Hungarians were gaining confidence. They were becoming cheeky and they had started to attack the partisans at night. In one of these attacks on a March morning in 1944, Zhenia Eichenbaum was killed.

The reason was that two divisions had been sent to conquer the town of Brest in order to block the German line of retreat from Smolensk. The Red Army advanced through the partisan territories of the Tshernak and Voroshilov troops and arrived twenty-five kilometres from Brest. But the Germans quickly brought reinforcements, intending to encircle the two divisions of the Red Army, closing off their retreat. After several days of battles, the soldiers began to retreat.

Shchors battalion at a lineup

On the banks of the Lahn River

Gregori A. Dudko (at the left)
Shchors battalion commissar

Abraham Bandt (on the right) 1944
Shchors's Patrol platoon commander

Boris Yudkovski (on the left) with his brother and sister in law (1946)

Group of partisans from the Pinsk division. Zvi Shepetinski kneels

A monument in the memory of the fallen partisans in the battles against the German Nazi occupier between 1941-1945 (Gantzevich 1963)

From fighting in the forests and swamps of Belarus to victory over Nazi Germany

On the Shchara banks. The partisan G.Gringhaus who photographed the site (1989)

The partisan Yacov Shepetinski, as a Red Army soldier, at the Brandenburg Gate and the Reichstag after the Berlin conquest. May, 1945

The monument at the valley of death in the Chepelovo fields
Burial place of thousands of victims of the massacre of Nov.41 & July 42

The valley of death in the Chepelovo fields

The monument at the valley of death at the Petralevich hill. Erected in 1964. Burial place of twenty thousand Jews of Slonim and the surroundings who were slaughtered in 1942

A group of partisans, mostly Jews - Pinsk (1945)
Zvi Shepetinski - lying on the right

A group of partisans from the Dzerzhinski battalion - Lenin brigade (1963)
Yacov Shepetinski - in the middle

Gathering of partisans from Lenin Brigade, Pinsk Division, in the forests where they fought in 1942-1944 (1963)

The death of Zhenia Eichenbaum

Zhenia was a partisan experienced in battles and a brave fighter. She was born in 1925 in the town of Poltusk. With the conquest of Poland, her family had fled to Slonim. There, she learnt of the German conquest in 1941 and was imprisoned, together with her family, in the ghetto. In the days of the massacres, she saw that people were disappearing from the ghettos and she enquired how she too could escape from the ghetto. She began to trace people who were attached to the underground, and she reached the carpentry shop in Podgurna (Street). The members of the underground brought her into their shelter and interrogated her. She explained that she wanted to take revenge the Germans, for she too had a right to revenge, like the members of the underground. After the massacre of 29th. June, she went out of the ghetto with the members of the underground and was accepted into the 51 group and began to work in the clinic. Eventually, she excelled as a fighter and took part in the troop's battles.

Until the troop's journey eastwards, Zhenia took part in the battles of the 51 group in Kosovo, Gavinovitch, and later, in Tchemyeli, Samitchin and on the Tenth Dam. She was a true fighter in the sabotage unit and took part in the conquest of Tchuchevitchi, Deniskovitchi and in the battle on the River Lahn on 5th.October. In February 1943, she fought in the battle of Putchini.

In 1943, she took part in blowing up trains on the railways, on the Baranovitch-Luninietz line and served particularly well there. She also took part in the operation on the Brest-Moscow line, and was active on the Brest-Pinsk line, near the Drohitchin and Gorodietz stations. Thanks to her, thirteen trains were blown up. As a sign of their appreciation of her activities in battle, the command gave her a machine gun, a weapon which was rare for partisan women.

Zhenia was a proud Jewish woman. Zerach remembers that once they encountered some partisans from the Pozharski troop of the Bobkov battalion and they, as they were accustomed, began to come out with anti-Semitic expressions, like, "What, the Germans haven't killed enough of you yet?" Zhenia drew her Nagan and called out, 'I'll kill these dogs!' Her comrades barely managed to separate her from these anti-Semitic partisans.

At the end of March, when the Kotovski troop was positioned at the meeting place between the canal and the Beloye Lake, Zhenia was badly wounded. Comrades managed to get her across the canal in a boat, but on the way, she breathed her last.

The twists and turns of liberation

Since May 1943, a partisan landing strip had been operating near the village of Korotchin. Here, planes landed frequently which were sent from the "Great Land" bringing newspapers, letters, military and medical equipment and also personnel for the partisans. The planes would fly those who were badly wounded back to the rear.

In April 1944, a group from the regional committee of the Bolshevik party arrived, headed by Mikhael Nikolaievitch Topichin. He had been appointed to fill staff posts in the Brest region in the renewed Soviet regime after liberation. In May 1944, Proniagin was flown across the front line to meet Topichin. He also met the commander of the regular army, General Dikan, whose H.Q .was then stationed near the town of Korostan. Proniagin reported on events in his division and received instructions to continue operations and returned after ten days.

Kommissar Yegorov was also invited to a meeting with Topichin. Two Soviet planes landed on the partisan landing strip of the Brest division, and on the night of 10th.June Yegorov took off in one of them. Enemy anti-aircraft hit the plane which caught alight and crashed into the River Pina. Yegorov was killed.

The summer days of 1944 were fiery days for the partisans. They were required to block enemy retreat lines. On 19th. June, the third stage of the railway track war, which was code-named 'Bagratyon', commenced and went on until the actual liberation. During the whole of this period, the partisans were laying ambushes.

On the night of 9th. July 1944, Topichin's group and the staff group of the liberation army, which was then situated on the border of the Brest region, joined up and reached the town of Antopol. And thus, the Belorussian war of liberation reached its end in July 1944.

However, the fighters of the previous 51 group continued their war. They still endured hardship and much suffering, and not only from the enemy, but also from those who had fought by their side.

Avraham Orlinski continued his partisan war in the ranks of the Budioni troop. He completed his partisan period in the Kartuz Bereza area at the end of July, but was discharged only in August. His wife, Dr Cheslava, finished her war in July, being the chief doctor in the troop. The couple left for Poland in 1945 and from there, on the 'escape' route to Germany, to the D.P. camps. There, Orlinski continued community work. They immigrated to Israel on 6th. October 1948.

Dr. Avraham Blumovitch, who served as Chief Medical Officer of the Brest division, completed his partisan war with the H.Q. of the division and reached the American sector of Germany, where he worked in the central committee of the She'erit Haplitah[144] in Munich. He immigrated to Israel in 1948, and during the war of independence in our state, he served as doctor in the northern command of Tzah"al (IDF) and after that, as Chief Medical Officer until September 1956, when he became known by the name of Avraham Atzmon.

---

[144] *Translator's note: This was the name for the Jewish survivors of the Holocaust.*

The odyssey of Archik Bandt

Nor were the sufferings of Archik Bandt over with his liberation from the forest, and many hardships came his way before he could rest from his struggles and his battles. Fate was not kind to him. Even after the liberation of many of his partisan comrades, he was moved around in far off places which he had never imagined, even in his wildest dreams.

After liberation, partisans were ordered to surrender any arms in their possession. Aharon went to the partisan command in Slonim to give up his submachine gun (P.P.D.) and his pistol. The commander, Anishchuk, who remembered that Archik had had a death sentence placed on him, ordered his detention in the camp where they were holding Italian prisoners of war, until his case could be clarified. On the other side of the road, they had set up a camp for partisans who did not know as yet where they would go and what they would do. The homes of many of them were in ruins and they had nowhere to return. On the day that Archik was detained, they came to the prison of war camp to take two Italians to work in the partisan camp kitchen. With the Italians, they took Archik as a translator. The commander of the partisan camp noticed his fluent Russian and asked about his origins. Aharon told him and the camp commander obtained a partisan certificate for him and he was released.

On 10th. July 1944, Aharon was recruited to the Red Army, sent on an H.G.V. driving course and stationed in Minsk. In the meanwhile, Nazi Germany had surrendered and Archik's unit had been sent to the Mongolia-Manchuria border, and was awaiting to attack Japan. The attack began on 5th. August 1945. Archik served in an anti-tank unit as a lorry driver transporting cannon and its ammunition. On 30th. August, he reached Port Arthur and stayed there until 5th. November 1946.

While he was staying in Port Arthur, he was interrogated as a suspect by Soviet intelligence. Aharon wrote a letter to Kalinin, president of the Supreme Soviet and sent it via a comrade who was going to Moscow, so that it would not pass through military censorship. The letter reached its destination and Archik received a reply from the presidential office saying that his case was being investigated and that they would forward their decision to the military regime. After he received this letter, they ceased to bother him.

On 15th.November 1945, Archik embarked on a ship to the port of Vladivostok and from there, he travelled on the trans-Siberian railway to Belarus taking about a month to reach Slonim. He approached the office of immigration in Baranovitch and went to Poland with his wife and son - a three year old who had been born in the forest and was called Ben Yaar - son of the forest, where he stayed until 1948. In this period, he worked as a driver for the 'Escape'(B'richah) [145] and would transport illegal immigrants (to Israel) to the Czech border, to Kletzko. However, even now, his troubles were not over. The

---

[145] *Translator's note: The Escape or Flight refers to the secret route/s devised to help Jews leave Europe for Israel.*

Polish secret service suspected that Mikolaichik[146] had been smuggled out of Poland with the help of kibbutz members who crossed the Czech border. They arrested Archik, who arrived with his lorry, and imprisoned him in the cellars of Warsaw prison. Archik stayed in prison six months until the establishment of the State of Israel, when he was released and left Poland. He arrived at the port of Haifa with his family, via France, on 14th. December 1948.[147]

Destinies

Itche (Yitzhak) Rabinovitch, who was also a partisan in the Budioni troop, was sent to the H.Q. unit. Most of the partisans in the unit, which numbered twenty-four men, were Jews. The division commander, Sikorski, trusted him, because, according to him, "Jews don't get drunk and you can trust them to carry out tasks." Itche, too, was liberated in the Kartuz-Bereza region, where the unit was dispersed. He reached Israel with the establishment of the state.

Twists and turns were also the fate of Shmuel Gutterman, who, on the way to the death pits from Slonim, had snatched the rifle from the guard on the lorry and disappeared in an alleyway. He reached the 51 group. After it was dispersed, he was transferred to the 55 group, and from there, to Kotovski troop.

Gutterman was quite obviously Jewish. He had a long Jewish nose (at least according to the ignominious 'Die Shturmer' style), and his faulty Russian accent aroused the scorn of non-Jewish partisans - indeed, they tormented him whenever they could.

When the 55 group received a mortar and Gutterman was transferred to its team, he was the man who knew how to work it and taught the rest of them. Here, his talent was revealed, and after a short time, he became known as a mortar expert.

This was a Russian mortar of 82 mm. diameter, but there were no shells. The German mortars, whose diameter was 81 mm. wouldn't fit, and using those shells caused the mortar to go off-target. Gutterman calculated an angle for aiming right which worked and his hits were always excellent. From now, they began to appreciate him and to treat him as he deserved, and prior to the liberation, he was well treated. When the troop was dispersed, Gutterman was recruited to the regular army and all trace of him disappeared. It's not known if anyone from his family survived, but he remains engraved on the memory of his Jewish partisan comrades from Slonim.

Zerach's Epilogue

---

[146] *Mikolaichik was a member of the exiled Polish government in London. He returned to Warsaw after the war and was a member of the temporary government.*

[147] *According to the evidence of Aharon Bandt.*

With liberation, Zerach Kremin's unit was dispersed among the villages in the Borki area, and the unit was allocated to guard the southern approaches to the River Pripiet. Their role was to prevent Germans infiltrating for intelligence. They were not supplied with food, and therefore, the comrades would carry out acquisitions at night in partisan style - with a rifle with a silencer, they would shoot a pig or a cow and divide the meat among them, and afterwards, blur their footsteps.

After some time, it was decided to send them back behind the lines. First, two battalions from the Voroshilov and Tscherniak troops were sent. They were equipped with radio equipment and were supposed to report when they managed to cross. After them, the fighters of the Kotovski troop were ready to cross. The partisans crossed to the opposite bank of the Pripiet, but there was no message from them. Apparently, they had decided not to make contact, for fear they would again have to live in the previous conditions of hunger. Thus it was decided to transfer the brigade from the Kotovski to which Zerach belonged, to a special battalion, whose role would be to fight the "Bandera" gangs[148]. Zerach says that they were to comb the marshes in order to catch deserters who were dodging military recruitment.

With the ending of their role, all the partisans were collected into the town of Manyevitch, and there they were ordered to surrender their weapons and join the regular army. Zerach, who was a teacher by profession, was released from recruitment and was sent to the town of Gomel to work in his profession, but there was nothing for him to do in this town. Food was in short supply and every night, they suffered German bombing.

One day, Zerach met Rachel Rozmarin in Gomel. Rachel was attached to the command of the Polish partisan movement. Through her, Zerach approached the Polish command, and he and his comrade Kersh were accepted. They were officially loaned out by the Belarussian movement to support the Polish movement. The next day, they were flown to Rovna, and transferred to the Polish army camp in Shepnov, where the Polish striking force was encamped, under the command of Polkovnik Toronchik.[149]

After a few days, they went out westwards to Poland on foot and entered the town of Chelm. At that time, the establishment of the state of Poland was

---

[148] *Stefan Bandera was one of the leading organisers and commanders of the Ukrainian Nationalist movement, who were pressing for separation from the Soviet Union and for the establishment of an independent Ukrainian Republic. With the German invasion his men collaborated with the conqueror and took part in the destruction of the Jews. Following liberation of the Ukraine by the Soviet army, his people organised themselves into gangs, and continued fighting their war in the forests against Soviet partisans and those active in the Soviet regime, murdering any Jews they encountered.*

[149] *The Polkovnik (Colonel) Henrik Toronchik was a Jew from Volotzlabek. He had taken part in the Spanish Civil War, as a commander in the Dombrovski Brigade. In 1943, in the forests of Belomoyet in the Soviet Union, he organised a striking force of paratroopers for partisan fighting in Poland. He died in Poland on 18th. January 1966.*

declared. Zerach and the others marched on until they reached the concentration and extermination camp of Maidanek. They still found there heaps of dead bodies which had not yet been buried and other evidence of the very recent functioning of this dreadful camp. They were equipped with new clothes and guns, but here they explained to Zerach that they wouldn't send him to Poland for partisan warfare because his "nose didn't fit".

These words hurt him deeply. Zerach decided to leave the Poles and to return to the Soviet Union. He came to the town of Brest, met most of his partisan comrades there and stayed to work as a teacher. He immigrated to Israel in 1948.

To the land, the land

Thus ends the story of the partisan war of the young people of Slonim and the experiences of the Jewish 51 brigade. Their bodies are at rest, the Jewish partisan fighters, who came from the ghettos of Slonim, Biten and Kosovo and the Polish refugees who also came from the Slonim ghetto, who rose up to avenge the Jewish blood which had been spilt, and in doing so, gave their own blood.

Their bones are scattered in the forests of Rafalovka, Volchye-Nori, in the forests of Polesia and its swamps, and on the paths along which the partisans from the Brest and Pinsk divisions passed.

Raise a prayer to the memory of courageous Jewish fighters who gave their lives smuggling the weapons for revenge, from the city to the ghetto and from the ghetto to the forest, who were killed in their attempts to break through the fences, who fell in battles of the partisans and were murdered by their "comrades in arms", haters of Jews. They fought with daring, they dreamed of liberation and they fell. They were not laid to rest in Jewish graves but were buried somewhere along the roads, and they have no headstones to mark their graves.

But their faces will hover before the eyes of their comrades in the struggle, and their names, their words, and sometimes their laughter or their last sigh will ring in their ears, as long as the survivors walk upon this earth.

May this book be a headstone of glory and a memorial to the Jewish fighters of the forest.

Appendices and Index
Appendix 1: From Enemy Dispatches

Arlt, commandant of a Waffen SS. Zug II unit centred in Minsk, reports on 3rd. October, 1942 on operations to annihilate the Jews and clashes with the partisans:

"On 26th. June the awaited transport of Jews of the Reich arrived.

"27th. June, almost the whole of our commando set out for the Aktzia in Baranovich. The outcome was, as almost always, negative.

In the course of this operation we cleared the Jewish ghetto in Slonim. 4.000 Jews were buried that day...."

On 2nd. July preparations were again made for the arrival of a transport of Jews, and pits have been prepared for their burial.

"On 10th. July we and the last commando were deployed against partisans in the forest of Kvidanov, we discovered an ammunition store. But we were suddenly attacked with machine-gunfire from the rear, in which a Latvian member was killed. We chased the partisans and killed four.

"On 17th. July a Jewish transport arrived and was eliminated.....

"On 28th. July an annihilation Aktzia was carried in the Russian ghetto of Minsk. 6.000 Jews were taken to the pits....

"On 29th. July 3.000 Jews from Germany were brought to the pits.

From Arlt's report of 25th. September, 1942 on the manhunts against the partisans and the extermination of Jewish transports:

"....my group, that is, Skobernik, Teichmann, Kempe, Auer and I, were transferred to the patrol commandos under the authority of Dr. Heuser. There were seventy-five men in the 'Heuser' commando, most of them Latvians heavily armed, with a light mortar and rifles.

On 23rd. August we were transferred to Shatzk, a distance of seventy-five kilometres from Minsk, in the direction Slutzk.

"On 28th. August the whole commando engaged with a partisan camp, which was supposed be located in a certain place in a swamp. The outcome was negative. We wandered for about an hour in the forest and got into a swamp which made progress impossible. After firing shells for fifteen minutes, we returned.

"This Aktzia was also unsuccessful, since the partisans, who were in the village, were well hidden and we couldn't find them. The village teacher, who tried to run away after he was interrogated, was shot dead by SS. man Kempe.

"Following several patrol trips the length and breadth of the Shatzk territory, we left the job to a unit of the First SS Brigade, and on 4th. September, moved a distance of about 150 kilometres to Biten, which is before Brest-Litovsk. The day we arrived, at nine o'clock in the evening, partisans attacked a village on the edge of the forest and burned eight houses. The Lithuanian guard which was positioned there opened fire....

"On the 8th. September we advanced towards Niekhchevo which is on the railway line, 130 kilometres from Brest. There we found billets ready for us. The next day, together with the First SS. Brigade, we attacked the town of Kosovo, twelve kilometres north of Niekhchevo, which was apparently in partisan hands. The partisans retreated and burned forty houses...."

"On 13th. September, at 1 o'clock, one of our convoys of five vehicles, going to Biten was attacked by the partisans. The Sharffuhrer SS Titz, travelling in the first, car was immediately hit by a bullet and died. The driver of the car, Haufstormfuhrer Yenner was hit in both arms...."

Following this, the report states that the SS. man Kirshner fell into partisan hands, and that they burned him.[150]

From the evidence of Alfred Metzner, the interpreter in the district administration in Slonim to an American investigator on August 10th., May 1947, concerning the slaughter in Slonim:

"....the second extermination operation in Slonim was carried out in the autumn of 1942, and its aim was the Final Solution of the Jewish problem in this region...

"I went to the ghetto with Muk and local police, as commander of the military unit. In this Aktzia we tried to turn the Jews out of the cellars with rifle butts and by throwing burning torches. When this wasn't noticeably successful, hand grenades were thrown into the cellars, which caused them to collapse. At one and the same time, incendiary bullets were fired into the houses, and whole sections of the town went up in flames. Any Jews who were in underground passages and cellars choked under the fallen houses..."

---

[150] *Kriegstagebuch des Kommandostabes Reichsfuhrers SS, Taetigkeitsberichte, s. 242, 244*

1.a

A character reference for the partisan Zerach Ben Avraham Kremin, given by commander of the Kotovsky troop in 1944.

:"While he served as saboteur and commander of a sabotage group. 22 trains were derailed with enemy manpower and wquipment. He has taken part in more than ten major battle missions, in the sabotage of telephone and telegraph communication and in the War of the Rail-track. He has supplied the Schors troop with eighteen machine-guns, ten submachine-guns and about ten thousand bullets. He is known among the partisans as a respected person of authority."

1.b

Medal "The Red Star"

Medal "Partisan in war for the homeland"

Certificate of medals of excellence granted to the partisan Zerach Kremin

CERTIFICATION
Headquarters of the partisan movement in Belarussia, August 5th, 1944
This is to certify that Zvi Shepetinski served as partisan in the Dzerzhinski
Battalion of the "LENIN" Brigade from June 30th, 1942 to July 31st, 1944

1.c

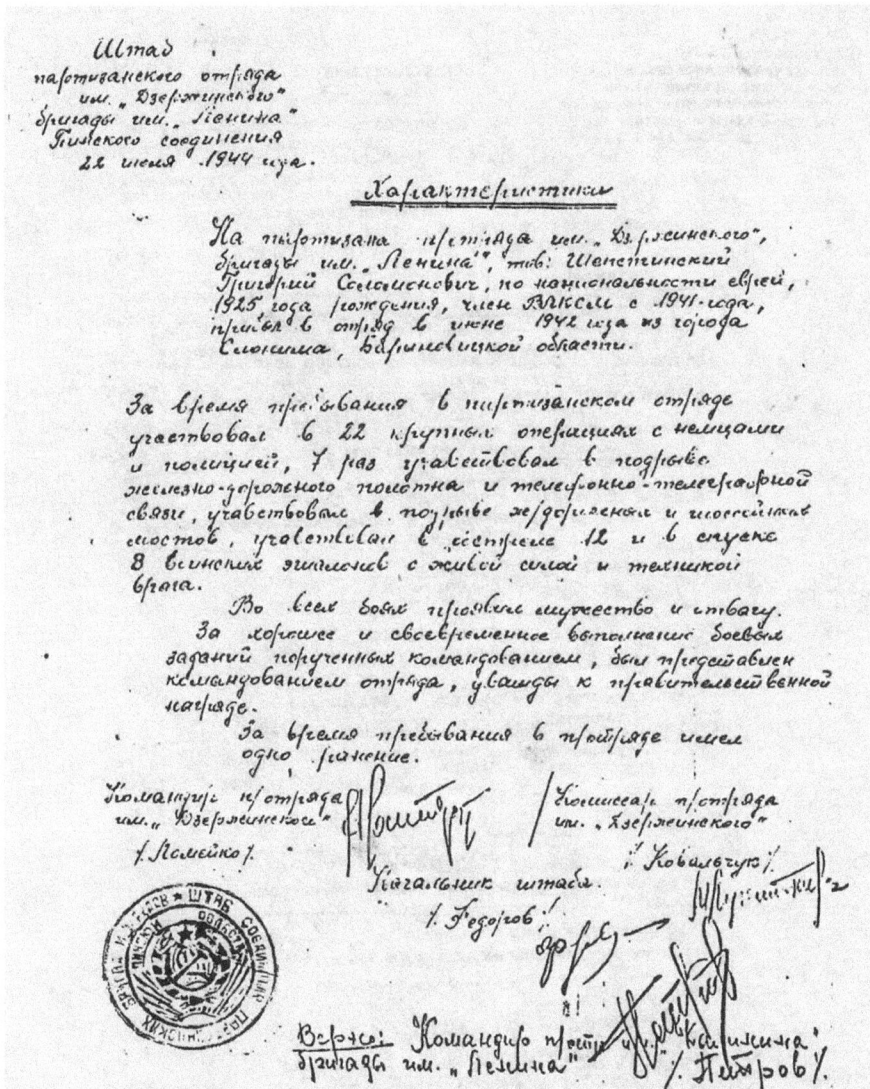

Character certificate for the partisan Gregory (Zvi) Shepetinski, awarded by commander of the Dzherzhinski Battalion of "Lenin" brigade, June 22,1944
"He participeted in 22 major battles against the german forces and the police. He took part 7 times in blowing up railroad ties and in sabotage of telephone and telegraph lines, participated in blowing-up and sabotage of 8 trains carrying enemy personnel and equipment.
In all these actions he exhibited daring and bravery. He was selected twice to recieve government medal of excellence. He was wounded once.

1.d

Character certificate for the partisan Jacob Shepetinski, awarded by commander of the Dzherzhinski Battalion, June 22, 1944
"He participeted in 22 major battles against the german forces and the police. He took part 5 times in blowing up railroad ties and in sabotage of telephone and telegraph lines, and has derailed three enemy military trains...
In all these actions he exhibited daring and bravery. He was wounded once.

Appendix 2

Report on the Extermination of Jews, Partisans and their Supporters in the Brest District Pinsk, Kobrin, Diwin, Molodita and Kartuz-ereza rest areas, period from 6th. September, 1942 to 21st. November, 1942[151]

Why they were shot	Type of victim			Total victims shot
	Men	Women	Children	
Partisans	104	5	4	113
Partisan Supporters	207	54	35	296
Partisan Families			(4 families) 14 persons	
Soviet citizens who had moved to Western Bielarus	776	124	103	1,003
Jews	Not known	Not known	Not known	41,848
Various				236
Total				**44, 837**

[151] Dokumenti obviniayut zbornik dokumentov o tshudovishchnikh prestuplenyakh nemetsofashistkikh zakhvatchikov na Sovetskoy teritorii Ogiz, Moskva 1945

Appendix 3
Document No. 314
From the Shchors Troop Logbook of Rail Track Operations – 1942[152]

22 August (1942)

We poured heavy fire on a train travelling from West to East with enemy military equipment and live personnel. Outcome – 17 losses and 9 wounded. The commander of the mission was Proniagin, troop commander.

26 August (1942)

On the night of the 26th. August the Brest-Moscow railway line was dismantled and transport was cut for a distance of 50 metres. The line guard's hut was burned. The same night communication was cut for a length of 200 metres and one Hitlerite was killed. The chief of staff was in command of the operation.

19 October (1942)

A military train was derailed on the Pinsk –Luninietz line. As a result of the explosion, the engine was sabotaged, 3 passenger carriages destroyed and 50 Hitlerites were killed, among them 13 senior officers. The 3rd., 4th. and 5th. divisions of the 51 group took part in the mission, under the command of Lofantzev and Sotchenko.

Document No. 236
From the operations logbook of the Shchors troop
For the period from 13th. July to 3rd. December 1943
(Names of Jewish partisans appear in the missions)

Night of 1-2 August (1943)

Enemy military train derailed on the Brest-Moscow line (in the 1,014th. kilometre from Moscow), in the Orantchitzi-Pavlovitchi area. Destroyed: engine, 6 coaches and 8 coaches with military equipment sabotaged. Transport stopped for 16 hours.

Aventisian was in command, participants: Boyko, Godzhayev, Gordei, Boldirev, Liker, Serko, Kutchmezov, Iliashenko, Murat, Riabin.

---

[152] Vsienarodnoye partizanskoye dvizhenye Beloruii, Minsk, 1978: Vol. II, Book 1, P.559, and Book 2, Pp. 511-514

5 August (1943)

Telephone/telegraph communication was completely wiped out between the villages of Zafrudi and Loyka on the Brest-Moscow road, for 1,500 metres.(13 poles were sawn down).

Commander - Avetisian, participants: Malakh, Romaniuk, Gordei, Navalayev, Ivan Radkin.

6 August

Enemy military train, with personnel, derailed on the Brest-Kovel line between Malorita- Khotislav stations. Engine destroyed, 10 coaches. Number of dead unspecified.

Participants: A.N. Shishkov, T.A. Ivanov, D. Sovivovitch, B. Rozmarin, Kersh, P. Koroli, B. Abit, Besmayev.

Night of 6 /7 August (1943)

Enemy military train derailed, with personnel, on the Brest-Moscow line in the Orantchizi- Pavlovitchi area. Destroyed: engine, 2 coaches; 4 coaches damaged. Number of dead unspecified.

Under the command of Avetisian, participants: Malakh, Kutchmezov, Romaniuk, Kobalevitch, Tchavai, Uvarov.

Night of 8-9 August (1943)

Two lines were blown up and 77 tracks damaged on the Brest-Moscow line in the Pavlovitchi-Zhabinka sector. Lines in this strip were unusable for 3 days.

Commanders: Konovaliev, Guzhevski.

3 October

Enemy military train derailed, with military equipment, on the Brest-Moscow line, in the 1,019th. kilometre. Destroyed: engine, 6 coaches, 3 coaches damaged. Transport stopped for 14 hours.

Participants: Malakh, Kotchemzov, Milikovski, Ismailov, Aveditchuk, Fashkevitch, Tchavai.

22 - 23 October (1943)

Brest-Pinsk line, in the Gorodetz-Vulka area - 225 tracks blown up.
Commander: Guzhevski.

29 October

Enemy military train derailed, on the Brest-Kovel line, near Malorita and Meliniki stations....
Participants: Zafrudni, Tcherefanov, Kersh, Duvenko, Milikovski, Mukasei, Sidoruk.

3 December 1943

Enemy military train blown up on the Brest-Moscow line, in the 1,018th. kilometre. Engine destroyed, 2 coaches, and 4 coaches with enemy military equipment badly damaged. Movement stopped for 12 hours.
Participants: Malakh, Liker, Kovalevitch, Ragimov, Rozmarin, Britch.

Document No. 23
From the combat logbook of the Kotovski troop in the Brest district,
For the period from 1st. to 31st. January, 1944[153]

12 January 1944

Ambush laid for German guards on Goroditz-Govrin line. 4 dead and 1 wounded. Loot: one rifle and ammunition.
Commander: Lieutenant Samyon, participant: Zhenia Eichenbaum.

13 January

On the railway line in the same site a banner bearing the slogan "Death to the German Conquerers" was mined. A German was killed dismantling it.
Squad commander: Kremin, participants: Guterman, Lomeiko

---

[153] *Shem (???), Vol. III, Pp. 58-60*

14 January

Unmined flag-posts were set up on the on the Gorodietz-Antopol line. The Germans thought that they were mined and opened fire, also throwing grenades. Movement was stopped for 3 hours.

Partisans responsible: Blizniok, Guterman.

14 January

Near Rodietz-Rasti: At 14.00 an enemy force of 400 infantry and 50 cavalry with artillery and mortars was moving towards the large village of Rodietz, with the objective of looting the population and destroying the village. In the battle which took off, 90 enemy were killed.

Under the command of the commander and the commissar of the troop. Participants: Gazin, Ditkovski, Potyomkin, Kremin, Blizniuk, Yankelevitch, Guterman, Lomeiko, Bibik.

25 January

At 11 o'clock an enemy train travelling from east to west was blown up on the Brest-Pinsk line between the stations of Gorodetz and Drogitchin in the fourth kilometre east of Gordietz. Outcome: engine destroyed, 2 coaches damaged with contents plus 8 tracks. Movement stopped 8 hours.

Group commander: Kremin, participants: Yankelevitch, Vulosiuk.

Appendix 4
List of Jewish Partisans in the 51 Brigade of the "Shchors", Numbering 172 Fighters

Name and Family name	D.O.B.	Place of Birth	Domicile
Abramchuk, Krusi	1920	Ostrov Mazovietzk	Israel
Abramchuk-Bandt, Liuba	1921	Ostrov Mazovietzk	Israel
Abramchuk-Epstein, Lisa	1926	Ostrov Mazovietzk	Poland
Abramovski, Eliyahu	1909	Slonim	Israel
Abramovski, Sonya	1925	Biten	Canada
Abramson, Lonka	1930	Leningrad	U.S.S.R.
Abramson, Vova	1922	Leningrad	Died in Slonim, July 1942
Akerman-Mishlevitch, Mania	1918	Lodz	Australia
Alpert, Chaya	1925	Slonim	Died in Israel, 1968
Alpert, Pesach	1898	Slonim	Israel
Alpert, Rivka	1901	Slonim	Died in Israel, 1955
Alpert-Rozenberg Hanna	1926	Slonim	Israel
Anuchnik, Yitzhak	1920	Slonim	Fell Volchye-Nory, 1942
Aronovich-Stein, Sima-Miriam	1916	Lodz	Died in Israel 1966
Bandt, Aharon (Archik)	1914	Slonim	Israel
Bandt, Avraham	1921	Slonim	Died in Israel, 1972
Beno, Vladek			

Name and Family name	D.O.B.	Place of Birth	Domicile
Berezin, Archik	1916	Medveditza	Fell in Bolsheye-Bolota, 1943
Berkovitch, Grisha	1914	Baranovitch	Executed by partisans, 8.12.42
Berkovitch, Shmaya	1920	Slonim	Israel
Berman, Yosef	1910	Kosovo	Fell in Gotzek, 1943
Birger, Aizik	1910	Lachovitch	Died in Israel, 1981
Blumenfeld, David	1914	Kalish	Fell in Battle of Kosovo, 1942
Blumenfeld-Liker, Lili	1918	Kalish	Brest (U.S.S.R.)
Blumovitch, Dr. Avraham	1909	Lumzha (Poland)	Died in Israel, 1972
Breskin, David	1904	Biten	Killed in Volchye-Nory, 1943
Bublatski, Avraham	1922	Slonim	Murdered in the forest
Burstein, Baruch	1920	(Polish refugee)	Fell at the front, 1944
Busel, Yehoshua	1925	Baranovitch	Fell Battle of the Lahn, 5.11.42
Buzin, Abba	1923	Zagiazh (Poland)	Fell in Telkhani, 1943
Delatitski, Anshel	1900	Slonim	Died in Slonim
Derchinski, Tzadok	1924	Slonim	Fell in the Red Army, 1944
Derechinski-Piletzki, Devorah	1922	Slonim	Died in Slonim
Doktorchik, Avraham	1916	Pabianitz	
Eichenbaum, Zhenia	1924	Polusk	Fell in battle, 1944
Einstein, Moshe-Peretz	1910	Derechin	Fell in Svietitza, 1943
Epstein (Zigmond), Edward	1920	Krakow	Killed in Volchye-Nory. 1942

Name and Family name	D.O.B.	Place of Birth	Domicile
Epstein-Bron, Musia	1924	Stanislauv	Killed in Volchye-Nory. 1942
Feitel, Aharon	1920	Warsaw	Fell E.Prussia, 1944
Feodorovitch, Yefim	1915	Gomel. U.S.S.R.	Fell Battle of 10th Dam
Finkel, Natan	1919	Suvalki	Israel
Finkel, Ze'ev	1921	Suvalki	Israel
Fischel		Slonim	
Galerstein-Imber, Tamar (Tanya)	1924	Biten	Israel
Galinski, Mendel	1923	Gavinovitch	Fell in Gavinovich, 1944
Gartchok, Yitzhak	1916	Darchin	Died in Minsk
Gertsovski-Doktortchik, Golda	1918	Slonim	Israel
Goldman	1913	Kosovo	Minsk
Goldman	1902	Lakhva	
Gringhauz, Grisha	1921	Slonim	Minsk
Gringhauz, Shepsel (father)	1893	Slonim	Died Israel, 1978
Gringhauz, Ya'akov	1923	Slonim	Fell in Battle of the 10th Dam
Grinshpan	1903	Ostrov Mazovietzk	Killed in Volchye-Nory, 1943
Grotchuk, Musia	1919	Derechin	New York
Guterman, Shmuel	1919	Tchenstokhova	Fell on the Visla, Red Army 1945
Imber, Aviezer	1918	Ostrov Mazovietzk	Israel
Imber, Yitzhak	1895	Ostrov Mazovietzk	Fell in Battle of the 10th Dam

Name and Family name	D.O.B.	Place of Birth	Domicile
Itzkovitch, Yitzhak	1926	Slonim	Fell at the front, 1944
Kagan-Marzon, Guta	1921	Sovalki	Israel
Kandelstein, Fima (Efraim)	1923	Bidgoshch, Poland	Executed in Puchini by partisans, 1943
Kersh, Yitzhak (Izak)	1918	Kotno, Poland	Lodz, Poland
Khatzkelevich, Yaakov	1922	Slonim	Israel
Khenchinska, Henya	1920	Lodz	Fell near Lake Vigonov-Samichin
Kohen, Mundek	1902	Kalish	Fell in Volchye-Nory, in the manhunt
Kosovski, Michael	1916	Slonim	Fell at the front, 1945
Kovarski, Dr. Fira	1918	Slonim	Committed suicide in the forest, 1942
Kremin, Dr. Anna	1895	Akerman, Bessarabia	Fell in manhunt in Volchye-Nory, 1942
Kremin, Dr. Moshe	1886	Zheludek	Fell in manhunt in Volchye-Nory, 1942
Kremin, Dr. Yasha	1918	Slonim	Fell in manhunt in Volchye-Nory, 1942
Kremin, Zerach	1921	Belitza	Israel
Kremin-Zakin, Batya	1920	Slonim	Fell in manhunt in Volchye-Nory, 1942
Krupeni, Efraim	1917	Biten	Fell in Gatchiza, 1943
Krupeni, Hershel	1922	Biten	Fell Volchye-Nory, 1943
Krupeni, Zhenia	1924	Biten	Fell Okinunova, in manhunt 1943
Kunitza, Rivkah	1922	Slonim	Murdered by partisans in Svietitza, 1943
Levitski, Gershon	1921	Slonim	Perished in1943
Leyzerovitch, Khona (Michael)		Slonim	Died Volchye-Nori, 1942
Leyzerovitch, Mordechai		Slonim	Died Volchye-Nori, 1942
Lichtenstein, Batya	1924	Slonim	Murdered in Volchye-Nory, 1942
Liepek, Dr. Yitzhak	1913	Warsaw	Died in Denmark, 1987

Name and Family name	D.O.B.	Place of Birth	Domicile
Liker, Natan	1910	Warsaw	Died in Brest
Lustig, Mietek	1921	Warsaw	Fell in Chemeli, 1942
Malakh, Heniek	1920	Ostrov Kieletzki	Fell at front nr. Bialystok, 1944
Malakh, Meir (Mayorek)	1923	Ostrov Kieletzki	Fell Battle of 10th Dam
Medbetski, Sarah (Sonya)	1920	Slonim	U.S.S.R.
Milikovski, Shimon	1920	Slonim	Fell in Puchini
Milikovski, Zelig	1913	Slonim	Fell at front, Red Army, 1944
Minkovitch, Mikhail	1908	Biten	Died in Bitan, U.S.S.R.
Mishelevitch, Yitzhak	1915	Slonim	Australia
Mishler, Ester	1923	Dlugo Siodla	Died in Nimerzhe, 1944
Mishler, Feivel (Felix)	1926	Dlugo Siodla	Israel
Modelevitch, Moshe	1898	Slonim	Died in U.S.A.
Moshkovski, Hillel	1922	Slonim	New York, U.S.A.
Moshkovski, Shabtai	1916	Slonim	Israel
Mudrik, Mordechai	1915	Kosovo	
Mukasei, Yokheved	1925	Slonim	Died Volchye-Nory, 1942
Mukasei-Moshkovski, Masha	1923	Slonim	Israel
Mukasei-Moshkovski, Rivkah (Rita)	1920	Slonim	Israel
Orlinski, Avraham	1903	Slonim	Israel
Orlinski, Dr. Cheslava	1907	Tchenstokhova	Died in Israel, 1966
Osek, Eliyahu	1916	Slonim	U.S.A.
Osek-Snovski, Sarah	1918	Slonim	U.S.A.
Perel, David	1913	Slonim	Fell at Bialystok front, 1944
Pertsov, Michael (Mishka)	1919	Osova	Israel
Pik, Mordechai	1910	Gantzevich	U.S.A. (?)
Podolski, (lieutenant) Fima	1923	Stalino, U.S.S.R.	U.S.S.R.
Rabinovitz, Yisrael	1924	Slonim	Fell in Battle of the Lahn, 1942
Rabinovitz, Yitzhak	1912	Slonim	Israel

Name and Family name	D.O.B.	Place of Birth	Domicile
Rapapport	1914	Lenin	
Ravitski, Avraham	1923	Lesnaya	Fell at Gavinovitch, 1944
Ravitski, Noah	1927	Lesnaya	Fell at Gavinovitch, 1944
Rodenstein-Zasun, Helinka	1920	Warsaw	U.S.S.R.
Rosa	1924	Ostrolenka	Fell in Volchye-Nory, 1942
Rosa, Yitzhak	1918	Ostrolenka	Long Island, U.S.A.
Rosenvasser, Miecheslav	1915	Warsaw	Fell at Telekhani, 1944
Rozmarin, Binyamin (Niomek)	1912	Zaveerche	Died Israel, 1985
Rozmarin, Rachel	1915	Zaveerche	Israel
Rubin, Mendel	1921	Poltusk	Israel
Sapirstein, Natan	1916	Warsaw	Shot by commander of Kotovski nr. Razdzialovichi, 1942
Sayet, Dr. Fima Efraim	1917	Grodno	Brest, U.S.S.R.
Servianski, Noah	1918	Ogostov	Died U.S.S.R.
Shabtai, Yehoshua	1924	Slonim	
Shefchuk, Karpel	1916	Slonim	Killed in Sporovo, 1943
Shelubski-Graf, Yehudit	1925	Slonim	Israel
Shepetinski, Fruma (Fanya)	1912	Slonim	Fell Volchye-Nory, 1943
Shepetinski, Hannah	1896	Zavershe	Fell Volchye-Nory, 1943
Shepetinski, Herzel	1922	Slonim	Fell in Chudino, 1943
Shepetinski, Reuven	1924	Slonim	Fell Volchye-Nory, 1943
Shepetinski, Shlomo	1898	Slonim	Fell Volchye-Nory, 1943
Shepetinski, Sonya	1923	Slonim	Fell Volchye-Nory, 1943
Shepetinski, Uri	1931	Slonim	Fell Volchye-Nory, 1943
Shepetinski, Ya'akov (Yasha)	1920	Slonim	Israel
Shepetinski, Yitzhak	1896	Slonim	Fell Volchye-Nory, 1943
Shepetinski, Yekhiel	1930	Slonim	Fell Volchye-Nory, 1943
Shepetinski- Ribatski, Hannah	1899	Slonim	Fell Volchye-Nory, 1943
Shepetinski-Rubin, Rayah	1928	Slonim	Canada

Name and Family name	D.O.B.	Place of Birth	Domicile
Shepetinski-Shefet, Tzvi	1926	Slonim	Israel
Shnur, Adek (Edvard)	1922	Warsaw	Fell on Red Army front, 1944
Shusterovitch, Zalman (Z'ama)	1921	Slonim	Killed by partisans at Puchini
Sibosh	1910	Warsaw	Fell Chemeli, 1942
Slonimski, Gita	1927	Biten	U.S.A.
Slonimski, Israel	1923	Biten	New York, U.S.A.
Smolinski, Dr. Leon	1908	Sovalki	Died U.S.A.
Smolinski, Miron	1918	Sovalki	Killed in forests of Michlin, 1944
Snovski, Matus	1908	Slonim	Fell Volchye-Nory, 1942
Snovski, Shimon	1915	Unknown	Fell nr. Kovrin, 1943
Sofer, Moshe	1923	Slonim	Fell on Polish front, 1944
Sokolik, Yisrael	1914	Ostrov Mazovietsk	New York, U.S.A.
Stein, Erich	1912	Frankfurt	Fell near Bodachye, 1942
Strikovski Dr. M		Lodz	
Tchapka, Yehoshua	1918	Slonim	Fell Siege of Samichin, 1942
Tchertok, Nahum	1918	Otvotsk, Poland	Settled in Israel
Timan, Ya'akov	1918	Ostrov Mazovietsk	Fell in Lushtcha, 1944
Tsirinski, Nionyia	1922	Slonim	Omsk, U.S.S.R.
Ugushevich, Yehoshua	1923	Slonim	Killed by Zhurbaliov, 1943
Ulanski, Yehoshua	1912	Biten	Byten (U.S.S.R.)
Volkoviski, Dr. Shlomo (Sioma)	1909	Slonim	Died in Israel, 1986
Volkoviski-Payevski, Mina	1916	Slonim	Israel
Waxman, Adolf	1917	Ostrov Kieletzki	Fell in ranks of Polish army, 1944
Weintraub		Polish refugee	Fell nr. Bostin, 1944
Weintraub (brother)		Polish refugee	Settled in Israel

Name and Family name	D.O.B.	Place of Birth	Domicile
Weiselfisch, Irka	1924	Warsaw	Miami (U.S.A)
Yakimovski, Avraham	1920	Slonim	Fell at the front, 1944
Yakimovski, Sonya	1926	Slonim	U.S.S.R.
Yakimovski-Ravitz, Zhenia (Zahavah)	1923	Slonim	Israel
Yankelvitch, Moshe	1918	Slonim	Died New York, U.S.A.
Yevshitski, Dov (Boris)	1910	Kosovo	Israel
Yoselevitch, Aharon	1922	Slonim	Israel
Zhagel-Factor, Liuba	1918		Died in Israel
Zilberhaft, Ya'akov (Kuba)	1920	Lodz	Israel
Zilberman, Hershel (Yitzhak)	1915	Unknown	
Zimnavoda	1919	Kalish (Poland)	Fell in battle of Puchini

Appendix 5

Partisan Leaflet

Document No. 189

This is a letter from partisans of the Pinsk Division appealing to Hungarian and Slovak soldiers in the service of the Germans, which was disseminated as a leaflet in the villages and towns in the area.[154]

2nd. November, 1943

For more than four years now the cannibal Hitler has been torturing you. He forces you, you who toil, to abandon your homes, your beloved wives and children, sends you to fight the Russian nation, to exterminate Russian women and children and to spill your blood in vain. Hitler promised you that he would ruin Russia quickly, but the situation now is this: the German army is already in a state of retreat, and has withdrawn to the other side of the Dnieper. The Red Army has blocked the German route to the Crimea, conquered Kakhovka, is attacking the towns of Nikolayev and Krivoi-Rog, has surrounded Kiev and Gomel and crossed the Dnieper south of Reczitza. The Germans are being forced to give up one town after another every day. The day of Russian victory over the Germans is approaching.

And now Italy is refusing to fight for Hitler. The whole Italian navy and air force have surrendered to the English and the U.S.A. The armies of England and America have reached Rome, and crossed the River Volturno. We know that it was the Germans who instigated this war, and that Hitler and the Germans alone are guilty of the murder and abuse of our people.

We, the partisans, defenders of the people and of labour, are taking revenge on the Fascists for their sins. We know that the Germans are forcing you to fight on foreign land. You are a people of workers like us. We call on you in friendship and mutual support. Let us then strike the Hitlerites, come let us fight together for the liberation of the homeland from the Hitlerite yoke, let us offer a helping hand to each other in a common struggle against Hitler and his gangs.

We await your reply and are ready for a cordial relationship and mutual aid.

Partisans of Pinsk

---

[154] Vsienarodnoye Partizanskoye Dvizhenye, Vol: II, Pp. 402-403

INDEX

Abdurozkov, Kahar	244, 245, 363
Abramchik, Krusi	17, 111, 112, 246
Abramchik, Leah (Lisa)	111, 120, 232, 246
Abramchik-Bandt, Liuba	17, 101, 111, 232, 246, 254, 282, 285
Abramovitch, David (Dodel)	17
Abramovitch, Liuba	17, 45
Abramovski, Eliyahu	1, 17, 74, 85, 94, 101, 102, 130, 221, 232
Abramovski, Sonia	196
Abramson, Lonka	232
Abramson, Vova	48, 85
Agayev	176, 177
Akerman, Manya	232, 245, 252
Alpert (family)	232, 246, 254, 261, 318
Alpert, Chaya	232, 246
Alpert-Rozenberg, Hannah	17, 232, 246, 254
Alpert Pesach	17, 41, 42, 71, 85, 87, 96, 100, 116, 157, 232, 246, 254
Alpert, Rivkah	186, 232, 246, 254
Andriosha	257, 258
Anishchuk	333
Antopol	3, 264, 266, 276, 283, 284, 332, 347
Anuchnik, Yitzhak (Itzel)	85
Arkadi	203
Artiom	89, 90, 92, 251
Astrinski, Max	298
Atlas, Dr. Yehezkel	11, 16
Avestisian, Artiom Samsonovitch	232, 345
Avramchik	see Abramchik
Azef, Haim	42
Azernitsa	xvii, 65
Bandera, Stefan	335
Bandt, Aharon (Archik)	4, 17, 45, 48, 59, 64, 66, 69, 71, 72, 75, 76, 78, 89, 91, 92, 95, 99, 101, 111, 112, 120, 122, 127, 154, 164, 171, 184, 202, 209, 210, 221, 223, 228-230, 232, 245-247, 252, 254, 333, 334
Bandt, Avraham	17, 69, 70, 76, 120, 222, 228, 229, 232, 252, 268
Bandt, Ben Yaar	333
Bandt, Liuba	17, 101, 232, 246, 254, 282, 285
Bandt, Matla	76, 252, 253
Bandt, Nechemah	76
Bandt, Yechezkel	76
Baranovitch	7, 29, 39, 59, 85, 165, 208, 213, 222, 224, 228, 235, 236, 243, 244, 246, 263, 264, 266, 267, 298, 299, 301, 305, 314, 331, 333, 337
Belgians	4, 307, 308, 311
Bell, Augustin	114
Belitza	58, 120
Belorussia	1, 6, 25, 26, 119, 147, 309, 321, 332

Belorussians ..... ix, 2, 9-11, 15, 16, 27, 34, 45, 102, 103, 108, 133-135, 148, 150, 153-155, 201, 203, 204, 211, 212, 260, 263-267, 271, 276, 291-293, 295, 298, 300, 309, 321

Beloye Oziero (the White Lake) 322

Ben Yaar 333

Bereskin, David 200

Berezin, Aharon (Archik) 232, 240

Berger, Dr. 65, 67

Berger, Yitzhak 232

Berkovitch, Grisha 3, 15, 224, 228, 229

Berkovitch, Dr. Lolek 204, 205

Bialystok 28-30, 44, 61, 121, 218

Bidgoshtch 237

Bistrov, Viktor 271

Biten 2, 3, 10, 12, 15, 17, 59, 69, 73, 108, 109, 114-117, 119, 127, 133, 136, 148, 149, 152, 153, 158-163, 165, 193-196, 198-203, 216, 255, 261, 266, 356-358

Blumenfeld, David 41, 72, 89, 93, 100, 120, 135, 136, 138

Blumenfeld, Lili 41, 93, 135, 232, 245, 252

Blumovitch, Dr. Avraham 16, 17, 42, 64-66, 69, 71, 72, 88, 89, 92, 99, 100, 102, 106, 109, 115, 119-122, 136, 162, 164, 178, 180, 181, 183, 184, 190, 209-212, 242, 244, 251, 261, 332

Bobkov, Nikolai Vladimirovitch 2, 15, 119, 163, 196, 197, 199, 200, 202-205, 252-254, 262, 264, 265, 331

Bobrov, Ivan Dmitrevitch 240

Bobruisk 220

Boretski, Yitzhak (Izya) 93, 190, 216

Borki 213, 335

Boroviki 211-213, 222, 291

Bostin 189, 298, 301, 315, 316

Boyosak, Stefan 125

Brakner, Yehudah 216

Brest 4, 17, 19, 20, 118, 119, 136, 161, 163, 165, 166, 235, 243, 244, 246, 259, 260-267, 269, 275, 279, 280, 282, 285-287, 289, 305, 321, 322, 331, 332, 336-338, 343-347

Brest division 3, 4, 19, 118, 191, 204, 219, 234, 246, 260-266, 275, 276, 299, 321, 332, 336

Brinski, Anton Petrovitch/Piotr ('Dyadya Petya') 2, 175, 176, 190, 191, 212

Bronna-Gora 203, 267, 277, 279

Bublatski, Avraham 3, 60, 71, 76, 85-89, 91, 93, 95-98, 101, 102, 107, 120, 232, 245, 246, 252, 253

Burshstein, Baruch 93, 94, 214-217

Busel, Yehoshua 224

Buzin, Avek (Abba) 113, 232

Chemeri 2, 39, 43, 121, 124, 164, 177, 216, 221

Chertikov, Alexei Petrovitch 165

Davidovitch-Stein, Miriam (Sima) 17, 232, 246, 252

Davoretzki, Alter 11

Delatitski, Anshel 41-44, 58, 69, 71, 73, 88, 100, 120, 128, 129, 177, 214, 232, 268

Deniskovitchi 3, 4, 223, 225, 226, 307, 310, 331

Derechin .... xvii, 11, 98

Derechinski-Piletzki, Devorah (Dora) 105, 147, 246, 251, 291

Derechinski, Tzadok 216, 291, 312, 316

Derechinski, Yasha 316

Derevnoye 33

Diatlovo 11

Diatlovitchi..299
Dikan..332
Ditkovki, Boma...162, 347
Dobromishi...164, 165, 167
Doktorchik, Avraham........17, 41, 60, 72, 74, 81, 85, 87, 88, 90, 93, 96-101, 114, 124, 127, 129, 132
 156, 164, 174-181, 183, 184, 186, 210, 211, 217, 232, 245, 247, 252, 254
Doktorchik, Golda......................... 2, 17, 175, 177, 180, 183-186, 188-190, 227, 232, 245, 252
Doktorchik, Rina..41
Dolgoye..164, 165
Domanovo..59, 169
Dombrovski, Anton...227, 236, 240, 299, 335
Dovnitskoya..235
Drogichin...266, 284, 347
Drogobuzh..262, 321
Drozdov, Nikolai Nikolaivitch...261
Dudko, Gregory Andreyevitch.........17, 39, 40, 47, 58, 88-90, 92, 118, 154, 157, 163, 164, 170, 175,
 180, 183-186, 188-190, 227, 229, 232, 249, 250
Dvoretz..xvii, 31
Dyadya Petya (Brinski)...2, 175, 176, 190, 191, 212
Dyadya Vasia (Vasilyev).....................3, 4, 218-220, 227, 236, 254, 255, 258, 259, 261, 291, 292,
 294-296, 298-300, 305, 307, 309, 312
Eichenbaum, Zhenia.. 4, 93, 97, 100, 177, 230, 232, 289, 322, 331, 346
Elioshka..90, 92
Epstein, David..42, 43
Erren, Gert..34
Faschenko, Michail...59, 60
Fedka..197, 202, 203, 257
Fedotov..95, 153
Fedya...15, 228-230, 255, 256
Feigenbaum, Fanya...41, 43, 71, 88, 120
Feitel, Aharon..216, 291, 294, 312
Feldman..232, 245, 252
Feodorovitch, Yefim..........119, 121-124, 127, 135, 137, 153-155, 164, 167, 168, 172-176, 178-180,
 190, 228
Fiedrik (family)...39, 58, 76
Fiedrik, Alexander Vlasowitz..1, 39, 40, 43, 47, 58
Fiedrik, Viktor..40, 59
Fiedrik, Volodya..65, 95, 98
Filentchik, Nikolai Filipovitch..59
Filko, Yosef Michalovitch..60
Finkel..184, 186
Finkel, Natan...17, 78, 93, 214-217, 224, 232, 245, 252
Finkel, Ze'ev..17, 64, 93, 104, 177, 216, 224, 232, 245, 252
Fisher, Yisrael..177
Fomin, Yefim Ben Moshe..20
Fyodorov, A.P...235
Gadzheyev, Morat...90, 92, 275
Galaztsev..277
Galinski, Mendel..93, 95
Gantzevitch...59, 185, 224, 226, 236, 240, 301, 307

Gavinovitch 2, 153-155, 183, 269, 331
Gavrilitchsi 222, 224, 225
Gellerstein, Mina 198
Gellerstein-Imber, Tanya (Tamar) 2, 3, 17, 114, 115, 147, 201-205
Germany .... xviii, 9, 13, 26, 29, 47, 63, 154, 252, 253, 255, 259, 270, 317, 318, 321, 332, 333, 337
Gertsovski-Doktorchik, Golda 2, 17, 175, 177, 180, 183-186, 188-190, 227, 232, 245, 252
Gildman, Misha 98
Goldin, Yekutiel 73
Gomel 121, 266, 275, 282, 335, 356
Gorodietz 255, 266, 331, 346, 347
Gotsk .... 190, 222, 226, 227, 236, 246, 249=251, 261, 298
Gratchuk, Masha/Musia 72, 216, 291, 292, 312
Gratchuk, Yitzhak (Itche/Ilya) 71, 72, 89, 186, 216, 291, 312
Greenstein 200
Gringhauz, David 216
Gringhauz, Grisha 60, 93
Gringhauz, Shepsel 93
Gringhauz, Ya'akov 93, 174, 175, 177, 216
Grishka 246, 268
Guterman, Shmuel 4, 81, 82, 232, 266, 334, 346, 347
Guzhevski, Viktor P. 165, 166, 178, 190, 191, 228, 229, 231, 261, 262, 285, 345, 346
Guzhinov, Pavel 275
Gvorin, Dr. Yosef 65, 80
Hantsevitchi 211
Heiman, Boris 2, 199
Hick 34, 77, 85, 86
Hirschler, Avraham 4, 305, 306
Holtz, Yosef 17, 32, 70
Honigstien, Dr. 82-84
Hungarians 4, 204, 283, 284, 307, 312, 322, 356
Huta-Mikhalin 197, 199, 202, 204, 265
Imber, Aviezer 4, 17, 44, 45, 72, 77, 85, 120, 123, 126, 175, 178, 180, 205, 216-219,
           232, 277-279, 281-284
Imber, Yitzhak 123, 138, 177
Irkutsk 281, 282
Iskrik, Yasha/Jacob 39, 43, 177, 221
Italians 4, 14, 306, 307, 333, 356
Itlis, Dr. 98
Itzkovitch, Hertz 32
Ivatsevich .... xvii, 158, 160, 165, 169, 200, 262, 268, 287, 288, 292
Kagan, Guta 232, 246
Kalish 32, 70, 120
Kalyuni, Kasian (Kigo) 137
Kalyuyev 218
Kandelstein, Efraim (Fima) 3, 237
Kaplinski, Dr. Noah 1, 17, 19, 27, 33, 45, 65-67, 82-84, 96, 104, 105
Kaplinski, Sonya 83
Kaplon 176
Kapusta, P.P. 3, 235
Kartuz-Bereza 179, 260, 277, 280, 281, 332, 334, 343

Katz, Liovek	77, 78
Kazakstan	121, 244
Kazanchev, Fedor	119
Kazantsov, Zhenia	92
Kersh, Yitzhak (Izak)	335, 345, 346
Kh., Ivan	182
Khatinichi	189, 211-213
Khatzkelevich, Ya'akov	4, 17, 137, 190, 239, 273, 284, 285
Khenchinska, Henya	85
Khokol, Pashka	160
Khoroshchanski, Me'ir	131
Khorostov	227, 234
Kistyunin	218, 220, 300
Kleshchev	118, 227-231, 233, 241
Kobani, Kazak	90
Kokoshitski, Cheikel	73
Koltava	234
Kolya	221, 222
Komarov	*see* Korsch
Kormuzh	213, 214, 216
Koroshcha	199
Korostan	332
Korotchin	331
Korsch, Yitzhak	232, 246, 247, 252, 266, 269
Korzh, V.Z (Komarov)	15, 118, 218, 224, 227-230, 233, 234, 236, 238, 240, 294, 310
Kosovo	2, 12, 59, 95, 103, 108, 109, 118, 131, 133-138, 149, 153, 155, 159-161, 163, 164, 193, 195, 196, 199, 201, 291, 331, 336, 338
Kotchiriganov, Vas'ka	299
Kotovski troop	4, 232, 261-264, 266, 275, 285, 286, 289, 321, 322, 331, 334, 335, 346
Kovaliov, Pavel Grigoryevitch	232, 261
Kovalski, Piotr Mamertovitz	262, 165, 167, 321
Kovarski, Dr. Fira	93, 97, 100
Kovel	321
Kovpak, Sidor Artemyevitch	3, 17, 234
Kozlovshchina	xvii, 16, 68
Krasnaya Sloboda	4, 236, 291, 292
Krasnostavski, Zhenia	17
Kremin, Dr. Anya	95
Kremin, Batya	195, 196
Kremin, Dr. Moshe	58, 95, 164
Kremin, Dr. Yasha	65, 72, 81, 93, 95, 116, 164, 195
Kremin, Zerach	1, 4, 7, 9, 45, 58, 66, 69, 71, 76, 89, 92, 95, 103, 104, 112, 114, 117, 118, 120, 122, 130, 132-134, 153-155, 164, 172, 174, 176, 181, 190, 191, 208, 210, 213, 214, 216, 223, 232, 240, 242, 243, 266, 275, 276, 285, 322, 335, 346, 347
Kribushin	3, 185, 208
Krivoruchko	213
Krupeni, Zhenia	201-203
Krusheinitzki, Drs.	213
Kunitza, Rivkah	232
Kursk	12, 234

Kvint, Gershon 43, 74, 112
Lapitchev, Kuzmitch 236, 261
Lekomtsev, Dr. Viktor, Alexeyevitch 16, 17, 136, 242, 243
Lenin brigade 4, 265, 300, 305, 312-315
Leningrad 48, 137, 255, 308
Lenino 236, 315
Leontiev, Andrei 90, 119, 120, 122, 134, 167, 176, 190, 233, 249, 261, 262, 265
Lesnaya 59, 165, 197, 246, 251
Liachovichi 234
Lichtenstein, Batya 203
Lichtenstein, Kalman .... xi, 17
Lida 273
Liepak, Dr. Yitzhak 232, 273, 286
Liker, Natan Yosifovitch 61, 175, 177, 223, 232, 240, 242, 243, 251, 261, 266, 285, 344, 346
Linkov, Gregory Matveyevitch. ('Batya') 3, 204, 234, 263, 301, 305
Linz 243
Lithuania .... ix, 25, 256, 257
Lithuanians 10, 27, 54, 55, 70, 74, 75, 120, 135, 159, 162, 171, 189, 201, 213, 300, 337
Lizhin, Nikolai Mikhailevitch 269, 275, 276, 286
Lodz 41, 120, 203, 238, 318
Logishin 236, 239, 298, 312, 315
Lomeyko, Naum Dimitrevitch 254, 255, 312, 314, 346, 347
Lomzha 42, 65, 120
Lopez, Justo 242
Lublin 25
Lugi 222, 225
Luninski, Chaim 76, 252
Luninski, Matla 76, 252, 253
Luninski, Tzilla 76, 252
Lushcha 4, 300, 312, 315
Lusino 314
Lustig, Mietek 136, 155, 166
Lvov 45
Malach, G. 60
Malach, Heniek 76, 91, 120, 177, 178, 223, 232, 266, 345, 346
Malach Me'ir (Mayorek) 93, 173, 175, 177
Malkovitchi 298, 301, 302, 314
Mariampol 1, 87, 88, 96-100
Marmuliov 220, 221
Mauthausen 70
Meirson, Gutta 93, 97
Melnik, Y.A. 235
Merzliakov 101, 118, 121, 137, 154, 163, 172, 178-180, 186, 187, 189, 191, 210, 211, 214-216,
222, 223, 228, 229, 237, 250, 251, 261, 264, 267, 276, 280
Metzner, Alfred 35, 358
Michailtchik, Vassili 59, 60
Mikolaichik 334
Milikovski 226, 256, 345
Milikovski, Shimon 3, 60, 112, 239
Milikovski, Yonah 111

Milikovski, Zelig 41, 45, 74, 86, 87, 94, 96, 102, 130
Minkovitch, Mikhail 127
Minsk .... xvii, 7, 29, 61, 70, 86, 161, 181, 212, 218, 221, 235, 246, 262, 264, 266, 269,
　　　　　　　　　　　　　　　　　　　　　　　　　　　　　275, 318, 322, 333, 337, 344
Mironchik, Yosif 125
Mirski 29
Mishelevitch-Akerman, Manya 232, 245, 252
Mishelevitch, Itche 126
Mishelevitch, Yitzhak 232, 245, 252
Mishka Pover ('the cook') 59, 89, 90, 95, 119
Mishler, Esther 232
Mishler, Feivel (Felix) 232
Misko 60
Misova 223
Mitia 177
Modelevitch, Moshe 132, 156, 177, 216, 224, 232
Mogilev 1, 7, 66, 67, 69-73
Molotov 29, 155, 271, 272
Moscow 134, 137, 156, 163, 165, 191, 209, 250, 251, 263, 264, 280, 285, 287, 289,
　　　　　　　　　　　　　　　　　　　　　　　　　　　　　308, 331, 333, 344-346
Moshkovski, Hillel 17, 65, 72, 123, 127, 232, 246, 252, 246, 252
Moshkovski, Masha Mukasei 2, 3, 17, 73, 116, 117, 200-202, 266, 346
Moshkovski, Rivka (Rita) Mukasei 2, 72, 73, 116, 117, 200, 201, 232, 246, 266, 346
Moshkovski, Shabtai 1, 17, 44, 45, 67, 72, 78-81, 93-95, 101, 175, 221-224, 232
Moshkovski, Tsvi 78
Mostova Street 1, 35, 74, 79-81, 84, 95, 116
Mukasei-Moshkovski, Masha 2, 3, 17, 73, 116, 117, 200-202, 266, 346
Mukasei-Moshkovski, Rivka (Rita) 2, 72, 73, 116, 117, 200, 201, 232, 246, 266, 346
Mukasei, Yocheved 2, 73, 116, 117, 200-202
Mutz 44, 46-49, 63, 64, 71, 77, 78, 277
Naumov, M.A. 235
Neuendorf, H.J. 35
Neushevski, Dr. 105
Niekhachevo 203, 278, 338
Nimerzhe 268, 271, 273, 282-284
Novgorod 255
Novogrudek 16, 58, 252
Novosilki 180-183, 185, 186, 189, 208, 213, 245, 248, 299, 300
Oginski, Mikhal Kazimiezh 25
Ogushevitz, Moshe 41
Ogushevitz, Yehoshua 232
Okuninovo 98, 196
Omsk 17
Orlinski, Avraham .. 1, 17, 19, 29, 30, 35, 51, 53, 65, 66, 70, 72, 82-84, 102-104, 123, 175, 177, 178,
　　　　211, 213, 226, 229, 230, 232, 236, 238, 244-247, 249-252, 264, 266-268, 270-272, 276, 332
Orlinski, Dr. Cheslava 1, 17, 29, 30, 51, 53, 65-67, 70, 72, 82-84, 102, 104-106, 123, 166, 175,
　　　　　　177, 180, 183, 184, 222, 226, 232, 238, 244, 245, 249, 251, 261, 267, 268, 276, 332
Orlinski, Pesach 104
Orlovski, Kiril Prokofievitch 3, 61, 153, 156, 240-243
Osak, Sarah 216

Osak, Yitzhak 216
Osovah 255
Ostrolenka 131
Ostrov Keletski 120
Ostrov Mazovietski 44, 72, 111, 120
Ozernitsa .... xvii, 65
Paretski, Dr. 65, 105, 106, 204
Pashka 200, 258, 259
Pavlovski, Pashka... 196, 197
Payevski, Yosef 81
Perel, David 44, 76, 78, 91, 92, 101, 120
Pertzov, Mikhael (Mishka) 3, 17, 255-259
Peski 3, 267, 271
Petralovitch 27, 84, 94
Philimonikha 253
Pik, Mordechai 232, 245, 252
Piletzki, Devorah (Dora) 105, 147, 246, 251, 291
Piletski, Volodya 105, 106, 147, 148, 246, 251, 291
Pinsk 2, 7, 118, 196, 213, 216, 218, 219, 227, 233-236, 238, 240, 255, 257, 261, 262, 264, 269,
    282, 286, 294, 298, 300, 307, 316-318, 321, 331, 336, 343, 344, 346, 347, 356
Pinski, Yitzhak 216
Pitkovski, Moshe 15, 160, 194, 199, 200
Plotnitza 236, 298
Podolski, Yefim Borisovitch (Fima) 101, 122, 124, 154, 232, 265, 252
Podorovski 137
Poland .... ix, xiii, xvii, xviii, 8, 10, 16, 23, 25, 31, 33, 41, 42, 44, 51, 58, 59, 63, 65, 77, 81,
    114, 115, 122, 176, 179, 220, 221, 225, 237, 252, 261, 291, 292, 318, 331-336
Polonski, Noah 198
Poltava 234
Poltusk 331
Pomin, Efraim Ben Mosheh 263
Ponomarenko 136, 265
Pripstein, Jacob 41
Proniagin, Pavel ...1, 15-17, 39, 40, 58-62, 70, 71, 88, 90, 92, 118, 124, 132, 134-137, 153-155, 157,
    165, 167, 171-173, 175, 176, 178, 181, 191, 213-217, 223, 227, 231-233, 239,
    243, 246, 254, 255, 250, 251, 259, 261, 262, 267, 268, 275, 286, 321, 332, 344
Pruzhani 104, 105
Pshenitchnikov 237
Pugachov, Yefremov 160
Pukhovichi 234
Putchini 3, 237, 238, 240, 331
Puzovitch 66, 67, 69, 70, 116, 161
Rabinovitch, Yisrael 73, 224
Rabinovitch, Yitzhak (Itche) 4, 17, 44, 74, 85, 93, 94, 97, 130, 138, 334
Rabinowitz, Max 44
Rafalovka 36, 59, 88, 90, 95, 118-121, 127, 131, 197-199, 216, 336
Ragimov 3, 212, 213, 346
Rapaport 245, 252
Rav Yitzhak 232
Ravitz 87

Razdzhalovitchi 132, 181-183, 185, 186, 189, 211-213, 245, 248
Ribatski, Chaya 54
Ribatski, Vovik 54
Ritmayer 34, 74, 83, 87
Rivka (Polish refugee) 54, 56
Rodenstein, Halinka 45, 73, 85, 139, 164, 186, 216, 217, 232
Rodietz 264, 347
Romanov 200
Rosa, Yitzhak 130
Rosakovo 39
Rovsani, Nikolai 221
Rozmarin, Benyamin (Nyumek) 179, 190, 221, 222, 232, 247-249, 266, 345, 346
Rozmarin, Rachel 186, 232, 246-248, 252, 335
Rubin, Mendel 216, 296
Rudenstein, Halinka 45, 73, 85, 139, 164, 186, 216, 217, 232
Ruzhani .... xvii, 83, 89, 94, 134, 176, 196, 197, 235
Samitchin 2, 165, 167, 169
Sankov, Vasya 155
Sapirstein, Natan 3, 208-210
Sayet, Dr. Avraham 208, 232, 245, 273
Schnur, Adek 72, 183, 232, 246
Schnur, Erich 105
Semutin, V.A. 235
Seriozha 89, 90, 92, 193-196
Servianski, Noah 41, 81, 93, 175, 177
Shabli 256, 257
Shabtai (shepherd) 46
Shalek (refugee from Lodz) 203
Shchors .... ix, 2, 3, 5, 15-17, 36, 39, 62, 92, 106, 109, 114, 115, 118-121, 123, 134, 136, 153,
155, 157, 160, 163, 165-167, 176, 185, 191, 193, 208, 211, 213, 219, 221,
225, 227, 228, 230, 232, 233, 236-238, 240, 242-244, 247, 248, 250-252,
254, 255, 259, 261-264, 266, 267, 269, 273, 275, 291, 292, 321, 344
Shefchuk, Karpel 87, 88, 93, 97, 232
Shefet, Zvi .... see Shepetinski, Zvi
Shelubski, Mendel 74
Shelubski, Yehudit (Judith) 2, 3, 17, 112-114, 147, 216, 219-221
Shelubski, Yosef 44, 73, 86, 116
Shelubski, Zelig 116
Shepetinski, Fruma (Fanya) 147
Shepetinski, Gita 318, 319
Shepetinski, Hannah (mother of Herzel) 76, 108, 115, 169, 202, 222
Shepetinski, Hannah (mother of Zvi) 76
Shepetinski, Herzel (Grisha) 1, 4, 30, 31, 39, 47, 57-60, 63, 64, 68, 69, 75, 76, 91, 92, 107, 108,
120, 124, 138, 147-149, 163, 166, 217-219, 291, 297, 299, 300, 312
Shepetinski, Rayah 30, 76, 115, 147, 183, 236, 291, 312, 318
Shepetinski, Reuven 30, 76, 108, 138, 147, 149, 163
Shepetinski, Sonia 76, 148, 150
Shepetinski, Shlomo 67, 76, 160
Shepetinski, Uri 30, 76
Shepetinski, Ya'akov (Yasha) 17, 19, 30, 31, 39, 47-49, 54-58, 62, 69, 76, 107, 108, 124, 135,

    138, 147, 149, 155, 156, 163, 165, 166, 173, 178, 183, 187, 213, 216, 219, 291, 292, 299-301, 312-314, 318

Shepetinski, Yechiel 30, 76
Shepetinski, Yitzhak 31, 67, 76, 108, 109, 115, 138, 149
Shepetinski-Shefet, Zvi (Hershel)... iii, xi, xiii, xiv, 4, 17, 19, 31, 53, 54, 67-69, 75, 76, 92, 107-109, 115, 138, 139, 147-150, 155-157, 160, 169, 178, 183, 184, 187, 188, 213-217, 234, 291, 292, 294, 295, 297, 298, 301, 302, 305, 310-312, 314-319
Shevchenko, Ivan Vasiliyevitch 312
Shpakovo 27
Shtchukin 272
Shtelle, Gunter 34, 82, 84, 93, 94, 125
Shulik 310, 311
Shulman 220
Shumilin 281-284
Shura 221, 223
Shusterovitch, Zalman (Zhama) 1, 3, 41, 60, 66, 71, 74, 87, 88, 90, 93, 97, 98, 120, 148, 232, 239
Sibosh 48, 85, 166
Sikorski, Sergei Ivanovitch 3, 118, 191, 204, 253, 254, 260-263, 265, 267, 268, 281-283, 286, 321, 334
Skolditch 59, 70, 97, 102, 111, 112, 122, 130, 252, 253
Slonim .... *passim*
Slonimski, Gita 216
Slonimski, Yisrael 12, 161, 162, 216
Slovaks 14, 356
Smasevo 236
Smolensk 322
Smolinski, Dr. Leon 65, 204
Smolinski, Miron 232
Snovski, Mitos 65, 71, 95, 103-105
Snovski, Shimon 223, 232
Sofer, David 280
Sofer, Moshe 190, 232, 237
Sokolik, Israel 45, 151, 152, 216
Sokolova 279
Solima, Danila 267
Sporovo 254, 260, 262, 264, 268, 282, 283, 286, 321
Stalin 8, 234, 282
Stalingrad 6, 234
Stalino 101, 122
Stalkov, Grigorai 275
Stalkov, Nicolai 275
Stein, Erich 47, 48, 60, 61, 63, 85, 120, 121, 123, 126, 127, 131, 132
Stein, Miriam (Sima) 17, 232, 246, 252
Steindam, Leah 131
Stenovski, Robert 235
Strikovski, Dr. M. 208, 232, 273
Sudovsky, Vladimir 125
Sushko, Yosef 59
Suvalki .... ix, 64
Svarin 254, 264, 269

Svyetaya Volya 3, 240, 245, 299
Svyetitza 132, 211, 242, 243, 245, 249
Tartatchok 155, 156
Tchemeri 2, 39, 43, 121, 124, 164, 177, 216, 221
Tchepelova 27, 81, 94. 125
Tcherniak, Dr. 266, 276
Tchernigovi, the .... *see* Fyodorov
Tchertok, Nahum 189, 216, 291, 294, 312
Tchuchevitchi 331
Telekhani 181, 211, 236, 245, 298
Timan, Ya'acov 45, 72, 85, 166, 174, 175, 183, 184, 186
Tokarikov, Seriozha 89, 90, 92, 193-196
Topichin, Mikhail Nikolaievitch 332
Toronchik, Henrik 335
Trabeniki 10
Tschorni 22, 190, 191, 209, 210, 234
Tsirinski, Nionia 17, 45, 58, 60, 61, 85, 87, 88, 132, 133, 164, 190, 213, 232,
　　　　　　　　　　　　　　　　　　　　　　　　　　　　　　　　266, 268, 273, 277, 279, 285
Tukhoviczi 182, 183, 185
Tushevitch 253
Tzuker, Dr. 201, 202
Ugushevich .... *see* Ogushevitz
Ukraine 122, 234, 235, 260, 315, 321, 335
Ukrainians 4, 9-11, 27, 47-50, 95, 101, 115, 120, 160, 212, 235, 245,
　　　　　　　　　　　　　　　　　　　　　255-257, 260, 265, 267, 271, 282, 285, 300, 315
Uriol 12
Valiuta 316
Vanka 258
Varshigora, P. 17
Vas'ca 295, 310
Vasiliyev, Vasili Alexandrovitch 3, 4, 218-220, 227, 236, 254, 255, 258, 259, 261, 291, 292,
　　　　　　　　　　　　　　　　　　　　　294-296, 298-300, 305, 307, 309, 312
Vasino 298
Vigonov (Lake) 3, 176, 212, 240, 299
Vigonovitchi 212
Vikhandler, Lipak 115
Vilchinski, Vatsek 42, 43, 60, 67, 103, 104
Vileika 7
Vilna .... ix, 65, 98
Vitebsk 7
Vizna 292
Volchye-Nory 3, 4, 11, 15, 24, 36, 59, 76, 88, 90-93, 95, 98, 107, 108, 114, 115, 117,
　　　　　　　　　　　　　　　120, 122, 130-133, 136, 138, 160-164, 171, 193, 196-199, 201-204,
　　　　　　　　　　　　　　　231, 245, 249-253, 262, 264, 265, 298, 300, 301, 318, 336
Volfin, Sheindl 131
Volfstein 58, 80, 81, 86, 87, 94, 96
Volkov, Vasili Andreyevitch 90, 103, 122, 154, 208-210
Volkovisk 28, 31, 84, 218, 235
Volkoviski, Mina 17, 147, 205
Volkoviski, Dr. Shlomo (Sioma) 205

Volodya 299, 313
Voronov, Volodia 239
Warsaw 4, 10, 28, 87, 120, 183, 252, 286, 289, 291, 312
Waxman, Adolf 81, 88, 93, 96-98, 214, 216
Waxman, Ya'akov 77
Weintraub 216, 296, 312, 316
Weiselfisch, Irka 76, 91, 100, 120, 139, 151, 152, 232, 246, 254
Wertzel 71
Wiesenfeld 65
Wohlin 191, 234, 235, 255
Wolka 167
Yakimovski, Avraham (Anton) 72, 120, 128
Yakimovski, Moshe 32
Yankelevitch, Moshe 116, 130, 221-223, 232, 266, 347
Yarmolenko, Grisha 121, 276
Yefremov 160, 193, 195
Yegorov, Sergei Yegorovitch 134, 232, 244, 247, 251, 261, 332
Yelishevitz 35, 43
Yevshitski, Boris (Dov) 216, 291, 292, 294, 312
Yochvidovitz, Henya 41
Yochvidovitz, Zlata 41
Yudelevitch, Abba 41, 79, 80
Yudelevitch, Motke 79, 80
Yudelevitch, Yisrael 70
Yudkovski, Boria 15, 198, 199, 266
Yudkovski, Sheina 199
Yudkovski, Uri 199
Yugolavia 16
Zablotye 213
Zachar 312, 313
Zagiezh 113
Zamoshtcha 46, 80, 81, 86
Zapolyeh 40
Zaretcha 162
Zavershe 39, 43, 47, 58, 76, 91, 92, 95, 97, 103
Zditovo 321
Zdzienciol 11
Zeifel, Hans 83, 84
Zelesye 62
Zhagel, Liuba 17, 81, 93, 94, 157, 223, 232, 246, 252
Zhatel 11
Zhirovitza 103
Zhuravliov 121, 228, 229, 244-246, 250, 261, 267, 268, 277
Ziborov, A.M. 291, 300
Ziborov, Ivan Vasilievitch 218, 220
Zilberhaft, Ya'akov (Kuba) 71, 216, 291, 292, 312
Zilberman, Yitzhak 216
Zimnavoda 238

369